Negotiati

Performan

D0127947

NEGOTIATING
PERFORMANCE

Gender, Sexuality, and Theatricality in Latin/o America

Diana Taylor and Juan Villegas, editors

DUKE UNIVERSITY PRESS   *Durham and London 1994*

© 1994 Duke University Press   All rights reserved
Printed in the United States of America on acid-free paper ∞
Typeset in Galliard by Keystone Typesetting, Inc.
Library of Congress Cataloging-in-Publication Data appear on the last printed page
of this book.
Parts of "Ethnicity, Gender, and Power in Cuban Carnaval" by J. Bettelheim
originally appeared in *African Arts* 24 (April 1991) and J. Bettelheim, ed. *Cuban
Festivals: An Illustrated Anthology* (New York: Garland Press, 1993). "A Touch of
Evil" by J. Franco is reprinted by permission of *The Drama Review*. "The
Multicultural Paradigm by G. Goméz-Peña is reprinted from *Warrior for
Gringostroika* by permission of G. Goméz-Peña. "Art in America con Acento" by
C. Moraga is reprinted by permission of C. Moraga. It appeared in *The Last
Generation* (Boston: South End Press, 1993) and an earlier version appeared in
Frontiers: A Journal of Women's Studies 12.3 (1992).

Contents

❏

Acknowledgments

❑

The idea for the Latino and Latin American theatre group residency at the University of California's Humanities Research Institute originated during Murray Krieger's visit to the School of Criticism and Theory at Dartmouth in 1987. Since then he has been a constant source of help and support. This volume would not have been possible without him.

Mark Rose, Director of UCHRI guided, debated, and coexisted with us during our residency, Fall 1990, for which we are grateful. The staff at UCHRI did the possible and often the impossible to make our stay pleasant and successful.

Nancy Millichap, of Dartmouth's Humanities Computing Center, was invaluable in turning all our essays — themselves written in diverse computer languages — into a manuscript. Gonzalo Lira, her student assistant, was always available to help. Colleagues Laurence Davies, Susanne Zantop, Marianne Hirsch, Annelise Orleck, and Silvia Spitta of Dartmouth College, have been generous in their comments and advice.

Eric, Alexei, and Marina Manheimer-Taylor were a wonderful part of this project from beginning to end.

Ken Wissoker, our editor at Duke University Press, has encouraged us throughout this process.

We thank you all.

Diana Taylor
Opening Remarks

❑

The idea for this volume on Latino and Latin American performance began in a group residency of theatre scholars at the University of California Humanities Research Institute in Irvine. Eleven of us had come together because, in theory at least, we had something in common. We identified ourselves as theatre specialists; we shared a personal and professional interest in U.S. Latino and Latin American drama and performance. Although we came from all over the Americas, we lived in the United States and all of us were associated with academic institutions. We each considered ourselves somehow marginal in relation to dominant Anglo society. We were all cultural mediators, living on the border (either literally or metaphorically) between cultures, moving among conflicting ethnic, linguistic, political, and experiential positionalities: Anglo, Latino, Latin American; Spanish, English, "Spanglish"; Marxist, feminist; straight, lesbian, gay, and so forth. We had agreed to focus on a common topic: *transculturation* — the mediation between and within cultures — and on questions such as the following: How do theories, literary schools and models, and intellectual currents travel from one sociopolitical context to another? How do "foreign" ideas impact on a culture? How are cultural influences assimilated or how do they displace autochthonous traditions?

For ten weeks during fall term 1990, the participants tried to hold on to the common goals and interests that had brought us together while debating and struggling with the many issues that put us at odds. The points of conflict ran along various divides: men versus women, Marxists versus feminists, those who studied "theatre" and those who defended the legitimacy of "performance," as well as between and among the multiple ethnicities we represented as a group. Whom were we referring to when we

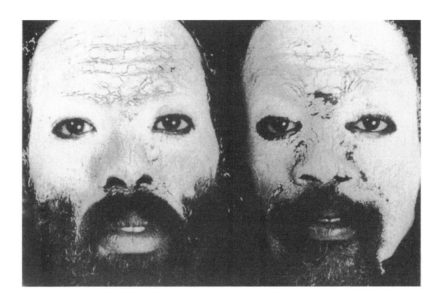

Figure 1. *Negotiating Differences, Negotiating Sameness,* Wayson Jones and Essex Hemphill, 6 and 7 January 1989. Sushi, San Diego. Photo courtesy of Guillermo Gómez-Peña.

used the terms "Latino" and "Latin American"? What did we mean by "culture" and "theatre" and whom, and what, did those categories leave out? What could we agree on, beyond this interest in Latino and Latin American theatre and performance which, we discovered, we could not even define to our satisfaction? Our discussions soon shifted from trans-culturation to a debate on negotiating differences. We tried to speak of and across the borders that united and separated us. How did *who* we were and *where* we were coming from shape our views of theatre and performance? Were we, as individuals, somehow representative of our diverse groups? Were we speaking *for* or speaking *from* a given position? We realized that while we had formally abandoned the subject of transculturation we were all transculturated and transculturators. We came to speak of ourselves as "double-agents" and "go-betweens."

As professors and practitioners associated to a greater or lesser extent with U.S. universities, we taught and "explained" and "performed" Latin American and Latino cultures mostly to students from the dominant one. Our research further served to disseminate and internationalize knowledge of and about our relatively marginalized cultures, a knowledge that some of our people claimed could only be used against us. Moreover, with regard to our own communities—if we still claimed to belong to them—we were also power brokers. We "introduced" the most recent theories generated in our academic circles. While there is a very positive, multicultural ring to our role as mediators, the task also proved difficult and conflictive for us, coming from communities and/or countries that have suffered from centuries of discrimination and cultural imperialism. Multiculturalism is fine, as Guillermo Gómez-Peña points out in his essay, when there is an *equal* exchange and dialogue. But the very real imbalances in political and economic power that exist between the dominant and marginal reproduce

Figure 2. Guillermo Gómez-Peña, "El Warrior for Gringostroika" (1992). Photo courtesy of Guillermo Gómez-Peña.

themselves in the cultural arena. As Alberto Sandoval's essay on AIDS theatre points out, Latinos are rendered practically invisible in the media — so while AIDS is ravaging men and women of color in the United States, it is represented almost exclusively as a threat to white, middle-class gay men. Ironically, the marginal are in danger of being neutralized and of losing their cultural specificity even in multiculturalism's move toward diversity. As Jorge Huerta explains, a Latino production often serves to satisfy demands for multicultural offerings in a theatre season — and so it is often cast cross-racially. Thus African Americans, Latino Americans, Native Americans, and Asian Americans have been known to compete for a few roles in a Latino play while all the traditional offerings of the theatre revert back to the star system and ethno-specific casting. The image of the cultural melting pot may have given way to the image of the interconnecting braid but that in no way assures that all strands enjoy equal visibility.

At the risk of seeming to represent the views of our group and creating a false sense of cohesion in regard to our discussions, neither of which I pretend to undertake, I will briefly point to the three issues which we found particularly problematic and which we encapsulated in our title, *Negotiating Performance: Gender, Sexuality, and Theatricality in Latin/o America:* (1) Who and what did we include under the rubric of "Latino" and "Latin American"? (2) What did we mean by *performance* — given that the term not only designates diverse phenomena in English but, to complicate matters, has no equivalent in Spanish. Does "theatricality," as Juan Villegas questions in his "Closing Remarks" better describe the phenomena we were dealing with? And, (3) given all our differences — gender and sexual orientation among them — was negotiation among us possible? Identity politics had failed, the politics of location was not working, coalition politics functioned in a few cases, and the politics of invitation, at least at the outset, seemed unthinkable.

Not all the issues I outline here are explicitly addressed in all the essays, yet negotiating the terms Latino, Latin American, gender, sexuality, theatre, performance, and theatricality was on some level a prerequisite for their articulation. Gender and sexuality, we found, could not be conceived as separate categories because they ran through each of these three major areas of discussion.

(1) Whom did we refer to when we used the term "Latino"? Historically, the term designates peoples of "Hispanic" descent who were born or live permanently in the United States. Politically, however, the term Latino is often used as antagonistic to, rather than synonymous with, the term Hispanic. Latinos, as defined by spokespeople such as Luis Valdéz, Cherríe

Moraga, Gloria Anzaldúa, Sandra Cisneros, Dolores Prida (to name a few), tend to identify ideologically with the so-called "third world," with "people of color," or economically and politically disenfranchised minorities. They take pride in their indigenous and African origins. Hispanics, on the other hand, emphasize their peninsular roots and often think of themselves as "white," European "First Worlders." This ideological divide has been complicated by the fact that Latinos come from very different cultures. Puerto Ricans are not the same as Nuyoricans—the former still live on the island or at least consider it "home" or home-away-from-home, while Nuyoricans have transplanted their culture to New York and feel more or less estranged both from the United States and from the island. On the island, they are considered "Americans"; in the United States, they are considered "Puerto Ricans." The displacement or *in-betweenness* Nuyoricans experience, however, is not limited to Puerto Ricans in New York. Thus, the term "Neoricans" has recently come into use to refer to those who live in other regions of the country.

None of those groups have much in common with U.S. Cubans but, again, for different reasons. Both islands have been under United States control for the greater part of this century, yet while many U.S. Puerto Ricans long for political independence, U.S. Cubans by and large adamantly oppose Cuba's break from the United States "sphere of influence" and its frustrated, though tenacious, pursuit of national autonomy. However, even the U.S. Cuban community, long considered the most politically conservative and economically successful "Hispanic" group in the country, is currently undergoing transformation. The younger generation, born and raised in this country, tends to be far more liberal than their parents.

Mexican-descended Chicanos, to name another Latino group, are themselves split between those recently arrived from Mexico and those who have lived in California, Arizona, New Mexico, and Texas before their land became a part of the United States in the nineteenth century. But again, as in the Latino/Hispanic case, the term "Chicano/a" is ideological rather than biological; it goes beyond the hyphenated, negotiated nationality-based, ethnicity of Mexican Americans to signal a relatively new ideological position of self-affirmation that took shape with the Raza movement in the 1960s.

In each one of the Latino groups, however, feminist members have been trying since the late 1970s to find a place for Latinas, for women who feel that issues of gender inequalities have too long remained shelved in the interests of what the men in their groups see as the overriding struggle to achieve ethnic (which too often means "male") equality. The homophobia of many Latino groups has also forced its gay and lesbian members to challenge the stereotypes of what it means to be a "man" or a "woman" in these communities. Thus the terms — Latino/a, Chicano/a, Hispanic — themselves have been the site of struggle and contestation, signifying everything from heritage to cultural consciousness, from an essentialist identity grounded in blood, color, sexual identity and orientation to a negotiated position — one could become Chicano/a, one could become "dark" as Cherríe Moraga says, one could choose to be "queer," in the words of Anzaldúa.

Given that the term "Latino" was so imprecise, what did that do to our subject matter? Who are the authorized Latino playwrights? Are Latino playwrights identified *biologically* as people of "Hispanic" descent born or living in the United States? Or are they identified *ideologically* as those who write about their specific ethnic experience in the United States as Jorge Huerta suggests? This latter position, however, can pose its own trap; it encourages Latinos to correspond to preestablished expectations of what an ethnic group should be writing about. There is the danger of thinking that Latino/as occupy any *one* positionality (be it in terms of ideology, class, gender or sexual preference, or race) or that they occupy it in any *one* way. There may be as many ways of being a Latina lesbian, let us say, as there are of being an Anglo, heterosexual male. "Sameness" cannot be assumed between those who share certain positions of proximity.

Moreover, the issue of language complicated our approach to Latino theatre and performance. What language(s) do Latinos speak? What language(s) do they write in? Spanish, for many Latino/as, is the language of resistance. It is the language of the community and of the home. While U.S. Latino writers often try to hold on to or recuperate Spanish as a "native tongue," in the words of Gloria Anzaldúa, for many groups in Latin America Spanish has been and continues to be the colonial language. The Mayan peoples discussed in Donald Frischmann and Cynthia Steele's essays in this volume are only one example of a group that does not consider Spanish the language of resistance. Language is part of a heated political debate in both continents. The imposition of Spanish in the Spanish-speaking Americas has historically deprived indigenous groups of their lands, their culture, and their right to active participation in society. Even today the members of rural indigenous communities that do the best economically are those (usually men) who have had access to some education and know enough Spanish to function in the marketplace. On the other side — geographically and politically — "English-Only" proponents in the United States seek to enforce rapid assimilation by ensuring that English be used in all official and public forums. There is more than a little jingoism in the calls for cultural "purity" underlying the "English-Only" project. The opposite tendency, evident in some academic institutions, also manifests itself in efforts to decree that all Latinos are fluent in Spanish — an expectation that belies a spectrum of sociopolitical obstacles facing Latinos that ranges from limited educational resources to racism and internalized racism. Thus it is over-simplistic to assume that Latinos make a conscious political decision whether or not to be fluent in Spanish. The fiery language debate has serious practical repercussions for artists: Whom do the dramatists write for — their own communities or mainstream audiences? If they write in English, does that signal a betrayal to their people or merely reflect their complicated reality? What do those choices mean in terms of their position and visibility vis-à-vis dominant culture, their chances of gaining access to funding agencies, theatrical spaces, publishing firms, and academic institutions? Is the choice simply one between assimilation or ghettoization? And who are the authorized critics? Is a shared ethnic *identity* a prerequisite for debate? If so, which *one*? And, consequently, what were some of us doing there? If not, could we overcome the notion of shared origins, identity, and destiny and negotiate a coalition, as Sue-Ellen Case proposes in her essay? Could we go beyond the limitations of identity politics and work out a politics of *community* in which those of us who share concerns, knowledge, and an ideological commitment to cultural dialogue (rather than dominance) could come together to discuss on equal footing? In short, could the concept of *cultural competence* allow us to speak across the ethnic, racial, gender, and sexual divides?

And who were the so-called "Latin Americans"? Among themselves, they have as little in common as U.S. Latinos and Hispanics. They come from twenty-five different countries as linguistically, racially, economically, and culturally diverse as any on Earth. As opposed to the Latinos, many have a sense of national independence; they have their own countries, their presidents and constitutions, their own official languages and religions. Many, but certainly not all. I remember as a child growing up in one of the northern provinces of Mexico in which people I knew could not name the country or the president and had no sense of any political organization beyond that of our immediate towns. Thus, class and cultural background become fundamental categories when discussing Latin America. Racial heritage also plays an enormous role, as the essays by Judith Bettelheim, Frischmann, and Steele make evident. Centuries of colonization have resulted, not surprisingly, in the valorization of the "white" race and European traditions. However, certain Latin American countries, especially those with predominantly mixed populations, have attempted to recognize the richness of their diverse racial and cultural roots. The Carnaval in Cuba after the revolution, as Bettelheim indicates, was a forum in which the population's Afro-Caribbean traditions could be officially celebrated. More ironical, perhaps, is the case of the Mayan theatre group examined by Frischmann and Steele. While Mexico has long officially honored, and at times mythified, its indigenous past, its indigenous groups have nonetheless continued to suffer from discrimination and exploitation. The recent uprisings in Chiapas demonstrate the depth of the hostilities. But under the auspices of Harvard specialists and the governor of Chiapas, as Frischmann documents, a group of Mayan men and women are being "taught" to recuperate their history and legends and turn them into theatre. Even in these experiments, as Steele points out in her feminist reading of this same theatre group, it is much easier for the community to recognize the racism directed at them than the sexism that exists both outside and within its boundaries.

Notwithstanding the very real history of oppression that unites all of these countries, most Latin American playwrights and scholars living in their home countries or in the United States belong to the affluent classes. They may not share the views that typify their own privileged classes but they do not generally identify themselves as "people of color" or as minority groups in their societies. In fact the term "people of color" is at best meaningless in Latin America; at worst, it reenacts U.S. dominance for it is only from the vantage point of the United States that all Latin Americans, regardless of race or class, are "people of color." The term occludes very real racial, class, and cultural tensions not only among the peoples of European, African, and indigenous descent but within these widely diverse groups as well. To return to the language of our debate, Latin American intellectuals may speak *for* the marginalized but not *from* the margins. However, there is also a tendency to wage accusations of "Yankee imperialism" at theorists who advance feminist or gay/lesbian thinking—although feminism particularly has a long, though often overlooked, history in several Latin American countries. In part, this deprecating stance has developed because liberation movements in Latin America have tended to be revolutionary ones organized around class conflict and "communist/capitalist" tensions. In part, too, the resistance to accepting feminist and gay/lesbian liberation movements is seen as displacing male intellectuals and leaders from center stage. The glorification of the revolutionary hero (in the tradition of Che Guevara, for example) casts the powerful (even *macho*) male as leader in the struggle for self-determination and relegates women to supportive but subservient roles. All of a sudden, then, this virile hero is stripped of his status as revolutionary leader of the oppressed and becomes seen instead as the oppressor of other oppressed groups — women, gays, and lesbians.

All of these issues are complicated by the fact that, in Latin America, there is less of a tendency to define oneself as a "Latin American" than, say, as a Mexican or Chilean, for example. Again, the monolithic vision of an undifferentiated Latin America can only be maintained by those outside it. The term itself is a foreign invention that derives from the mid-nineteenth century French coinage *Amérique Latine*. The sense of collective identity ("Latin America") stems less from a history of shared community than from the shared history of *opposition to* the colonial powers. Latin Americans may not all know about or like each other, but by and large they feel intense animosity toward the United States, which has become the latest in a long history of colonizers.

This animosity creates an ambivalent attitude toward Latinos, by virtue of their living in "the belly of the monster." Cherríe Moraga's essay, "Art in América con Acento," enacts the mixed loyalties and confusion on both sides of the divide for those who value ethnic over national ties. There is no easy Latino/Latin American separation, no monolith on either side of that slash. Moraga may well wonder how Latinos can participate in U.S. military aggression against "our América" as José Martí called the Spanish-speaking communities of these two continents. Moreover, some Latin Americans scorn Latinos for being between cultures, between languages, neither-here-nor-there. That is precisely the space that Latina/o writers claim as their own and occupy/theorize with pride. Gómez-Peña, a Mexican who migrated north to Tijuana/San Diego speaks of the borderization of culture as a utopian project: "Today, if there is a dominant culture, it is border culture."

So how did we come up with Latin/o American? Was our desire to expand and move borders simply wishful thinking? The links were necessary, we felt, in order to explore the historical, political, ideological, and artistic connections between these areas that all but disappear when we divide them into two, oppositional blocks — the so-called "First World" and "Third World," one "American" and one *foreign* or, in the language of U.S. horror films and the immigration service, *alien*. The aim of this volume was to break down these divides, to explore the many worlds, languages, traditions, ideologies, and positionalities that coexist — at times peacefully, at times not — and that have, over the centuries, come to constitute a *latino america* across two continents.

(2) Our next stumbling block, having to do with the meaning of performance, theatre, and theatricality seemed no easier than the first.

In one of our first discussions we recognized the rift between those who dedicated themselves to the study of "theatre" in a traditional sense and those who focused on "performance." The debate was of course tied into the whole question of "culture," implicit in our original topic, transculturation. Were we looking at "high" culture (and theatre as its maximum expression) in the traditional Western sense as something separate from daily life? Did "theatre" necessarily conjure up classical notions of a mimetic art, based on a written text, represented in a special, separate space to delight and instruct an exclusive, generally economically privileged, audience? This disciplinary rigidity has rapidly lost valence over the past three decades, undermined by revolutionary and liberation movements in Latino America and the onset of postmodernism, feminism, and cultural studies. Moreover, the generic limitations are particularly problematic for our communities because they are tied into our history of colonialism, gender inequality and racism. If we limit our understanding of theatre to written texts designed to be staged we enter into an economic network that excludes the vast majority of our populations. Who can afford to produce and consume these texts and productions? We find ourselves left with a canon that, at least superficially, reflects Western dramatic models and styles. Given the destruction of autochthonous art forms and the imposition of new ones throughout the conquest and five hundred years of colonization, how could it be otherwise? Yet, rather than looking beyond the apparent similarities and analyzing the original uses to which these acquired models are put (i.e., their transculturation), critics trained in Western drama too often conclude that Latino theatre is amateurish or that Latin American theatre is derivative and undeserving of further attention. This attitude, still prevalent today, further marginalizes our communities and reproduces the colonial relationship that maintains the supremacy of the cultural metropolis over the impoverished periphery. Furthermore, most Latin American and Latino communities do not have the economic infrastructure to put our playwrights, productions, and audiences in contact with each other. So while we all know Shakespeare and Ibsen, our populations can seldom name our own playwrights, let alone other Latino or Latin American ones. This economic limitation contributes to the internalization of the feelings of worthlessness and inferiority associated with neocolonialism. If we haven't heard of our own plays, they must not be any good. Finally, the cultural products we have to show for ourselves fail to represent the contributions of women and disenfranchised minorities. Thus, it seems logical to conclude that women do not participate in theatre or that indigenous or Afro-Caribbean or Latino communities are "primitive" and have no "culture."

As these essays illustrate, in order to appreciate Carnaval (Judith Bettelheim's essay), or indigenous performances (Donald Frischmann and Cynthia Steele), or women's use of spectacle for political organizing (Marguerite Waller, Diana Taylor), or the casita culture of the Nuyoricans (Juan Flores), we had to abandon traditional notions of theatre and culture. We had to replace the word theatre with *performance,* a term that allowed us not only to include all sorts of spectacles that "theatre" leaves out but to look at theatre itself from a more critical perspective. The word performance, of course, presented its own problems. First, there is no equivalent in Spanish. In English, moreover, the word most commonly refers to two antithetical phenomena. Traditionally, theatre has been written of as a hybrid art form, and until the 1960s, performance referred to the representation or mise-enscène of the dramatic text. Furthermore, it was placed in a secondary and subservient relationship to the script, which independently enjoyed the status of a literary work. Since then, the word has also come to mean almost the opposite of theatre. Performance has claimed its autonomy both from the dramatic text and its representations to constitute itself in various antitheatrical forms—among them performance art, public art, and what we might call public performance.

These various forms of performance often overlap to a significant degree. Each, in its own way, destabilizes traditional notions about "culture" and "art." Most share a common goal; they reject the institutionalization of theatre and they attempt to subvert a system of representations accused of supporting repressive, hierarchical, and patriarchal societies. But it is nonetheless useful to differentiate among the various phenomena that come together in this volume as performance in its most global sense, for they depend on different aesthetics of presence, they set up a different perspective and evoke a different critical response.

Performance art tends to be based in the actor rather than the text; it tends to be personal and grounded in narrative (rather than traditionally dramatic forms). The comparatist scholar Laurence Davies, for example, speaks of performance art as a kind of performed essay. The relationship between actor and audience in performance art, however, more often resembles the one established in traditional theatre than in public art—that is, the actor is usually there, in person, in front of the audience; the audience generally pays admission to the show; the critical emphasis is on the show. As in traditional theatre productions, performance art emphasizes process rather than product. Yet the critical response is to the art piece, rather than to the audience. Often, too, the focus of performance art is on the hermetic and private rather than the public. None of this is to suggest that performance art is less political than public art or public performance. But it is often political in a different, more private way. And while performance artists commonly emphasize the private over the communal, Latino artists such as Gómez-Peña (who recently won the MacArthur "genius award" for his work) and John Leguizamo (of *Mambo Mouth* and *Spic-O-Rama*) bring the Latino community onstage through a series of impersonations. Jesusa Rodríguez, whom Jean Franco writes about in her essay, uses performance art to trace the history of the Mexican people, and the occluded and distorted role of women in that history.

Public art—such as billboard art (María Teresa Marrero), and the living installations (Juan Flores) presented in this volume—emphasizes product over process. The artist is absent and the relationship is between the work and the audience. Generally, public art, as the name suggests, is located in public spaces where an unpaying audience has access to it at any time. Public and community concerns and aspirations usually take precedence over the artist's more private ones. The Latino public art studied here, much like its counterparts in Latin America (the famous murals by the revolutionary painters of the 1920s and 1930s for example), takes art out of elitist circles, out of "cultural spaces" in the strictest sense of the word and posits, on the contrary, that society as a whole is culture—the site in which symbols and identity are forged, negotiated, and contested. The focus in public art shifts from the notion of culture in elite spaces to that of the everydayness of culture. María Teresa Marrero's essay shows how artists try to deal with and provoke this shift. She demonstrates how predominantly white, middle-class audience members become the "show" as 1,200 of them line up in the midst of the homeless and disenfranchised inhabitants of the poor Latino neighborhood of the Million Dollar Theatre in Los Angeles. As the audience finally entered the theatre, its members realized that their street experience as unwitting objects of the gaze was in fact part of the spectacle, the programmed prelude to the show they were paying to see. And Juan Flores, in his essay on the Puerto Rican casitas (workers' shacks constructed on the island in the 1940s and 1950s), illustrates how both the meaning of culture and cultural meaning undergo radical change as the casitas are reconstructed in the Bronx during the 1980s and 1990s to give Nuyoricans a feeling of home. These same houses, complete with their porches, *bateys,* gardens, and chickens, are cultural centers in which people play music, dance, cook, eat, and interact. Some casitas provide medical or legal services for the community. In the Bronx these houses represent a nostalgic "going back" to the island of earlier times, but they also serve as symbolic "making home" out of New York, of reforging community, making *familia,* to quote Cherríe Moraga, and to overlay the northern cityscape with a rural, tropical map. This example of what I would call "performing culture" or "culture as performance" becomes transformed, as Flores indicates, when the casita was officially recognized as a cultural product by the Smithsonian Institution in Washington. A perfect casita was put on display in an exhibition called "Las Casitas: An Urban Cultural Alternative." But even as they were being lauded as cultural alternatives, the city of New York threatened to bulldoze them for being illegal structures. The casitas were simultaneously valorized and repudiated by dominant culture. What happens — we had to ask ourselves — when the culture and art of one group are attacked and disauthorized on the level of daily life and, on another level (as cultural objects) appropriated by authorized cultural institutions? Separating "art" from daily life — as if they were antithetical — proves disempowering to marginalized groups that do not have access to what, traditionally, has been a separate realm of "art" and "culture."

A different kind of performance that we explore here, which I will call public performance, includes organized and repeated action that takes place in a public space and that may or may not have artistic aspirations. As Janelle Reinelt and Joseph Roach write in *Critical Theory and Performance,* performance can be understood in the encompassing terms used by Richard Schechner, as "restored" or "twice-behaved behavior": "The concept of restored behavior embraces theatrical performances, sacred and secular rituals, and social displays of many kinds, from sporting events to shamanism" (12). Under this category we can include Carnaval, but we can also include Jorge Salessi's study of drag in the construction of the male homosexual subject in Argentina and my analysis of the gendered performative strategies as instrumental in political resistance, as seen in the case of the Madres de la Plaza de Mayo. Salessi and I followed the theoretical lines traced by Judith Butler to look at gender itself as performance, as socially constructed roles that men and women are forced to assume and reenact on a daily basis. Our interest was in seeing how far those roles could be redefined or subverted in order to allow individuals to continue functioning in oppositional roles. The concept of performance made it not only possible, but necessary, for us to place 'roles' within a larger socioeconomic system of representations.

The broad concept of performance, then, allowed us to explore numerous manifestations of "dramatic" behavior in the public sphere which tend to drop out of more traditional approaches to theatre. But the notion of performance also allowed us to reexamine theatre itself as one of various systems of representation in patriarchies which push women and popular audiences to the margins. Kirsten Nigro charts how Mexican feminist playwrights of the last twenty-five years have challenged the subservient role of women in representation. Performance, seen as a deconstructive strategy in much feminist theory, enabled us to look at theatre in a way that critiqued its own staging.

The fact that no exact equivalent for "performance" exists in Spanish did not dissuade us from using the term, primarily because there is a long and very rich tradition of performance in Latin America. Evidence of pre-Hispanic rituals, dances, and plays exists in the *codices* (indigenous manuscripts), the bas reliefs on temples and buildings, and the journals of the fifteenth- and sixteenth-century explorers and conquerors. In order to be able to appreciate the plethora of spectacles native to our cultures, we have to retrain ourselves to look beyond the term "theatre," a term that was imposed in the early colonial period along with the obligatory adherence to Spanish models, themes and styles.[1] Performance differs from theatricality — the term that Juan Villegas prefers — in that it signals various specific art forms common both to Latinos and Latin Americans (from performance art to public performance) but also in that it encompasses socialized and internalized roles (including those associated with gender, sexuality, and race) that cannot really be analyzed as "theatrical discourses" (which Villegas holds as synonymous with theatricality). Additionally, the term performance, and especially the verb performing, allow for agency, which opens the way for resistance and oppositional spectacles. Theatricality, I agree with Villegas, may be the closest approximation to performance available in Spanish, but it is limited in that it is a noun with no verb and therefore no possibility of a subject position. Furthermore, the term theatrical discourses further precludes the possibility of anti-hegemonic agency — who directs and manipulates theatrical discourses? Thus, while both "performance" and "theatricality" appear in the book's title, each of the terms illuminates and delimits our subjects in different ways.

(3) What did we mean by "negotiation" and was such a thing possible among us? While we thought of ourselves as "others" of sorts, we were all so different, culturally, ideologically, and politically. Attempts to focus on certain kinds of "otherness" displaced and threatened to erase other kinds of differences. We could talk openly enough about national and ethnic conflicts, but tensions arose when we brought up issues of gender and sexual orientation. It became clear that traditional ways of thinking about culture along national and ethnic lines not only excluded the issues of gender and sexual orientation but were in fact predicated on their exclusion. (See essay

by Sue-Ellen Case.) Was "culture" then some privileged space of aesthetic and philosophical debate removed from daily life and relationships of domination? Or was culture the arena in which these relationships and exclusionary practices could be fought out, or, more optimistically, *negotiated*. Literally we had come together to "do business," as the term negotiation implies. After all, we do this for a living. We had agreed to share space — to interact at the Institute and to share our fields of academic interest. Negotiation rings of bargaining, political give-and-take, peace talks, mediation, diplomacy. In this respect, I'll borrow from Marguerite Waller's introduction to "Border *Boda* or Divorce *Fronterizo?*" when she cites one of the members of Las Comadres, the multicultural performance group: "We hoped to become closer to each other through telling our stories and weaving them into a performance. Ironically we failed, although the show was successful and beautiful." Our biweekly meetings at the Institute raised more questions than we were able to answer, either during our residency or in this volume. As Juan Villegas makes clear in his "Closing Remarks," many issues remain unsolved. We cannot all speak the same language — literally in the group or figuratively and academically as in this volume. Not all the participants, unfortunately, are represented here. Our backgrounds, personal and disciplinary, are very different. And these differences among us, which originally we had hoped would contribute to the intellectual diversity of the group threatened, at least at times, to make for irreconcilable difference. Many us left feeling that we had failed to weave our stories together. Yet, ironically, most of our stories are here, together. While we never pretended to be all-inclusive or representative in our approach to our subject matter (as if this were possible in a field as vast and diffuse as this one), it was clear that our concerns were part of a wider debate that we wanted to be part of. So we invited other scholars, not present at the Institute, to participate in the project by contributing to this collection of essays. Our original politics of identity gave way, in theory and in practice, to a politics of invitation, a politics of community. This volume, then, not only reflects but reenacts our aspirations to shift and expand borders, to re-envision a Latin/o America (a play on the Spanish version of *latinoamerica*) as a shared space, as an inclusive "América" home to all Latino/Americans which does not pit nationality against ethnicity and in which dialogue and negotiation might be possible. By inviting more and more people to join our debate we did not aim to arrive at a consensus or exhaust this dynamic and expanding field but rather to draw more people into our border experience. Readers, like spectators, contribute to the dialogue, to the production of meaning and to the shifting of ideological borders that the authors included here observe in their essays. As Guillermo Gómez-Peña puts it, "as you read this text, you are crossing a border yourself."

NOTE

1   For further discussion of this issue see "The Making of Latin American Drama," chapter one of my book, *Theatre of Crisis*.

Guillermo Gómez-Peña
The Multicultural Paradigm: An Open Letter to the National Arts Community

❑

THE PARADIGM SHIFT

Today in this troubled continent accidentally called America a major paradigm shift is taking place before our very eyes. The East Coast/West Coast cultural axis is being replaced by a North/South one. The need of U.S. culture to come to terms with the Latino American "cultural other" has become a national debate. Everywhere I go, I meet people seriously interested in our ideas and cultural models. The art, film, and literary worlds are finally looking South.

To look South means to remember: to recapture one's historical self. For the United States, this historical self extends from the early Native American cultures to the most recent immigration from Laos or Guatemala.

The current Latino and Asian immigration to the United States is the direct result of international conflicts between the so-called First and Third Worlds. The colonized cultures are sliding into the space of the colonizer, and in doing so, they are redefining its borders and its culture. (A similar phenomenon is occurring in Europe with African immigration.)

The First and Third Worlds have mutually penetrated one another. The two Americas are totally intertwined. The complex demographic, social, and linguistic processes that are transforming this country into a member of the "Second World" (or perhaps Fourth World?) are being reflected in the art and thought produced by Latinos, blacks, Asians, Native Americans and Anglo-Europeans. Unlike the images on television or in commercial cinema depicting a monocultural middle-class world existing outside of international crises, contemporary U.S. society is fundamentally multiracial, multilingual, and socially polarized. So is its art.

Whenever and wherever two or more cultures meet — peacefully or violently — there is a border experience.

In order to describe the trans-, inter-, and multicultural processes that are at the core of our contemporary border experience as Latino artists in the United States, we need to find a new terminology, a new iconography, and a new set of categories and definitions. We need to re-baptize the world in our own terms. The language of postmodernism is ethnocentric and insufficient. And so is the existing language of cultural institutions and funding agencies. Terms like Hispanic, Latino, ethnic, minority, marginal, alternative, and Third World, among others, are inaccurate and loaded with ideological implications. They create categories and hierarchies that promote political dependence and cultural underestimation. In the absence of a more enlightened terminology, we have no choice but to utilize them with extreme care.

My artistic sensibility as a deterritorialized Mexican American artist living a permanent border experience cannot be explained solely by accepted historical notions of the twentieth century Western vanguard (from Dada to techno-performance). I am as Western and American as Laurie Anderson or Terry Allen. Yet my primary traditions are Chicano and Latin American art, literature, and political thought. We must realize that the West has been redefined. The South and the East are already in the West. And being American today means participating in the drafting of a new cultural topography.

Let's get it straight: America is a continent, not a country. Latin America encompasses more than half of America. Quechuas, Mixtecos, and Iroquois are American (not U.S. citizens). Chicano, Nuyorican, Cajun, Afro-Caribbean and Quebeqois cultures are American as well. Mexicans and Canadians are also North Americans. Newly arrived Vietnamese and Laotians will soon become Americans. U.S. Anglo-European culture is but a mere component of a much larger cultural complex in constant metamorphosis.

This pluralistic America within the United States can be found among other places, on the Indian reservations, in the Chicano barrios of the Southwest, the black neighborhoods of Washington or Detroit, or the multiracial barrios of Chicago, Manhattan, San Francisco, Los Angeles, or Miami. This sui generis America is no longer part of the First World. It still has no name or configuration, but as artists and cultural leaders we have the responsibility to reflect it.

Despite the great cultural mirage sponsored by the people in power, everywhere we look we find pluralism, crises, and non-synchronicity. The so-called dominant culture is no longer dominant. Dominant culture is a meta-reality that only exists in the virtual space of the mainstream media and in the ideologically and aesthetically controlled spaces of the more established cultural institutions.

Today, if there is a dominant culture, it is border culture. And those who still haven't crossed a border will do it very soon. All Americans (from the vast continent America) were, are, or will be border-crossers. "All Mexicans," says Tomás Ybarra Frausto, "are potential Chicanos." As you read this text, you are crossing a border yourself.

INTERCULTURAL DIALOGUE

The social and ethnic fabric of the United States is filled with interstitial wounds, invisible to those who didn't experience the events that generated them, or who are victimized by historical amnesia. Those who cannot see these wounds feel frustrated by the hardships of intercultural dialogue. Intercultural dialogue unleashes the demons of history.

Arlene Raven once told me, "In order to heal the wound, we first have to open it." Now we are just beginning to open the wound. To truly communicate with the cultural other is an extremely painful and scary experience. It is like getting lost in a forest of misconceptions or walking on mined territory.

The territory of intercultural dialogue is abrupt and labyrinthine. It is filled with geysers and cracks; with intolerant ghosts and invisible walls. Anglo-Americans are filled with stereotypical notions about Latinos and Latino American art. Latin Americans are exaggeratedly distrustful of initiatives toward binational dialogue coming from this side, or *el otro lado*. Bicultural Latinos in the United States (be they Chicanos, Nuyoricans, or others) and monocultural citizens of Latin America have a hard time getting along. This conflict represents one of the most painful border wounds, a wound in the middle of a family, a bitter split between two lovers from the same hometown.

Fear is the sign of the times. Americans are a culture of fear. Everywhere I go, I meet Anglo-Americans immersed in fear. They are scared of us, the other, taking over their country, their jobs, their neighborhoods, their universities, their art world. To "them," "we" are a whole package that includes an indistinct Spanish language, weird art, a sexual threat, gang activity, drugs, and "illegal aliens." They don't realize that their fear has been implanted as a form of political control; that this fear is the very source of the endemic violence that has been affecting this society since its foundation.

Border culture can help dismantle the mechanisms of fear. Border culture can guide us back to common ground and improve our negotiating skills. Border culture is a process of negotiation toward utopia, but in this case, utopia means peaceful coexistence and fruitful cooperation. The border is all we share/

La frontera es lo único que compartimos.

My border colleagues and I are involved in a tripartite debate around separatism. Some Chicano nationalists who still haven't understood that Chicano culture has been redefined by the recent Caribbean and Central American immigrations feel threatened by the prospect of intercultural dialogue and Pan-Americanism. Meanwhile, sectors of the Mexican intelligentsia viewing themselves as guardians of Mexican sovereignty see in our proposals for binational dialogue a disguised form of integration and pull back. Ironically, the conservative Anglo-Americans who are witnessing with panic the irreversible multiculturization of the United States tend to agree with Chicano and Mexican separatists who claim to speak from the left. The three parties prefer to defend "their" identity and culture, rather than to dialogue with the cultural other. The three parties would like to see the border closed. Their intransigent views are based on the modernist premise that identity and culture are closed systems, and that the less these systems change, the more "authentic" they are.

We must realize that all cultures are open systems in constant process of transformation, redefinition, and re-contextualization. What we need is dialogue, not protection. In fact, the only way to regenerate identity and culture is through ongoing dialogue with the other.

Then, the question is, what does dialogue mean? Some thoughts in this respect.

Dialogue is a two-way ongoing communication between peoples and communities that enjoy equal negotiating powers.

Dialogue is a micro-universal expression of international cooperation. When it is effective, we recognize ourselves in the other and realize we don't have to fear.

Dialogue has never existed between the First and Third Worlds. We must not confuse dialogue with neocolonialism, paternalism, vampirism, or appropriation.

Dialogue is the opposite of national security, neighborhood watch, racial paranoia, aesthetic protectionism, sentimental nationalism, ethnocentrism, and monolinguality.

In order to dialogue we must learn each other's language, history, art, literature, and political ideas. We must travel south and east, with frequency and humility, not as cultural tourists but as civilian ambassadors.

Only through dialogue can we develop models of coexistence and cooperation. Only through an ongoing public dialogue in the form of publications, conferences, and collaborative intercultural art and media projects can the wound effectively heal. It will be a long process. It might take 30 to 50 years. We cannot undo centuries of cultural indifference, domination, and racism overnight. All we can aspire to is beginning a dialogue. This document is a humble contribution. I ask you to join in.

A whole generation of artists and intellectuals has begun the dialogue. It is mostly artists, writers, and arts administrators (not politicians, scientists, or religious leaders) who are leading this effort. And from these people, the most vocal and enlightened are women. They are the true cultural leaders of our communities.

THE OTHER VANGUARD

U.S. Latino culture is not homogeneous. It includes a multiplicity of artistic and intellectual expressions both rural and urban, traditional and experimental, marginal and dominant. These expressions differ, depending on their creator's class, sex, nationality, ideology, geography, political context, degree of marginality or assimilation, and time spent in the United States.

California Chicanos and Nuyoricans inhabit different cultural landscapes. Even within Chicano culture a poet living in a rural community in New Mexico has very little in common with an urban *cholo*-punk from L.A. Right-wing Cubanos from Miami are unconditional adversaries of leftist South American exiles. The cultural expressions of Central American and Mexican migrant workers differ drastically from those of the Latino intelligentsia in the universities, ad infinitum. Even this document that attempts to present multiple voices and concerns cannot possibly reflect all sectors of our communities. There is no such thing as "Latino art" or "Hispanic art." There are hundreds of types of Latino American art in the United States. Each is aesthetically, socially, and politically specific.

The United States suffers from a severe case of amnesia. In its obsessive quest to construct the future, it tends to forget or erase the past. Fortunately, the so-called disenfranchised groups who don't feel part of this national project have been meticulously documenting their histories. Latinos, blacks, Asians, women, gays, experimental artists, and non-aligned intellectuals have used inventive languages to record the other history from a multicentric perspective.

"Our art functions both as collective memory and alternative chronicle," says the San Francisco–based Chicana artist and critic Amalia Mesa-Bains.

In this sense, this other art, if nurtured, can become a powerful tool to recapture the desired historical self. The great paradox is that without this historical self, no meaningful future can ever be constructed.

Métier is being redefined. In Latin America, the artist has multiple roles. He/she is not just an image-maker or a marginal genius, but a social thinker/educator/counter-journalist/civilian diplomat/human rights observer. His/her activities take place in the center of society and not in specialized corners.

So-called minority artists in the United States have also been forced to develop multidimensional roles. In the absence of enough institutions that respond to our needs, we have become a sui generis tribe of community organizers, media interventionists, and alternative chroniclers. And the images, texts, and performances we produce are an integral part of these extra-artistic activities.

These models are much more pertinent to our times than those of the established art world.

Unlike the avant-garde of modernist times, today's avant-garde has multiple fronts. Or, as Steven Durland has stated, "the avant-garde is no longer in the front but in the margins." To be avant-garde today is to contribute to the decentralization of art. To be avant-garde means to be able to cross the border back and forth between art and politically significant territory, be it interracial relations, immigration, ecology, homelessness, AIDS, or violence toward women, disenfranchised communities, and Third World countries. To be avant-garde means to perform and exhibit in both artistic and non-artistic contexts: to operate in the world, not just the art world.

In order to articulate our present crisis as cross-cultural artists, we need to invent and reinvent languages. These languages have to be as syncretic, diverse, and complex as the fractured realities we are trying to define.

Postmodernism is a crumbled conceptual architecture, and we are tired of walking among someone else's ruins.

Border artists use experimental techniques and performance-derived practices to intervene directly in the world. The permanent condition of political emergency and cultural vulnerability we live in leaves no other choice. If our actions are not daring, inventive, and unexpected, they won't make a difference, and border reality, with its overwhelming dynamics, will supersede us in an instant.

In this sense, the experimental nature of border art is informed more by political and cultural strategies than by postmodernist theory.

Like artists operating in other politically sensitive parts of the world, border artists understand that formal experimentation is only worthwhile in relation to more important tasks such as the need to generate a binational dialogue, the need to create cultural spaces for others and the need to redefine the asymmetrical relations between the North and the South and among the various ethnic groups that converge in the border spiral. Confronted with these priorities, the hyper-specialized concerns of the art world appear to be secondary.

Much of the contemporary work produced by the Latino community is often regarded as anachronistic and traditional by the art world. Why?

Innovation for innovation's sake, New York's art obsession, doesn't really make sense to us. Innovation is not a value per se in our culture. What we consider "original" generally deals with extra-artistic concerns or concerns related to our traditions and the historical moment we live in. Because of this, our art never seems experimental enough to a monocultural observer.

The misunderstanding increases when the art world discovers that most of us aren't that interested in the gratuitous use of high technology or in the creation of special effects as an end in itself. Our rejection of unnecessary technology is seen as technophobia rather than a political stance.

There are, in fact, many Latino artists working in computer art, media art, video, audio, and sophisticated multimedia languages, but they utilize technology in a socially responsible manner to reveal the contradictions of living and working between a preindustrial past of mythical dimensions and a postindustrial present in permanent states of crises.

When validating contemporary Latino artistic expressions (and this can also apply to African American, Asian American, and Native American art), critics must take off the ethnocentric glasses of innovation and approach the work within its own framework. To understand this framework, they have to do their homework.

Artistic quality is also relative. Hegemonic centers like New York, Paris, and Mexico City have manufactured sacred canons of universality and excellence that we are expected to follow in order to break out of regionalism or ethnicity. But these dogmas are crumbling. The multicultural process that the United States is presently undergoing implies a shift of center, a decentralization of aesthetic canons and styles, and therefore a multiplication of validating criteria.

Today we must always use multiple repertoires to analyze and appreciate a work of art or literature, especially if it comes from a non-Anglo-European source. Cultural multiplicity and aesthetic relativism must be familiar notions to contemporary curators, critics, journalists, arts organizers, panelists, and funding agents.

THE LATINO BOOM

What exactly is the "Latino Boom?"
The artists' answer (choose one of the following):
A. A kind of smoke screen to hide reality.
B. A prestidigitation act to distract us from politics.
C. The green light for us to become rich and famous.
D. A major opportunity to infiltrate and speak from within.
E. A contemporary version of the "good neighbor" policy toward Latin America.
F. The logical result of the Chicano and Nuyorican movements.
G. A caprice of a Madison Avenue tycoon.
(Choose one of the above answers and mail it to the education department of your local museum.)

In 1987, just like in 1492, we were "discovered" (rediscovered, to be precise). We have been here for more than 2,000 years, yet, according to *Time* magazine and many other publications, we "just broke out of the barrio." Today Latinos are being portrayed as the new "up and coming" urban sofisticados. We are suddenly in, fashionable and grantable, and our ethnicity is being commodified. Why?

According to theorist Gayatri Spivak, "otherness has replaced postmodernism as the object of desire." We are undetermined "objects of desire" within a meta-landscape of Mac Fajitas, La Bamba crazes, MTV border rock, Pepsi ads in Spanish and Chicano art without thorns.

In the same way the U.S. government needs and wants a cheap undocumented labor force to sustain its agricultural complex without having to suffer Spanish language or unemployed foreigners wandering in their neighborhoods, the contemporary art world needs and desires the spiritual and aesthetic models of Latino culture without having to experience our political outrage and cultural contradictions. What the art world wants is a "domesticated Latino" who can provide enlightenment without irritation, entertainment without confrontation.

"They don't want the real thing. They want microwave tamales and T-shirts of Frida Kahlo." They want ranchero music sung by Linda Ronstadt, not Lola Beltran (the "queen" of Mexican ranchero music); the Mexicorama look of *Milagro Beanfield War* and not the acidity of Chicano experimental video.

We must politely remind the art world that image is never a substitute for culture. It is reality that must be addressed, no matter how painful or complex it might be. Like the border graffiti says: "Simulacra stops here" (at the border).

In this Faustian moment of perplexity and sudden attention given to "Latinos" by major cultural institutions and mainstream media, we are concerned about the way "Latino art" is being presented and re-presented.

Some frequent mistakes include homogenization ("all Latinos are alike and interchangeable"); decontextualization (Latino art is defined as a self-contained system that exists outside Western culture); curatorial eclecticism (all styles and art forms can be showcased in the same event as long as they are "Latino"), folklorization and exoticization (needless to explain).

Latino artists are being portrayed as "magical realists," "pretechnological bohemians," "primeval creatures in touch with ritual," "hypersexual entertainers," "fiery revolutionaries," or "amazing success stories." Our art is being described as "colorful," "passionate," "mysterious," "exuberant," "baroque," etc., all euphemistic terms for nationalism and primitivism.

These mythical views only help to perpetuate the colonizing notions toward the South as a wild and exotic preindustrial universe ever awaiting to be discovered, enjoyed, and purchased by the entrepreneurial eye of the North.

It is mainly the artists who voluntarily or unknowingly resemble the stereotypes who end up being selected by the fingers of the Latino boom, but where are the voices of dissent who delineate the boundaries of the abyss? Where are the artists experimenting with the new possibilities of identity? Where are the artists working in performance, video, or installation, the more political ones? And where are the Latinas? Women have been instrumental in the creation of a Latino culture in the United States. Why are all these key artists being left out of the blockbuster Hispanic shows and the all-encompassing Latino festivals?

Some people think that these questions are an expression of our permanent dissatisfaction and ungratefulness. My response to them is simple. By asking out loud, we are merely trying to clean the mirror of true communication.

Many of us are ambivalent about the effects of the boom. On one hand, it has opened doors to many talented artists whose work was practically unknown outside the Latino milieu. On the other, it has brought foreign values to our milieu. Those who are chosen are pressured to become more slick and "professional" and therefore more individualistic and competitive, and to produce twice as much as before. The result is devastating: museum-quality art framed by cultural guilt and spiritual exhaustion. And on top of that, it has produced a confused community, divided into those who were chosen and those who weren't. Those left behind are slowly poisoned by jealousy and defeat.

Many of us don't aspire to make it in Hollywood or New York. We want something even more ambitious. And that is to be in control of our political destiny and our cultural expressions. What the boom has done is to provide us with a handful of opportunities to "make it" at a very high spiritual cost. But it has not contributed to the betterment of the conditions of our communities.

There is a fatal discrepancy between the colorful image of prosperity broadcast by the boom and the sordid reality that no one wishes to address. Today Latinos have the highest school drop-out rate. We are the largest population in the prisons of the Southwest. The majority of babies born with AIDS are Latino and African American. Police brutality, alcoholism, and drugs are quotidian realities in our communities. Even our physical space is being threatened. Gentrification is pushing our families and friends outside our barrios as we witness with melancholy and impotence the arrival of real estate lords, insensitive yuppies, trendy restaurants, and commercial galleries. So, what exactly is booming?

The Latino boom is clearly a media-produced mirage: a marketing strategy designed with two objectives: to expand our consumer power and to offer exotica to the American middle class. Our participation in national political and cultural processes remains restricted to token individuals who are generally conservative.

"We want understanding, not publicity." We want to be considered intellectuals, not entertainers; partners, not clients; collaborators, not competitors; holders of a strong spiritual vision, not emerging voices; and, above all, full citizens, not exotic minorities.

THE MULTICULTURAL CRAZE OR
"WE ARE THE (ART) WORLD" PART II

"2 Latinos + 2 Asians + 2 Blacks = Multicultural" — (conceptual T-shirt)

A multicultural fever of epidemic proportions is afflicting the art world. Everywhere we look, there are cultural institutions organizing events that feature artists from various ethnic communities that have almost nothing in common aesthetically or ideologically. "The only thing that binds us is otherness," says Amalia Mesa-Bains, "a threatening otherness that must be rationalized and made accessible."

"Multicultural" is the hip word of today. Everybody agrees it is politically correct. Few know what it really means.

It is an ambiguous term. It can mean a cultural pluralism in which the various ethnic groups collaborate and dialogue with one another without having to sacrifice their particular identities to the Big Blob. But it can also mean a kind of Esperantic Disney World, a tutti-frutti cocktail of cultures, languages, and art forms in which "everything becomes everything else," and nothing is really indispensable. This is a dangerous notion that strongly resembles the bankrupt concept of the melting pot with its familiar connotations of integration, homogenization, and neutralization. It is why so many Latino organizations are so distrustful of the term.

Many key questions are still unresolved: Can "minority" groups or organizations who only produce work relevant to their milieu be considered multicultural? Given that Chicano culture is a culture of fusion between the Mexican and Anglo-American, can we say that all Chicano spaces are by definition multicultural? Are Anglo-American women and gay groups part of this project? Can a group formed by a majority of Anglo-Americans, say eight out of ten, be considered multicultural? What is the difference between fusion, hybridization, synthesis, and appropriation? What is the difference between cross-, inter-, and multi-cultural?

The debate is open and we should all participate in sharpening the meaning of the word.

During the past twenty years, a number of pioneering nonwhite artists, writers, and institutions have been quietly but tenaciously paving the way toward the present multicultural craze. Yet they aren't getting recognition or funding. Some are even giving up for lack of support. Meanwhile, monocultural organizations with absolutely no track record of multicultural involvement have adopted the rhetoric of multiculturalism as a strategy to obtain substantial program funding. They often use this funding to commission Anglo artists who work with appropriated imagery.

What should be done? If a monocultural organization wants to apply for funding to produce "multicultural work" (and no one is questioning their right to do it), they must at least have the dignity to contact the various ethnic communities around them, ask for assistance, invite them to collaborate, and, if possible, hire people of color for permanent staff positions. To hire bilingual clerical staff and multiculturally literate archivists could be extremely helpful.

A provocative model is being implemented based on the temporary relationship between an alternative space and a local community organization with the common goals of sharing audiences and producing a specific event, an exhibit, or a publication. Other models must be brought forward.

Am I asking too much? Multiculturalism must be reflected not only in the programs or publicity of an organization, but in its administrative structure, in the quality of thought of its members and eventually in the audience it serves.

I'm becoming exhausted repeating it: multiculturalism is not an art trend, not a grant language, nor a new investment package for art *maquiladoras*. It is the very core of the new society in which we live!

PARADOXES AND PROPOSALS

We are living in a paradoxical moment. At the peak of the Latino boom and the multicultural craze, we witness in utter perplexity the most arrogant behavior of the current administration perpetrated against "minorities," immigrants, and Latin American countries.

In the very moment Eddie Olmos, Luis Valdez, Ruben Blades, and Los Lobos are becoming national celebrities, the U.S. government is threatening to dismantle bilingual education and affirmative action and proposing to build a ditch on the U.S.-Mexico border.

Just as my colleagues and I are being asked to perform and exhibit in the main spaces of Manhattan and San Francisco, the border patrol is dismantling labor camps in North County (San Diego) and the police in California are declaring open warfare against Latino gangs.

On the same TV channels that show us glamorous commercials for Taco Bell, Colombian coffee, or Mexican beer, we also witness sensationalist accounts of Mexican criminals, drug dealers, and corrupt *politicos* on the evening news. The current media war against the Latino cultural other is intercut with eulogies to our products. Blood and salsa, that's the nature of this relationship.

It's all very confusing, but we are determined to find the underlying connections between these facts. For these connections can reveal important information about the way contemporary United States culture deals with otherness. In this context, my colleagues and I encourage our fellow artists, writers, journalists, curators, and cultural organizers to participate in this continental project, to collaborate (truly collaborate) as much as possible with the cultural other, inside and outside our borders, and to learn to share decisions and power with the people of non-Anglo-European descent. Only through a continuous and systematic rejection of racism, sexism, and separatism can we come to terms with otherness outside and the otherness within. From within, we must help the United States become an enlightened neighbor in this continent and a respectful landlord in its own house.

Cherríe Moraga
Art in América con Acento

◻

I write this on the one-week anniversary of the death of the Nicaraguan Revolution.

We are told not to think of it as a death, but I am in mourning. It is an unmistakable feeling. A week ago, the name "Daniel" had poured from Nicaragüense lips with a warm liquid familiarity. In private, doubts gripped their bellies and those doubts they took finally to the ballot box. Doubts seeded by bullets and bread: the U.S.-financed Contra War and the economic embargo. Once again an emerging sovereign nation is brought to its knees. A nation on the brink of declaring to the entire world that revolution is the people's choice betrays its own dead. Imperialism makes traitors of us all, makes us weak and tired and hungry.

I don't blame the people of Nicaragua. I blame the U.S. government. I blame my complicity as a citizen in a country that, short of an invasion, stole the Nicaraguan revolution that el pueblo forged with their own blood and bones. After hearing the outcome of the elections, I wanted to flee the United States in shame and despair.

I am Latina, born and raised in the United States. I am a writer. What is my responsibility in this?

Days later, George Bush comes to San Francisco. He arrives at the St. Francis Hotel for a $1,000-a-plate fund raising dinner for Pete Wilson's gubernatorial campaign. There is a protest. We, my camarada and I, get off the subway. I can already hear the voices chanting from a distance. We can't make out what they're saying, but they are Latinos and my heart races, seeing so many brown faces. They hold up a banner. The words are still unclear but as I come closer closer to the circle of my people, I am stunned. "¡Viva la paz en Nicaragua!" it states. "¡Viva George Bush! ¡Viva UNO!" And my heart drops. Across the street, the "resistance" has congregated — less organized, white, young, middle-class students. *¿Dónde 'stá mi pueblo?*

A few months earlier, I was in another country, San Cristóbal, Chiapas, México. The United States had just invaded Panamá. This time, I could stand outside the United States, read the Mexican newspapers for a perspective on the United States that was not monolithic. In the Na Bolom Center Library I wait for a tour of the grounds. The room is filled with norteamericanos. They are huge people, the men slouching in couches. Their thick legs spread across the floor, their women lean into them. They converse. "When we invaded Panama. . . ." I grow rigid at the sound of the word, "we." They are progressives (I know this from their conversation.) They oppose the invasion, but identify with the invaders.

How can I, as a Latina, identify with those who invade Latin American land? George Bush is not my leader. I did not elect him, although my tax dollars pay for the Salvadoran Army's guns. We are a living breathing contradiction, we who live en las entrañas del monstruo, but I refuse to be forced to identify. I am the product of invasion. My father is Anglo; my mother, Mexican. I am the result of the dissolution of blood lines and the theft of language; and yet, I am a testimony to the failure of the United States to wholly anglicize its mestizo citizens.

I wrote in México, "Los Estados Unidos es mi país, pero no es mi patria." I cannot flee the United States, my land resides beneath its borders. We stand on land that was once the country of México. And before any conquistadors staked out political boundaries, this was Indian land and in the deepest sense remains just that: a land sin fronteras. Chicanos with memory like our Indian counterparts recognize that we are a nation within a nation. An internal nation whose existence defies borders of language, geography, race. Chicanos are a multiracial, multilingual people, who since 1848, have been displaced from our ancestral lands or remain upon them as indentured servants to Anglo-American invaders.

Today, nearly a century and a half later, the Anglo invasion of Latin America has extended well beyond the Mexican/American border. When U.S. capital invades a country, its military machinery is quick to follow to protect its interests. This is Panamá, Puerto Rico, Grenada, Guatemala. . . . Ironically, the United States' gradual consumption of Latin America and the Caribbean is bringing the people of the Americas together. What was once largely a chicano/mexicano population in California is now Guatemalteco, Salvadoreño, Nicaragüense. What was largely a Puerto Rican and Dominican "Spanish Harlem" of New York is now populated with mexicanos playing rancheras and drinking cerveza. This mass emigration is evident from throughout the Third World. Every place the United States has been involved militarily has brought its offspring, its orphans, its homeless, and its casualties to this country: Vietnam, Guatemala, Cambodia, the Philippines. . . .

Third World populations are changing the face of North America. The new face has got that delicate fold in the corner of the eye and that wide-bridged nose. The mouth speaks in double negatives and likes to eat a lot of chile. By the twenty-first century our whole concept of "America" will be dramatically altered; most significantly by a growing Latino population whose strong cultural ties, economic disenfranchisement, racial visibility, and geographical proximity to Latin America discourages any facile assimilation into Anglo-American society.

Latinos in the United States do not represent a homogeneous group. Some of us are native born, whose ancestors precede not only the arrival of the Anglo-American but also of the Spaniard. Most of us are immigrants, economic refugees coming to the United States in search of work. Some of us are political refugees, fleeing death squads and imprisonment; others come fleeing revolution and the loss of wealth. Finally, some have simply landed here very tired of war. And in all cases, our children had no choice in the matter. U.S. Latinos represent the whole spectrum of color and class and political position, including those who firmly believe they can integrate into the mainstream of North American life. The more European the heritage and the higher the class status, the more closely Latinos identify with the powers that be. They vote Republican. They stand under the U.S. flag and applaud George Bush for bringing "peace" to Nicaragua. They hope one day he'll do the same for Cuba, so they can return to their patria and live a "North American-style" consumer life. Because they know in the United States they will never have it all, they will always remain "spics," "greasers," "beaners," and "foreigners" in Anglo-America.

As a Latina artist I can choose to contribute to the development of a docile generation of would-be Republican "Hispanics" loyal to the United States, or to the creation of a force of "disloyal" americanos who subscribe to a multicultural, multilingual, radical restructuring of América. Revolution is not only won by numbers, but by visionaries, and if artists aren't visionaries, then we have no business doing what we do.

I call myself a Chicana writer. Not a Mexican-American writer, not a Hispanic writer, not a half-breed writer. To be a Chicana is not merely to name one's racial/cultural identity, but also to name a politic, a politic that re-

fuses assimilation into the U.S. mainstream. It acknowledges our mesti-
zaje — Indian, Spanish, and Africano. After a decade of "hispanicization" (a
term superimposed upon us by Reagan-era bureaucrats), the term Chicano
assumes even greater radicalism. With the misnomer "Hispanic," Anglo-
America proffers to the Spanish surnamed the illusion of blending into the
"melting pot" like any other white immigrant group. But the Latino is
neither wholly immigrant nor wholly white; and here in this country, "Indian" and "dark" don't melt. (Puerto Ricans on the East Coast have been
called "Spanish" for decades and it's done little to alter their status on the
streets of New York City.)

The generation of Chicano literature being read today sprang forth from a
grassroots social and political movement of the sixties and seventies that
was definitively anti-assimilationist. It responded to a stated mandate: *art is
political.* The proliferation of poesía, cuentos, and teatro that grew out of El
Movimiento was supported by Chicano cultural centers and publishing
projects throughout the Southwest and in every major urban area where a
substantial Chicano population resided. The Flor y Canto poetry festivals
of the seventies and a teatro that spilled off flatbed trucks into lettuce fields
in the sixties are hallmarks in the history of the Chicano cultural movement.
Chicano literature was a literature in dialogue with its community. And as
some of us became involved in feminist, gay, and lesbian concerns in the late
seventies and early eighties, our literature was forced to expand to reflect
the multifaceted nature of the Chicano experience.

The majority of published Chicano writers today are products of that era
of activism, but as the Movement grew older and more established, it
became neutralized by middle-aged and middle-class concerns, as well as by
a growing conservative trend in government. Most of the gains made for
farm workers in California were dismantled by a succession of reactionary
governors and Reagan/Bush economics. Cultural centers lost funding.
Most small press Chicano publishers disappeared as suddenly as they had
appeared. What was once a radical and working-class Latino student base
on university campuses has become increasingly conservative. A generation
of tokenistic affirmative-action policies and bourgeois flight from Central
America and the Caribbean has spawned a tiny Latino elite who often turn
to their racial/cultural identities not as a source of political empowerment,
but of personal employment as tokens in an Anglo-dominated business
world.

And the writers. . . ? Today more and more of us insist we are "American"
writers (in the North American sense of the word). The body of our literary

criticism grows (seemingly at a faster rate than the literature itself), we assume tenured positions in the university, secure New York publishers, and our work moves further and further away from a community-based and national political movement.

A writer will write. With or without a movement.

Fundamentally, I started writing to save my life. Yes, my own life first. I see the same impulse in my students — the dark, the queer, the mixed-blood, the violated — turning to the written page with a relentless passion, a drive to avenge their own silence, invisibility, and erasure as living, innately expressive human beings.

A writer will write with or without a movement; but at the same time, for Chicano, lesbian, gay, and feminist writers — anybody writing against the grain of Anglo misogynist culture — political movements are what have allowed our writing to surface from the secret places in our notebooks into the public sphere. In 1990, Chicanos, gay men, and women are not better off than we were in 1970. We have an ever-expanding list of physical and social diseases affecting us: AIDS, breast cancer, police brutality. Censorship is becoming increasingly institutionalized, not only through government programs, but through transnational corporate ownership of publishing houses, record companies, etc. Without a movement to foster and sustain our writing, we risk being swallowed up into the "Decade of the Hispanic" that never happened. The fact that a few of us have "made it" and are doing better than we imagined has not altered the nature of the beast. He remains blue-eyed and male and prefers profit over people.

Like most artists, we Chicano artists would like our work to be seen as "universal" in scope and meaning and reach as large an audience as possible. Ironically, the most "universal" work — writing capable of reaching the hearts of the greatest number of people — is the most culturally specific. The European-American writer understands this because it is his version of cultural specificity that is deemed "universal" by the literary establishment. In the same manner, universality in the *Chicana* writer requires the most Mexican and the most female images we are capable of producing. Our task is to write what no one is prepared to hear, for what has been said so far in barely a decade of consistent production is a mere bocadito. Chicana writers are still learning the art of transcription, but what we will be capable of producing in the decades to come, if we have the cultural/political movements to support us, could make a profound contribution to the social transformation of these Américas. The reto, however, is to remain as culturally specific and culturally complex as possible, even in the face of main-stream seduction to do otherwise.

Let's not fool ourselves, the European-American middle-class writer is the cultural mirror through which the literary and theatre establishment sees itself reflected, so it will continue to reproduce itself through new generations of writers. On occasion New York publishes our work, as it perceives a growing market for the material, allowing Chicanos access to national distribution on a scale that small independent presses could never accomplish. (Every writer longs for such distribution, particularly since it more effectively reaches communities of color.) But I fear that my genera-tion and the generation of young writers that follows will look solely to the Northeast for recognition. I fear that we may become accustomed to this very distorted reflection, and that we will find ourselves writing more and more in translation through the filter of Anglo-American censors. Wher-ever Chicanos may live, in the richest and most inspired junctures of our writing, our writer-souls are turned away from Washington, the U.S. capi-tal, and toward a México Antiguo. That is not to say that contemporary Chicano literature does not wrestle with current social concerns, but with-out the memory of our once-freedom, how do we imagine a future?

I still believe in a Chicano literature that is hungry for change, that has the courage to name the sources of our discontent both from within our raza and without, that challenges us to envision a world where poverty, crack, and pesticide poisoning are not endemic to people with dark skin or Span-ish surnames. It is a literature that knows that God is neither white nor male nor reason to rape anyone. If such ideas are "naive" (as some critics would have us believe), then let us remain naive, naively and passionately com-mitted to an art of "resistance," resistance to domination by Anglo-America, resistance to assimilation, resistance to economic and sexual exploitation. *An art that subscribes to integration into mainstream Amerika is not Chicano art.*

All writing is confession. Confession masked and revealed in the voices and faces of our characters. All is hunger. The longing to be known fully and still loved. The admission of our own inherent vulnerability, our weakness, our tenderness of skin, fragility of heart, our overwhelming desire to be relieved of the burden of ourselves in the body of another, to be forgiven of our ultimate aloneness in the mystical body of a god or the common work of a revolution. These are human considerations that the best of writers presses her finger upon. The wound ruptures and . . . heals.

One of the deepest wounds Chicanos suffer is separation from our Southern relatives. Gloria Anzaldúa calls it a "1,950-mile-long open wound," dividing México from the United States, "dividing a *pueblo,* a culture." This "llaga" ruptures over and over again in our writing, Chicanos in search of a México that never wholly embraces us. "Mexico gags," poet Lorna Dee Cervantes writes, "on this bland pocha seed." This separation was never our choice. In 1990, we witnessed a fractured and disintegrating América, where the Northern half functions as the absentee landlord of the Southern half and the economic disparity between the First and Third Worlds drives a bitter wedge between a people.

I hold a vision requiring a radical transformation of consciousness in this country, that as the people-of-color population increases, we will not be just another brown faceless mass hungrily awaiting integration into white Amerika, but that we will emerge as a mass movement of people to redefine what an "American" is. Our entire concept of this nation's identity must change, possibly be obliterated. We must learn to see ourselves less as U.S. citizens and more as members of a larger world community composed of many nations of people and no longer give credence to the geopolitical borders that have divided us, Chicano from Mexicano, Filipino-American from Pacific Islander, African-American from Haitian. Call it racial memory. Call it shared economic discrimination. Chicanos call it "Raza," — be it Quichua, Cubano, or Colombiano — an identity that dissolves borders. As a Chicana writer that's the context in which I want to create.

I am an American writer in the original sense of the word, an Américan *con acento.*

Jorge Huerta

Looking for the Magic: Chicanos in the Mainstream

❏

Let me begin by defining my terminology. My focus in this article is on Chicano as opposed to Latino or Latin American plays and playwrights. For me, the term Latino applies to those descendants of Latin American parents born and/or educated and living in the United States. The largest groups are the Mexican American, or Chicano, the Puerto Rican, and the Cuban American. More often than not, "Chicano" is used as a political label, a badge which connotes a sense of otherness. Just as there are biological and cultural aspects to being a Mexican American, it must be understood that not all Mexican Americans call themselves Chicano regardless of whether or not they have felt marginalized in this society. However, with few exceptions, those playwrights writing about the Chicano experience do refer to themselves as Chicanos. Chicano plays were initially produced only by Chicano *teatros*; now, groups that are dominated by other Latinos, particularly in the Midwest and on the East Coast, are also producing Chicano plays.

There are many Latino theatre companies in this country, from New York to Los Angeles and Seattle to Miami. If I refer to Latino theatres, this includes the Chicano *teatros* as well, in contrast to the mainstream theatres which are generally Anglo-dominated. While I will concentrate on the phenomenon of mainstream theatres producing Chicano plays, in many cases the word Chicano can be altered to Latino, for all Latinos face virtually the same problems as we attempt to take our rightful place in the development and history of "American" theatre.

Until the early 1980s Chicano theatre in this country could only be found in the Chicano communities that had spawned their own *teatros*, playwrights, directors, and actors. Mainstream theatre companies did not produce plays that dealt with the Chicano experience, either out of apathy, or, perhaps, because they assumed that much of that theatre was being expressed in Spanish.

This attitude began to change when the New York Public Theatre produced Miguel Piñero's *Short Eyes* in 1974, and the Center Theatre Group coproduced Luis Valdez's *Zoot Suit* in Los Angeles in 1978. Motivated by the critical and financial success of these two plays, other mainstream theatre companies began to show an interest in what Chicanos and Latinos were writing and began to produce their plays. I will assess this trend from the viewpoint of an active participant in many of these programs in an effort to reevaluate this practice; a process which can be termed either "mainstreaming" or "infiltrating," depending upon one's viewpoint as well as on the results of such alliances.

Major questions arise when non-Latino theatres produce Chicano plays: Which playwrights get produced and why? Which directors are allowed to direct and why? What actors are cast and why? Further, what audiences are being reached and why? Finally, we can ask the larger question of each of these categories: Why not? But first let me briefly trace the evolution of Chicano theatre since 1960.

Prior to the mid-1960s, aside from Spanish religious folk drama, most of the theatre produced in the Chicano community consisted of theatre of exile or relocation: plays from the mother country, Mexico. These productions were generally in Spanish and often reflected an attitude of reverence for the homeland rather than an expression of what it meant to be the "other" in the United States. There were certainly plays about Mexican/Chicano dislocation prior to the 1960s, but they have not survived the test of time.

It was not until 1963 when Luis Valdez wrote his first play, *The Shrunken Head of Pancho Villa,* that a Chicano playwright began to explore the idea of being marginalized in this country. When this play was presented by San Jose State College in California in 1964, it became the first produced play written by a Chicano about being Chicano. This production motivated Valdez to continue in the theatre and after a year with the San Francisco Mime Troupe, he founded the legendary Teatro Campesino in 1965. Valdez guided his troupe in the creation of *actos,* or political skits about the farm worker crisis. These *actos* later inspired other Chicanos to form their own *teatros,* collectively creating *actos* relevant to their particular struggles. Luis Valdez can thus be credited with inspiring a national movement of Chicano theatre groups; a movement that perseveres, under much different circumstances, to this day.

Chicano theatre groups, mostly community-based or university-affili-ated, continue to exist from the Midwest to the West Coast. Now, however, there are also a handful of companies with funding sufficient to pay full- or part-time salaries to administrators and artists. Thus, the *teatro* movement has evolved into a full spectrum of theatre groups reflective of national trends, though much more modestly funded. Some *teatros* insist on total autonomy from funding agencies while others, such as the Teatro Campe-sino and Teatro de la Esperanza, include staff who participate as panelists in the funding processes of local, state, and national agencies.

Whereas the original Chicano theatre movement was represented by groups rather than individuals (aside from Luis Valdez and a few others), Chicano theatre today is actually a diverse assortment of companies and individuals who cannot be categorized into a single genre or theme. The collective process, once an integral and vital aspect of this movement, is no longer the norm. The anonymity of early collective creations has given way to recognition of individual playwrights and directors who are making their marks both within the *teatros* and outside the Chicano communities.

Although Chicanos have their roots in Mexico, their plays have focused on the diaspora of Mexicanos who have emigrated to this country. This is not so much a theatre of exile as it is a theatre of relocation and negotia-tion — how to survive in a hostile society. When I first began to research Chicano theatre in 1970, there was not one play in print; now there are many. Every Chicano play or adaptation produced to date can be termed political theatre, for they all assert a commitment to the Chicano commu-nity by revealing injustices in such institutions as the schools, the police sys-tem, the courts, and the workplace while also often exposing a search for identity within the dominant culture. During the 1980s, the Chicana play-wrights came to the fore, exploring gender and sexuality as they exposed sexism, patriarchy, and homophobia in the Mexicano/Chicano community.

Although themes may vary, it is the context that determines whether or not a play is, indeed, Chicano. Neither the ancestry of its author, nor the fact that it is written in a particular language, determines whether or not a play is Chicano. If the theme explores the nature of being Chicano, I would call it Chicano and more particularly, ethno-specific theatre. The majority of plays about the Chicano are original scripts rather than adaptations. To date, all Chicano plays take place in the United States.

A Chicano play can be adapted from non-Chicano plays, such as Arthur Miller's *A View from the Bridge,* or Osvaldo Dragún's *Historias para ser con-tadas,* which have been transferred to the barrio. Thus, plays can *become* Chicano by virtue of contextualization, changing locales and adding Spanish to the dialogue. In the case of *A View from the Bridge,* originally written about Italian Americans in Brooklyn, the shift to San Diego's Logan Heights, under the Coronado Bridge, made obvious sense and proved the universality of the immigrant experience in this country. Certainly not all plays can be adapted to the Chicano *ambiente* by simply translating some of the dialogue to Spanish, but language is the most obvious identifier of culture and has often been crucial to the contextualization of a Chicano play.

Very few Chicano plays have been written exclusively in either Spanish or English, revealing, instead, the Chicano's bilinguality. Initially, the plays were very bilingual, written in a combination of English and Spanish and often sprinkled with *caló,* or street slang. During the 1980s the language evolved from an almost equal amount of Spanish and English to a majority of English. One reason for this linguistic shift was the rise of the individual playwrights who were without a *teatro* to produce their works. Some of these playwrights chose to court the mainstream theatres which had begun to show an interest in Latino projects. For most theatres, the concern was sincere; an effort to plumb the well of Latin American and Latino plays that might be of interest to their audiences.

In 1985, the South Coast Repertory Theatre, in Costa Mesa, California, initiated the Hispanic Playwrights Project under the direction of José Cruz Gonzales in an effort to develop Latino plays and playwrights. This theatre company's commitment to the development process is firm, but following the first year of the project, the theatre has not produced any of these plays in their main-stage or second-stage seasons. When I asked Gonzales why the theatre had discontinued producing Latino plays in their season after the first year, he answered cryptically: "Taste." Perhaps wisely, the producers chose not to invest in mainstage Latino productions, inadvertently illustrating the potential danger when a non-Latino theatre produces Latino plays. Let me explain:

The first year of the Hispanic Playwrights Project, the theatre optioned *Birds* by Lisa Loomer and *Charlie Bacon and his Family* by Arthur Giron. Both of these plays deal with Chicano/Mexicano themes. José Luis Valenzuela directed the first play and I directed the second, as readings for the public. However, when the theatre decided to produce fully-mounted versions of these plays the directors were non-Latinos. One was the artistic director of the company and the other a director with whom they were familiar. This decision is understandable, given the financial risks; however, neither production reached its full potential. I would posit that neither of the directors had a firm grasp of the culture of the plays.

In his direction of the reading of *Birds,* Valenzuela had brought years of experience in Chicano/Mexicano theatre to his concept, giving a life to the text that enhanced its vision, the sociopolitical issues, and the characterizations. It was his Mexicano/Chicano consciousness that enabled the director to embrace the material with a clear understanding of the communities represented. The action flowed freely from scene to scene as required by the script. We could sit in the audience and recognize the people in Loomer's play as representative of our community. Months later, when I entered the theatre for the fully-mounted production, however, my apprehensions grew when I saw that the set looked like a monumental Taco Bell restaurant. The fluidity of the text was forever lost on a ponderous set that hampered the rhythms of the writing. Apparently the director of *Birds* felt that the "mission style" would capture the setting of a play that takes place in the world of a Mexicano/Chicano/Anglo family. It was a Hollywood cliché that was embarrassing as well as frustrating. The entire production team must have an understanding, a sensibility of the people and situations being portrayed. Otherwise our plays are not about us; they are about them.

In addition to examples of cultural incompetence, there is another danger: the disturbing trend among some regional theatres to produce Latino plays as their "multicultural" events, using these productions to illustrate their alleged commitment to cultural diversity. The Center Theatre Group of Los Angeles has seldom been noted for its adventurous casting, usually falling into the star system and traditional typecasting. But when the theatre produced Ariel Dorfman's *Widows,* set in Latin America, in 1991, suddenly the company was multicultural. The Magic Theater in San Francisco produced Octavio Solís's *Man of the Flesh* — a Chicano Don Juan — in 1990. However, the actor playing the central figure of Juan was neither a Chicano nor even a Latino; he was black, but not a black Latino and not even bilingual in a role that demands a bilingual actor. In 1992, the Marin Theatre Company produced Arthur Girón's *A Dream of Wealth,* about the exploits of the United Fruit Company in Guatemala and again, the cast was multicultural. The list goes on, but the reader gets the point. Why are some theatre companies casting only their Latino plays with multiethnic casts? Why not their other productions as well? It is too convenient for these companies to take care of affirmative action goals only when producing a Latino play. Of course they would not dare to cast an African American play with white actors.

Another curious and politically sensitive area is the trend to hire Anglo women to direct Latino and Latin American plays. Female directors of any background are grossly underrepresented in the regional theatres, but why should non-Latinas be chosen to direct ethno-specific plays that have nothing to do with their own backgrounds? It seems that just as we were complaining about the white, male directors attempting to interpret our cultures, the artistic directors saw fit to bring in the white women. Thus, ethno-specific theatre offers mainstream artistic directors the opportunity of relegating all "others" to minority status—be they women, Latinos, blacks, Asian Americans or Native Americans. In other instances, Latino directors have been contracted to direct the children's productions; a very worthy cause, but, once again, a form of secondary status.

The two mainstream theatres that demonstrated a firm commitment to producing fully mounted productions of Latino plays each season were the Los Angeles Theatre Center and the San Diego Repertory Theatre. The border city of San Diego is an obvious site for bilingual theatre and the Rep's artistic directors initiated its Teatro Sin Fronteras to produce and promote plays in both Spanish and English. This program continues and the Rep's audiences are being exposed to a variety of Latino and Latin American plays.

In Los Angeles, José Luis Valenzuela led the "Latino Lab" to national prominence, directing Latino plays under the aegis of the Los Angeles Theatre Center until that institution's demise in 1991. The Lab's collectively created homage to the Chicano Moratorium of 1970, titled *August 29,* was perhaps the most significant Chicano production of the 1980s, which premiered exactly twenty years after the event for which it is titled.

August 29 brought Brechtian documentary face-to-face with a ghost story as it dramatized a fictitious romance between the ghost of Ruben Salazar and a Chicana professor while she prepares a book about his life and death at the hands of a Los Angeles sheriff on August 29, 1970. *August 29* has only been produced by the Los Angeles Theatre Center and will hopefully be presented in other theatres as well, for it challenges its audiences to think about inequities, leaving no one free of criticism, regardless of ethnicity. *August 29,* however, was a rare exception, exposing villains outside of the Chicano community.

While the early *actos* and plays boldly presented injustices perpetrated by the power structure, usually Anglo-controlled, most of the Chicano plays that have been produced by the regional theatres demonstrate problems confined to the microcosm of the barrios. These plays can be termed "safe theatre," that is, nonthreatening for the dominant culture. The five Chicano plays most produced by mainstream theatres are Luis Valdez's *I Don't Have to Show You No Stinking Badges!*, Milcha Sánchez-Scott's *Roosters*, Octavio

Solís's *Man of the Flesh*, Edit Villareal's *My Visits With MGM (My Grand-mother Marta)*, and Josefina López's *Real Women Have Curves*. Valdez's play is certainly critical of Hollywood stereotyping but we never see the (non-Latino) enemy. With the exception of Solís's piece, there are no Anglo characters in any of these plays; no villains outside their own circle. It appears that mainstream theatres are more interested in Chicano plays that do not attack the power structure.

A central issue in López's play is the threat of deportation but we never see the representatives of the INS, who might, in fact, be Chicano. The Anglo characters in *Man of the Flesh* are caricatures, not to be taken seriously, while the villain is a Chicano. All five of these plays deserve to be produced, but is it a coincidence that they leave the audience free to blame the Chicanos' problems on the Chicanos?

The danger here is that Chicano theatre and Chicanos in particular are being defined by the theatres that produce their plays. Milcha Sánchez-Scott's *Roosters* is a case in point. This is a delicately written piece about a Chicano family in the Southwest in which the adolescent daughter is a devout Catholic, the mother an all-suffering wife, and the sister an old prostitute. In other words, the virgin, the mother, and the whore. These three women are contrasted with a humble Mexican *campesino* and an ex-con father in mortal battle with his poetic son. The characters are not stereotypes — they are *real* — but in the hands of the wrong director or producers, the plays can be a devastating portrayal of Chicano culture. Do all of the members of the production team understand this Chicano play that defies common notions of reality by using dancers to portray fighting cocks and ending with a climactic Ascension?

I saw the New York production of *Roosters* and was quite moved by the finale as Angela, the daughter, rose above the rooftop. Whether this was a metaphor or whether we were being asked to believe that inexplicable phenomena are still possible, I understood that my community could believe in miracles. Sánchez-Scott told me later that one of the potential directors she had interviewed for the New York production had asked her if Angela was on drugs. Clearly, this non-Latino director had no understanding of Chicano spirituality.

The San Antonio production of *Roosters* was directed by José Guadalupe Saucedo, a founding member of El Teatro de la Esperanza, a Chicano who understands his community's language and spirituality. His actors were all Chicano or Mexican and his audience was mostly the same. In fact, Saucedo bilingualized his production since he knew that the San Antonio audience would not only understand Spanish but appreciate a production that reflected the bilingualism of its community. They did. A non-Latino theatre company would lose the majority of its audience if the director attempted to add Spanish to this play. Indeed, if the author had included more Spanish in the text it would not have attracted the attention of non-Latino producers in the first place. This brings us to the crucial question of language in Chicano theatre.

Very few regional theatres have produced plays in Spanish for the obvious reasons. Therefore Chicano playwrights who wish to get produced by the regional theatres cannot present their scripts to literary managers *en Español* or even in Spanglish. Few literary managers would be able to judge these texts. The majority of Chicano playwrights who wish to see their plays produced by mainstream companies are writing either entirely in English or with very little code-switching. Because of a linguistic ignorance on the part of certain producers, Chicanos are being defined as monolingual English-speakers, rather than the bilingual community they actually represent.

One playwright who has insisted on writing her plays bilingually is Cherríe Moraga, whose most recent play is titled *Heroes and Saints*. Moraga is a poet and her simple yet stunning imagery permeates the language of her characters. The degree of bilinguality she uses as well as the images she employs enable her to differentiate between subgroups in the community according to class, gender, age, and ethnic identification. The older characters are more bilingual and communicate in a form of poetry that reflects their dual languages and cultures. The language is truly Chicano in its use of code-switching from English to Spanish within a single sentence: *"Por eso, te digo* she better learn to keep her damn mouth shut. *Ella siempre* gotta be putting *la cuchara en la olla."* Neither the monolingual English-speakers nor the Spanish-speakers appreciate this bilingualism as do Chicano audiences. And the effect is totally lost in translation whether to a single English or Spanish text; neither language alone can duplicate code-switching effectively.

Moraga has made a very conscious choice to capture the nuances of working-class Chicano dialogue. She may, therefore, have to accept limited production opportunities for this play since theatre companies that have not developed bilingual audiences may be reticent to produce such a text. Moraga's initial inspiration, Luis Valdez's very bilingual *The Shrunken Head of Pancho Villa*, has only been produced by *teatros* or by universities with Chicano audiences. Only time will tell if Moraga's play will appeal to non-Latino producers or suffer the same fate as Valdez's first play. To date *Heroes and Saints* has been very successfully produced at the Mission Cultural

Center in San Francisco and the Guadalupe Cultural Arts Center in San Antonio, two major Latino organizations which have developed bilingual audiences who go to and support their theatrical productions.

"If the people do not go to the *teatro*," Chicana/o *teatristas* wrote in 1971, "then the *teatro* must go to the people." And we did, performing our *actos* wherever there was an audience: school auditoriums, union halls, community centers, colleges, prisons, universities, and the like. Admission was seldom charged; *teatros* either performed free of charge, passed the hat, or charged a modest fee from the presenting organizations. This was community-based theatre, not a profession yet, therefore the *teatro* members basically donated their time for the cause. Audiences were always grateful for an opportunity to see a performance that reflected their community and for most *teatristas* that positive response was sufficient.

Most Chicano *teatros* had not followed the regional theatre model of high-powered boards, capital fundraising for major facilities, and the season subscription base. The community-based *teatros* were modest organizations and the regional theatres had little in common with them, particularly the audiences either attracted. But when the regional theatres began to look for Latino plays to produce, they were quite frank in their desire to build a Latino audience, eager to bite into the Latino dollar.

As the regional theatres have developed their economic base, the cost of producing professional theatre has made ticket prices inaccessible to the working class. Therefore when they produce Latino plays, they generally attract middle- and upper-middle-class Latinos. This creates a distinction between the audiences in a regional theatre and the working-class audiences the *teatros* enjoy. Those of us who direct in the non-Latino theatres welcome the new Latino audiences but suffer the mixed blessing of being able to pay our artists while having to say good-bye to our usual grassroots public. When we direct in Chicano theatres, on the other hand, we can produce plays that might not be successful outside *La Familia,* as it were.

It is said that good theatre is universal, yet there are Chicano plays that cannot effectively reach non-Chicano audiences even though they work extremely well in their respective communities. Luis Valdez's *The Shrunken Head of Pancho Villa* serves as an example. I have seen this very bilingual, ethno-specific play work quite well in the Chicano community but I cannot imagine it making sense to a non-Latino audience. This play, which revolves around the central figure of Belarmino, a bodiless head who claims to be Pancho Villa *sin cuerpo,* taxes the understanding of even a *Chicano* audience but I have seen Chicanos loving it.

Valdez's first effort at playwriting succeeds within the context of the

Chicano community precisely because his characters are mirror images of the people in the audience. They are types as well as distortions in Valdez's surreal vision, but they are readily recognizable to a Chicano/Mexicano audience. Any bilingual, middle-class or working-class Mexican/Chicano can relate to and appreciate the trials and tribulations of the family in *The Shrunken Head of Pancho Villa*. Non-Latinos may not be as enthusiastic because they might feel left out due to all the Spanish and might also be unable to relate to some of the issues. Nothing could be worse than a play that leaves a non-Chicano audience thinking that Chicanos do not make sense.

Another example of how linguistically distinct audiences differ were their responses to a production of Octavio Solís's *Man of the Flesh* which I co-directed for the San Diego Repertory Theatre in 1991. The theatre commissioned a Spanish translation titled *Ladron de corazones* as part of its Teatro Sin Fronteras project. The Spanish version of the play had some English dialogue, just as the English version had some Spanish. In other words, both versions were actually bilingual. The play received totally different reactions from the distinct audiences.

Perhaps because they knew the play was also being presented in Spanish, the majority of Latinos came to the Spanish version of the play and always reacted openly and positively. The English performances were attended by mostly Anglo audiences, presumably non-Spanish-speaking, and they were never as enthusiastic as the Spanish-speaking audiences. We discovered that in the Spanish performances the audiences were entirely bilingual, reacting to the dialogue in either language, while the same could not be said of the English-speaking audiences. In fact, some audience members watching the English version said they felt excluded because they did not understand many of the jokes in Spanish. I would caution any other mainstream theatre to be very careful when selecting a very bilingual play and to be aware of cultural and linguistic barriers.

The major question the regional theatres ask is: "How do we attract a Latino audience?" as they ponder why there are so few Latino season subscribers. Latinos who are interested in Latino theatre will find their way to a Latino play, especially if that play addresses their specific community. However, after a decade of courting the Latino audience, the regional theatres have to face the fact that one Latino play per season is not going to effectively build a year-round Latino following. This is not to say that non-Latino theatres should therefore avoid producing Chicano plays. They should produce them. But they must understand why they are producing a play about a particular ethnic group. This is what good theatre is all about:

understanding a community. They must also be cautious of which Chicano plays they produce.

San Diego theatre critic Welton Jones raised the hackles of the Latino theatre community in that city when he wrote that he wanted to see *less* "Latino theatre produced by non-Latino theatres." We were all appalled by this seemingly insensitive remark; angered that this white, male critic could be so bold as to suggest taking Latino theatre out of the non-Latino theatres. But I am virtually suggesting the same thing, if not for the same reasons. Ultimately it all has to do with the audience one is trying to reach.

I believe that "good theatre" requires a "good audience" of people who go to the theatre looking for more than entertainment; people who want to be enlightened and challenged; to be made to think. I believe that the best theatre has always inspired people who share a belief in the theatre as a communal process. As I travel around this country, witnessing groups of people who gather for a play, few are believers any more and if "theatre is a temple," it is now dedicated to corporate America.

The real believers are those people with a sense of community, a sense of purpose, and yes, even a sense of "otherness" that has brought them together seeking renewal of some sort. For AIDS activists, the theatre is a place for education and compassion when it is permeated with the positive energy of like-minded people. For Chicanos, that renewal may be as simple as hearing their language and seeing their icons on stage. We have all experienced it at one time or another in the theatre and it is what keeps us coming back, doing what we do either as performer or audience, hoping for that incomparable satisfaction. We keep searching for the magic that comes when we can feel everyone around us in equal pleasure.

Many Chicano/Latino actors have told me they perform on film or television, usually playing negative stereotypes, because they need the income. Yet they long for the opportunity to perform on stage for the unequalled fulfillment it gives them. And though they welcome the possibility of acting in any play, nothing can compare to the satisfaction they get from a Latino audience.

Ultimately theatre is about communication: through words and images, through music and rhythms, through story and character. If Chicano plays are to survive in non-Chicano theatres then it is incumbent upon those companies to educate themselves to guarantee that they are culturally competent. They must understand that Chicanos are not Cubans, that Puerto Ricans are not Dominicans; that Latin America is as varied in cultures as the English-speaking world. The theatre must not be like Hollywood, throwing all Latinos into one cauldron and coming out with some "hybrid" that is based on generalizations. The theatres must be as sensitive to Latino audiences as to their own patrons, careful not to be too timid while not wanting to offend either group. These theatres must take risks, but their risks will be far less if they bring together the right collaborators to express Latino themes on stage.

Finally, the presence of Chicanos in the non-Latino theatres is neither "mainstreaming" nor "infiltrating." It is not mainstreaming because this connotes a current that carries everybody to an all-encompassing ocean. Most Chicanos do not want to become a part of that amorphous body of water; further, we are too often asked to swim upstream anyway. Nor is it infiltrating because that conjures images of eventually taking over those major regional theatres — not a bad idea, but a rather idealistic one at best. No, our presence should be no different from that of any of the other theatrical migrant workers: to be treated with respect and allowed artistic freedom. Otherwise, the Chicano theatre artist is no better than an affirmative action statistic.

Alberto Sandoval
Staging AIDS: What's Latinos Got To Do With It?

❏

We don't need a cultural renaissance; we need cultural practices actively participating in the struggle against AIDS. We don't need to transcend the epidemic; we need to end it.
—*Douglas Crimp,* AIDS: Cultural Analysis/Cultural Activism

The unspoken rule is that you can exist only as one thing at a time—a Latino or a gay man—with no recognition of reality's complexity. Add an H.I.V. *diagnosis to this mix and it gets complicated.—Dennis deLeon, "My Hopes, My Fears, My Disease,"* New York Times, *May 15, 1993*

Art is a lot of things: it's an educational tool, a grieving tool and a healing tool.—Max Navarre, "Art in the AID*ies: An Act of Faith,"* High Performance

To Hector Santiago, for his courage and *deseo de vivir.*

AIDS is not only a medical crisis but a crisis of representation. Two issues complicate the AIDS crisis: Who gets AIDS? How is the person with AIDS represented? The diversity of AIDS cases becomes problematic when we consider that dominant cultural representations of AIDS are produced by an Anglo-American population with access to the mainstream. By the year 2050, when there will be a cure for AIDS (I hope) and the cultural archives of the plague are reviewed, the researchers will recover an archipelago of cultural constructions that registers who was infected and affected by AIDS in the 1980s and 1990s. The record will show that mainly white gay middle-class males contracted, experienced, suffered, and died of the virus. Critic Richard Goldstein has acknowledged the silences of all "others" on Broadway in the following declaration: "AIDS is increasingly a disease of impoverished people of color. Yet, if one were to describe this epidemic from works of art alone, one would have to conclude that only white women and gay men have been people with AIDS (20).[1]

In this essay I will examine how issues of representation and relations of power, agency, and intervention are important factors that contribute to the response and imagery of AIDS in society at large. I will limit myself to the theatrical space in order to expose how groups in power and with access to power have unintentionally marginalized and silenced other groups such as women, Latinos/as, gay Latinos, lesbians, and working-class drug addicts. The latter have been underrepresented, rather mis(s)represented, because those with access to power (Broadway and Off-Broadway) have taken the lead and outlined the paradigms of staging AIDS. In this essay, my goal is to raise consciousness that AIDS as a crisis of representation (of language, imagery, and discourse) is also a crisis of representation in terms of who is represented, when, where, why, and how. When staging AIDS, what's *Latinos* got to do with it?

A look at AIDS theatre reveals the absence of people of color. Plays about AIDS center on white gay and often Jewish males: Larry Kramer's *The Normal Heart* (1985), William M. Hoffman's *As Is* (1985), Harvey Fierstein's *Safe Sex* (1987), William Finn's *Falsettos* (1992), Tony Kushner's *Angels in America* (1993), Kramer's *The Destiny of Me* (1993), Paul Rudnick's *Jeffrey* (1993). All these plays deal with the personal drama of AIDS in specific communities. Nonetheless, they establish the paradigm of AIDS as a universal experience when in fact their particular experience pertains to one ethnic group: white Jewish gay males. My point is not that white Jewish gays should not stage their experiences. We must recognize that AIDS activism challenging the silence and prejudices surrounding the disease was mobilized by Jewish gays, especially by Larry Kramer. Kramer credits his experience as a Jew in touch with the horrors of the Holocaust in developing his comparison between gays with AIDS and Jews. His book, *Reports from the Holocaust: The Making of an AIDS Activist* (1989), outlines his philosophy and position, as he speaks out as a Jew and a gay man: "Perhaps because I am both, I find it remarkable how many similarities I notice between homosexuals and Jews . . . History recently made a pretty good attempt to destroy the Jewish people, and as I think history now has an opportunity to do (and is already doing) pretty much the same to homosexuals . . ." (233).

Yet as the theatre on AIDS was defined by gay men it became a theatre of exclusion. The first anthology on AIDS theatre, *The Way We Live Now: American Plays and the AIDS Crisis* (1990) does not contain any African American, Asian American, Haitian, or Latino voices.[2] Although Michael Feingold's introduction is well-intentioned, he falls in the trap of universalizing the experience of one ethnic group: "In this volume you will find a range of human possibilities as wide and complex as the reach of the epidemic itself . . . You will also find a record of the numbness, the shock, the fright, the immobility I have mentioned. There is no way to overcome these things without viewing them straight on" (xv–xvi). How "wide and complex" is the experience he is referring to? Who has a voice? When? Why?

If we trace the history of oppression of gays, the issue of class and race cannot be left out. Not all gays have access to power. The problem is that gay identity has been universalized and essencialized as a "white" ethnicity without making room for difference. Not all gays experience racism and marginalization. Oppression tends to be limited to homophobia, as exemplified by Larry Kramer's statement: "Why is it that white heterosexuals prefer not to think about or deal with AIDS? For the African and the black and the Hispanic American cases, it's because of racism. For the gay male cases, it's because of homophobia" (*Reports* 238). The way Kramer defines oppression reveals that "gay males" equal "white males" in a given social class and location, i.e., the Village in New York City.[3] Is whiteness invisible? Or is gayness?

What do people of color have to do with AIDS theatre?

The first decade of cultural representations of AIDS was led by gay white males who had access to Broadway and Off-Broadway. Little attention was paid to other experiences such as those of drug addicts, Haitians, hemophiliacs, and even heterosexuals with AIDS.[4]

The first attempt to include diversity in AIDS theatre was Joe Pintauro's *Raft of the Medusa* (1992), a kaleidoscopic rainbow of people coping with AIDS in a therapy session. The characters were merely types, lacking psychological development. In its effort to show a diversity of experiences, including those of class, sex, and race, this play was almost tokenist in nature, even including a deaf female character with AIDS. Only one African American play on AIDS, *Before It Hits Home* (March 1992) by Cheryl L. West, has been staged Off-Broadway and received critical attention.[5] The play is about a bisexual jazz musician who returns home to die. The reviews were not very favorable. The one in the *New York Times* by Frank Rich, entitled "A Black Family Confronts AIDS," stated that it was crudely written, predictable in plot, full of archetypes, and melodramatic. Indeed, the play did not fulfill Rich's expectations and he frankly suggests that it should have been (a docudrama?) on television where its "aesthetic failings would be less apparent" (C22). However, he concludes: "For the moment, this particular slice of the AIDS story is one that the theatre may be in a position to tell best, and that it may yet tell better." Whose theatre is Rich talking about? Who is the

. audience? And what does he mean by "aesthetic failings"? When Rich enters the territory of aesthetics he falls in the trap of Eurocentric, phallogocentric, and ethnocentric ways of doing, seeing, and reviewing theatre. Are critics like Frank Rich and John Simon equipped to evaluate alternative theatre (i.e., African American, Asian American, women's theatre, gay theatre, AIDS theatre, Latino theatre)? What does Rich's aesthetic platform stand for when faced with George Whitmore's statement that "AIDS is about shit and blood."⁶ Indeed, AIDS is a minefield in the arts, as cultural critic Jan Zita Grover has stated provocatively: "AIDS brings an already existing social debate — What is the purpose and value of art? — to a crisis point. It throws into relief the irreducible fact that artwork is based not simply (or romantically) on personal visions, but on social realities." There is an urgency in AIDS writing, an urgency to write about AIDS that cannot wait for aesthetic distancing, as AIDS activist John Preston has mandated: "The purpose of AIDS writing now is to *get it all down* . . . To repeat: The purpose of the writer in the time of AIDS *is to bear witness* . . . To live in a time of AIDS and to understand what is going on, *writing must be accompanied by action*" ("AIDS Writing," 61).

Given that the dominant paradigm of AIDS theatre has been shaped by white, middle-class, Eurocentric standards, it is hard for other minorities and people of color to enter into this realm of representation. Do they have anything else to add? Has it all been said? How can people of color keep up with the development of AIDS in the theatre when they have not even made it to Broadway and scarcely Off-Broadway?

If we trace the development of white gay theatre on AIDS, there are three stages: (1) anger and accusation; (2) safer sex campaigning; (3) the creative stage. The first plays are educational and want to voice the gay experience. These are agit-prop pieces full of terror, anger, and fury. They vociferate discrimination, compassion, frustration, pain, confusion, grief, death, loss, helplessness, and activism. As the plague sits in the theatre around the clock all season long, a search for creative spaces begins. In this way AIDS theatre moves from propaganda to creative theatrical and poetic forms. Aesthetically diverse plays appear — musicals like *Falsettos* which is a show about a new understanding of the family and masculinity, or plays which mediate and transfer AIDS to other illnesses like *Marvin's Room,* or hybrid plays combining poetic imagery, spectacle, and political issues like *Angels in America,* and plays with humorous, escapist, ludic overtones like Vogel's *The Baltimore Waltz.* In 1993, AIDS theatre entered a new phase when *Jeffrey* opened Off-Broadway. The message now is that AIDS has become a part of life and all that can be done is accept it, move on and laugh about it. There is cynicism here, yet laughter also has its cathartic effect — that is, uncontrollable laughter releases emotional pressure, as Rudnick has expressed: "Only money, rage and science can conquer AIDS, but only laughter can make the nightmare bearable" (21). With *Jeffrey*, AIDS has entered the realm of comedy leaving behind its lugubrious phase. Also, Anglo-American AIDS theatre has started to search for utopia, a longed-for-cure in the future. Such is the case with two solo performance monologues by white men: Tim Miller's *My Queer Body* and David Drake's *The Night Larry Kramer Kissed Me*. Although they articulate a gay identity and a gamut of subject positions in the white gay community, at the end even utopia could erase historicity and the reality of AIDS.[7] Where is the theatre of people of color and AIDS? Off stage? Backstage? In order to center-stage, in this case, Latino AIDS theatre, we must move from commercial theatre to community-based theatre.

II

In Latino communities the theatre of AIDS usually takes the form of workshops. There is an urgent need to educate our people who are currently the group hardest hit by AIDS in the United States. Among the issues at stake are prevention and education: using condoms and clean needles, protecting women and teenagers. Latino AIDS theatre has a didactic intention: its purpose is to raise consciousness. Teatro Pregones in the Bronx and Teatro VIVA in Los Angeles, for example, promote education and raise consciousness about the virus. In the skits and workshops produced by these theatres, AIDS is represented as a web with many strands. Racism, classism, sexism, homophobia, ethnocentricity, nationalism, migration, and cultural differences must be tackled. Indeed, in these webs of action, transaction, and interaction, identity is multiple and heterogeneous. The sexual revolution goes hand in hand with oppression, racism, and the need for social change. It is not conceivable to separate art and politics. Neither can this theatre be approached with bourgeois concepts of aesthetics, refinement, taste, and literary elitism. It is unpolished and crude.[8] It has only a social purpose for being, and a political agenda: a ritualistic performance and collective effort that allows the community to promote AIDS awareness, to learn about AIDS, to carry on condom-usage campaigns, to deliver an activist agenda, and to cope with the devastating epidemic. Theatre is a matter of survival, not entertainment or leisure.

At a critical moment when Latino communities are "epicenters of AIDS," the impact of the disease has mobilized both heterosexuals and homosexuals. Teatro Pregones creates AIDS awareness by making the audience participate in the development of the dramatic plot. In this way the audience can learn how to cope with AIDS and to deal with sexuality, machismo, and homophobia. The audience is expected to interrupt the play any time a case of oppression is detected. Audience members are supposed to change the course of the action: to rewrite the "play" by replacing the character with their own acting and lines. This direct participation allows for a better understanding of oppression. The production is followed by a panel discussion which provides information on AIDS. In words of Jorge B. Merced, member of the group El Abrazo, a component of Teatro Pregones, this kind of theatre has its artistic and political value: "If AIDS demands that we take the bull by the horns, then theatre about AIDS demands that we topple the fourth wall and that we reject distancing in order to allow for dialogue by means of the theatre."[9] Of course, the issue here is promoting a different politics, and a different way of doing theatre which is influenced by Latin American theatre of liberation, particularly Augusto Boal's philosophy and techniques underlying the Theatre of the Oppressed. The goal is to take theatre to the people. Theatre is not only for leisure and profit but a part of life, a ritual of participation, a rite of passage to political action, social change, and survival.

Teatro VIVA in L. A. is designed to bring safer-sex information to a target gay and lesbian population. It is designed to encourage people at risk to get tested for HIV. The program humorously and frankly presents a series of theatrical short skits in bars, festivals, community centers, and colleges. These contain important information and techniques for HIV intervention and prevention. The project directors are gay and lesbian artists Luis Alfaro and Monica Palacios.[10]

There are also community agencies and dedicated leaders who work directly with the Latino communities on issues of AIDS, sexism, homophobia, and discrimination, such as Hank Tavera and Felipe Barragán in San Francisco. Presently Tavera is the director of the Fourth AIDS Theater Festival, which took place in San Francisco October 19–23, 1993, in conjunction with the Sixth National AIDS Update Conference. His goal is to give more exposure to local and national talent and more visibility to Latinos and other people of color. Felipe Barragán promotes HIV education and prevention through theatrical skits directed at teenagers in the Bay Area schools.

In charting community-based Latino theatre on AIDS we cannot leave out Puerto Rico. Why? Because Puerto Rico has the nation's highest per capita rate of new cases — at least every tenth resident has been exposed to AIDS.[11] By the year 2000, one third of the island's population will be HIV-positive. As American citizens we can come and go freely. Given that Medicaid does not cover medical treatment and expenses in Puerto Rico, as it does in the United States, Puerto Ricans come to the United States starting yet another new pattern of migration. We also migrate, as I did, to escape Catholic terrorism and stigmatization by the family. (How can we forget Cardinal Luis Aponte Martínez's criminal statement of ignorance: "It is more sinful to wear a condom than to have AIDS.") As Puerto Ricans get sick with AIDS, the moribund in terminal stages return to die and be buried in Puerto Rico. The ultimate drama of the deathbed scene, indeed, takes place in the air. The air bus is a floating theater.

In Puerto Rico, the theatre of Rosa Luisa Márquez performed by Los Teatreros Ambulantes de Cayey (in collaboration with Antonio Martorell) has taken the lead in raising consciousness about AIDS. Márquez's theatrical imagery and aesthetics are in constant dialogue with Latin America theatrical expressions. Her piece on AIDS, *El sí dá*, is not simply a workshop: what we have here is a working philosophy of doing and seeing theatre. "*El sí dá* (AIDS) is a Theatre/Image that intervenes in classrooms to provoke a reflection about the epidemic in Puerto Rico" (48). "We don't want to put together a melodrama or a manual of instructions. In spite of the severity of the problem, we don't want to terrify the spectators nor to assault or offend them. We want to raise consciousness by the most direct means possible" (49).

Besides Márquez's theatre, a play was produced in Puerto Rico in 1992 on the subject of AIDS, *El amor en los tiempos del SIDA* (*Love in the time of AIDS*). The play was adapted by playwright José Luis Ramos Escobar from a poetry book with the same title by Eric Landrón. The action centers on raising consciousness among heterosexuals. It is allegorical and poetic. At times, it even seems like a commercial for AIDS prevention. Its structure is fragmented; its genre is hybrid. In one of the fragments there is a gay man asking for respect, but he is just a marginal voice which is excluded from the play's central mission — to educate the heterosexual community.

III

As I map out Latino theatre on AIDS, an archipelago of art forms, styles, theatrical models, and diverse audiences emerge. This mapping delineates the spectrum and diversity of Latinos in the United States and how they cope with AIDS in their communities by means of theatre. Now I would like to move to a more "literary theatre," a theatre that, without becoming explicitly apolitical, has an aesthetic literary dimension. "Literary theatre" does not participate in the spontaneity and direct political action that char-

Figure 1. *El sí dá,* Los teatreros ambulantes. Rosa Luisa Márquez, director. Photo by Miguel Villafoné.

acterizes Latino community-based militant theatre. The plays are rehearsed and written to be published and eventually staged. Although theatre is ephemeral, published theatre pretends to be ever-present through the written word—the script aspires to a future production. With these publications (if their potential is realized), the Latino theatre of AIDS would enter the realm of literature (drama). But in my quest for Latino AIDS theatre, I found that none of the plays have been published.

In my search for manuscripts of Latino AIDS theatre, I was surprised by the number of playwrights with plays on the subject. It dismayed me to hear from these playwrights that they were struggling to write about AIDS while their relatives and friends were dying of the disease. In these cases, as described for example by playwrights Dolores Prida and Migdalia Cruz, there was no distance between life and drama. It was all a matter of waiting and processing the shock, the pain, and the losses.

I found myself surrounded by a growing body of AIDS plays. Latinos were mailing me their work from locations nationwide, from California to

Puerto Rico. Obviously Latino theatre on AIDS was alive and doing well in our communities but it had yet to see the light of day in mainstream culture, theatres, and publications. I discovered and recovered plays in English, Spanish, and Spanglish about heterosexuality and gay issues. Plays with political and aesthetic dimensions were being written, not necessarily produced, by Cubans, Chicanos, and Puerto Ricans. These plays are vivid testimony to the pandemonium and the spiritual struggles of our Latino communities confronting AIDS. Indeed, AIDS in these works is not only at the heart of the communities but at the heart of the family. Education, prevention, and survival are the main coordinates structuring the plots as the characters fight oppression, dismantle taboos, and search for acceptance. Truth and honesty, fear and pain, force the characters to define their subject positions and their identities in relation to HIV people, people with AIDS, people dying of AIDS, and those affected by AIDS. The plays that I have compiled are the following: Juan Shamsul Alam's *Zookeeper,* Rane Arroyo's *Wet Dream With Cameo by Fidel Castro,* Ofelia Fox and Rose Sánchez's *Siempre intenté decir algo* (or *S.I.D.A., I Always Meant to Tell You Something*), Hector Santiago's *Camino de angeles* (*Road of Angels*), *Un dulce cafecito* (*Sweet Coffee*) and *Al Final del Arco Iris* (*At the End of the Rainbow*),

Figure 2. *El sí dá*, Los teatreros ambulantes. Rosa Luisa Márquez, director. Photo by Miguel Villafoné.

Alfonso Ramírez's *The Watermelon Factory,* Cherríe Moraga, *Heroes and Saints,* Eric Landrón, *El amor en los tiempos del sida* (poetry and theatrical adaptation), José Rivera's *A Tiger in Central Park,* Pedro R. Monge Rafuls's *Noche de ronda* (*Night Rounds*), Louis Delgado, Jr.'s *A Better Life,* Teatreros Ambulantes de Cayey, *El sí dá* and my own work, *Side Effects.*[12]

From these, I will analyze *Noche de ronda* and *A Better Life* as two examples of Latino theatre on AIDS where a new paradigm of Latino identity is in formation. I will explore how AIDS has pushed the limits to reconfigure political and sexual identities in the theatre and in the communities at large to deal with the crisis. In these two plays a new Latino ethnicity is articulated within the parameters of a politics of representation, a politics of identity, and a politics of affinity. By a politics of representation I mean the deconstruction of negative stereotypes and degrading images of Latinos in the dominant culture, and the need to reconstruct new images, especially, in the theatre for a self-representation. I define a politics of identity as the articulation of subjectivity-in-process both in language and discourse — the constitution of the subject position as a speaking subject in relation to all kind of discursive formations and power. I understand a politics of affinity as the move to break away from labels and divisive barriers (racial, class, ethnic, sexual, gender, ideological, political, religious, generational) in order to discard stereotypes, to de-center oppression, and to recognize difference as a fact of life. Only through equality, mutual respect, and tolerance of difference in our democratic society can we achieve a politics of affinity.

Noche de ronda by the Cuban exiled Pedro R. Monge Rafuls at first sight is an updated version of Mart Crowley's *Boys in the Band* (1968).[13] It is a party of gay men, this time Latinos. The protagonist, Eladio/la Chicana, has decided to celebrate his last birthday because he has convinced himself that he is HIV-positive and is going to die. He has been tested and is afraid to find out the results. This party is a farewell to life and friends. All ethnicities and Latin American nationalities make up his gay circle of friends: the Dominican, the Cuban, the apparently assimilated Puerto Rican who comes with his Anglo boyfriend, a Colombian, a "new Hispanic." There is a spectrum of gay identities and sexual preferences: *la loca,* the closet case, the U.S. gay clone, the straight acting one, the coming-out one. As the party goes on, and as they wait for Juana la Cubana — who is in a hospital dying of AIDS but they do not know it — an uninvited guest arrives. It is Eladio's father from Mexico — a super macho who cannot believe the scene. His son is surrounded by *loquitas* and a stripper — a Nuyorican bisexual — who they rented for the occasion. He is in shock to find out that his son is a *loca* himself. Eladio hates his father's machismo. He left Mexico because the father embodies homophobia and chauvinism. His exile was a conscious choice to run away from his father and machismo.[14] For this reason, as an "orphan," Eladio's main crisis in the play is his relationship with his father and patriarchy. Looking for an alternative position, he identifies with the lyrics of a *ranchera*, Nobody's daughter: "I too am nobody's daughter / I have only one last name / I have to thank my mother for that one / for I don't even know my father / I think he must be a coward / one of many that the world has known / the cruelest fathers are guilty / they don't even deserve to be men / they go around deceiving women." *Noche de ronda* centers on the dismantling of machismo and how Latino gays move across national, state, and barrio borders to urban areas in search of a new identity. Eladio's group of friends form an extended family of gay men who are cast out from their homes and family. As the play evolves it articulates a sense of belonging, self respect, pride.

Noche de ronda is a comedy which comes close to being a tragicomedy because of the AIDS epidemic. Given that AIDS has destroyed all hope of sexual liberation, the play must promote the prevention and education of AIDS without being propagandistic. Among other critical issues covered are promiscuous sexual behavior, incestuous relationships with *primitos* (little cousins), bisexuality, homosexual encounters with married men, and internalized homophobia. Sexual identities intersect constantly with ethnic, class, racial, national identities. For example, Eladio is Mexican but they call him *la Chicana,* as he explains he got the name from: "a Latin American boyfriend I had that didn't understand the difference between a Chicano and a Mexican woman like me." Miguel, who is a "Hispanic" without any specific national label, responds: "We Hispanics are a big mixture which we don't even understand." Eladio defines his nationality with pride: "I'm not Hispanic. I'm Mexican." Of course, Eladio is an immigrant who defines his identity in relation to Mexican paradigms of nationality rather than in relation to U.S.-born Latinos. As we can see, the subjectivity of each is in process as the men struggle with labels and challenge sexual and ethnic stereotypes.

In *Noche de ronda* dismantling stereotypes through laughter and campy feminine behavior transgresses gender roles. At the same time the spectrum of Latino subjectivities and nationalities is staged to the fullest. Even language is at stake with the formation of a U.S. Latino identity, as Miguel says: "The United States is a bilingual country. We are a fast growing community. Soon we will be the majority in this country . . . I can't understand how it is that you live here for so many years and don't speak English."

Note that Miguel defines himself as a gay man who is a member of the Latino community. Ethnicity and sexual identity are not incompatible. He negotiates his political and social identity with his sexual one without producing further dislocations, marginalization, and exclusion. Such a process of inclusion is further personified in Gustavo, who is gay, Caribbean, black: "The black beauty from the Caribbean has arrived. Cuba, Santo Domingo and Puerto Rico are united in my beauty . . . My love, I am international by injection." Between the lines s/he exposes her/his promiscuity and sexual preference of anal penetration. What is a joke reveals a crossroads of gay identity, sexual preference openly expressed, and ethnicity.

On the subject of AIDS, the play is educational but with humor. It is not dogmatic. It is human and emotional as the characters deal with their terror, fear, anguish, pain, their friend's agony and the loss of friends. In the middle of all this catastrophe, a good joke on the subject is always welcome to relieve the pain and break the taboo:

Have you heard the story of the little asshole who was being pursued by AIDS? (Making the appropriate gestures.) A little asshole was running and running and AIDS was just behind him, trying to catch him. Run, little asshole, run and puuum, he jumped into a church. And my dears, the Priest was there. And the little asshole says, "Help me, Father, help me." And the Priest asks "What's wrong?" "Oohh, Father! AIDS is after me. Work a miracle, Father." And the Priest said, "Let us pray" and puuum, the miracle was performed. The little asshole turned into a little bird. "Now go, little bird," said the Priest, and the bird flew away. But outside, AIDS was still waiting for him. "Where are you going? Who are you?" "I'm a little bird. Look at my wings flapping." "Let's see, prove it to me. Sing!" AIDS said. And the little asshole began to sing. (He makes great gestures with his mouth and puckers his lips as if he were blowing wind.) Ffffffuuuuuusssssss.

It is no coincidence that the joke takes place in the church. The desacralization of the Catholic church is an act of appropriation in order to fight back Catholic homophobia and terrorism against gays and people with AIDS. The miracle of the church, the prayers to be heard did not work: people are dying of AIDS. The priest did not do anything to save the bird as the church has been indifferent to people with AIDS. Furthermore as for the image of the "little bird," it is a metaphorical, ironic and euphemistic displacement of *pato* (duck) and *tener plumas* (have feathers). To the person with AIDS, "their feathers fall out" once a gay Latino is diagnosed HIV-positive. AIDS pushes his sexual identity to the extremes: he can not hide his/her *patería*.

In the play the fact that Juana la Cubana never shows up is very significant. S/he has always kept in secret her/his illness and is alone dying in a
hospital. The pressure of a prejudiced society causes her/his exile up to a
point that s/he must die on her/his own alone and isolated. On the other
hand instead of Juana showing up at the party, it is Eladio's father who
arrives. In this way, the prejudiced society that kills Juana is exemplified in
the figure of the father. He insists after his arrival that his son is straight and
that he is going to give him grandchildren. Ironically the father says that he
came to see him because his mother was worried that he was sick. (You
know, mothers always *know*.) The father identifies the group of friends immediately as *locas* but he denies that his son is gay. He pretends that the
behavior is part of the U.S. ways of being: "Look at you, Jairo. I really like
you. It's true you're a little effeminate, but it doesn't matter. You're young
and modern. I know that the people in this fucking country are different
than in mine, but that's OK." Once you cross the borders tolerance is acceptable; at home it is unacceptable. Finally the father reveals the fear that
Eladio had contracted AIDS and convinces himself that his son is not gay:
"Your mother told me she was worried you'd have AIDS but I told her,
'Lupe, that's a fag's disease and my son's no fag.' Right, son?"

What has happened is that AIDS has pushed identities to the extreme.
Because of AIDS Eladio is forced to accept his gay identity. The father must
face reality: he is not going to have any grandchildren to perpetuate his last
name. Machismo and patrilinearity have come to a halt as the play highlights the oppressiveness of traditional roles and of the family unit. His
father's heterosexual, sexist, and homophobic dreams have totally disinte-
grated. At this point, Eladio comes out of the closet and defends his mother.
When Gustavo joins in, the father, full of anger and hatred, expresses his
racism and homophobia: "Shut up. The worst thing in the world is to be
black and a fag." Eladio has no other choice but to show pride, ask for
respect, and defend his gay friends. When he says, "You've forgotten that
this is my house and these are my friends," he decides to "send his father to
hell" and to unite with his friends — his community — as a family. The father
faces the challenge of accepting his son's gayness rather than view it as
"God's punishment." Unfortunately, the father's machismo is too strong to
accept it. He has no language, no discourse, no room to make room at
home for his gay son. His last words are fragmented and halting; he cannot
articulate the identity of a supermacho father who happens to have a gay
son: "No . . . when he came . . . I . . . today . . . I now go . . . when I return to
Mexico . . . to . . . No . . . your mother . . . If . . . she knew that . . . he . . ." It is
Gustavo, the *loquita,* who has a voice to enunciate the crisis of the father and

patriarchy: "Poor idiot. He thinks that his world has come to an end, that his life is over because he won't have grandchildren . . . Poor idiot. It doesn't matter if his son dies, just that he's been deceived. That matters. (Pause. With dignity.) Being a man is more complicated than just opening a woman's legs." At the end machismo/patriarchy has no discourse after Latino gays become stronger and proud of their identities. Eladio's party ends on a bad note but the real party of being honest and proud of himself and his new family has just begun.

Noche de ronda stages a diversity of identities among the Latino gay community. It is ironic that the title refers to Agustín Lara's bolero. *Noche de ronda,* a song dedicated to prostitutes, highlights sexual marginality in its lyrics. With AIDS the song acquires a new reading, the rereading of an illness that kills people. Nightlife has once again allowed for the underworld to inhabit the areas of desire and sexual satisfaction.[15] Gay visibility with AIDS in a way is registered in the song because a prostitute's promiscuous sexual life and marginality can be compared to a gay's lifestyle. AIDS puts gays and prostitutes at risk, situating them on the verge of tragedy: "these night rounds are not good / they cause harm / they cause pain / And one ends up crying." Outside heterosexual gender relations and outside marriage, according to conservatives and religious fanatics, gays participate in a continuous *noche de ronda.* Like prostitutes, gays symbolize a sexual threat, and a freedom from family responsibilities that the mainstream can easily associate with all the dreaded stereotypes of the Other.

Lara's song, in a way, puts in the open the marginalized identity of the prostitute as Monge's play center-stages gay identities. The dialogue between the song and the play have a point of contact: sexuality, sexual preference, and the eroticism associated with the *noche de ronda.* Lara's song, like the play, voices an unconventional yet unconditional love, a love that does not dare to speak. After AIDS, the unsaid is spoken, the taboos are broken as we all hope for tolerance, mutual respect, and acceptance, not only in boleros or in the campy appropriation of those boleros, but in the search for a better life after AIDS.

A Better Life by Louis Delgado, a Puerto Rican playwright who grew up in the Bronx, is the only play about AIDS by a Latino that has achieved critical acclaim. It opened August 1993 Off-Broadway at the Theatre Row Theatre. This play stages the interaction between macho streetwise Marty, an African American intravenous drug user and pusher, and the upper-middle-class Howard, a gay Asian American dancer, as they share a room in a hospital's AIDS ward. After their diagnosis, both men are abandoned by their respective lovers. Their condition of abandonment is a double one: it means an end to their love relationships and an exile from a healthy life to the world of opportunistic diseases. Sharing a room leads to a better understanding of each other and mutual respect. The play looks for a key to cross-racial understanding and coalition, an image that is represented literally by the set of keys that the Asian American gives to the African American when he invites him to move into his apartment after he leaves the hospital. Marty has no family and may be homeless. Howard may never make it out of the hospital. They must learn how to live together, to share the key to life although they are from different worlds in terms of social status and lifestyles. As Howard says: "The point is, I don't like your lifestyle any more than you like mine. But the fact of the matter is that I can't do anything about it right now. I've got enough things on my mind without having to listen to put-downs and your abuse. You want to kill me? Go ahead and kill me, I'm going to die anyway." AIDS erases those differences and pushes toward togetherness in order to dismantle homophobia, machismo, and social prejudices. With AIDS there is no time for dishonesty. Marty and Howard are there to support each other, to take care of each other, to survive together, to fight together for a better life. At the end of the play both characters have gone through a process of transformation, as Marty tells Howard's sister: "not once did he put me down. He just listened and understood. I've never been able to do that with anyone." Because of AIDS, mutual care and respect lead to social change. That new beginning is founded when Pat, Howard's sister, gives Marty a set of keys: "Howard asked me to take care of something for him. He asked me to make you a set of keys to his place." Utopia? Yes. But why not? A sign of hope is welcome at the end, especially when Howard was taken away after he has a coughing attack and difficulty in breathing. Like his sister says: "is he going to die?" Howard may die but there is a new beginning: a new politics of cultural representation and difference has only just begun.

Both characters represent a new politics of affinity despite class bias, racism, homophobia, and social prejudices. In these terms the playwright trespasses ethnic and racial boundaries by representing characters with different sexual, racial, class, and ethnic backgrounds. For example, Howard's lover is an upper-class white man who is married and in the closet. This character gives testimony to inter-racial relationships as well as depicting the possibility of bisexuality in heterosexual marriages. One might ask why there are no Latinos in the play. But why should there be any? What is at stake here is diversity: a new politics of representation articulated by a consciousness of ethnicity. New identities result from more inclusive politics of affinity. All these articulations, definitions, and identity formations of subjectivities-in-process are possible because of AIDS. Once again AIDS is the factor that pushes individuals to forge new hybrid identities which are multiple, porous, and heterogeneous. Indeed, diversity and multicultural- ism are possible only through the recognition and acceptance of difference. In the play difference is ironically contained in Howard's humorous and honest line when he explains that they contracted AIDS in different ways, ways which mark their differences: "It's almost the same . . . We both put foreign objects into our bodies." In a multicultural society difference is the recognition of pluralism and multiplicity of identities. As in *Noche de ronda,* the cultural politics of difference results from new representational prac- tices, what Stuart Hall calls "the recognition of the immense diversity and differentiation of the historical and cultural experience of black subjects" (28). This also applies to what Hall sees as a new politics of ethnicity: "The term ethnicity acknowledges the place of history, language and culture in the construction of subjectivity and identity, as well as the fact that all discourse is placed, positioned, situated, and all knowledge is contextual. Representation is possible because enunciation is always produced within codes which have a history, a position within the discursive formations of a particular space and time" (29).

The importance of *A Better Life* is not limited to the issue of inclusiveness and representation of difference. The play is also based on personal experi- ence. The play center-stages marginality and gives a voice to Louis Delgado, a recovered drug user. As in the play, for him there is always hope, a better life. There will be a time for reconciliation and unity, as Marty sings: "We got to get out of this place, if it's the last thing we ever do. We got to get out of this place, girl there is a better place for me and you." Getting out means crossing boundaries, breaking ground, dismantling machismo, debunking taboos, coming out, coming to terms, finding a new home away from home. In order to reach freedom, that is social change, we must accept and understand each other for what we are, for our differences. Acceptance and tolerance also must take place in the heart of the family as Howard's sister Pat demonstrates in her visits to the hospital with love, support, and care.

To conclude, Latino theatre on AIDS is diverse. Playwrights stage the per- sonal, social, political dimensions of the crisis in a variety of forms within a theatrical spectrum from workshops, street theatre, protest plays, agit- prop, documentary, and popular theatre to conventional models of theatri- cal genres and staging. Latino theatre on AIDS is all about articulating a new politics of representation as it maps new ethnicities in a global postmodern society. People of color can only intervene in this historical process with our own cultural representations as long as we practice a politics of affinity.

NOTES

I am grateful to my colleague Julie Inness for her careful reading and editing. I would like to thank Diana Taylor for her editorial help, for translating the quotes from Spanish, and for her support.

1   A similar remark was made by Michael Cunningham in "After AIDS, Gay Art Aims for a New Reality": "Still, if you go to a show that touches on AIDS, the odds are good you're going to be seeing a lot of gay white males" (17).

2   Only two plays by white women appear in this anthology: Paula Vogel's *The Baltimore Waltz*, 1990, and Susan Sontag's *The Way We Were*, 1986. In a review of the anthology, Joseph Cady made some illuminating comments on white gay representation: "The gay community was hit first and hardest by AIDS in America . . . and because, as social outcasts even before AIDS, they had nothing left to lose in taking up the stigmatized subject, gay men have predominated in, and written, almost all our AIDS literature to date." On minority underrepresentation and silence, Cady states the following: "The complex reasons for this silence need exploring. One is surely the prior devastation of IV-drug users by poverty and racial prejudice; another is the ironic reluctance of heterosexuals to acknowledge AIDS because of their traditional status as social insiders (in contrast to the impetus that gay men's status as outsiders has given them to confront the disease" [24]). Another important issue that Cady notes is the absence of any popular, group, or documentary theatre in the volume. He closes the review with a brilliant remark: "Does this distribution simply represent the best work available, or does it, at least in part, express a cultural choice, an attempt to detoxify the stigmatized subject via association with famous writers?" (26).

3   Kramer also limits difference to sexuality putting aside class and race: "Invariably the first thought is that people hate *difference*. They're frightened because they *can't* see us, they can only sense our threat" (*Reports*, 238). Hazel V. Carby has theorized on race: "if we try to recognize that we live in a special formation that is structured in dominance by the politics of race, then, theoretically, we can argue that everyone has been constructed as a racialized subject. It is important to recognize the invention of the category of whiteness as well as blackness and, consequently, to reveal what is usually rendered invisible because it is viewed as the normative state of existence" (85).

4   During this period the AIDS experience was stereotyped on stage. Instead of showing people living with AIDS, they are seen dying of AIDS. Their life is a death sentence and anger and rage do not allow for negotiation and alternative experience. And, as gayness and AIDS have not been disassociated, even culturally diverse representations of AIDS have been framed by misogyny.

5   There is a stand-up comedy group composed of gay African Americans that stage the AIDS experience in their communities, POMO AFRO HOMOS; their shows *Fierce Love* and *Dark Fruit*.

6   Bumbalo's *Someone Was There*, quoted by David Bergman (132).

7   Other (white) plays about AIDS are Victor Bumbalo's *Adam and the Experts* (1990), Robert Chesley's *Jerker, or the Helping Hand* (1986), and Alan Bowne's *Beirut* (1985). Plays about AIDS that never mention the disease explicitly are Scott McPherson's *Marvin's Room* (1990), Craig Lucas's *Prelude to a Kiss* (1990), and Manuel Puig's *The Kiss of the Spider Woman* (1993) in the Broadway musical adaptation by Terrence McNally.

8   David Richards writes about AIDS theatre in general: "If you are looking for enduring art,

most AIDS plays don't qualify, which doesn't mean that they don't serve a purpose. They tell us what the temperature is right now and capture the current state of our fears and prejudices. That's useful information to have. As sociological documents, filed from the edge, they can still hit hard."

9   "AIDS, Theater, and the Community," a testimonial account read at the 1992 MLA Convention (NYC), on a panel entitled "AIDS and Puerto Rican Literature and Arts: A Dialogue."

10   Luis Alfaro, Monica Palacios, and Beto Araiza are Latino performers bringing AIDS to the stage through their solo performance monologues. Cultural critic David Román has written on their pieces as well as on Teatro VIVA. The essays are "*Fierce Love* and Fierce Response: Intervening in the Cultural Politics of Race, Sexuality and AIDS" and "Teatro Viva!: Latino Performance, Sexuality, and the Politics of AIDS in Los Angeles" (forthcoming). I would like to express my gratitude to David Román for sharing with me parts of the manuscript of his forthcoming book on theatre and AIDS, *Acts of Intervention*.

11   As of January 1993, there were 8,959 reported cases of AIDS in Puerto Rico. The Oficina Central para Asuntos SIDA in San Juan provided me with this information and further documentation. In the United States, according to the *HIV/AIDS Surveillance Report* (July 1992), there were 37,162 AIDS cases reported among Latinos.

12   Pedro Monge Rafuls and I are preparing a special issue on Latino AIDS theatre for *Ollantay Theatre Magazine* to appear in 1994. Some of these plays will be published in this issue.

13   It is interesting to note that Cuban exiles are out of the closet more often than other Latinos. In their plays the criticism of compulsory heterosexuality is overt and direct. The logic behind such a liberal position is that for Cuban exiles leaving Cuba meant total freedom. Consequently, in the U.S. democratic society, freedom of speech goes hand in hand with freedom of sexuality. The goal of Cuban exiles is to dismantle homophobia as inherited in the U.S.-Cuban communities and practiced in Cuba (before and after Castro). Also, there is a questioning of gender roles at work and the invention of new identities in exile as well as for a second generation identity-formation. For these new identities homosexuality is no joke, *la loquita* is no laughing matter. On the other hand, traditional values are caricatured. The audience can laugh at old ways of seeing and doing by portraying how racist, homophobic, classist, sexist Latino culture can be. I am grateful to Nancy Saporta Sternbach for helping me formulate this interpretation.

14   Unlike many Latino AIDS plays, *Noche de ronda* shows the protagonist migrating to avoid the cultural stigmatism of his homosexuality. A large number of plays deal with AIDS when it hits home because many Latinos lack the financial independence to move away from their intolerant communities. There is no place like home to start dismantling oppression, machismo, and homophobia. These plays are breaking the silence and deconstructing degrading depictions of Latinos. They attack gender binarism, affront machismo, and question Catholic oppression and homophobia. It should not be forgotten that Anglo-American males migrated to the cities leaving their families behind because of their economic independence. For Latinos the heart of the family is where acceptance and tolerance needs to begin.

15   See Carlos Monsiváis's cultural analysis of Agustín Lara's boleros (*Amor perdido* 61–86). Monsiváis places the bolero in its sociohistorical context in order to examine the representation of prostitution, marginality, and sexuality in urban Mexico in the thirties and forties.

Marguerite Waller
Border Boda *or Divorce* Fronterizo?

❏

This assembly is not one where severed or separated pieces
merely come together. — Gloria Anzaldúa

BORDER FEMINISM

"We hoped to become closer to each other through telling our stories and weaving them into a performance. Ironically we failed, although the show was successful and beautiful." One year later, this was the assessment of her experience offered by one participant in *Border boda* (Border Wedding), a performance/ritual conceived and performed by members of the multicultural women's group Las Comadres, active in the United States/Mexico border region that includes Tijuana and San Diego. *Border boda* was part of Las Comadres' multimedia installation, "The Neighborhood/La Vecindad," which opened at San Diego's Centro Cultural de la Raza in October, 1990, and subsequently traveled to the Bridge Center for Contemporary Art in El Paso, Texas, where it became part of their "Border Issues/La Frontera" exhibition. For some, *Border boda* became a "real" wedding — a sudden quantum leap in intimacy after perhaps too brief a courtship. The group, according to this analogy, is now struggling through the first bumpy year of what may or may not turn out to be a successful "marriage." What everyone involved seems to agree upon is that the group show and performance constituted a genuine effort to work and to learn interculturally, that the effort unleashed tremendous creative energies, that it broke hearts and changed lives, and that no one foresaw what terrible difficulties would be encountered in the course of working collaboratively against the grain of four centuries of racist, misogynist colonial and postcolonial history.

I write this account of the group's collective creation of visual and performance art from a decidedly non-expert, non-neutral, non-unitary position. By this I do not mean to say, as if it explained anything, that I am Anglo, have only a rudimentary knowledge of Spanish, and videotaped rather than performed in *Border boda,* though all these are the case. Rather, after four years as a member of Las Comadres, I find that the effort to locate positions too often involves reifying some interpretive systems at the expense of others, reinscribing the framework and psychological effects, if not exactly the content, of cultural imperialism. It may seem self-evident to some members of the group, Anglo and Latina, for example, that we should all know or be learning Spanish. This, surely, is the fundamental gesture one should make in trying to evolve a new, hybrid "border subjectivity," akin to Donna Haraway's "cyborg subjectivity," which escapes the monolingual logic of self and other, original and alien.[1] But where does that position the Chicanas, raised perhaps in the agricultural Midwest or on U.S. military bases, who themselves do not speak Spanish? What of their daily battles with the disapproval of Spanish-speakers? With Anglos who take them for nonnative speakers of English? What of the Chicana who has tried to learn Spanish, but has a block against learning the language that in her Kansas childhood would have isolated her from friends and community and that now swamps her with the pain of the catastrophic loss of her grandparents?[2] How might she, or, for that matter, a rural, Midwestern Anglo woman, feel about bilingual meetings called for by urban, middle-class women (of any nationality or ethnicity), for whom bilingualism is the result of a relatively privileged education? I still feel that Spanish is central to my understanding of the place and the time that I am living, but I do not think that it will allow me to represent anyone or anything more authentically. I represent others in the group only in the sense that my position is different from, and therefore analogous to, that of each of them. The complexities of my position, such as I can begin to appreciate them through our collective experience, serve, like the complex positions of each of us, to point to what Comadre Emily Hicks has described as "the multiplicity of languages within any single language" (*Border Writing* 1). The border subjectivity to which Las Comadres was trying to give birth in its installation and performance involves, not reducing history to a narrative, or position to an identity, but practicing a "multi-dimensional perception . . . informed by different sets of referential codes" (1). In what follows I will do what I can not to imply that there is an absolute place, trajectory, or moment against which other places, motions, and moments can be determined. To keep the multiple dimensions of our story in play, though, I depend upon readers to participate in the process of discovering that positions, including their own, are multiple, even contradictorily, readable (and constantly being read) within an unforeseeable range of codes and frames.

The group's beginnings seemed simple enough. In the fall of 1988 several women artists decided to counteract the isolation they felt, as a result, they thought, of jobs, family responsibilities, and the male domination of the arts community, by meeting once a month to read some texts together, get feedback on their work, discuss current shows, and support each other's artistic growth. This group considered itself bilingual and multicultural. It included several current and former members of the Border Arts Workshop/Taller de Arte Fronterizo group, who had been making and theorizing art of the border region for several years, as well as artists, writers, performers, and curators, many of them also teachers or students, who had lived and worked for varying lengths of time in the Tijuana/San Diego area. We showed each other our own art, read each other's theoretical papers, and grazed among the visual and written works of an international array of other women creators. Most meetings took place in San Diego, despite our intention to belong to both sides of the border, but there were a few memorable gatherings in a beautiful garden belonging to a compound of artists' cottages (where one of the Anglo members was living) in Tijuana. In San Diego we met in art galleries, university screening rooms, and people's living rooms.

But, in retrospect, and through the lenses provided by two articles we read after the experience of "La vecindad" and *border boda* — bell hooks's "Third World Diva Girls: Politics of Feminist Solidarity" and Donna Haraway's "A Cyborg Manifesto" — this idyllic stage of our involvement was not unproblematic. We were, I would say, what Haraway and Chela Sandoval have called an "affinity" group (Haraway 155–56). That is, what we had in common was our sense of invisibility, claustrophobia, isolation, or exploitation in relation to the webs of sociality and power within which we usually operated. It was a profound relief to arrive at a meeting, see the quantities of food everyone had brought, and nourish ourselves for the next several hours on both that and the brilliance, originality, and daring of each other's imaginations. Because nothing was apparently at stake, there were few if any overt conflicts. I enjoyed a sensation of "learning" a great deal — about the art scene, about the two cities, and about where I wanted to take my own critical and theoretical work. This learning, though, was more additive than deconstructive. It gave me a sense of enlargement and accomplishment. While I became acutely aware of my lack of knowledge and experience, my psychic borders were not particularly threatened. Nor, I think, were those of most of the other women in the group, even, ironically, those of us who felt put down or silenced and those who left because they found us too academic, too loud, or too anarchic. While some of us enjoyed the romance of feeling adventurous, open, and politically engaged, others felt, but did not talk much about, a sense of exclusion that, though uncomfortable, was familiar. As a group (though not for everyone individually), we were in what bell hooks has dubbed the "nice nice" phase of multicultural feminist interaction (89). The social and cultural codes of middle-class white culture predominated, however spiced by the language, food, and politics of the various Latino American cultures we also represented.[3]

I do not mean to imply any of this was "wrong," that from the start the group should have been willing, and should have known how, to court the "swamping of . . . psychological borders" that Gloria Anzaldúa has represented as an inevitable part of the struggle for a new, *mestiza* consciousness (*Borderlands* 79). Pragmatically speaking, our way, for a while, seemed to work. Several exhibitions, panels, papers, classes, even books were nurtured by this interaction. What is so difficult to accept, especially perhaps for committed political activists, is that one cannot know in advance, or once and for all, where the borders are going to be and how they are going to operate. One cannot therefore begin to appreciate and to think in border logic until, in whatever form it happens, the power differentials, the historical wounds, the ongoing ways we are heard and seen differently, begin to score the beautiful surface. When the lines of force begin to present themselves visibly, tangibly, painfully, they can then be deepened, the beautiful surface opened and transformed into the potentially also beautiful, multi-dimensional, non-Euclidean, "heterochronic" (Haraway, 156) space/time of multicultural border subjectivity.[4]

Two events and an invitation propelled us into the activism and activist art-making that pushed us beyond thinking of our respective oppositional consciousnesses as common ground. First a highly touted show, "Los vecinos/The Neighbors," at the San Diego Museum of Photographic Art (MOPA), raised our hackles. Consisting of seven photographers' and two video artists' responses to the social and economic arrangements of the San Diego/Tijuana border region, the show, we felt, exemplified the mainstream art world's appropriation of the effort that local activist/artists had, for many years, poured into articulating and transforming border "realities."[5] All but two of the artists were from elsewhere (New York, Mexico City, Boston), their work supported by generous NEA grants and exhibited steps away from, but without reference to, the Centro Cultural de la Raza in San Diego's Balboa Park. As Comadre Berta Jottar put it "One more time big institutions were bringing in big artists to a place they did not know; again history was being written by corporate institutions." We knew, furthermore, that the local artists, had they received these grants, would have given a significantly different picture of the "neighbors." In the MOPA show, "neighbors" meant almost exclusively undocumented workers, who were either crossing the border illegally, getting arrested and deported, or working at construction sites in San Diego. Anglo Americans, insofar as they appeared at all, were represented by police officers, foremen, and tourists. That is, the photographs perpetuated the marginalization they imaged, conceptualizing "neighbors," not from within the shared space of a "neighborhood," but from the exoticizing vantage point of those at "home" looking out at something across the fence, down the street, or on the other side of the proverbial tracks.

Most of our students (many of them Chicano and Mexicano) who saw the show also reacted strongly. While they could see that the show was intended as a forceful exposé of the harassment and exploitation of Mexican workers and appreciate the stunning photographic star turns with which this intention was carried out, they found some of the images almost unbearable. An image of U.S. Immigration officers (*la migra*) handcuffing restaurant workers, for example, which could be read by an out-of-towner or an Anglo viewer as politically sensitive, might register as more like a threat to the Chicano(a) whose sense of vulnerability is reinforced by this bruising reminder of how people like him/her are seen and treated legally and politically. The "illegal alien" image is precisely the image of themselves that some Comadres must confront everyday — in school, in the media, on the street, in the workplace. Worse, it can become an internalized self-image of powerlessness, perhaps the most pernicious form of psychological and spiritual, as well as economic, oppression. Comadre Ruth Wallen speculated that, conversely, there might be a quasi-sexual pleasure involved for some Anglo-identified spectators of images of Mexicans as abject. The incessant repetition of images of Mexicans as universally helpless and downtrodden could stimulate a not unpleasant sensation of dominance, offering a perverse reassurance that to be Anglo is to control rather than to be controlled. Represented as not having lives and neighborhoods of their own, the people in these photographs become the objects of a voyeuristic gaze that fetishized the undocumented worker as the sole and appropriate figure for the border. This displacement amounts to yet another form of exploitation; the workers are perhaps the smallest part of the story of the political, economic, and symbolic construction of a constitutive "difference" between Mexico and the United States.

The second event was a right-wing, populist campaign, called "Light Up the Border," begun in the fall of 1989 and continuing through the summer of 1990. To protest the crossing by "illegal aliens" (mostly Native American *indios*) of a border that blocks a centuries-old migration route, a border that was nonexistent until 150 years ago and entirely open through the 1970s, Muriel Watson, a town councilwoman from the suburban/agricultural community of Encinitas, and Roger Hedgcock, a local radio talk show host and former mayor, urged the "Americans" living in San Diego to converge at a prearranged point on the border on the third Thursday of every month. There they would line up their cars at dusk and send a wash of light into the no-man's land marking the boundary between the two countries. The demonstrations were intended to discourage the 2,000-plus undocumented workers who negotiate the border every day and to signal the U.S. federal government that the border needed more lights, more INS officers (or better, an armed military presence, according to some of the demonstrators), more detention centers, and a better fence. From numerous conversations in which members of Las Comadres engaged demonstrators, and from Hedgcock's own broadcast conversations with listeners who called in, it became evident that neither the demonstrators nor their organizers knew the Indio, Spanish, and Mexican history of the region, let alone the current Mexican political and economic situation, and least of all the complex, self-serving, and immensely profitable games U.S. business, manufacturing, agriculture, and government have been playing with Mexican labor for generations. Instead, Watson and Hedgcock promulgated, uncynically it seemed, a racist (and implicitly sexist) fantasy of a beleaguered United States threatened with inundation by a "flood" of polluting "aliens" pouring through its leaky border.[6]

A coalition of community activists, teachers, artists, and students from both sides of the border devised a performance art piece in response to this scapegoating of Mexican workers for the economic and emotional deficits of the local Anglo community. Members of the Border Arts Workshop/ Taller de Arte Fronterizo, the Union del Barrio, members of our reading group, and several hundred other activists, artists, and students positioned themselves opposite the headlights of over a thousand cars, and by holding up mirrors and mylar- or aluminum-covered cardboard reflectors, returned the wash of light back on the vehicles' owners. Doubling the gaze, undoing the Watson-Hedgcock faction's implied monopoly of the power to "illuminate" the border, the counter-demonstrators made looking, at least symbolically, reciprocal and interactive.

For the April demonstration, Las Comadres (naming ourselves for the occasion) hired a plane to fly before the evening's light show, towing a banner that read, "1000 Points of Fear—Another Berlin Wall?" This provocative reference to current events in Eastern Europe brought a perceptible gasp from demonstrators, some of whom drove away after they read it, apparently moved by the analogy to reconsider what they were doing. This left a larger proportion of White Supremecist groups, like the "WarBoys" and "The Holy Church of the White Fighting Machine of the Cross," to be faced by the counterdemonstrators, and a hostile, potentially dangerous confrontation ensued.[7] Though cause and effect are impossible to determine in such situations, it seems likely in retrospect that the counterdemonstrators' upping of the ante on this occasion thus contributed to the subsequent decline of the "Light Up the Border" movement over the summer. Neither its leaders (two politicians, after all) nor their more moderate followers wanted to be associated with physical violence, a feeling shared by the counterdemonstrators who on subsequent occasions merely stood in silent witness or quietly recorded the event on film and videotape.

The tense April "Light Up the Border" demonstration also catalyzed significant internal changes in our group. Some apprehension of the spiritual and political power that could be tapped by working together despite and through the "interference" of the historical and political divisions that unite and separate us was born that night. Comadre Aida Mancillas subsequently wrote about the new depth of communication that occurred when she confronted some of her own childhood demons in the company of another Comadre, Cindy Zimmerman. As she and Cindy drove to the designated border location together, they discovered that each was contending with her own point of fear, that they shared a dread of reactivating trouble from the past in the scene that lay ahead of them:

In an hour we would meet our individual nightmares across a police barricade. Mine was about the Ku Klux Klan and how they would ride into the Mexican neighborhoods in Santa Ana, California where my mother's family lived during the 1920s. My anger was part of a collective anger, huge because at the base of it was the shame of knowing the obscenity had gone unchallenged. I could smell the hate of the nightrider's descendants as we got closer to the gathering of cars, and I was grateful for the television crews whose presence somehow protected me from harm. Her nightmare was confronting the racism of her own kind; of seeing her people, the neighbors so like those she had grown up with in Oklahoma, lining their cars up along the road, headlights pointed at Mexico to shine light on the problem of foreigners. . . . She was ashamed of their ignorance and bigotry; ashamed of them and for them. And as we gazed into our respective mirrors, we both hated and loved what we saw there because it was part of us, part of our inheritance, our burden and responsibility. (2)

Surprisingly, the evening created a space where something wonderful occurred. Cindy found the courage to cross the road and converse calmly with the demonstrators about what they were doing. Aida found the tenor of her family story subtly changing:

I learned her people had come West from Oklahoma during the years of the Dust Bowl and the Great Depression. I had heard of these people coming to work in the fields and factories of California from my mother and aunts. In many places they replaced the Mexican field hands in a struggle between the disinherited. But in my idealized memory I like to think her people worked alongside mine in the groves of walnuts and apricots of Southern California. Perhaps they worked a swingshift at the local defense plant. Perhaps they showed up at the same dancehall. Perhaps the wall between them was only a window. (3)

In the spring of 1990, Aida was also invited by the Centro Cultural de la Raza to curate a visual art exhibition of her own design. She asked Las Comadres if they/we would like to accept this invitation collectively. We decided we would. The time seemed right to respond to "Los vecinos" and "Light Up the Border" on our own terms and in our own media — as women and as artists — and to make good on the promise held in our name. This name, subsequently criticized within and outside the group for suggesting that we are all Chicanas, referred for us at that moment to the existence of nonbiological, but nonetheless familial, ties — like those of godmothers and godfathers. In using it, we meant to portray ourselves as a "border family" of women who, though coming from very diverse backgrounds, had chosen to become responsible to each other. The exploration of this "family" relationship, of which Aida's and Cindy's experience was an instance, became, in fact, the particular purpose of our seventy-minute performance piece, *Border boda*, conceived of as inseparable from the visual installation, "La vecindad/The Neighborhood," through which we entered the public discourse on borders and border subjects.

PERFORMING THE BORDER

My "stories" are acts encapsulated in time, "enacted" every time they are spoken aloud or read silently. I like to think of them as performances and not as inert and "dead" objects (as the aesthetics of Western culture think of art works.) — Gloria Anzaldúa (Borderlands 67)

Both the visual art and the performance that emerged from the several months of intense preparation that followed our acceptance of Aida's invitation defy the ability of any one participant or witness to describe them. That is ideally a purpose as well as a consequence of a collaborative creative process. Like a carnival or circus, or like the civic pageants once popular in Europe and still an important part of the ritual life of many societies, our performance emerged as the kind of spectacle/ritual/text Mikhail Bakhtin, the Soviet theorist, characterized as "heteroglossic" (*Rabelais* 154; *The Dialogic Imagination*). Heterogeneous and non-hegemonic, such texts interlace not only different perspectives, histories, and psychologies, but also different languages, genres, and registers. Spectators, under these circumstances, become themselves virtual participants, as their experiences and literacies focus the web of visual, tactile, audial, political, and historical elements of such spectacles. And, as "spectators" participate in the construction of meanings from their own shifting and disparate perspectives, these different readings complement each other in a second collective, interactive process (Pietropaolo 350–51). "La vecindad/The Neighborhood" and *Border boda,* then, set the scene for the collapse of the objectifying relationship between observer and observed that we noted in "Los vecinos" and tried to subvert at the "Light Up the Border" demonstrations. As the counterdemonstrations had tried to do at the border, the installation and the performance, in many ways, made spectators into part of a spectacle which was *about* the community that staged and observed it.

The strategy of destabilizing subject/object relationships operated in Las Comadres' work with astonishing consistency and incalculable cumulative effect. Visual as well as performance aspects of the show extended images in time and space, giving them dimensions and voices that foregrounded and interrogated the relationship between spectator and spectacle. A large vertical painting, for example, picturing horizontal nude bodies lying prone in a border canyon where bandits prey upon border-crossers, loomed over a pile of the shoes the bandits would have confiscated, arranged on the floor, preventing the viewer from standing in the traditional contemplative position in front of the work. A piece of hate mail sent by a neo-Nazi group call-

Figure 1. Las Comadres' production of *Border boda*. Photo courtesy of Lynn Susholtz.

ing itself the "WarBoys" was stenciled onto a large cloth rug that visitors had to walk on, or detour around, to get from one part of the installation to another. One entire room, the "library," made spectators simultaneously into readers of, and figures in, its design, as they sat at a long, multicolored table, reading through the collection of feminist and border-related materials that had been significant to us over the past two years, surrounded by our banners from "Light Up the Border" counterdemonstrations, a photographic essay on bilingual education, and wooden and metal artists' books mounted on the wall.[8] One of the most striking pieces, and a crucial prop/ metaphor in *Border boda,* was a multidimensional sculpture made of painted wood, a section of chain link fence with a window cut out of it, a small mirror, and pink and yellow stage lights. The figure of the Virgen de Guadalupe was evoked by a huge, mandala-shaped aura painted on wood, which was hinged down the middle. A toothed circular saw had started its descent through the center of this icon, headed for a mirror, hung at eye level across the hinged cut. A few feet in front of the mandala stood the chain link fence with its window and, suspended from it, a painted bodice reproducing one of Frida Kahlo's images of invisible physical and psychic pain. María Teresa Marrero, Chicano/a theater and performance historian, has described the spatial effects of this piece as follows:

The image Las Comadres create is based on the Oriental principle of the "empty middle." Here La Virgen de Guadalupe is deprived of a literal body. . . . Since the space is empty, it suggests that any woman can occupy it by positioning herself there. The border, then, can be seen as a construct, a state of being, which those who literally "place themselves" there can experience. Furthermore, once positioned, the opportunity exists for seeing oneself, since a mirror is the only object placed inside this middle space. . . . The iconography of filling in a sacred space with the body of an "ordinary" woman is a powerful one. Meanings shift in both directions: it places woman towards the sacred, as the sacred shifts into the human. The Virgin, taken out of the institutional patriarchies of the Catholic Church and the Mexican government, and also taken out of the sanctity of the Mexican traditional home altar, becomes an appropriated icon. (*Self-Representation* 85–86)

The director of *Border boda,* Laura Esparza, envisioned a performance that would similarly renegotiate relationships between past and present, sacred and secular, performers and audience, women and institutions. She saw *Border boda* as a bridge between two theaters — the great Chicano *campesino* theater of the sixties and seventies and the avant-garde performance art of an emerging group of more multicultural, urban performers like Luis Alfaro and Guillermo Gómez-Peña. The visions of both, she feels, are needed in a Chicano theater that addresses the improvisational realities of a decidedly nonmonolithic Chicano culture — that speaks to the Chicano living in Ohio, to the monolingual, English-speaking Chicana who cannot talk easily to her Spanish-speaking parents, to the bicultural child of a bicultural marriage, or to the descendants of the four-hundred-year-old *tejano* family, a family colonized four times, by four different countries — Spain, Mexico, Texas, and the United States — without ever having left the neighborhood. The stories and traditions of the elders are more than ever relevant to this diasporic, self-alienated (non)community, which needs post-national, yet historical reference points to support its members' daring and necessary departures from the past into the future.

Performed in two different spaces, the seventy-minute performance piece explores two asymmetrical cultural spheres, which meet and interpenetrate, often violently and/or painfully, across the border area of the border fence sculpture. In a colorful kitchen area a Mexicana grandmother and her sister try to prepare their Chicana granddaughter/great niece for her wedding to "Ted," a gringo, while struggling with their own deeply mixed feelings about this marriage. The grandmother unfolds an associative series of stories about herself, their family, and its acquaintances, while her mute sister expressively chops and cooks fruit, sugar cane, and cinnamon for a *calientitos* that will be served to the entire audience at the end of the performance. The *tía* also, on four occasions, becomes magnificently vocal, singing a series of history-laden Mexican border songs that comment mordantly on the grandmother's stories. The meanings of these songs (at least the denotative meanings) are, of course, lost on the monolingual niece, as well as on non-Spanish-speaking spectators and performers, a dimension of the performance I will say more about below. In an adjacent black and white "conflict" or "media" room, a space in which roles and perspectives are inhabited somewhat differently, two apparently Anglo performance artists interrogate official U.S. culture's representations of Chicano culture. Intermittently they assume the personae of journalists, one an idealistic liberal and the other a hard-boiled cynic. Through a series of skits, debates, poems, and videos, the two philosophically and politically incompatible figures discover the inadequacies of both their positions to the job of reporting on the border. Entangled within the logic of Anglo representations and appropriations, they try ineffectually, but always interestingly, to formulate satisfying interpretations of historical and contemporary events.

At several points the two spaces of the performance connect with shocking potency. In the Kitchen, for example, the grandmother has recounted the story of her and her sister's marriages and her own difficulty getting pregnant, but nothing has been said about her daughter and son-in-law, the border bride's mother and father. The *tía*, rather incongruously in the light of the warm tone and happy ending of the pregnancy story, then sings the rigorously unsentimental song, "*Arrieros somos*," It translates loosely:

> We are all shepherds and we are all on the same road of life. And each one of us will have what he deserves. You will see that at the end of your journey you will be bitter about having been born.
> We all come from nothing, and to nothing we will all return. I laugh at the world because even the world is not eternal. We simply pass through this life.

While the aunt sings, the woman playing the bride takes her place in the border fence sculpture, and enacts through dance movement the feeling of being torn in two directions — between emotions of joy and sorrow, as well as between the two cultures whose relationship to each other underlies this family's emotional and psychological turmoil. After the song concludes, the video monitor in the Conflict/Media room begins to show images of present day Mexican farmworkers toiling in what are obviously large U.S. agri-

business fields. Simultaneously, performer Ruth Wallen delivers a harrowing rendition of Gloria Anzaldúa's dramatic monologue "We Call Them
Greasers." At the end of the poem, whose final stanza recounts the rape and
murder of a *tejano* rancher's wife by an Anglo landgrabber, the granddaughter's voice from the Kitchen asks curiously, "What happened to Mama?" As
the pieces of the puzzle fall into place for the horrified audience member,
the apparent non sequiturs of the sequence metamorphose into a starkly
obvious narrative of violence and loss.

Later in the performance the flow of energies and complexities between
the Kitchen and the Media/Conflict room works to render a more positive
figure for border subjectivity. On the monitor in the Media/Conflict room,
a Mexican woman, Mrs. Vásquez, tells a story about being seized and
beaten by United States INS agents while she sold tacos near the border.
Speaking with great self-possession, she denounces the hypocrisy of Americans who want no one to enter their territory without authorization, but
feel entitled to invade Mexico and brutalize Mexicans. As the tape ends, the
lights come up on the granddaughter/niece, played by Comadre Eloise De
Leon, again standing in the middle of the aura of the border fence sculpture,
this time delivering Mrs. Vásquez's story in English. For a moment, at least
media technology works to create rather than to inhibit community. The
granddaughter/Eloise, who has an uneasy relationship with Spanish in
both the fiction of *Border boda* and in real life, is able to become part of Mrs.
Vásquez's story and Mrs. Vásquez's story part of hers *because* the story is
on videotape. Electronic reproduction allowed another Comadre, María
Kristina, to translate Mrs. Vásquez's words into English, which in turn
enabled Eloise to perform them. The inclusion of both the tape and Eloise's
mandala-framed reenactment of it in the performance further complicates
the notion of representing the border, replacing the notion that such a reality is susceptible to mimesis with an example of a complex, composite practice of deterritorialization and translation. Each of the women involved in
this segment of the performance was a mediator, a translator, and the willingness of all of them to serve as such created its own kind of community.

Mrs. Vásquez's appropriation of the video apparatus and Eloise's ability
to act as a bridge between the Spanish-speaking Mexicana and non-Spanish
speakers of whatever ethnicity thus displaces the Manichean impulse to see
(in *Border boda* or elsewhere) a simple opposition between a "bad," oppressor, Anglo side and a "good," if oppressed, Mexicana side (or, conversely, a
"good" Anglo side and a "bad" Mexican side) — precisely the impulse that
has historically put *la chicana* in such an untenable psychosocial position.
Such binary thinking, emblematized by the black and white enlargements

of newspaper articles and photographs that constituted the decor of the Media/Conflict room, is belied when the media performers eventually cross to the colorful Kitchen where they are discovered to "be," not "Anglo" (whatever that is) but Jewish and Italian and German and English. The "Mexicanas" were themselves not only *Indio* and Spanish, but also, we learn, Romanian and Jewish. Conversely, when the "grandmother," who was played on different occasions by Aida Mancillas and Laura Esparza, enters the black and white Media/Conflict room, she metamorphoses into a racist media hack, Heddy Rodgcock (i.e., a female Roger Hedgcock). The division between these two asymmetrical performance spaces is presented, in other words, not in terms of any essential, racial difference, but in terms of a cultural/conceptual incommensurability. Ironically, insofar as one reduces this incommensurability to a moral binary, one remains caught on the binary side. One is missing the critique of such moral binarism even as, on another level, one may be condemning the black and white thinking that underwrites the self-destructive habit of binary self-definition.

By the end of *Border boda,* the impasses of cross-cultural representation are not so much resolved as thoroughly exacerbated, clearing a space for a freer circulation of cultural influences — names, stories, ideas, fashions, emotions — that flows both ways. The performance concludes, significantly, with performers moving into each other's spaces and out from both spaces into the audience, a movement that is followed by the audience's being invited into the newly reconfigured Kitchen to drink the aromatic *calientitos,* whose preparation has paralleled, and in some sense stands for, all the other action of the performance.

Anglo critics, interestingly, tended not to grasp the significance of this choreography. Most notably the *High Performance* reviewer carefully re-isolated the Kitchen scenes from the rest of the performance, criticizing the "secondary" Media Room episodes for introducing too many issues, endangering the continuity of the storytelling going on next door. She concludes generously: "Fortunately this did not reduce the impact of the Kitchen scenes: the threads of the grandmother's stories wound around one another to create a rich tapestry. . . . the family's stories were personal, with abundant detail, and told in a setting enriched by ritual and metaphor" (44). Such isolation and aestheticization of traditional elements of Chicano culture were, needless to say, precisely what the director and her collaborators *aimed* to disrupt, to render discontinuous, so that what might appear to be a beautiful and safe "tapestry" from the colonizer's point of view could also be seen, heard, and felt, as a living, ongoing, historically and politically fraught struggle for economic, cultural, and psychological survival.

The *tía* (created and performed by Rocío Weiss) is mute for good reason. Her rage is so great, her distrust of how she will be heard is so profound, that she cannot or will not speak while she is north of the border (though she is known to become loquacious the moment she sets foot in Tijuana). Instead she sings. Coming into the performance as if from a great distance, each of her songs delivers an ironic comment on the stories being told and the story unfolding in front of us. The ironies of her final song are characteristic, if atypical in their abjuration of grief. In response to a tragically structured story of genocide and abuse of the land in Oklahoma told by Cindy, who has come from the audience to join the storytellers in the Kitchen, the *tía* bursts into a rousing rendition of "Adelita," a *corrido* from the Mexican Revolution. Very upbeat, "Adelita" tells the story of the women soldiers who fought valiantly and successfully with Zapata and Pancho Villa — especially one in particular whom the song's singer would follow to the ends of the Earth even if she left him for another man. By juxtaposing Cindy's story, with its potential to demoralize the *Indias* even as it condemns their oppressors, and this empowering *corrido*, the *tía* refuses to allow Chicana psychological borders to be "swamped." The language "barrier" becomes a rich communication resource, allowing the story to resonate differently in relation to the different linguistic and historical backgrounds of members of the audience.

For the audience, here and throughout, there is, then, no unequivocal place to stand, and that is the point. Moral and cognitive mastery, or what Donna Haraway calls "the manic compulsion to name the Enemy" (151), gives way to a sense of the partiality and limitation of one's focus of attention and the multiplicity of the stories and events that make up the community. The performance ends, for example, not with any resolution of the conflict over the granddaughter's wedding or answers to the question of how to represent border stories in the U.S. press, but with a proliferation of foci and interactions among spaces, which fills the gallery with the energy of ritual rather than the catharsis of Aristotelian drama.

The trouble with Aristotelian catharsis, according to Comadre Emily Hicks, and with any theater that cannot come to terms with multicultural experience, comments Laura Esparza, is that it reinforces the naturalization of a single reality. *Border boda* is not about knowing or not knowing. There are no great recognition scenes where "real" identities and relationships are uncovered. Nor are there any epiphanic scenes in which the niece finally understands how to stabilize her relationships. The experience of *Border boda*, for both performers and audience, is instead about what Gloria Anzaldúa in her recent anthology calls "making face" (*"haciendo caras"*), which she explains as "expressing feelings," and by extension, making politically subversive gestures. "Face," she says, can be "the piercing look that questions or challenges, the look that says, 'Don't walk all over me,' the one that says, 'Get out of my face.'" (*Making Face* xv). We thought of *Border boda* not as representational theater, but as a ritual/performance, pressed out of our collective (if heterogeneous) memories, to give ourselves and our audiences the strength and spirit to come to terms with our painful histories and conflicted relationships to each other.

BORDER CONFLICT

All five performers assumed that a collective version of the discipline of performance art, in which the artist pushes and deepens her own conflicts in order to make them accessible, would realize the intentions of "La vecindad/The Neighborhood" with particular effectiveness. This assumption proved both "right" and "wrong." Having said so much about what went well, I feel a responsibility to say a little more here about the problems we encountered.

First, we were not ourselves exempt from the visual politics we were criticizing. In some video footage of border-crossers being arrested on San Diego's Imperial Beach, recorded by us for use in *Border boda,* our analysis of the "Los vecinos" show hit home in a new way. Again there were images that were extraordinarily painful for some Comadres to watch, even when they were heavily contextualized within a critique of media representations of Mexican and Chicano culture. But this time the pain was more "personal" since the images were made by "friends." It was then painful for other Comadres, for whom these images were new and revelatory, to acknowledge, with such utter specificity, the chasm separating the consciousnesses and sensibilities of some of us from the consciousnesses and sensibilities of others of us. Theoretically this difference serves as a way to understand with great immediacy the subtle effects of racism. To discover and use these differences was one of the motives of our collaboration. But *living* this separateness was, and continues to be, felt by some as also tragically threatening to collaboration. In the heat of making art ourselves, we discovered the flaws in, and had to do without, those shared, monolithic, critical positions that had originally infused us with so much energy. This development, which did not necessarily occur along ethnic lines, undoubtedly contributed to the "success" of the show aesthetically, but having to live and breathe the daily reality of conflicting perceptions and points of view also drastically undermined our new, fragile sense of well-being. It felt, as one Comadre characterized it, like a "psychotic break."[9]

Our own capacity to undercut each other also occasionally shocked us. I thought at first that we might be suffering from a variation of bell hooks's "diva girl" syndrome, a tendency toward "abusive and dominating behavior by . . . 'feminist' thinkers, even if our work is based on a critique of domination" (99). Hooks observes that, mimicking the forms of power that have shaped us, we have not yet learned how to present and to recognize different cultural standpoints without feeling defensive or usurped. The implied solution to this problem is "to know and respect boundaries," using power to support and affirm (102). Recently, though, I came across a diagnosis of what sounds like an experience even closer to ours that suggests a process less directly accessible to conscious direction. In the introduction to her book *Epistemology of the Closet,* theorist Eve Sedgwick describes a graduate seminar she taught on gay and lesbian literature in which half the students were men and half women. All the women including herself, she writes, were intensely uncomfortable and at first attributed this discomfort to "some obliquity" in the relations between the men and the women (61). Eventually, though, it seemed clear that the problem lay among the apparently homogeneous, and feminist, women, who were caught up in what Sedgwick calls a circuit of "intimate denegation." "[I]t appeared that each woman in the class possessed (or might, rather, feel we were possessed by) an ability to make one or more of the other women radically and excruciatingly doubt the authority of her own self-definition as a woman; as a feminist; and as the positional subject of a particular sexuality" (61). Sedgwick then surmises that most people involved in forms of politics that touch on issues of identity—race as well as sexuality and gender—have observed or been part of such circuits—some "consolidating," some "denegating." She stresses that such dynamics are not "epiphenomenal to identity politics, but constitute it" (61). The reason she offers has to do with the complexities of identification—because it always involves identification "against" as well as the vagaries of identification "as" and identification "with." The latter is, as she points out, in itself "quite sufficiently fraught with intensities of incorporation, diminishment, inflation, threat, loss, reparation, and disavowel" to generate tensions (61).

Our biggest blowups, in regular meetings as well as during the intense evolution of *Border boda,* did not occur *between* Anglos and Chicanas, but *within* those groupings. For example, it was an arduous but relatively straightforward matter for the Media/Conflict room performers to criticize overly didactic skits that stereotyped rather than analyzed the "gringo" media. It was harder and less straightforward for Emily and Ruth to know where and how to take their stylistic and conceptual disagreements with each other.

In this regard, I find it especially significant that the character whom the performance group had the most difficulty focusing on was that of the granddaughter/niece, the one closest to the position of all the performers in the Kitchen. The underdevelopment of this character may have been due partly to Eloise's coming to the role late when Comadre María Kristina had to resign for family reasons. But Eloise and the rest of the performers all sensed that there was, as well, some unarticulated resistance to developing this character's rebellions and conflicts, to making her more than the vessel of her family's vivid stories and gestures. As Laura later commented, "We *are* that character, clearly. She is dear to my heart, that border person who has great relevance to what other Americans of color experience, too. But why is she so inarticulate? Why can't she speak up? Once we are able to cope with her, we might be able to claim the power of this position." Part of this inarticulateness was due, several others suggested, to the reluctance of Chicanas to air their differences in front of Anglo women. (When Anglo Comadres point out to Laura that she and other Chicana Comadres don't *seem* inarticulate, she replies, "We're overcompensating.") But the aversion to developing the granddaughter also seemed rooted in the dynamics of the Kitchen space itself. Everyone, in her way, wanted to love this figure, and it may be that this very love helped reduce the role to a cipher. If her beauty and strength had been more specified, she might have acquired the unfortunate power to undermine those who identified with/as her most. In a sense her "failure" was inevitable. How could she represent what the whole performance insisted was a multiple, and "unrepresentable," position?

I see no easy way to push beyond this impasse. (And, as I hope I have indicated, it is not an impasse unique to, but thrown into relief by, the problematics of Chicana identity.) The difficult way beyond it, to the extent that *Border boda* found one, proved very difficult indeed — nothing short of a transformation in the way "identity" is formed and felt. *Border boda* seems to have led its performers, at least temporarily, to a state of much greater than usual fluidity, a state that was encouraged and supported by the ritual and discipline of the project. On stage and off, people *changed*, or "moved," in Gloria Anzaldúa's sense of shedding the skin. Theoretically this is the kind of movement that obviates the framework of representation and identification that I am suggesting kept the granddaughter's creators from applying more critical pressure to her role. But what I am calling fluidity sometimes just felt painful to us — difficult to accept in others and difficult to live with in ourselves — even with the supporting web of group improvisation. And, the so-called "real" world always remained to be dealt with, where fluidity could easily translate into a frightening vulnerability. Once the performance was over and the ritual gone, it was worse. "We felt embarrassed, as if we had been at an orgy, not a wedding," was Emily Hicks's earthy observation.[10] Comadres found themselves in a *terra incognita* of mutual nonrecognition in which no one felt at home. At this writing, the question remains whether we, or others, can make this potentially fertile, deterritorialized *terra* collectively habitable. We would welcome the participation of other collaborative groups, theoreticians, artists, activists in discovering how to make that next move.

NOTES

Members of Las Comadres who collaborated on "La vecindad/The Neighborhood" and *Border boda:* Kirsten Aaboe, Yarelli Arizmendi, Carmela Castrejon, Frances Charteris, Magali Damas, Eloise De Leon, Maria Eraña, Laura Esparza, Emily Hicks, Berta Jottar, María Kristina, Aida Mancillas, Anna O'Cain, Graciela Ovejero, Lynn Susholtz, Ruth Wallen, Margie Waller, Rocío Weiss, Cindy Zimmerman.

1   Emily Hicks extends and concretizes Donna Haraway's widely admired postulation/ description of a nonessentialist "cyborg subjectivity" to describe a border subject whose perception and writing are "holographic." As Hicks writes in the "Introduction" of her book *Border Writing: The Multidimensional Text,* "What makes border writing a world literature with a "universal" appeal is its emphasis upon the multiplicity of languages within any single language; by choosing a strategy of translation rather than representation, border writers ultimately undermine the distinction between original and alien culture" (xxiii). See also her essay, "Border Performance Texts."

2   My understanding of the complex, conflicted linguistic position of the non-Spanish-speaking Chicana is greatly indebted to conversations with Eloise De Leon and Laura Esparza, and particularly to De Leon's videotape on the subject, *Reaching In.* Esparza is working on a new performance piece that puts the issue squarely in front of, and even in the mouths of, the audience.

3   In her essay "Third World Diva Girls" bell hooks contrasts the relatively easy feminist pleasure of analyzing the way patriarchy manifests itself in everyday life in *male* behavior, and the more difficult "recognition of the way in which patriarchal sexist thinking distorts women's relation to one another" (99). By implication the analysis of the oppressive structure, be it "patriarchy" or be it "racism," is itself problematic, colored by the same thinking that it seeks to understand and dismantle. If groups like (and unlike) ours do not move through and past the first phase, its distortions will keep coming back to haunt us.

4   In *Border Writing* Hicks refers to and extends the term "deterritorization," familiar to readers of Gilles Deleuze and Felix Guattari's *Anti-Oedipus: Capitalism and Schizophrenia,* to describe the subject position of the border writer/reader. See especially their chapter "Territorial Representation" (184–92). She also refers to Deleuze and Guattari's work on

Kafka's writing (in *Kafka: pour une littérature mineure*) to characterize "a kind of realism that approaches the experience of border-crossers, those who live in a bilingual, bicultural, biconceptual reality" (*Border Writing* 5). Las Comadres have worked, ideally, toward a collective version of such a deterritorialized sense of our language(s), culture(s) and reality(ies).

5   For a scathing critique of this appropriation, see Guillermo Gómez-Peña's "Death on the Border: A Eulogy of Border Art" in the Spring 1991 issue of *High Performance*. The twentieth anniversary exhibition (October–November 1991) at the Centro Cultural de Raza, "Counter-Colon-ialismo: Contemporary Manifestations of Colonization/Manifestaciones Contemporaneas de la Colonizacion," suggests that a eulogy is premature, but, as the name also suggests, resisting what Gómez-Peña calls the gentrification of border aesthetics, the turning of border culture into "a consumer monstrosity" that distracts attention from, rather than focusing it on, political and human rights issues, is felt as an added pressure by the artists and activists involved in (and in need of) the border art movement.

6   See Klaus Theweleit's book *Male Fantasies, Volume 1: Women Floods, Bodies History.* Theweleit has detailed the figural association of Jews, social democrats, communists, anarchists, with an image of woman-as-flood in the rhetoric of poems and novels written by proto-Nazi German Freicorpsmen in the years between World War I and World War II. He reads this otherwise irrational conflation as a "fear of flowing," a fear, that is, of dissolution or limitlessness, on the part of male subjects under increasing pressure to live within "an impregnable body armor" (380). The images and figures he discusses resonate suggestively with Anzaldúa's metaphor of "floundering on uncharted seas" and having one's psychological borders "swamped" (*Borderlands* 79). The fascist, it appears, projects his fear of the female/flood onto whomever he has constructed as other; the "other," who may have internalized this fear just as strongly, not only does not have the same opportunities for projecting it, but must also contend with being treated as its embodiment. For Anzaldúa, the person who finds herself in this classic double bind must, for survival, bushwhack her way out of "the subject-object duality that keeps her a prisoner" toward another mode of subjectivity altogether (80). Theweleit's argument suggests to me that no one is particularly comfortable in the subject position that fantasizes and fears flooding.

7   The rhetoric of these groups startlingly recapitulates the conflation of "others" in a single category and the sexualizing of that category analyzed by Theweleit. Part of a letter sent by "The Holy Church of the White Fighting Machine of the Cross" to Roberto Martínez, a human rights activist, goes as follows: "The cops are going to start shooting you Mexicans wholesale soon, and there will be nothing you can do about it. Go back to T.J. (Tijuana) and watch the mule fuck the whore that will be better for you. . . . Stop criticizing the border patrol and the whites who are trying to save our white country from the Jews and the Gay stooges in the government who will not act in behalf of the white Aryan race."

8   On March 5, 1993, a reconstruction of the "library" was included in an exhibition entitled "La Frontera/The Border: Art About the Mexico/United States Border Experience," jointly curated by the Museum of Contemporary Art, San Diego and the Centro Cultural de la Raza, San Diego. This exhibition will travel to the Centro Cultural Tijuana, the Tacoma Art Museum, Washington, the Scottsdale Center for the Arts, Arizona, the Neuberger Museum, State University of New York, Purchase, and the San Jose Museum of Art, California.

9 A less sensationalizing but essentially similar diagnosis of what *la mestiza* must go through in order to move "Towards a New Consciousness" is offered by Gloria Anzaldúa in her call for "a tolerance of ambiguity": "numerous possibilities keep *la mestiza* floundering in uncharted seas. In perceiving conflicting information and points of view, she is subjected to a swamping of her psychological borders. She has discovered that she can't hold concepts or ideas in rigid boundaries. . . . *La mestiza* constantly has to shift out of habitual formations: from convergent thinking, analytical reasoning that tends to use rationality to move toward a single goal (a Western mode), to divergent thinking, characterized by movement away from set patterns and goals and toward a more whole perspective, one that includes rather than excludes" (*Borderlands* 79).

10 Perhaps our reaction should be read as an encouraging sign. Note how precisely and economically the figure of the orgy combines fascism's two nemeses, engulfment and sexuality.

Sue-Ellen Case
Seduced and Abandoned: Chicanas and Lesbians in Representation

❑

Seduced and abandoned is a condition articulated in the passive voice. It marks an inherited condition, an object position that traces, after the fact, a sexual encounter of pleasure and pain, of bonding and of tearing apart. I learned the phrase in the sixties in the lesbian bar scene, where it was a kind of throw away, slung out, usually by some butch number, who was attempting to tough out her pain of loss by expressing it as a cliché — a word formation that emphasized its common, serial quality over its specificity. The phrase usually produced a laugh, for it succinctly performed the social experience in the bars of short-term relationships and the practice of serial monogamy,[1] the subculture of the bars, and, often, internalized homophobia, which mitigated against any lasting sexual alliances because they were proof that one was, indeed, the despised lesbian. "Seduced and abandoned" marked off the territory of lesbian encounters in contradiction to those of dominant culture, gesturing a kind of backslap to the world of dates, engagements, and lifetime models — abandoning "forever and ever" for "quick and dirty." The phrase played like a line from a script everyone knew, for the bars were theatres of seduction, where the scenarios of desire and loss were played out — where the tirades of pain, anger, love, and loss were delivered. "Seduced and abandoned" was the lesbian tragedy and farce: the tragedy of love and loss and the farce of its repetition. The laughter that the phrase engendered signalled a community which survived through the very process of seducing and abandoning itself.

In this chapter, "seduced and abandoned" is also slung out: here, to tough out the pleasure and pain politically, critically, and personally experienced in the coalitions and confrontations among Anglo lesbians and Chicanas concerning the politics of representation. As "seduced and abandoned," this phrase articulates the serial nature of their encounters, the circulation of desire among them, and the constant performance of inclusionary/exclusionary strategies. As expressed in the passive voice, it marks here as well, an object position — the inherited condition of appearance and invisibility in the system of representation. The racist and homophobic dynamics in the system hail these identities as if simple and transparent. These are identities assigned to inclusion in the representable as sites of exclusion — through their denotation, they are abandoned. "Chicana" and "lesbian," in dominant discourse, are object positions masquerading as subject positions; they lose their agency as they reveal. Whereas Anglo, or "white" and "heterosexual" consume agency as they veil their identity.

Identity politics calls for these abject identities to be inhabited as subject positions with agency — subject positions which claim for themselves the right of self-identification. In this insistence on their right to self-identification, to reclaim the identity from its exclusionary utility, these "subjects" maintain a central, stable site in the discourse: a fixed location from which they might appropriate the discursive "properties" of the dominant system of representation. In this case, the materialist practice of appropriating the dominant for the oppressed does entail claiming the center and holding it, rather than doing the dance of displacement at the masked ball of decentered subject positions. More crucially, within this argument, these subject positions maintain a stable site from which they might enter into coalitions with other identity-based positions.

Recently, the deployment of identity politics has been termed "strategic essentialism" as if to accommodate the misconception that these identities were ever perceived as ontological categories rather than social, experiential ones. The charge of "essentialism" that has been leveled against identity politics presumes that any claims on the system of representation by "real" people proceed from an ontological base — as if to claim the identity "lesbian" or "Chicana" presumes a metaphysical order rather than a materialist analysis. The sense that to maintain a stable identificatory subject position is to claim derivation from some system of idealism is a testament to the way that the category of experience has fallen out of certain current political analyses. Ironically, the practice of embedding a specific materialist history in the subject position, which is the function of identity politics, specifically by invoking the category of experience has been perceived as asserting some unchanging order of things. Without any record of experience as the historical, material mark of participation in an ethnic community, subculture, or grass-roots movement, there is no referent outside critical analyses to which they must be *accountable*. In point of fact, political systems without such a referent are essentialist in their self-referentiality. Experience marks the way in which a subject position is more than a structural cipher, a formalist point in a discursive field; rather, it accounts for a material history of oppression within which the fear of danger, the pain and anger of censure, or the hope for pleasure may be registered, and more, become the base for political strategies, such as separatism, or activism in the streets. What has been termed "presence," a damning concept in post-Derridean terms, has actually meant showing up in the community.

In this way, identity politics construct, as well as have been constructed by, dynamic inclusionary/exclusionary practices at base, for, without the experience of oppression and the pain of its particularities, access to the subject position of that identity is denied. Likewise, exclusionary and inclusionary boundaries secure a place for protection; they bring with them the promise of a contingent security within a community which shares fear, pain, hope, or a dream. Nested among others who share the identity, they are buffered from the direct attack of exclusion deployed by the dominant order. From that location, secured by inclusion/exclusion, coalition politics may be negotiated: it is the "home" one must sense in order to leave it. As Bernice Johnson Reagon said about coalition politics in a speech to feminists: "The first thing that happens is that the room don't feel like the room anymore. (Laughter) And it ain't home no more. It is not a womb no more. And you can't feel comfortable no more" (359). Yet, as Reagon emphasizes: "The 'our' must include everybody you have to include in order for you to survive. . . . That's why we have to live in coalitions." And her language is also a tough one: " 'Cause I ain't gonna let you live unless you let me live. Now there's danger in that, but there's also the possibility that we both can live — if you can stand it" (365).

The presumption of experience undergirds Reagon's concept of coalition, with the emphasis on what it "feels like" to be home or leave it, and the sense of "danger" which determines who "gets to live." The laughter included in the quotation signals both the oral nature of the address and its community. It is similar to the kind of laughter I described earlier as occurring in the bar — experiential, the sound of living through the threat and promise of coalition. While standing threateningly at the entrance of her identity position, like butch bouncers at the bar, Reagon nevertheless calls for considered inclusion: "Anytime you find a person showing up at all those stuggles . . . one, study them, and two, protect them. They're gonna be in trouble shortly because they are the most visible ones. . . . They can teach you how to cross cultures and not kill yourself" (363). So, while identity politics have determined a critical agenda which problematizes the

Anglo feminist critic's access to the position of women of color in representation, the heterosexist Anglo feminists' or women of color's access to the lesbian subject position, or the lesbian's access to works addressed to and received within an ethnic community which may be homophobic, there is also some kind of cross-over dynamic of the displaced that is mandated.

Critically I will move along this exclusionary/inclusionary axis of identity to read cultural texts, while also accommodating the category of experience. The order of displacement of identity, or "leaving home" I want to employ, begins with a selection of texts which represent the Chicana or lesbian, not as any politically viable subject position, or location, but display in their very construction of that subject position the contradictions and displacements, or worse, the suppression of one identity, be it ethnic or lesbian, at the expense of the other. This practice of a critical coalition, then, for the Anglo lesbian and the Chicana here resides in abandoning the centered subject position from which others may be marginalized and inhabiting instead a coalition position which unseats that centrality by its own contradictory animation of racism or homophobia. By this I mean that the subject position for one identity is gained by its deposition of the other one. It is a form of an "I" for an "I," or a inverse form of Reagon's " 'cause I ain't gonna let you live unless you let me live." Thus, to mobilize homophobia for the construction of "lesbian" in a Chicana text, or racism to construct "Chicana" in an Anglo lesbian text allows access across those identities through an inclusionary/exclusionary move.

Of course, the danger in such an analysis resides in the retention of an invisible category, which absorbs agency by assigning locations to other identities while remaining omnipresent. "Whiteness" and "heterosexuality" are most often the invisible categories which control the "others." From this perspective, one could perceive my critical project, which is seemingly in search of coalition, as actually concealing the hidden category of "white" in its construction, securing its hierarchical hold. As Norma Alarcón reveals it: "Anglo-American feminist theory assumes a speaking subject who is an autonomous, self-conscious, individual woman. It takes for granted the linguistic status which founds subjectivity. In this way it appropriates woman/women for itself, and turns its work into a theoretical project within which the rest of us are compelled to 'fit' " (363–64). Complementary to Alarcón's assignation of such a subject to Anglo American, one might also ascribe it to the assumption of liberal democracy or capitalism as the context. Thus, it is a bourgeois Anglo notion of the subject position which operates as the catalyst for the entire critical method of coalition, hierarchizing the identities by the construction of the subject position.

Alarcón de-authorizes such critical projects by locating them within the social struggles for supremacy.

I would like to further de-authorize the seeming intellectual terrain of this project by revealing its dependence upon my own social, historical construction. The narrative of my own experience is employed to illustrate how my own construction of "lesbian" as an identity was fueled by racism — specifically by my relation to Chicanas, and is enlivened by racism — specifically regarding Chicanas. In other words, the author must claim home and leave it in order to write the theory.

The texts, then, are the following: Estela Portillo's *The Day of the Swallows,* a homophobic play, yet with an Indian lesbian as the main character; the narrative of my own lesbian, racist awakening, and a consideration of the work of Cherríe Moraga, which brings together lesbian and Chicana along an acute axis of in/exclusion.

THE DAY OF THE SWALLOWS

Estela Portillo was the first Chicana playwright to gain recognition within the Chicano cultural movement. Her play *The Day of the Swallows* was written in 1971, during the early years of the movement. It was included in the first anthology of Chicano plays and Portillo was awarded the Quinto Sol prize for her contribution to Chicano literature. Portillo also worked as a cultural activist in her community, promoting the Chicano Cultural Arts Program in El Paso and founding the first bilingual theatre in that city.

The Day of the Swallows begs the question of what defines Chicano theatre. Jorge Huerta, the most noted historian of Chicano theatre asked: "What makes a work of art *Chicano?* Is *Day of the Swallows* a Chicana play simply because it was written by a Chicana from El Paso? Even though there are no Chicano politics in her play, is it yet Chicano since it deals with Mexican or Chicano characters?"[2] For Huerta, the ethnic identity of the author does not constitute a Chicana play. He feels that the play should be bilingual, a common feature of the Chicano subculture, or stage, as Huerta defines it, the social, material conditions of Chicanos. Other such critics have interrogated the play's mythic setting and themes, asking whether they are drawn from the Chicano interest in Aztlán (the reimagined Aztec Empire), or from the European authors who influenced Portillo in her studies as an English major.[3]

Notably, the above doubts were raised by male critics of Chicano literature. The feminist critics consider the text somewhat differently — particularly in light of its focus on the experience of a lesbian. The feminist analysis attends to the narrative of Josefa, the victim of the community's homophobia, who commits suicide. Janice Dewey directly confronts Huerta's category of social action by asserting that: "a woman's suicide in the face of an entire town's condemnation of her lesbian love. . . . is the culmination of theater for social protest" (40). Likewise, María Herrera-Sobek concludes that "In Hispanic communities and in the heterosexual population in general" there is a homophobia which this play addresses in a "balanced combination of myth and social protest," suggesting to the community that "to repress those differing from us in sexual habits and preferences is an invitation to unleash violence and tragedy" (Unpublished ms.). In other words, the ethnic politics of the play are contingent upon its representation of the lesbian and the confrontation of homophobia within the community.

What interests me here is a further displacement in political positioning. For while these feminist critics make ethnic politics consonant with a politics of gender and sexual preference, their recuperation of the lesbian's suicide as political situates her death within the heterosexual community which has something to learn from it. From within one kind of traditional lesbian critique, that suicide marks a distance from the gay and lesbian community and is politically irredeemable. The negative portrayal of the lesbian life, which ends in suicide is like Lillian Hellman's *The Children's Hour,* or other plays in which the lesbian is sacrificed to the uses of the heterosexual community, which would use her suffering to adjust its own homophobia. The narrative structure reinforces this negative, distant perspective on the lesbian, creating a sense that there is something frightening, dark, and terrible about her. The play opens with blood which has been mysteriously, but sinisterly spilled by Josefa. We later discover that she has cut out the tongue of her young ward, so that he could not tell the community that he witnessed one of her lesbian acts—a kiss. Thus, lesbian critics may find the play homophobic, citing Portillo's own description of her motivation for writing the play: "When my first book was rejected, someone told me to do fiction. I had just seen the movie *The Fox* . . . and someone said, why don't you write something like that and make millions? I'm always thinking of a buck. So in a month and a half I wrote *The Day of the Swallows* and I put everything in. The plot is about lesbians; I knew nothing about them, but I was going to sell it."[4]

At the same time, the Chicana lesbian writer Cherríe Moraga reads Portillo's play this way: "I've always loved *Swallows* although it is a 'classic' lesbian work in the worst sense of the 1950s view. . . . In this play . . . Portillo as author is the obedient daughter. Those who follow the law of the father will be rewarded. . . . those who transgress are punished (the lesbian suicide)" ("Obedient Daughter," 161–62). *In the sense of ex/inclusionary critical positions, I am interested in Moraga's ambivalence when she writes "I've always loved Swallows although."* While I cannot know what pleasure Moraga found, I can certainly claim my own lesbian pleasures in the text which operate alongside my displeasures. I take a great deal of pleasure in reading a lesbian character in the midst of elegant lyricism—a lyricism I can claim not as Romantic, but as one grounded in the homosexual lyric tradition of Lorca, Cherríe Moraga, Francisco Alarcón, Whitman, Wilde, and Tennessee Williams. Josefa's house, far from the pueblo, is in the desert, set within an eroticized landscape: "Then the maguey thickens with the ferocity of chaotic existence. Here the desert yawns. Here it drinks the sun in madness" (207). The moon is a "werewolf" by which Josefa bathes in the lake, when "passions are hard and fierce" (208). And the burning light, another of Josefa's lovers, will be inhabited by her own desire after her death. Josefa's erotic relation to the land and her suicide, a final coupling with the land, are common in homosexual writings, in which the desire which dares not write itself to another person, or within the community, but is displaced to a celebration of place becomes dispersed within the elements, as in Whitman or Lorca. What may be regarded as mythic or romantic may also be perceived as a survival tactic for homosexual desire, which continues to come into a sexual relation to the world in spite of its constant rejection within the heterosexual community. Listen to Josefa's final exit into an orgasmic coupling with land and light. "So still your water. . . . but I know your passions underneath. Deep . . . deep . . . for all time. Hush! I'm coming. . . . my burning lake" (243). From a lesbian perspective, then, the play is both homophobic and pleasurable in the way that it situates the lesbian character in relation to erotic elements. However, while reading with the text in this way, the lesbian critic becomes caught in confirming the negative portrayal of Josefa as well.

There is another way to read the play, which unites lesbian and ethnic concerns, precisely in displacement. Portillo's dramatic and political investment in the Indian/land/colonization politics becomes displaced onto the lesbian character. In other words, the lesbian narrative displaces what is actually the Indian one. The dramatic form of the play constructs a subtext of native representational systems over which a Eurocolonial shape is laid— both in narrative structure and in discursive style. Josefa works like a totem for race, or a stand-in for the idol worship of the ancient peoples: she is isolated, the people come to her, adore her, she provides for them, and, with her walking stick, punishes them. She even cuts out a tongue—a practice not uncommon among the ancient peoples and, in the end, practices self-sacrifice. She lives outside the hacienda, the Spanish colonial presence, and she rejects the Catholic ritual for an older, native one. Thus, her social status organizes a ritual dramaturgy that both reveals and conceals the native practices beneath it.

Perhaps more accurately, Josefa the lesbian does not stand for Indian, so much as for the abolition of Indian. As lesbian, she represents that which should not be seen — that which ultimately must be eradicated, in this case, by suicide. Her eradication is set among varying kinds of colonial ownership practices which she transgresses. Her suicide is a final deadly transformation by drowning, but by joining the forces of light she also returns into the landscape/light/lake that both marks the loss of those places to the native peoples and a kind of violent reclaiming of them. While heterosexual colonizing operates much differently than colonial practices against native peoples, the drive to eradicate communities through legal ownership, such as marital and familial rights against homosexuals creates a consonance between the position of Indian and lesbian. It is reminiscent of a poem by the Native American author Paula Gunn Allen entitled "Some Like Indians Endure":

> i have it in my mind that
> dykes are indians. . . .
>
> indian is an idea some women
> have of themselves
> the place where we live now
> is idea
> because whiteman took
> all the rest . . .
> like indians
> dykes have fewer and fewer
> someplace elses to go
> so it gets important
> to know
> about ideas and
> to remember or uncover
> the past
> and how the people
> traveled
> all the while remembering
> the idea they had
> about who they were

indians, like dykes
do it all the time
(298–301)

LOWER CASE WHITE

Raised as a poor white (white trash) in Southern California, I grew up in the neighborhood of what we then called "Mexicans," or derogatorily, "*cholos*." From the ages of eleven to thirteen I was the head of a white girls' gang that fought the "Mexican" girls' gang over issues of territory and "honor." Spanish was the enemy language, though we all knew the "bad" words. In fact, Spanish served as my original profane language, marking it with racism, sexuality, and transgression. In this way, its taboo status later became associated with my own repressed homosexuality.

The Spanish language and the history of Mexican and indigenous peoples filtered through all our local representational systems. My racist father, Frank, was nicknamed Pancho; the basically Anglo annual parade in our town was opened by five Spanish land-grant sisters, the Camarillos, sitting in silver saddles and wearing black lace, while the mission and the statue of Father Serra dominated the downtown sightlines. My father worked alongside "Mexicans" in the citrus groves and the oil fields, and my mother and aunts worked alongside the women in the packing house. We lived with these people, but were obsessed by hating them.

My longtime rival Gloria Valenzuela led the "Mexican" girls' gang. Our days at school and on the streets were consumed with breaches of honor and territorial incursion that set up our fights. Only much later did I realize what a sexual activity the gang violence promoted: I was obsessed with Gloria's body. One of the most crucial incitements was when she tore open my blouse on Main Street. The humiliation of the exposure and the violence of her tearing at my breast promoted a heady mix of racism and lesbian desire. Imagining her hidden weapons, such as the razor blades slipped into the back of the shoe heels, prompted hours of planning on my part for our next encounter: just where and how I would grab her. Supremacy was the narrative, however. The "Mexicans" (actually an apt phrase for these people since California was, at one time, part of Mexico) just had to lose. This is an obsession currently at the forefront of California politics since, demographically, it seems they are "winning." Nevertheless, that supremacy was physical for me and Gloria—we pulled each other close in order to illustrate just who would emerge on top. Our fights were prohibited by school authorities, so they were secret affairs arranged in back lots.

For my family our racist hatred served as the amulet with which we held the promise of upward mobility. And it worked. When I was 13 my father was promoted and we moved to the "nice" part of town. On the privilege of my whiteness, I left the gangs and the "Mexicans" just in time to get through high school. My lesbian awakening, at 15, was limited to other "Anglos." By the time of graduation, I was able to enroll in a private college in Stockton. Afraid of censure in the dorms, and isolated as a lesbian, I repressed my sexual desires and attempted to become heterosexual. At the same time, I became a worker at a migrant settlement and spent that summer with the Friends' Society living and working with the migrant field workers, while studying their legal and economic situation. The first member of my family to attend college, I also set out to learn the gestural and discursive strategies of the educated "class." I worked at losing my working-class accent, my tomboyish gestures, and my white trash sense of fashion.

This is the point at which my class/color/sexual experience became sublimated into political, critical theory. My academic success resulted from the repression of my experience and the silencing of my emotions. My social acceptance and my feeling of safety depended on the repression of my homosexuality. Forsaking the arms of Gloria Valenzuela in the dirt lot, I wrote my way into political analysis. Identity politics and the feminist movement later, I began to critically reinhabit these positions from out of the subculture of the primarily Anglo lesbian bar scene. With the discourse of the intellectual class in place, I tried to intervene into the structure with my own experience. A retrograde project, the battle was to rediscover a way to write that integrated these elements. I succeeded, to some extent, in establishing a camp style for lesbian theory—a way to bring subcultural discourse into the writing.

Then, I brought out a heterosexual Chicana and we became partners for several years. While she yearned for a lesbian identity by embracing the relationship, my Anglo attitudes as her lover drew her away from her Chicana identity. While I was enflamed by my historical past, now regained, my old amulet of upward class mobility still kept me from learning Spanish, or comfortably participating in the ethnic community. Moreover, the homophobia in the ethnic community terrified me and the separatist, cultural nationalism, while familiar to me as lesbian separatism, excluded me in painful ways. Thus, we once again seduced and abandoned one another, and, after riding the roller coaster of inclusionary/exclusionary dynamics, finally relegated our experience together to the line dance of serial monogamies.

The fires of racism, lesbian desire, its repression, and the wild oscillations between discursive strategies and experiential memories conflagrate this writing. My project of coalition, of reading the wrestling depositions of lesbian and Chicana subject positions across texts is a form of fetishism. The dirt lot sex fight reads *The Day of the Swallows.* The play's homophobic dramaturgy, which produces Josefa's image at the expense of "lesbian" allows my desire of the Chicana/Indian to circulate as lesbian, while deposing, through my racism, Indian; as the play deposes lesbian for desire for the Indian. In these dark spaces of exclusion and inclusion, the images can circulate together — both marked as transgressive and sexual. Yet my own narrative discloses the hidden white privilege in my writing of this critical account. The seeming symmetry of examples belies a white supremacy in the racist animation which fires my own Anglo lesbian subject position. My critical discourse is my amulet of upward mobility, deployed to secure the dominance of whiteness even in the imagined coalition of lesbian and Chicana.

With Anglo at the axis of this bifurcation, the coalition, the crossing-over depends on deposition. The writhing struggle for supremacy is marked in the uneven access to privilege the Anglo category intrudes. Without Anglo the two identities, lesbian and Chicana operate in a different manner. While I have no access to the synthetic nature of their relationship, I can perceive some contradictions which seem similar to the operations in the critical strategies outlined above.

CHERRÍE MORAGA

No access is available to me for extricating Cherríe Moraga's subject position as Chicana lesbian. It is in a certain history of the reception of her work which is available here as a site of in/exclusion along this axis. From her earliest works onward, Moraga has sketched out the way that lesbian and Chicana, when together, move each of the identities out of their communities. When she was criticized by her ethnic community for achieving her initial national visibility through Anglo feminist organizations and publications, her answers indicated that her lesbian perspective distanced her from the heterosexist organization of alliance: "I did not move away from other Chicanos because I did not love my people. I gradually became anglocized because I thought it was the only option available to me toward gaining autonomy as a person without being sexually stigmatized" ("Long Line of Vendidas" 174).[5] "You are a traitor to your race if you do not put the man first" (177). "What looks like betrayal between women on the basis of race originates, I believe, in sexism/heterosexism" (173). "Heterosexism [is] — the Chicana's sexual commitment to the Chicano male — is proof of her fidelity to her people" (178). Moraga's identity within the Chicana community is decentered by her lesbian identity.

Within the lesbian feminist community, Moraga represents the ethnic voice, along with Gloria Anzaldúa, Paula Gunn Allen, Audre Lorde, and Michelle Cliff. In both communities Moraga inhabits an insider/outsider position — an intercultural, multiple location from which her work produces uncomfortable coalitions.

The production history of her play *Giving Up The Ghost* illustrates the same kind of positioning. In spite of its specific address to the Chicano community, and its bilingual language (Spanglish), its first two staged readings were by an Anglo feminist theatre, At the Foot of the Mountain, in 1984 and a lesbian theatre, The Front Room Theater, in 1986. Only later was it performed by a Chicano theatre, El Teatro de la Esperanza at the Mission Cultural Center, in 1989. Within the feminist community, the play was exceptional for its material and multiple identity construction, in contrast to the few white lesbian plays which had appeared, without class or race specificity — taking for granted the bourgeois, white lesbian as normative.[6] Within the ethnic community, its representation of lesbian sexuality, which implicates even heterosexual women, was singular.

The major character, Marisa, is split within herself: her adult self and her young self, Corky. When Corky comes on stage: "*una chaparrita*' who acts tough, but has a wide open sincerity in her face which betrays the toughness. She dresses in the 'cholo style' of her period (the '60s): khakis with razor-sharp creases; pressed white undershirt; hair short and slicked back" (*Giving Up The Ghost* 1). The historical, class, and butch specificity of her identity speak to the lesbian and the Chicana in the audience in a material, experiential way. While the lesbian spectator may embrace this image, the heterosexist Chicana may not. Yvonne Yarbro-Bejarano has described it this way: "[her] subjectivity as [a] sexual being is shaped in dialectical relationship to a collective way of imagining sexuality. The text explores the ways in which Chicanas, both lesbian and heterosexual, have internalized their culture's concepts of sexuality" (145).

In the play, the border between Anglo and Chicana rests between the two lovers: Corky/Marisa is from a mixed-neighborhood in the United States and Amalia has Mexico in her past, her erotics, and her imagination. Sexuality is also situated on the border: Marisa/Corky's sexual history is lesbian while Amalia's is heterosexual. Seduced and abandoned is definitely the motif here. Marisa is both seduced by Amalia, the heterosexual, ethnic woman and abandoned by her. Here is a passage, using Mexico, the desert, and seduction, which also marks the abandonment.

AMALIA: Desert. Desierto.
Maybe in the desert, it could have turned out
differently between La Pachuca and me.
I *had* intended to take her there,
to México.

She would never have gone alone,
sin gente allá.

For some reason, I could always picture
her in the desert
amid the mesquite y nopal.
Always when I closed my eyes to search for her,
it was in the desert where I found her

Amalia continues, relating how she imagined Marisa in the desert, as a little
girl singing "*Desierto de la Sonora/Tierra de mi memoria,*" which, of course,
Corky would never have sung. Then, she comes up behind Marisa, wraps
her arms around her, and sings a song of race and love to her.

MARISA: (unmoved) answers:
I've just never believed
a woman capable of loving a man
was capable of loving a woman
me. . . .

AMALIA drops her hands from Marisa's shoulders, coming toward THE
PEOPLE.

She tells of her love for a man, who was Mexico to her. In the end, she leaves
Marisa. Seduced and abandoned is the movement of the narrative; the
dynamics of the verse.

But Moraga does not leave it there, as the above examples have. Marisa is
not only the Chicana lesbian, she is the Chicana writer, who through representation can intervene in the system as well as in her own internal composition. The wetness of lesbian desire is her ink, and being seduced and abandoned is making *familia*. Lesbian *familia* is not necessarily of the blood, but
of the heart. As Moraga has written it:

It's like making familia from scratch
each time all over again . . . with strangers
if I must.
If I must, I will.

I am preparing for the worst,
so I cling to her in my heart,
my daydream with pencil in my mouth,
when I put my fingers
to my own
forgotten places.

Moraga can claim an agency in the synthesis of lesbian and Chicana which has recently animated her introductory in her forthcoming book. The essay, entitled "Queer Aztlán," celebrates the integral role of the homosexual in the Chicano community. On the other hand, after *Giving Up The Ghost,* Moraga's second play, *Shadow of a Man,* focussed on the family unit, while the third, *Heroes and Saints* included a gay man, but no lesbian. At the same time Moraga was producing her lesbianless plays, which were centered in and performed for the Chicano community, she published a short piece entitled "La Ofrenda," the lyric story of a bar butch in the gay and lesbian journal *Outlook.*

"Chicana lesbian" plays more complex roles of in/exclusion in the synthesis. The agency to create *"familia"* is there in the writing, if not in the publishing reception, though there is a move toward a final kind of hard-won partnership. Perhaps the most promising hope I can, at this point, articulate is that Chicana lesbians and Anglo lesbians could hope, after much diligent and long labor, to change their respective communities so that the fires of racism and homophobia may be put out and the wrestling match could become something more like a dance.

NOTES

1 See, for example, Madeline Davis and Elizabeth Laposky Kennedy, "Oral History."
2 Jorge Huerta, quoted in Janice Dewey, 40–41.
3 See Eliud Martínez, "Personal Vision."
4 Estela Portillo quoted in Dewey 40.
5 This article is quoted from a feminist, predominantly white anthology. The original publication by South End Press was also not a Chicano Press.
6 See, for example, the plays by Jane Chambers, or the award-winning *8x10 Glossy.*

María Teresa Marrero
Public Art, Performance Art, and the Politics of Site

❏

Performance art and conceptual public art are two hybrid artistic media employed by Los Angeles Chicano Daniel J. Martínez. In Martínez's work, these hinge upon the key element of *urban site* as both a physical and ideological locus where artistic and social concerns intersect. The subtext of the micro-urban performance opera *Ignore the Dents* is the story of the "invisible" people within the context of contemporary downtown Los Angeles (Martínez, Interview, October 1990). The "invisible people" in *The Dents* and in Martínez's public art projects (such as the downtown Seattle banner project "The Quality of Life") are those *other than* those who can afford to be in the specific places where "art," "art objects," and "culture" are produced by those whose economic interests behooves their commodification (exclusive art galleries, collectors, museums, etc.).

The concept of socio-artistic intervention through the use of public space works well for a mixed media artist who emerged from a Los Angeles barrio[1] but whose intellectual frame of reference defies ready-made ethnic labels. Martínez stays far away from the common appropriation of kitsch ethnic and cultural signs.[2] As a matter of course in his work, Martínez ignores any element of the stereotypical in his creative vocabulary. He does, however, show a marked preference toward the appropriation of already existing forms (performance art/opera, billboards, city street banners) in order to incorporate images and messages which provoke semiotic shifts.

In this essay I will discuss Martínez's work in conjunction with some of his interethnic collaborative public art and performance pieces. They are contextualized within the overall twentieth century avant-garde art and performance movements with which the artist chooses to identify on ideological and aesthetic grounds. Martínez's creative endeavors aim to alter prevalent notions of public space through the use of either the written or spoken word in strategically selected urban sites. These endeavors tend to raise controversial questions about circulating notions of cultural power relations. His long-term collaboration with African American experimental musician Vinzula Kara provides another vital element: the integration of sound into the visual experience.

First, I will establish an overall frame of reference for Martínez's work as a visual artist, in which his public billboards, banners, and bus shelters predominate. Then, I will consider the dynamics of the micro-urban opera *Ignore the Dents* within the context of the "multicultural" Los Angeles Arts Festival during the Summer of 1990. As with Martínez's other artwork, the movement of *The Dents* is a deconstructive/regenerative one. The work's particular regenerative process encompasses the (re)creation of identity constructs of a city bent — until recently — upon ignoring its long history of multiculturalism.

As Martínez transforms city spaces into the site of public debate through the controversies that they provoke, questions of (in)access,[3] (lack of) privilege, and social memory[4] become visible. I propose that Martínez's oeuvre can be apprehended as an attempt to ground (but not simplify) human experiences within the postindustrialist construct of the public sphere.

ABOUT THE PUBLIC SPHERE AND ART IN PUBLIC PLACES

The very concept of the "public sphere" is an unstable and changing historical construct, as perceived within Western European political history.[5] In *The Structural Transformation of the Public Sphere* Jurgen Habermas traces the relationship between authority and the public sphere. The marked shift toward modernity in the concept of the "public man" is associated with the emergence of the bourgeoisie and the consolidation of nation states (Habermas 18). By the end of the seventeenth century the concept of "public opinion" arose in France with the advent of journals and printed media. The "reading public" (i.e., "critical public") included clergy, professors, lawyers, and doctors who came together to form "a public" of citizens. Their duty was to compel public authority to legitimize itself before the public opinion (the term arose from the French *opinion publique,* which is also associated with *publicité*) (Habermas 25–26). The term meant: "whatever was submitted to the judgement of the public, gained publicity" (Habermas 26). Within the current context of electronic worldwide media image and news dissemination, the concept of "public opinion" cannot be so naively

constructed. In postindustrial economies, where space and time are defined primarily in terms of market values, concepts of the "public sphere" have necessarily shifted as well. The targeting of all sectors of society for the consumption of the "spectacle" (mass media) has generated an illusion of a classless society, equalized by its participatory roll as "consumers." As such, we have all been visually educated to identify images with product values.

A semiotic shift occurs when the function of a public advertising system (such as billboards, bus shelters, or banners) is appropriated through art in public places. In the Seattle banner project, "The Quality of Life," a series of socially discrepant conditions were uncovered. Strategically hung along downtown Seattle's high-end shopping sector, these banners used clear statements[6] to underline the apparent dichotomies which exist between "the haves and the have nots" (Martínez, Interview, October 1991). The Downtown Seattle Organization, a group of businesses which riled against the project, believed that the banners were to be "colorful, cheerful and enjoyable as is Seattle's tradition" (Hackett). In other words, they are to be "neutral" of any political or social commentary, and neutral enough to stimulate shopping.[7]

Figure 1. Daniel Martínez, "Guerra de las culturas," commissioned by the San Diego Museum of Contemporary Art, the Dos Ciudades, Two Cities billboard project, 1990. Photo by Daniel Martínez.

In these illustrated instances the move *against* dominant socioeconomic and political values is foregrounded. The attitude of resistance incorporates a regenerative attitude built into the defiance. New meanings emerge from the displacement of one type of common visual sign by another. This is particularly so when the form remains familiar but the content is made "strange," not unlike Brecht's alienation effect. The billboard messages are strategically placed in highly visible sites, in which normally one would find a positive marketing advertisement message. This fact offers a shift of signification within the established parameters of the medium. The medium obeys the status quo, the content and public reaction subvert.

Martínez's art installations can be perceived as "staged" works which aim to provoke public dynamic, controversial dialogues. They involve the careful selection of site as a formal vehicle for social observations. The works themselves are intended as counter-hegemonic practices which elicit strong reactions from the viewers; subsequently, these reactions stimulate dialogue among sectors of society which usually do not intersect. The entire series of actions which accompany each artwork can be perceived as causing a dynamic dialectic in time and place. This dialectic relationship

Figure 2. Daniel Martínez, "Ignore Dominant Culture," bus shelter project for the Los Angeles City Window Grant, in collaboration with Gannet Transit. Photo by Daniel Martínez.

between the spectators and the artwork, between the artwork and the site, and among spectators themselves establishes a strong link within the history of the U.S. avant-garde, particularly with the 1960s Environmentalists, the Happenings, and Fluxus. As with Abstract Expressionism in painting, the focus is upon the process between the artist and the elements, rather than a focus upon a polished, "museum quality" end product (Haskell).

It is in this sense that Martínez identifies with the European Situationists (1957–1972). Their point of convergence can be located within the perception of art as a life process, in which there is no separation between the "artistic" and the "sociopolitical." In 1967 one of the founding members of the Situationists, Guy Debord, wrote in *Society of the Spectacle:* "The spectacle is the moment when the commodity has attained the "total occupation" of social life. Not only is the relation to the commodity visible but it is all one sees: the world one sees is its world" (Sussman 8).

Methodologically the Situationists International devised a series of key ideas: *dérive,* unitary urbanism, and psychogeography (Sussman 9).[8] Of these the concept of unitary urbanism has been the most influential for Martínez's creative thought process (Martínez, Interview, October 1991). It is defined formally as "the theory of the combined use of arts and techniques for the integral construction of a milieu in dynamic relation with experiments in behavior" (Sussman 9, 143–47, 199).

The intent here, however, is not the subversion of standard artistic aesthetics for the sake of innovation alone. Instead, Martínez's appropriation and subversion of form through content is a social intervention upon the environment which "Explores the possibilities of disorder. . . . The evolution of the works are designed to exist, transform the environment, alter perceptions, and then to be dismantled into a formless disarray of objects, thereby ceasing to exist. . . . My role as an artist is to serve as the catalyst who senses and captures the multi-layers of my socio-physical environment" (Martínez, *Vitae*).

A MICRO URBAN OPERA: *IGNORE THE DENTS*

While Martínez's public art projects infiltrate areas of affluence, his micro-urban opera, staged in a former Latino vaudeville theater, forces the displacement of an affluent audience into an area of underprivilege. The dimensions of conflict need to be taken within a series of circles of sociopolitical contexts, particularly the growing tension between conservative and liberal arts and humanities sectors. Neoconservatism in contemporary U.S. politics has been firmly entrenched by the Reagan and Bush administrations. In broad terms the consequences have been felt in two major areas of public life: the economic recession and growing unemployment, and the strengthening of neoconservative and Christian right-wing organizations. The latter came to a pinnacle during the 1989–90 National Endowment of the Arts crisis.[9] The 1990 appointment of Diane Ravich as Assistant Secretary of Education, and the 1991 appointment of conservative Harvey C. Mansfield, Jr., to the National Endowment of the Humanities' Advisory Council posed a significant threat to the advancement of women's and ethnic multicultural studies in university curricula (Winkler, A5).

Within this conservative agenda, the cultural productions of "marginal" groups — blacks, Chicanos, Nuyoricans, Native Americans, Asian Americans, gays and lesbians — are viewed as "the new tribalism"[10] in the arts and humanities. It is within this national debate that the Los Angeles city project of (re)defining itself as an administrative paradigm of "multiculturalism" has taken place.

The Los Angeles Arts Festival (Summer 1990) commissioned *Ignore the Dents*.[11] It was one of three pieces by or about Latinos. The others were Guillermo Gómez-Peña's *1990*,[12] and Iranian-born Reza Abdoh's *Pisadas en la obscuridad*.[13] The issues reflected in *The Dents* continue in the line of social confrontation which characterizes Martínez's public art projects. The work hinges upon a deconstructive attitude, particularly challenging circulating notions of the definition of Los Angeles's identity as a multicultural city. This factor is better understood if taken within the city's history of ethnic and racial segregation. In order to consider Los Angeles's cultural identity, it is necessary to conjure a sense of social memory. Definitions created out of current demographic and bureaucratic needs may be expedient, but not "representative."[14]

The Dents's (re)creation of social memories is not approached as a venture into the recuperation of "lost" origins through indigenous (Aztec, Maya) iconographies or motifs, and therefore not identifiable by critics as "ethnic" or "minority" art. Martínez's project of (re)building social memory is closely associated with Johannes Birringer's postmodern reading of Italo Calvino's *Invisible Cities*. Calvino's parable of the imagined city of Zobeide requires "interminable work of building and rebuilding the city, the construction site of culture and history" (Birringer 120). This assessment is relevant to the city of Los Angeles, by merely considering the transformation of its proper name: from *La ciudad de Nuestra Señora de Los Angeles* (the city of Our Lady of the Angels) to "L. A." In the gap between the poetic and spiritual Spanish to the functional brevity of the English acronym, lies the crux of the city's history.

In considering Los Angeles from a Chicano literary perspective, UCLA Chicano scholar Raymund A. Paredes ascertains that one must begin with a fundamental fact: Los Angeles has been, since the mid-nineteenth century, a city uneasy about its Mexican-ness:

> The first several generations of Anglo settlers sought either to obliterate the prevailing Mexican character of the city or to make it over in their own preferred conceptualizations, both responses deriving from the widespread belief that actual Mexican culture was unworthy of recognition and preservation. By 1920, when the great surge in Los Angeles growth began, Mexican culture had either effectively submerged or relegated to specified neighborhoods. (Paredes 209)

I believe that a fundamental aspect of *Ignore the Dents* addresses these aspects of urban space as a site of the social process of memory (by those whose presence precedes current bureaucratic fads) and forgetfulness. This is a fundamentally confrontational position in light of the Los Angeles city project to create a "multicultural" image of the city. In particular, Los Angeles is being established as a *worldwide* paradigm of the multiculturalism that is being forecast as the wave of the future in post-Soviet Western Europe.[15] Says Martínez: "Los Angeles has been a multicultural community from way before the term "multicultural" was attached to it. The problem is that dominant culture refused to allow the integration of culture to exist. They set up a class system and segregation in a way that keeps people in their neighborhoods, keeps them illiterate, "pregnant," keeps them in extremely working class conditions" (Martínez, Interview, October 1990). The unmasking of the multicultural rhetoric has itself become a heated political issue in the Los Angeles arts community (Breslauer and Mitchell 6). Multiculturalism has turned into a battleground of art's administrative politics. Faced with the sheer number of "minority" population growth,[16] the predominantly elitist museum, gallery, and grant managers find it necessary to address questions of the (lack) of representation of alternative artistic production visible in the city cultural "palaces." Minority leaders, however, have pushed the issue one step beyond. They are now bringing into the bargaining table years of experience from their own community arts management experience to bear upon the touchy question of *access* at the fundamental administrative and decision making levels, in other words, *self*-representation.

Within this context *Ignore the Dents* was commissioned to participate in the Los Angeles multicultural arts festival. Festival director Peter Sellars invited Martínez to a series of discussions, upon which several factors were ascertained. Sellars assured Martínez that the piece could be staged in any venue that the artist wished (Martínez, Interview, October 1990). Martínez chose the Million Dollar Theater on Broadway and Third Streets in a Latino business sector of downtown Los Angeles. The Million Dollar Theater, now a Spanish-language movie house, had been one of the cultural centers of Mexican vaudeville during the first half of this century (Kanellos 21, 38). This particular area is now rather rundown, particularly if seen in the shadows of landmark buildings such as twin opaque glass towers of businesses like the high-end Bonaventure Hotel. If, as Martínez states, historical domination has been keeping the various cultural and ethnic groups segregated through zoning gerrymandering, the way to subvert this is to erase the geographic lines.[17] This was achieved by provoking the Angelino art public to cross the boundary between the upper-middle-class business urban spaces into the working-class, predominantly Latino, sector of town where the Million Dollar Theater is located. This subversion of class concepts of public space in effect erases the usual consistency between the sectionalizing aims of urban "cultural" zoning and the viewing of "cultural" events.[18] This relatively "unsafe" urban location normally not frequented by the mostly white, upper-middle-class and "sophisticated" Angelinos provoked a face to face confrontation with the local residents — the late night transients and homeless persons whose homes *are* the streets.

The latter assumptions about the audience composition is reasonable on two accounts. First, *Ignore the Dents* was advertised in the English-language[19] press (the *Los Angeles Times, The Downtown News, The L. A. Weekly*) as a "micro-urban opera" experimental performance piece. This type of billing normally attracts a specific type of public: people interested in experimental performance (other performers, theatre people, critics, journalists, and academics — like myself). Secondly, as a spectator during the Friday, September 7, performance, I was able to visually ascertain an overall impression of those in attendance that evening.[20]

As the line of 1,140 spectators (on Friday, September 7, 1990) and of 1,270 (the following night)[21] wound around several city blocks, they became the spectacle for the local residents, transients, and corner drunks. This mix made an uneasy situation for some of those in line, as the street persons made no qualms about randomly speaking to those in line. After all, this is their "territory." In a society that constantly attempts to walk past, not see, and ignore its downtrodden, this was a profoundly political and personal act. The kind of confrontation orchestrated by *The Dents* provoked not only looking at the "other" but a profound inner look at ourselves. How each person reacted in light of the situation revealed much about the subject position of each.[22]

The Dents focused upon the dislocation of several common binary oppositional ways of perceiving physical space and reality. As a notion pertaining to the ordering of life, the outside is usually rendered "public" and the inside is rendered "private." As a notion pertaining to psychological space, the outside is rendered "other" while the inside is rendered "self." Self-reflection, normally conceived as an "inner" activity, was forced to take place in public. In this sense, the appropriation of the urban space as a temporary symbolic construct relates to the Situationist aspect of psycho-geography and unitary urbanism. However, it is also linked with the conceptual experiment of cognitive re-mapping. According to architectural theorist Jon Lang, "cognitive maps are not exact replicas of reality, they are models of realities" (Lang 136).[23] Within their creative model of reality construction, *The Dents* reconceptualizes notions of urban borderlines as a culturally and economically permeable area (Flores and Yúdice).

Attracted by the spectacle, the middle- and upper-class audiences crossed normally taboo, invisible downtown L. A. boundaries. The sense of public spectacle was highlighted by two large spotlight reflectors illuminating the night city sky, simulating the razzle dazzle of a Hollywood movie premier. The excitement grew as we approached the theatre entrance. Liz Young's lobby and theatre design established an indeterminacy between the outside/street and inside/theatre spaces. The lobby, itself designed as an art installation, funneled the spectators through monitored turnstiles, giving each spectator a small, cardboard cutout of a human head. On each "head" was the printed city map of the area, Broadway and Third.

As the spectators entered into the 1,200 seat movie house, the first image visible was a large split screen. On one side people moved toward the left, on the other toward the right. Upon a closer look one became aware that the persons on the screen were those in the lobby, passing through the turnstiles. Closed circuit video provided the "insider" a close look at those still "outside." The voyeuristic thrill was immediately tainted with the awareness that a few minutes before, *my* own image had been stolen from me and made available to another voyeuristic public. Helpless to prevent it, the principles of social surveillance were made visible more quickly than any Orwellian or Kafkaesque rendition of *The Trial*. By this time the program informed us that we were in the overture, or third part of the opera. The prelude had taken place on the street, the *Antefatto* while traversing the lobby.

The musical element is essential in *The Dents*. Vinzula Kara calls his compositions popkret (a combination of pop rhythms, the French movement of *musique concrete*,[24] and the innovations of John Cage) (Kara, Interview).[25] Cage's incorporation of chance and of sounds (and silence) traditionally considered nonmusical respond to Kara's aesthetic of popkret. The *musique concrete* style incorporates the "concrete" daily sounds of urban life — such as that of police helicopters, automobile traffic, footsteps, laughter, etc. — into the psychological structure of the piece. Kara's emphasis in what he calls sound "cymbolism" (a combination of "symbolism" and "cymbal") shapes his composition's layers (the audible and the barely perceptible) in order to "reshape the perception of the ear and the mind" (Kara, Interview).

Each of the thirteen scenes was based upon the musical deconstruction of operatic tropes and scores selected from the history of the opera. For instance, the *Antefatto* was based upon the medieval Gregorian chants of Machaut, the overture used segments of Monteverdi, the *Dramma giocoso* used Purcell, the *Aria a tres* used Bach, the *Deux ex machina* used Wagner, the *Lamento,* Verdi, and so forth until coming to the most contemporary represented by Phillip Glass, who is followed by Kara for the closing scene.

As an assault upon the traditional highbrow pretensions of the opera, Vinzula Kara's electronic score permeated the theatre. Through a computerized instrument called a sampler, virtually *any* sound (musical or environmental) can be recorded and analyzed as a computer *byte* of information. The sound bite can be deconstructed by several means: by separating its parts, by altering its tempo and rhythm, by playing it backward, etc. An "original" musical score can incorporate layers of pretaped sound bites, which are organized nonlinearly to respond to the perceived sense of *chance* which — to the artists — accompanies life in general, urban (and specifically ghetto) life in particular. In this way Vinzula Kara's creative process parallels Martínez's: that of appropriation, deconstruction, and regeneration of meaning. A mix of city ambient sounds and repeated layers of operatic and pop music and popular culture jingles (the "Lone Ranger" and the "Felix the Cat" themes) stimulated the nervous system into a state of dissonant, yet melodically repetitive anxiety. For instance, the incorporation of helicopter sounds into one of the layers of the overture connoted the unnerving monitoring activities of city police. Within the context of the ghetto, it could mean that they are "either protecting somebody, or just as likely, hassling somebody"[26] (Kara, Interview). Contradiction was made musical.

Kara's layered multiple scores created an atmosphere at times of irritation and anguish, at others of sublime beauty. For instance, scene nine, the *Aria col de capo,* or Asphalt Aria, incorporates the vocal virtuosity of tenor Charles Lane and alto-soprano Luz María García with bass Andrew Koch. This powerful segment juxtaposes asphalt as the primary texture of life for those who live on the street. It makes a powerful contrast between the beauty of the singers' voices — lofty, sacred in character — and the harsh, profane reality of street life. With repetitive, lulling sacred sounds against concrete, abrasive ones, a male Black Virgin (Charles Lane) emerges singing in Spanish,[27] making this one of the most memorable aural and visual images of the performance.

The scenes which took place inside the theatre (from scene four, or the *Dramma giocoso*) to the last (scene thirteen), the action defied lineal narrative structures. However, I maintain that the scenes were interconnected by the types of oppositional relationships performed. Each segment was designed to reveal the dynamics of a set of binary power relationships.

In the prelude, it is Us/Spectators and Them/the Street people (or vice versa). The locus is the city block, where while waiting in line, We become visible to each other in the street encounter. In the *antefatto* the relationship explored is Us and the Invisible Them (those who control the surveillance): power is defined in terms of access to technology. We are invisible to ourselves (we cannot "see" ourselves), yet visible to the invisible controllers (we cannot see them). In the overture, We recognized the projected image of Others and recognized Ourselves as having been manipulated: all of Us present. By the time traditional notions of dramatic "action" begin with scene four, or the *Dramma giocoso,* the public has already participated as "actors" and viewers in the first three movements of the performance piece. Both seeing and being seen have been manipulated.

The remainder of the scenes move the performers in and around the aisles and the exposed theatre stage. For instance, in scene five, the *Aria a tres* (Aria for Three), a multiracial cast of three (Lin Osterhag, Fernando Castro, and Michele Mais) offer a powerful statement about the role of the individual within a market economy: members of society are seen as largely disposable commodities that can be bought and sold. In light of a man's real hunger (Castro), he is told by Authority (played by Osterhag) to consume himself by cannibalizing his various body parts. Society as a consensus of its members requires that the members allow or not allow themselves to be abused by the rules and rulers.

A powerful solo by Chicano bilingual poet Manazar Gamboa is described as a *Lamento,* or Tragic Aria, in scene seven. Gamboa articulates cultural survival as an act of poetic courage. Gamboa's is the sound of memory as he reaches back into the history of this place now being "renamed" as multicultural: Gamboa is a living witness of the 1940s Los Angeles zoot-suit wars in East Los Angeles, upon which Luis Valdez's renowned play and film is based (Martínez, Interview, October 1990). Gamboa articulates his individual history as the history of a people. Likewise Martínez holds the view that cultural survival has been a manner of cultural war (Koehler).

The *Provo* (scene eight) simultaneously addresses two types of hierarchical structures: the musical conductor who directs while the orchestra must obviously follow, and other types of political structure which demand a similar response. Vinzula Kara deconstructs the sanctity of this traditional relationship by "conducting"[28] a polyphonic array of individually created sounds which evidently do not obey the rules of unity. The orchestra convenes and disbands carelessly, chaotically and at will. "This was our Dada section," says Kara playfully (Kara, Interview).

For *Duette da camera* or Chamber Duet Especially for Lovers (scene ten) Patrick Miller and Dana Nelson form a triangle between the Ideal (Love), Thanatos (Death), and Eros (Desire) locked in a cycle of creation and destruction repeated ad infinitum.

The *Pastorale* (scene eleven) incorporates nonperformers in order to expose the fundamentally violent relationship between society and its downtrodden. The violence, institutionalized by the inequalities of the social conditions, and perpetuated by sheer neglect, is reenacted on the streets. This is an antithetical scene of juxtaposing the idyllic "pastoral" with the city "jungle." And lastly, the *Cosa,* or *Aria di sortita* (Exit Aria), depicts the Watts riots as a foreshadow of the riots in South Central Los Angeles that were the result of the police beating Rodney King. It resonates with people's willingness to create public chaos in response to sustained oppression. At the end of the performance Martínez came on stage and literally threw the audience out on the street, by aggressively telling us to leave the safety of the theatre and go out into the real streets where this is not art, but life.

THE DENTS, THE CRITICS, AND SOME CONCLUDING THOUGHTS

However, as in the case of Martínez's public art installations, a particular type of spectator — the critics — again played a significant role. The aggregate discourse about *The Dents* has become part of its profile.

From *Los Angeles Times* classical music critic came derisive comments about the Million Dollar Theater itself. Evidently the incongruity of the "opera" with a working-class barrio movie theatre made the experience uncomfortable for the critic: "the house has seen better days . . . gum-laden chairs . . ." The comments become revealing: "the micro-urban agenda included . . . a pity the homeless interlude, a siege mentality escapade, an agit prop exercise. There even was a symbolic divertissement, in which a globe descended from the balcony and celebrants, mistaking it for a piñata could run the aisle and beat it with a stick" (Bernheimer). The trivializing comment about the piñata is an insidious ethnic slur thinly veiled under the guise of a formal, performance critique. The recurring argument emerges: the politically conservative critic's inability to perceive the possibility of a communion between "art" and "politics."[29]

Alternative papers like the *L. A. Weekly* offered a less emotional and more accurate reading: "*Ignore the Dents* spoke best to those in the audience attuned to the potent images and episodic, contradictory, even hallucinatory sense of (dis)continuity originally found in the Philip Glass-Robert Wilson masterpiece [*Einstein on the Beach*]. Anyone looking for your usual story, music, acting, or just plain spectacle was bound to be disappointed" (Frank).

However, it was a performance art critic who revealed a more troubling and deeper problem in evaluating some fundamental elements of *The Dents*. By bracketing it within the overall politics of the L. A. Festival, the piece was perceived as:

Trapped between opposing goals. It was a protest against several kinds of cultural hegemonies, including high-art definitions . . . Yet it reverted to theatrical convention. Similarly its overtly "political" subject matter overshadowed its covertly political underpinnings . . . making the overt material work theatrically would have required subsuming Martínez' grassroots community politic [*sic*] to a different artistic goal . . . Had the piece relinquished its didactic rhetoric and fully embraced a visual ritual form, many in the community it was supposed to represent would have protested, claiming their voice was again being excluded or silenced (Apple 17).[30]

The "covertly political underpinnings" mentioned obliquely poses the question of *The Dents*'s authenticity as representative of the (unnamed) "Latino" community (vague as the defining terms may be). Concluding with the implication that had *The Dents* assumed a more "ritual" (less overtly political?) stance it would have pleased the palate of art critics more. However, this more poetic/ritual version — somehow — would have been interpreted (a priori? a posteriori?) by the Latino community as contradictory to their interests (as defined by . . . ?). The question which arises out of this argument is indeed one of representation: Who is the critic speaking *for* in this type of critical discourse?

I find the construction of this argument perturbing. The problematic function of establishing the "representability" of a cultural group by a particular artist here is reduced to a set of implied assumptions. Furthermore, it betrays a hegemonic cultural bias of looking for *individual* "spokespersons,"[31] which implies the simplification of the complex notions of "minority" "Latino" communities in the United States. Oversimplifying notions lead directly to the emergence of stereotypes.

Furthermore, the appropriation and deconstruction of a hegemonic art form (the opera) is perceived as a contradictory and incompatible reversion. Nevertheless, the tactics of appropriation and subversion are recurring, common, and successful practices, not only in Martínez's work, but in that of previous avant-garde artists.[32] The decontextualization of Martínez's work from the historical avant-garde and from the artist's own creative trajectory marginalizes it. Perceived as outside of the aesthetics of Western radicalism, *The Dents* also does not fit into preestablished notions of Chicano performance (Teatro Campesino–style). This performance piece, as well as the work of other experimental performance artists included in this volume — Las Comadres and Gómez-Peña[33] — does not respond to faded definitions of a unitary and binding Chicano experience. These artists are involved with the rearticulation of a perpetually unfixed identity construction.

The emerging model for the Chicano/a performers is that of educated, articulate, and sophisticated artists who are willing and quite able to dialogue with their own communities as well as with the (high) art establishment. Is it entirely impossible, then, for even "liberal" Anglo critics to integrate Chicano/a (or any so-called "marginal") artists whose technique and style fall squarely within prevalent Western European twentieth century social art history because s/he is considered primarily ethnic? Are "ethnic" and "conceptual" mutually exclusive categories? Is the fundamental threat, then, the one posed by the implied possibility of "minority" artists redefining and even surpassing Western standards of artistic/cultural production? Or is creative "interculturalism" — at the level of critical discourse — a one-way street reserved exclusively to celebrate the "genius" of Western, white males (i.e., Brooks, Artaud) who appropriate colonized, "exotic" cultural productions (India's epic tales, Balinese theatrical technique)?

By not taking the structure, content, or context of *Ignore the Dents* seriously, a fundamental oversight is implied. The placing/locating/fixing of Martínez's work within the canons of the "postmodern aesthetic" clearly dislocates the recurring movement of Martínez's work, which in my opinion is to ground the experience of the urban site within social, economic, and historical factors. The privileging of the postmodern focus upon fragmentation, lack of unity, or linearity clearly obliterates the anti-postmodern thrust of social memory grounding. The postmodern project of the "eternal present" and historylessness (Birringer) is antithetical to Martínez's oeuvre. *Ignore the Dents* and Martínez's public art projects pose a fundamental challenge to circulating constructs of the identity of "ethnic" or "marginalized" artists living within hegemonic national territories such as the United States. Martínez's conceptual art aims toward the displacement of the individual within a given social context. This directs the observer to look at questions of social (non)privilege and (in)access which go beyond divisive ethnic or cultural differences. This strategy has systematically been met with strong responses from a variety of institutional forces (the Seattle Downtown Business Association, the Los Angeles arts critics, etc.). These adversary responses tend toward the devaluation and erasure of the work.

The appropriation of the public sphere by Chicano/Latino visual artists serves a variety of immediate functions: it creates high visibility for artists and for their particular type of expression; it makes certain issues visible, and generates consciousness and discourse (artistic, social, political, economic) around issues relevant to that community (as identified by class, and not race); it displaces ethnic-specific labels to a given artist's work, since its placement in anonymous sites dispenses with the usual personal publicity generated by art-show openings.

However innovative this new generation of experimental, conceptual artists may be in their individual or collective work, vestiges of their work will disappear if qualified performance historians and art critics do not meet the challenge to engage in its critical discourse. The junction between the historian and critic provides essential secondary material. This is particularly important with ephemeral artistic productions such as the work just discussed. The junction between the public and the private, and among interethnic collaborations can provide new creative alliances for articulating social, cultural, and political issues of common concern; the creation of a critical discourse around it will buffer the Chicano/Latino artistic expression — among others — against erasure, and memorylessness.

NOTES

I would like to express my appreciation to Daniel J. Martínez, whose collaboration in this essay is fundamental. I would also like to thank Chicana poet Helena María Viramontes, whose recommendation made the introduction to the artist possible in the first place; and to Vinzula Kara for his musical expertise. This article was made possible through a University of California, Irvine Humanities Dissertation grant. Special thanks to Juan Villegas, John White, and Jacki Apple.

1   Martínez grew up in Lennox, California, a lower working-class neighborhood bordered by the cities of Watts and Inglewood.

2   The appropriation of kitsch ethnic signs is an approach that Guillermo Gómez-Peña adopts quite well. He manages to (de) and (re)construct the "ethnic" by means of a carefully articulated fictional persona, the Border Brujo.

3   The parenthetical prefixes denote the exclusionary nature of signs which follows a process of presence/absence: the presence of one denotes the absence of the other, and vice versa.

4   My perception of "social memory" is informed by the works of sociologists Norbert Elias in *The History of Manners* (in German 1939, English translation 1978) and Paul Connerton in *How Societies Remember* (1989). Both construct the concept of social memory as the cumulative — yet temporal and dynamic — *performative* (physical) habits or practices by a given group of individual people who share a particular set of historical and social circumstances.

5   I believe that the philosophical kinks between Western Europe and the United States are justified, not as an appeal to hegemonic authority but as a useful historical construct.

6   As an artistic convention, artists can engage in either abstract or representational art forms. Artwork which employs written language is considered "representational." This is the case with the public art project in Time Square, *Messages to the Public,* in which language and/or images are flashed onto an electronic digital color board. Some visual artists involved in this project are Jenny Holzer (1982), Keith Harig (1982), Antonio Muntadas (1985), Anton van Dalen (1987), Alfredo Jaar (1987). Sources include Jeffrey Cruikshand and Pam Korza, *Going Public* (1988) 21; Diane Waldman's *Jenny Holzer,* 30–31, and *ARTnews* (October, 1991) 105.

7   A major portion of the Downtown Seattle Organization of business' efforts to *prevent* the banners from being hung concentrated upon the fact that the banner's social commentaries might prove prejudicial to the area's most profitable shopping season: Christmas. A compromise reached between the Seattle Arts Commission (the funding agency for the public art project) and the DSO had the banners come down prior to the Christmas shopping season! (Commentary based upon correspondence between the named organizations and Martínez, courtesy of the artist.)

8   *Dérive* (drift) "was defined as a mode of experimental behavior linked to the conditions of urban society: a technique of transient passage through varied ambiances. Psychogeography meant the study of the specific effects of the geographical environment, consciously organized or not, on the emotions and behavior of individuals. See Elizabeth Sussman (ed.), *On the Passage.*

9   See Marrero, "Chicano-Latino," particularly the subheading "The NEA Controversy, Censorship and the Cultural Climate," 149.

10 *The New York Times*'s R. Bernstein has a number of articles opposing what he terms "the new tribalism" and "political correctness" in the arts.

11 The eleven-member core group consisted of: writer Harry Gamboa, Jr., composer Vinzula Kara, assistant director and choreographer Patricia Pretzinger, producer Josephine Ramírez, dramatist Erica Bornstein, costume and prop designer Diane Gamboa, lobby and theatre designer Liz Young, sound engineer Paul Chávez, lighting designer Aubrey V. Wilson, sound technician Mitchell B. Frank, and graphic designers Jim and Gibran Evans. Eighty persons were involved in the project.

12 In the Festival guide Gómez-Peña's piece appeared under the "Off the Streets" section, however there was nothing street-like about it. *1990* was a one-man show, performed

through the artistic persona of the Border Brujo in the Mexican tradition of *teatropoesía* (narrative, performed poetic text). The dense narrative, rich as it was in concepts and images, was performed and read from the static position of sitting midstage surrounded by an ingenious mix of stereotypical Mexican "ethnic" signs worn as a costume. It was performed at the Museum of Contemporary Art (MOCA).

13   Abdoh's piece, *Pisadas en la obscuridad*, is described as a "poetic spectacle and environmental morality plays [*sic*] that traffic in the invigorating lowlife of Los Angeles . . . it's a murder-mystery, horror musical performed by drag artists and body builders" (Los Angeles Festival Calendar, 12).

14   The problem of an individual artist being "representative" of a particular community is a pervasive one within funding organizational structures. In the attempt to address racial, social, and cultural imbalances often further ones are created. See Jacki Apple's "Politics, Performance and the Los Angeles Festival."

15   For an extensive look at Europe's immigration and intercultural problems see Judith Miller, "Strangers."

16   In 1990 the Los Angeles (city) population was 38 percent white, 36 percent Latino, 15 percent African American, and 12 percent Asian. Yet 93 percent of the city's museum visitors are Anglo. See Robin Cembalist.

17   For an excellent in-depth study of the effect of shifting geographic lines upon the semiotics of urban cultural life as seen through the theatre see Klaus van den Berg, "The Geometry of Culture."

18   The comment is directed toward the consistency in the United States for the urban zoning of cultural districts (for theatres, galleries or museums) in often artificially "safe" urban environments. The importance that city councils place upon the arts as a boost to urban renewal of rundown urban areas can be excellently observed in the 1990–91 controversy over the now defunct Los Angeles Theater Center.

19   Martínez, along with a number of other collaborators, doesn't speak Spanish. *The Dents* was performed entirely in English.

20   In Los Angeles, which is known for its tolerance and even fostering of "difference," it is difficult to make appraisals about people from their appearance. I saw extravagantly punk-looking people and I saw middle-aged, conservatively dressed persons at the performance. I did get the impression, however, that the majority were Anglo.

21   On Saturday, 8 September 1990, the performance was oversold by 70 seats; the Million Dollar Theater has a 1,200 seat capacity. According to Daniel Martínez no one was turned away.

22   For instance, upon leaving the theatre, a man slurring his words in Spanish began making some comments about my anatomy. My female friends and I ignored the remarks, becoming tense. He then rushed toward me and secured a handful of my behind. Angry, I turned around and pushed him away, saying — in Spanish — how he wouldn't like for this to happen to his mother, his sister, or his wife, so why was he doing this to me. Surprised, he immediately backed away. I used a well-understood code of *machismo:* I evoked the virgin-like reverence observed for mother figures. In this sense my cultural link with this man gave me a protective advantage. I did not speak to him as a *drunk,* I related to him as a *fellow Latino,* in our mother tongue.

23   Cognitive mapping is a basic component of human adaptation. It is a generally unconscious activity directed at making sense out of one's environment. In this aspect, a place is said to be "legible or imaginable" if its physical or psychic characteristics are strong

enough to make an impact upon memory. See Jon Lang's *Creating Architectural Theory*, 135–45.

24   *Musique concrete* is defined as "a type of music current . . . in which musical and non-musical sounds are assembled on recording tape" (Richard Middleton in *Pop & the Blues*). Vinzula Kara disagrees slightly with this definition: he believes that any sound can be considered "musical" (Kara, Interview).

25   Cage's 1952 untitled piece performed at Black Mountain College is considered by some performance historians as "the putative father of the mixed-means theatre" (Kostelanetz 50). Theatre of mixed means is just one of the many nomenclatures given to the innovations in performance/theatre in the latter 1950s and 1960s. Alan Kaprow's *18 Happenings in 6 Parts* (1958–59) placed the word "happening" in circulation. (Kostelanetz xi). The term "events" was later used by the international (and non-fixed) group Fluxus. See Barbara Haskell, 49–60.

26   The 1991 videotaped and nationally televised beating of African American Rodney King by Los Angeles police testifies to what many minority civic leaders have been alleging of the Los Angeles police under Chief Darryl Gates.

27   According to both Kara and Martínez it is an allusion to the Afro-Caribbean religious belief system of Santería.

28   The "orchestra" members were local high school performing arts students.

29   This recurring argument by newspaper journalists and critics comes to bear upon the case of the Seattle banners, "The Quality of Life." See Regina Hacket, *Seattle*.

30   Ms. Apple is a respected performance artist and critic, and contributing editor of *High Performance* magazine. It was she who graciously sent me a copy of her article "Politics, Performance and the Los Angeles Festival."

31   This is an element with which Gómez-Peña must surely be concerned. The prophetic overtones of his Border Brujo persona work well as a culturally critical voice, but its very poetic style and philosophical discourse can be quite digestible by the high arts factions (particularly since he has been selected as Latino/Chicano "representative" recipient of the MacArthur Foundation Award in 1991).

32   Asger Jorn, a member of the Situationist International extensively built his work upon the concept of *détournement* (semantic shift) by building upon canvases previously executed by other known painters, thus altering its meaning.

33   Limitations of space prohibit a comprehensive contrastive analysis between the work of Martínez, Las Comadres, and Gómez-Peña. Let it suffice to reiterate that other than sharing the "label" of experimental performance artists, each denotes marked methodological and ideological differences. For further information on Gómez-Peña's work see Gómez-Peña, "A Binational Performance." For Las Comadres see my dissertation chapter entitled "Performance and the Politics of Site."

Juan Flores

"Salvación Casita": Puerto Rican Performance and Vernacular Architecture in the South Bronx

❑

The casita people had the Smithsonian jumping that night. It was 2 February 1991 and the occasion was the opening celebration of the new Experimental Gallery, a space within the Smithsonian Institution's Arts and Industries Building intended to "showcase innovative artists, scientists, educators and designers from local, national and international communities." As stated in the invitation, "The Experimental Gallery pushes the edges of our museum knowledge by encouraging risk-taking in exhibition technique and style." Care is taken to assure us that the experimentation is to be that of the exhibit makers, and that "Content and Subject are not the Experiment!"[1]

Yet, with all these cautionary distinctions, the central space of the new gallery was dedicated to what was clearly the featured inaugural exhibit, "Las Casitas: An Urban Cultural Alternative." What an experiment in content and subject for the "national museum" of the United States! For on display was the world of those little houses, modeled after the humble dwellings in Puerto Rico of years gone by, which have sprung up in the vacant lots in New York's impoverished Puerto Rican neighborhoods over the past ten years. Wherever you go in the South Bronx and East Harlem ("El Barrio") these days you're liable to catch sight of a casita, in its design and atmosphere magically evocative of the rural Caribbean and now serving as a social club or cultural center for inhabitants of the surrounding tenements.[2]

I'll never forget the feeling I had as I made my way through the crowd of art-world professionals and museum officials hobnobbing in the huge domed rotunda and first set my eyes on that spanking, bright turquoise casita. "Rincón Criollo" (roughly, "Hometown Corner"), so familiar to me from my forays to Brook Avenue in the South Bronx, transplanted to such an unlikely site! The program called it a "built environment," a "living installation, a living space of rescued images that reinforce Puerto Rican cultural identity." Clearly the innovation was not just that of the gallery staff but of the people who built the casita "environment" in the first place. To me, the sight of a casita in the Smithsonian was an uncanny example of the title of the book I happened to have with me that night, Sally Price's *Primitive Art in Civilized Places.*

The little building assumed an imposing but somehow uncomfortable presence there in the center of that gaping, uncluttered space, and seemed intruded upon by the oohs and ahs of its sophisticated visitors as they filed up the "cute" porch and into the "quaint" interior. Lining the walls, the life-scale photos of "real" casitas in their "real" home setting helped bridge the gap somewhat, as did the explanatory captions, the decorative and functional "objects" of casita culture, and the video showings set off in the far corner.

But what made the difference, and brought this "experimental" representation in the nation's capital back in touch with the South Bronx, was the presence of the casita people themselves. There was José Rivera, one of the original builders of Rincón Criollo and for some years its president. There was his brother Ramón ("Papo"), who helped José build the replica and install it in the Experimental Gallery. There was Cepeda (hardly anyone knows him by his first name), another long-time Rincón Criollo mainstay, who aside from his regular role as cook and MC at casita events has taken on the joyful task of documenting everything on video. So there, too, was Cepeda, with his contagious toothy smile, tilted Panama hat, starched *guayabera* shirt, and camcorder tucked under his chin. Norma Cruz and Benny Ayala, the casita's resident teachers of music, instrument-making, and dance, were also present, as was José Manuel Soto, or "Chema" as everybody knows him, the founding and guiding spirit behind the casita since even before the lot was cleared. In fact, people from the neighborhood even call Rincón Criollo "la casa de Chema." And sharing the excitement were other familiar faces, those of the friends of casita culture like Beti-Sue Hertz, the director and curator of the project, Bill Aguado, director of the Bronx Council on the Arts, project photographer Martha Cooper, consulting urban anthropologists Joe Sciorra and Susan Slyomovics, and participating architect Luis Aponte-Parés.

The initial awkwardness and incongruity of the scene then began to give way to congeniality and, as we drifted into the rotunda to partake of

Figure 1. "Las Casitas" at the Smithsonian. Photo courtesy of Juan Flores.

the abundant food and drinks, to an air of festivity. And when "Manny Oquendo's Libre" took the stage and started blasting its hot *guarachas* and *plenas,* that venerable rotunda of the Smithsonian Institution seemed like a casita party, transposed and out of its habitat, but still exuding that bois- terous human energy which only comes of living vernacular performance. Tweed suit jackets and lush evening gowns swirling to those irresistible salsa sounds, museum administrators trying vigorously to keep up with the confident steps of South Bronx street people, "Libre's" congas and trom- bones filling every cranny of the Institution's vast halls with tropical sound straight from New York City—beyond anyone's expectations, the casita had indeed proven itself to be "a living installation, a living space of rescued images that reinforce Puerto Rican cultural identity."

A month or so later, on a day in early spring, José Rivera called to invite me to a special event at Rincón Criollo. They were calling it "Salvación Casita" ("Save the Casita!") and there was a sense of urgency in his voice. It seems that the developers and housing authorities were hounding them once again, not with any explicit threats but by floating the idea that they were considering use of the "vacant" land for some kind of construction and development. The purpose of "Salvación Casita" was to show, by force of sheer human presence and activity, that the space is not at all vacant and is

Figure 2. "Las Casitas" at the Smithsonian. Photo courtesy of Juan Flores.

already being put to valid use. As at eviction parties of years gone by, casita members recognize that the best way to keep the authorities at bay is to celebrate the blatant fact of collective occupancy.

I arrived early, in the late afternoon, to the smell of barbecued chicken wafting from the backyard and the bustle of people, men and women, old and young, setting up for the event. Inside the casita was like a dressing room, with Norma Cruz seeing to the makeup and costumes of her young dance students as they got ready to perform. On the porch, José, Benny Ayala, and some of the other musicians were testing microphones and tuning instruments, while Cepeda was already at the mike welcoming arriving friends and neighbors and announcing future casita events and "salvation" plans. In this homegrown performance space, the front porch is the stage, or rather the bandshell, as the formal and spontaneous dance presentations take place among the public in the yard directly in front of the porch. José even told me once that they built the porch a little wider than casita custom would have it precisely with this stage function in mind, extending it so as to accommodate all the musicians, instruments and sound equipment needed for full participation in *bomba* and *plena* performance.

The front yard, or "batey," gradually started filling with people — casita regulars and associates, guests invited and uninvited, neighbors from the surrounding tenements and friends and family from El Barrio, Brooklyn, and other parts of the Bronx. Though nearly everyone was Puerto Rican, it would be difficult and even pointless to generalize in any other sense about the assortment of people gathered for the casita event. There were as many women as men, there were blacks and whites, toddlers and elders, and everything in between. Though dress tended to be very casual, the range of styles was strikingly varied as well: baseball hats and panamas, linen blouses and tank-tops, full dresses and cutoffs, tattered jeans and baggy slacks, Nikes, dance flats and even a few spike heels.

The human atmosphere, despite the supposedly "forbidding" location and the expressed urgency of the occasion, was consistently relaxed, congenial, and respectful. Not a trace of fear, anger, or aggressiveness was evident, nobody seemed inclined to get "out of hand," and even the unknowing interloper could not help but feel welcome and comfortable. Lively gestures and hearty laughter accompanied casual conversation, toddlers danced on their parents' laps, youngsters flipped motley colored skateboards, a young couple strolled over to the improvised bar to buy beer, bystanders stood idly along the chainlink fence, passersby congregated on the street and sidewalk to look on and wave, now and then drifting in when they recognized a familiar face.

The hub of these many disparate styles and activities, drawing them together into a single shared event, was the presence of the casita itself. Architectural shape and detail, extemporaneous and crafted decor, spatial arrangement and location conspire to lend the casita and its environs a unifying emblematic weight, and to convert the easy occasionality of the scene into an occasion of community history. Leisurely playfulness and everyday sociability, when in close range of the casita, become performance.

Cepeda finishes his welcome and announcements by promising *"un poquito de salsa."* Carefully he places the mike in front of a Sanyo tape player, puts on his favorite cassette and takes to circulating with his trusty Camcorder. Technology is clearly no stranger to the casitas, which are often equipped with refrigerators, television sets and VCRs, stereos, and even jukeboxes. The gathering crowd delights in the first sounds as they wait, with growing anticipation, for the musicians and dancers to assemble. As the sun sets behind the buildings on Third Avenue, the scattered groups begin to take shape as an audience, and the glow of a single lightbulb sets off the porch as a theatrical stage.

Four hours of live music were interrupted only by further announcements, calls for donations to support the casita, and the introduction of new groups. Of the variety of songs played — there were merengues, boleros,

Figure 3. Plena musicians playing panderetas entertain at party at Rincón Crillo, a casita in the South Bronx. Photograph by Martha Cooper.

seises, sones, guarachas — by far the most common and favorite were *bombas* and *plenas*. It was these African-based forms of Puerto Rican popular music that got everyone moving, clapping, and shouting in chorus. Increasingly as the night progressed, the line between audience and performers faded, so that by the last hour the porch was overflowing with men and women of all ages singing and keeping the beat with *panderetas, güiros,* or whatever else was at hand. What had first seemed like a picnic or block party, and then a concert, took on the air of a carnival.

Who were these *pleneros* that served as the catalysts of such an outburst of collective participation? The answer is close at hand: José, Papo, Benny, Chema, the same people who founded and built Rincón Criollo. As one *plena* chorus puts it, *"Le cambiaron el nombre / a la* casita *de Chema / ahora la están llamando / la institución de la plena"* ("They changed the name / of the casita of Chema / now they're calling it / the institute of the *plena"*). The *plena* is the musical expression of the casita and its cultural habitat; its tones and themes seem to mesh perfectly with the collective needs and moods of the people. It is no accident that the most celebrated *plena* group in New York for some years now, "Los Pleneros de la 21," was formed and based at Rincón Criollo.

Though it originated and gained its initial popularity in the coastal towns of Puerto Rico early in the century, the *plena* has a long history in New York. Since the beginnings of the emigrant Puerto Rican community and through the decades, *plenas* have been a favored genre of musical entertainment at social clubs, house parties, and political and social gatherings for all occasions.[3] A key person to influence the grounding of the *plena* in New York's Puerto Rican neighborhoods, especially the down-home, street variety, is the legendary Marcial Reyes. For some thirty years Marcial was known throughout El Barrio and the South Bronx for his unique style of *pandereta* playing and his hundreds of *plena* compositions.

Marcial was also one of the founders of Rincón Criollo. He was there, always raising hell, throughout the clearing and building process and even before, when Chema's hangout was still a storefront social club across the street. He was a fixture in all the jams on the porch in the first years, and around 1983 he helped draw together some of the most accomplished practitioners, many of them regulars of Rincón Criollo, to form "Los Pleneros de la 21." Identifying the members of the group was made easier because, like other forms of traditional popular music, *plena* performance has often been shared from generation to generation along family lines. Even among the Rincón Criollo mainstays, several are from families of *pleneros* and *bomberos;* most notably José and Papo are the sons of Ramón "Chin" Rivera, the renowned *panderetero,* vocalist, and composer who played with the likes of Rafael Cepeda, Mon Rivera padre, Vicente Pichón, and "Bumbún" Oppenheimer.

The worlds of the casita and the *plena* are thus symbiotically related as forms of performative expression of working-class Puerto Ricans, especially those of Afro-Caribbean origins from the coastal areas of the Island. Both are rooted in the everyday life of the participants and their improvisational quality make both optimally inclusive as to the terms of involvement. Just as anyone of good will is welcome at casita events, so taking part in plena jams is open to any newcomer who can keep a beat. One of Chema's compositions says it clearly: "*Oye todo el que llega / sin instrumento desea tocar / coge hasta una botella, un cuchillo de mesa / y pega a marcar*" ("Anyone who shows up wanting to play / even without an instrument / pick up a bottle and knife from the table / and keep the beat").

It seems that this affinity between architectural and musical expression goes back a long way, to the origins of both practices at the beginning of the century. An early photo of Barrio San Antón in the southern coastal city of Ponce, considered the birthplace of the *plena,* shows an unpaved street lined with casitas. The structural concept is the same as that evident in New York today, most notably with the front porch facing out onto an open public space. It takes no great stretch of the imagination to place a group of *pleneros* behind the porch railing and people socializing and dancing in the front yard.

Despite their conscious adherence to early traditions, both casita and *plena* practice undergo inevitable adjustments in their contemporary New York setting. With the casitas this change is obvious, because of such impinging factors as land-use codes and the winter climate. In one of his compositions, a take-off on the well-known song "Los carboneros," José Rivera remembers being in the casita before it had heat, and playfully complains to the negligent "super" to provide some coal: "*Super, hace frío, carbón / me levanto por la mañana / pa' irme a trabajar / el super no se levanta / y a mí me pasmá*" ("Super, it's cold, burn some coal / I get up in the morning / to go to work / the super doesn't get up / and I'm here freezing to death"). The irony in this song refrain is of course double, since unlike their antecedents in Puerto Rico the casitas here are not intended, nor allowed, to be lived in. And as that icy winter scene suggests, the immediate reference-points for New York casitas, everything from construction materials to furnishings and décor, all pertain to the surrounding urban setting.

The changes in the *plena* involve not only the role of amplification, recording, and thematic references to life in New York. Here there is also a mingling of vocal and instrumental styles which in traditional, Island-based *plena* remained differentiated according to region or individual artist. In speaking of the members of "Los Pleneros de la 21," for example, José readily identifies styles from Mayaguez or Santurce, or the trademarks of Mon Rivera padre or Emilio Escobar.

Another interesting and important difference is the role of women. While *plena* musical presentation has traditionally been an overwhelmingly male experience, with women only present as dancers or an occasional vocalist, the women of Rincón Criollo came forward as instrumentalists. At "Salvación Casita" the women were slamming away at the *pandereta*, a sight which I'm told is virtually unimaginable in the Puerto Rico of recent memory. Maybe this is still another throwback, like casita architecture, to very early times, since history has it that two of the first masters at the *pandereta* were women: Catherine George, known as Doña Catín, and her daughter Carolina Mora Clark, who went by the name of Carola among friends and neighbors in her native Ponce.[4]

Though live *bomba* and *plena* music is the central activity at the casita event, the musical porch/stage is situated spatially between two other performance areas, the dance floor/yard directly in front and the casita interior backstage, each of which bears its own relation to the musical presentation. The space for dancing allows for immediate, kinetic interaction with the rhythms and flows emanating from the porch; in the *batey,* physical communication with the musicians and instruments is all but inevitable. Inside the casita, on the other hand, even when the carnival atmosphere reaches its highest pitch, there always seem to be people just sitting around talking, children playing on the floor or watching television, apparently heedless of the whole boisterous affair.

The front yard of Rincón Criollo is paved with bricks, unlike other casitas in New York where the *batey* is either bare earth or covered with cement. This special effect came about accidentally, it seems, when one of the associates, a bricklayer by trade, started placing down bricks he had gathered from a demolished building nearby just to see what it would look like. Everyone liked it right away, José recalls, because of what they called the "Old San Juan effect," and before you knew it, after they all pitched in to help, the *batey* of Rincón Criollo was fashioned with colonial-style pavement.

Dancing at the "Salvación Casita" party, as in other casita activities, took on the full range of forms, from individual and couple to open group participation, from inconspicuous head-bobbing and foot-tapping to the formal presentation, in folkloric costume, of the young women in Norma Cruz's *bomba* and *plena* class. At several points in the evening, most notably during this rehearsed display of coordinated shimmying and traditional movements, the crowd in attendance was an audience. They also moved aside to admire and cheer when a particularly adept couple, like Norma Cruz and her husband Consorte, took to the center of the *batey* to demonstrate the perfect synchronization that comes of years of dancing *plena* together. Another memorable and more unusual display, which brought hilarious delight to the party, was when a man in his sixties, clearly one of the neighborhood personalities, got out there and danced a whole number by himself. Sporting a weathered, hip-length leather jacket and a black baseball cap turned slightly to one side, he shimmied, twisted, and jerked his way through the entire ten-minute piece with remarkable timing, all the while oblivious to the friendly snickers and guffaws of the onlookers.

Aside from these moments of choreographic exhibition, most of the crowd was out there on the brick floor. There was none of the self-consciousness that sometimes prevails at dance clubs and even house parties, as people moved about in every which way, young with old, tall with short, gliders with hoppers, women with women, even, at some points, men with men. As the energy level rose those seated on the sidelines joined in as well, clapping and swaying in their seats, and groups of onlookers outside the fence took to dancing on the sidewalk. The energy of collective performance radiated outward from the incandescent wooden porch filled with waving *panderetas, güiros, congas* and accordions.

Inside the casita was like another world, though only a thin wooden wall and a few yards separated it from the porch trembling with percussive sound. Two women and an elderly man sat at a kitchen table talking. Four or five children were watching *Saturday Night Live*. A toddler was playing with a cat on the floor. A teenage couple was whispering and giggling in the back doorway. Another woman was busy rearranging some of the wall hangings: a calendar with the Puerto Rican flag, a picture of Nationalist leader Pedro Albizu Campos, a leaflet with the face of the woman poet Julia de Burgos. Out through the back door you could see a few people lined up waiting to use the outhouse. There was a tranquility and everydayness that offered a welcome respite from the eventful intensity outside. And yet, despite the contrast, this peaceful scene was also, in some remarkable way, an integral part of the performance. The completeness of the event required somehow this space for the nonevent, as though it were a reminder that when the party is over the casita itself, the community's home away from home, will still be there.

In Puerto Rico the casitas were often clustered at the mouths of rivers. Peasants and rural workers displaced by the abrupt economic changes under American rule, and again at mid-century by the beginnings of industrialization, found along the riverbanks and marshy deltas the only land available for them to settle. There, removed from the facilities of the nearby towns and cities, they would patch together their makeshift shanties and eke out their subsistence by fishing, truck gardening, and seasonal stints on the huge sugar plantations. As they built their humble dwellings these squatter families always knew that their days there were probably numbered, and that at any moment agents of the government or the corporations could lay claim to the land and send them packing.

Papo and José Rivera remember such moments from their childhood in "El Fanguito," the crowded slum in the mangroves of Santurce where they grew up in the fifties. When the eviction notices came, they and their neighbors would disassemble the casitas, transport the wood planks and panels to the other side of the lagoon, and set them up again. And life, they recall with a wry smile, would return to normal, as though nothing had happened. "What did we care which side of the water we lived on?"

Since its earliest use, casita architecture has been eminently portable; casita settlements were built more with the dream than with the real prospect of settling in mind. With displacement the most pressing fact of life, the illusion of permanence becomes paramount. The same is true of the cultural world of the casita people: while the music, dancing, pig roasts, and everyday activities give the impression that they are rooted there and always have been, they are lived with the knowledge that it had all occurred somewhere else yesterday, and could well be happening somewhere else tomorrow.

This duality between apparent fixity and imminent relocation may account for the special appeal of casita design among the impoverished and disenfranchised residents of the South Bronx. Under the present conditions of inner-city life they too, like their nomadic ancestors in Puerto Rico or at some earlier time in their own lives, face the constant threat of removal, of having to pick up and do it somewhere else. Potential displacement is especially the condition of their gathering sites for cultural and recreational activity. For while they may enjoy a semblance of stability, however tenuous, in their tenement apartments or housing projects, over the years economic circumstances have forced them to move their public get-togethers from the dance halls to the storefront social clubs to the vacant lots. And from the vacant lot where to but another vacant lot?

The scramble for public space converged with the need to clean up the rubble and treacherous abandon left by the demolition ball, and to plant and harvest. In some cases the first little structures were intended as tool sheds for the neighborhood gardeners, who were then spurred on by a reluctant nod from the city agencies in the form of Operation Greenthumb. The transition to the present casita as cultural center with adjoining mini-farm was only a matter of time and lively cultural memory, but at the price of stricter official vigilance, more elaborate security measures and, of course, a far heightened sense of impermanence.

Such social conditions, in addition to their dense historical symbolism, make the casita settings themselves into acts of performative expression. Whatever may be going on at any given moment, the whole scene — casita, garden, *batey,* outhouse, people milling and playing — is like a moveable stage, an array of theatrical props that can readily be packed up and reassembled in some other place and time. The chainlink fence around the yard, aside from its obvious security function, goes to accent the sense of enclosure, of boundedness and fixity within certain marked-off confines. Here we are, it seems to say, nestled between these particular buildings on this particular block, and we're comfortable and having a good time here. But this insistence on demarcation and spatial specificity is actually a performative response to the very fluidity of cultural and social borders characteristic of their historical experience.

The aesthetic of casita performance thus needs to be viewed from two perspectives: performance at the casita and the casita itself as performance. Spatially, there is an angle on the multiple levels and zones of performative expression inside the fence, and an angle from outside the fence, where the casita and its enclosure appear as though from aerial range in their larger architectural context. It is from this second optical approach, where the surrounding buildings, sidewalks, and streets and the whole urban design come into play, that performance refers to an act of imaginative transposition, or construction as anticipated provisionality and recontextualization. For the community, building and being at the casita kindles a performative sense of vividly imagined place and time: it is "as if" we were in Puerto Rico or Puerto Rico were here, or "as if" Puerto Rico were still as it was back in the days when people like us lived in casitas. But from the wider angle the constructed illusion means that casitas exist "as if" there really were a set place proper to the community. Either place engenders metaphor, or place itself is metaphor.

Beyond its practical and symbolic functions for the community in which it is located, the casita stands as a highly suggestive emblem of contemporary Puerto Rican culture, and of migrant vernacular culture in general. For peoples caught up in circulatory, back-and-forth migratory motion and thereby subject to the constant renewal of personal and historical ties, culture is experienced as dramatic movement and change, adaptability and resilience. Uniqueness, stasis, and even the inexorability of territory and sequence give way to a logic of negotiation and interchangeability. The performance act, object, and site are all eminently transferable, replaceable, mutable; borders, however vigilantly patrolled, are traversable and ultimately collapsible. If economic and political conditions forbid such transactional mobility, performative memory makes it possible, or even necessary. We did this back then, over there, so let's do it again now, over here. In fact, we'd better if we're going to survive.

As emblem, the casita is intended to mean many different things to different people. It is no wonder, then, that artisans in Puerto Rico are making plaster-cast miniature casitas for home adornments, that there are casita T-shirts and casitas in ads for all kinds of products, that a town festival in Cabo Rojo featured a "real" casita and casita kiosks in the plaza, or that additions atop some flat-roof "urbanizaciones" are designed after casitas. Nor is it an incongruity that when it could no longer afford a regular site the former Black and White in Color Gallery in the Bronx decided to become mobile as the Casita Gallery, or that Puerto Rican artist Humberto Figueroa's exhibit at the Museo del Barrio a few years ago included two pre-fab casitas in the center of the gallery floor.

Nevertheless, despite the casitas' seemingly boundless, protean adaptability, there are still grounds for some serious misgivings about the sight of a replica of Rincón Criollo in the halls of the Smithsonian Institution in Washington. The tourists from middle America and the D.C. cultural elite will surely never make it up to Brook Avenue and 159th Street, and it is unlikely that they will come to appreciate the pressing human conditions that made this "quaint" little structure possible, or necessary. Of course if they are willing, even for an hour, to give themselves over to the intense performance energy of "Manny Oquendo's Libre" and "Los Pleneros de la 21," maybe they will be able to listen in on casita language in a way that will dramatize their own relationship to the people of the South Bronx. But when I saw those fancy coattails and evening gowns flying to the rhythms of salsa and *plena,* and José and Cepeda grinning, I was able to sense more deeply than ever the irony in the phrase "primitive art in civilized places."

Even as a happy recollection, that euphoria of conviviality and taste of carnival could only be momentary and, in view of the historical meanings of casitas, ultimately illusory. For however benevolent and "innovative" the intentions guiding the inauguration of the Experimental Gallery, the very format and location of "Las Casitas: An Urban Alternative" only serve to illustrate with particular poignancy the ideological weight surrounding the concepts "primitive" and "civilized" and any account of their supposed conciliation. The very idea of limiting "risk-taking" to exhibition style and technique and the emphatic disclaimer that "Content and Subject are not the Experiment!" fits perfectly into analyses of hegemonic cultural theory and practice like that of Sally Price.

As tenaciously as those die-hard dichotomies of the "civilized" and the "primitive" and "technique" and "content" continue to hold sway in cultural discourse, it is the other paired terms of the title, "art" and "places," which suggest more fruitful lines of thinking about casitas and their contextual transformations. On what grounds and to what end are casitas to be considered "art," and what role do shifting and contrasting "places," understood spatially and temporally, play in deepening our critical involvement? Both in the Smithsonian and in the South Bronx, and even in its "original" appearance in Puerto Rico, casitas mark off "alternative spaces," scenes and practices which diverge from and as such challenge prescribed arrangements and uses of social space. But clearly they are "alternative" in different ways, and it is close historical attention to the changing relations between "art" and "place," expressive practice and sociocultural geography, that allows for some insights into these critical distinctions.

In their passage from Puerto Rico in the first half of the century to the South Bronx in the 1980s to the Smithsonian in 1991, casitas have occupied three different "places," and their construction and use constitute, or relate to, "art" in three different ways. Between its primarily functional, habitational presence in Puerto Rico of not-too-distant memory and its recreational, nostalgic reincarnation in the Bronx and El Barrio in recent years, and between these home-grown community centers and "Las Casitas" in a museum gallery, two major transformations occur in the meaning of casitas as sites and forms of cultural practice. Though both attest to the seemingly limitless adaptability and negotiability inherent in what I have termed a casita "aesthetic," these changes are obviously of a very different order. In broad terms, but with the idea of "place" in view, the first move is one of de-alienation, the second of alienation. Casitas like Rincón Criollo have the effect, and surely this is their intention, of bridging distances of space and time, and of providing a respite from the unhospitable and atomizing con-

ditions of their tenement apartments. With its heightened symbolic reference, the "home" for poor families in Puerto Rico of yesteryear becomes a
"home away from home" for poor Puerto Rican communities in the U.S.
inner-city today.

The Smithsonian's "Rincón Criollo," on the other hand, is the casita
as sheer display, disengaged from any community-based needs and desires. Though in relation to their "originals" in Puerto Rico the new casitas
also have a museum-like sense of preservation and exhibition, the "public"
served by its construction and use is in sociological terms the same population, only at a later chapter in its history, and the casita's functionality for
everyday collective life, while re-articulated, is still present. What was, at
least in part, the casita as community museum is now the casita "installed"
in a museum; if not exactly a commodity, it has become an artifact, an
object, and in any case no longer a process and ongoing expressive and
representational practice. And again, though the intention may be to bridge
the disparate worlds of the museum-goers and the casita people, whatever
proximity is achieved is itself a simulation. The net effect, after the inaugural
ball is over, is an accentuation of distance, difference, and ultimate incom-
patibility based on hierarchies of cultural power. The museum casita, with
all its rhetoric of welcoming respect, amounts to cultural tourism of a
special kind: instead of intruding on turf by going to it and interloping, the
museum exhibit of vernacular culture does so by "installing" the cultural
turf on display in one's own turf. Even the casita people themselves, whose
presence did so much to enliven and authenticate the encounter, were there
as part of the display, as "performers" in a masking, scripted sense rather
than as participants in a process of cultural creativity and reenactment.

For it is clear, when the historical trajectory of casita life is brought to
bear, that the other face of the validation and celebration of community
culture by the dominant society is its repudiation and eventual suppression.
By analytically juxtaposing casita as community museum and casita within
institutional museum we can recognize how powerless folkloristic fancy is
in detaining the advances of the bulldozer. The "preservation" of the community's own cultural preserves, the act of "salvación casita," finally falls to
the casita community itself.

So far at least, since the 1970s, the "Salvación's Casita" campaign has been
a success: Rincón Criollo is still there, literally holding ground against the
constant incursion of the developers and housing authorities. The surrounding lots, vacant over the years and allowing for a sense of open space
and wide horizons, are now filled in with new housing units, of the three-
story, "post-projects" variety, harbingers of bigger, better, and—for the

casita people — more threatening developments ahead. Yet not a Mother's Day or New Year's season goes by without that embattled corner turning into a party. Dance classes and membership meetings continue, and time and again Cepeda is back at the microphone to rally new rounds of support in defense of the casita. A copy of the brochure from the Experimental Gallery's opening exhibit has its place on the wall inside, one memorable but not particularly consequential page in the life-story of "an urban cultural alternative," Rincón Criollo.

NOTES

1   Brochure for exhibit "Las Casitas" An Urban Cultural Alternative," Experimental Gallery, Smithsonian Institution, Washington, D.C., 2 February 1991.

2   For an excellent analysis of the casita phenomenon and its place in Puerto Rican and Caribbean architectural history, see Luis Aponte-Parés and Joseph Sciorra. Both essays and several others, including the present one, are intended for publication as part of the larger casita project directed by Beti-Sue Hertz and the Bronx Council on the Arts.

3   About Puerto Rican music and musicians in the earlier decades of the New York community, see Ruth Glasser.

4   This point and other useful information about the early *plena* tradition may be found in Felix Echevarría Alvarado and my own piece, "Bumbún and the Beginnings of Plena Music," in *Divided Borders*.

Kirsten F. Nigro
Inventions and Transgressions: A Fractured Narrative on Feminist Theatre in Mexico

❑

We Mexican women who have gone down in history
are so few. — The Eternal Feminine, *Act II*

Although women have had a long history of playwriting in Mexico dating from colonial times (Sor Juana's plays being the most brilliant example), that history is hardly a straight or uninterrupted line. Instead, it is badly broken up, with long periods of silence, sometimes because women were not writing, at others because what they were writing had no access to staging or publication and so were lost to the historical record. This all-too-familiar story is part of the larger one that Jean Franco follows in *Plotting Women: Gender and Representation in Mexico,* where she speaks of a master narrative in which women have either not been emplotted at all, or emplotted according to an experience or definition that is not their own. As Franco reads this narrative from colonial times she underscores how the discourse first of religion and the Church, and then of official nationalism, and more recently of modernization in Mexico have placed women in two seemingly contradictory but in the end very logical poles: the first makes them an absence by erasing their presence or nullifying their potential power in the public sphere, by denying them the right to authorship; the second appropriates Woman as a sign to be used strategically, if not cynically, in a male-authored project. Because of this, Franco notes that *Plotting Women* does not so much tell the story of a coherent process as it does record momentary deviations, eruptions that briefly open up spaces in that other story that works so hard to keep women out.

The specific narrative to be traced in this essay is fractured for all the same reasons and in all the same ways, as will become clearer further on. But it is fractured in another significant way, for it purposely begins in medias res, in 1976, with the staging of Rosario Castellanos's *The Eternal Feminine*.[1] This point of departure, however, is not altogether arbitrary, as *The Eternal Feminine* can be considered a liminal text, a threshold between plays written by women about women's problems, mostly in a realistic manner, to "show how things are," to ones that dissect and deconstruct the institutions and social practices that "make these things the way they are," including their chosen medium, the theatre. This is a fundamental move that allows for plays that, rather than representing women as trapped in and by ways of life whose reformation (if it is to come at all) must be, as usual, a male enterprise, instead open up spaces where women can position themselves as agents of action and radical change.

The Chilean feminist poet, Marjorie Agosín has commented that "When we read works written by Latin American women of only a generation ago, we discover a commonality in the themes they have bequeathed us. The prevailing features are passivity, reserve, hidden eroticism, and very little humor. . . . Their works convey images of confinement and diffidence. Their landscapes and metaphors [are] about absence and things missing" (420). Agosín, along with many other critics, sees the mid-1970s as a moment when this legacy begins to be replaced by another, one that is still in process and in which many women are no longer considered nor consider themselves in the passive voice. The present narrative will look at how this shift, this fracture in a tradition, opens up new ways of doing feminist theatre, first in *The Eternal Feminine*, and then in two later texts which take up where Castellanos left off.[2] All three have as a clearly feminist strategy the transgression of patriarchal boundaries — social, sexual, and artistic — which have isolated Mexican women within confining, if not asphixiating, spaces. In each instance, these transgressions are both destructive, in that they break down barriers, and constructive, in the way that they refocus, re-define fundamental issues concerning women's subjectivity — how women experience themselves; concerning their representation — how others, especially men, construct them; and concerning their self-representation — how they construct themselves.

In the following discussion I want first to emphasize how Castellanos, Sabina Berman, and Carmen Boullosa each renegotiate definitions of gender. Therefore, my use of terms like "woman," "female," "subject," and "sex" will at this point be more an appropriation of the playwrights' use (or abuse) of them. But because who defines what becomes such an issue in the plays themselves, my own speaking position must also be a consideration here. Thus this essay has a more self-reflexive nature as it moves toward its conclusion. This move seems fully in line with what, in the last instance, these playwrights make amply clear — the extent to which the "offstage I" (the reader, the critic, the theatregoer) is implicated in the gender construction of every speaking, moving "I" on stage.

II

My song I now begin,
a very well-known hit;
the subject found therein
is the eternal feminine,
about which wise men write,
in books, on parchment thin.
— *"Ballads,"* The Eternal Feminine

The Eternal Feminine is part of a process, part of a long journey in which Rosario Castellanos never ceased to explore and to grapple with the consequences of being a woman, and of being a woman in Mexico. But it also fits into and reflects a particular moment in Mexico, when feminism, or "women's liberation," as it was then called, had become a visible and controversial presence. While certainly Mexican women had organized and fought for their rights well before then, the movement begun in the 1970s had very particular origins and characteristics that set it apart as what Ana Lau Jaiven has called "the new wave of feminism" (141).[3] The year 1968 is a key one in understanding this movement, for the student protests and bloody events of Tlatelolco mark the beginning of a serious questioning of and outright rebellion against the policies and rhetoric of the Mexican government. In its earlier phase, oppositional/confrontational politics, especially as practiced by university students, was apparently coalitional, with men and women joined together in common cause. However, what became clear was that these radical movements, like so many others, ended by replicating patriarchal structures. The realization of this and an awareness of what women across the northern border were doing combined in the early 1970s to produce a specifically *women's* protest movement. As Jaiven has written:

The new wave of feminism in our country surged beginning with the knowledge that its members had of what was going on in North America and at a time when the Mexican political system was fighting to recuperate a lost image of credibility among many sectors of the population because of the repression of the student movement. . . . If the participation of women in that movement was equal numerically to that of men, this was not the case with what they did. Women were in charge of printing and distributing flyers, of cooking food for their male comrades on guard duty, of cleaning the places where the different committees met, of filling up the ranks of demonstrators. (16, 76; translation mine)

Thus *The Eternal Feminine* appears at a key moment, when Castellanos's own long-term feminist project dovetailed with the much broader one of the new Mexican feminism. It is not coincidental then that this play incorporates many of the themes that were then topical: the oppression of the bedroom and home, the need for women to have a voice in their own decision-making, etc. In this *The Eternal Feminine* is of its time. Yet, it was also very much ahead of it, in the way that Castellanos problematized gender. The play's very title places it squarely within the debate still going on between essentialist and materialist feminists, a debate of far-reaching consequences, for whether women are seen as eternal and unchanging, or as shaped by and shapers of their everyday experiences makes a great difference both to the specifics of women's lived reality and to the political project that would improve or modify it.[4] Castellanos certainly understood and knew firsthand the consequences of living in a country whose symbolic order and social practices have been predicated on essentializing notions of Woman. *The Eternal Feminine* is her answer to this, a counter-text that identifies where these notions come from, and shows them up for what they are (at least as Castellanos sees them): inventions, something made up for a reason and with very concrete, palpable results. Castellanos's strategy consists of three key maneuvers: 1) she creates a non-narrative theatre piece, as an effective way of eluding the pull of Mexico's master cultural narrative; 2) she allows women to tell their own stories, which positions them as active subjects within the "big story," while at the same time giving them the pleasure of subverting it; 3) she dismantles almost all the images of the Eternal Woman held very dear or vilified in Mexican society by blowing them up into caricatures, revealing their very constructedness; 4) she theatricalizes gender, and in so doing, implicates theatre practices in the gendering process.

In her essay "Refusing the Romanticism of Identity: Narrative Intervention in Churchill, Benmussa, Duras," Elin Diamond discusses the dangers of narrative for a feminist project: that it excludes female representation; that in the emplotment of the male quest, women are merely obstacles or objects of pleasure; that it tells itself as progressive and inevitable, which satisfies the reader/audience's own desire for order and closure; that in a parallel move, the reader/audience also constructs a narrative that, as Diamond says, is a "causal chain of events moving towards a telos or completion" (94). History is equally suspect for its complicity with narrative. It too pretends to simply tell itself through a disinterested author, ordering its content in a straight line toward closure, passing over or moving through women. But, according to Diamond, the understanding that history *is* narrative constitutes a key move for feminists, as it makes clear that women's absence in history or her secondary, passive role in it are a consequence of narrative itself.

Not surprisingly, then, a major concern in some feminist theatre has been to disrupt narrative on stage, and challenge the audience's own desire to create tidy and closed narratives. While there is no general agreement as to what the best strategy for doing this might be, one of them has been to reject the conventions of stage realism, with the argument that it shares and replicates the processes and structures of narrative. Jeannie Forte sums up why realism is suspect in a feminist project: "It poses an apparently objective or distanced viewpoint from which both the narrator and the reader can assess the action and ultimate meaning of the text, a pose which makes the operations of ideology covert, since the illusion is created for the reader that he or she is the source of meaning or understanding, unfettered by structures of culture" ("Realism, Narrative" 115). Realism, therefore, can reaffirm the dominant order by making it seem that all is clear and in its place; it can erase contradiction and perpetuate the illusion of a centered, integrated (male) subject who is both creator and interpreter of knowledge. The challenge, then, as Forte and others see it, is to destabilize this apparently stable order, to show the ideological seams that hold it together. Just how and if this means throwing realism off the stage for good, is still up for debate.

In *The Eternal Feminine,* Castellanos is certainly concerned with many of these same issues, as she had been in much of her other writings. Her solution here is to have a story line that is so unbelievable and so constantly interrupted that it loses authority, the latter understood in the sense of displaying logic and coherence. The narrative, such as it is, involves Lupita, who goes to a beauty parlor to have her hair done on her wedding day. Unbeknownst to her, a magical dream-inducing apparatus has been placed in the hairdryer and during most of the play she goes in and out of dream states. In Act I Lupita is catapulted into what proves to be her not-so-rosy future, as she moves from deflowered bride to little old lady. In Act II, she visits a circus tent where a group of women who have had the dubious fortune of being included in the official discourse of Mexican history come back to life and tell their version of how things really were. At the beginning of Act III the gadget in the hairdryer has caused a short in the salon's electricity. To cover up her still soggy hair, Lupita tries on a variety of wigs, each of which turns her into a prototype of the Mexican Woman — the Old Maid, the Hooker, the Other Woman, the Aggressive Professional.

This is clearly such an outrageous sequence of events that there is no question of it holding together as coherent narrative. Even in Act I, where there is a narration of sorts, Castellanos deauthorizes it by showing that within the supposedly and paradigmatically happy story that is written for women by Mexico's master cultural text, there is embedded another one, in which marriage and motherhood are not so blissful, and being a widow is a final, much-longed-for liberation. This story, however, cannot permanently displace the other. As Castellanos goes on to suggest in Act II, narrative is interpretation, or as one of the characters says, "versions of what we think we were" (304).[5] For example, in Sor Juana's telling of who she was, she suggests that she was a lesbian, or at least that she had once loved another woman erotically. When her listeners react with confusion and even outright displeasure, Sor Juana, "*taking things lightly*" says: "But what you have seen is only an entertainment. It's perhaps, just one version" (315). Before telling this story, Sor Juana had already confessed "to a penchant for disguises" (310), insinuating that she is not one but many, or perhaps that she *can* be many, and therefore purposely deceptive. With this, Castellanos would seem to be saying that however important it is for Mexican women to enter into historical discourse — subverting, rewriting, or totally rejecting it — this does not mean that narrative itself should no longer be suspect. It is just that it has been opened up to other voices, like Sor Juana's, which by her own account, speaks not necessarily the truth. It is not then simply a question of making a his into a her story, but rather of understanding how stories come to be in the first place, and how they work to make themselves seem transparent.

If Sor Juana questions whether the "I" speaks as one subject, for Lupita the experience of multiple subjectivity is lived on stage, where, in addition to being who she thought she was, she also becomes at least thirteen other women. And if Lupita is multiple, then she cannot be essential, but rather, contingent. The distinction between a condition and a state of being, between *ser/estar* in the Spanish language, is fundamental in *The Eternal Feminine,* and owes much to Castellanos's readings of Simone de Beauvoir, who posited woman as a process, as something that is made, and not born. In this play Castellanos views such a process of becoming in theatrical terms that end by destabilizing the theatrical metaphor itself, making of it a method of freezing women into essences, but at the same time a potentially liberating one. For example, in Act II, the Empress Carlota engages in a dialogue with Maximilian that sounds suspiciously like moments from Rodolfo Usigli's *Corona de sombra* (*Crown of Shadows*), the classic playtext on the Hapsburg empire, authored by the one playwright who is considered something of the *pater* of modern Mexican drama. The topics of discussion, the tone, language, and phrases are all as remembrances of this past text, an intertextuality that points to the way that male-authored theatre itself has helped to codify and perpetuate the meanings associated with women in Mexico. Castellanos's Carlota reproduces this meaning in the dialogue she evokes, but undercuts it by adding something that is not in the Usigli text — that once she returned to Europe, Carlota quite simply forgot Maximilian, and expresses disappointment at finding out that he died a death as *declassé* as execution by firing squad in a place with such an ordinary name as Bell Hill. With just this one small stroke, Castellanos demystifies not just the "Carlota narrative," but the one that the stage specifically has helped to write and to inscribe into the popular imagination in Mexico.

Whereas in this scene theatre is seen as an accomplice in the creation of falsehoods, in the one where Sor Juana recreates her past, it proves also to be an ally, a space where women can destabilize fixed gender identities. Having shorn her hair and changed her courtesan's dress for a page's habit, the young Juana Inés becomes a character in a *comedia de enredos* in the manner of those she herself had written: as a girl in drag who has another of the same sex attracted to her. When the young woman Celia walks in, she mistakes Juana Inés for her male lover, to whom she had "opened her virgin door" (312). What ensues is an ambiguous courtship dialogue in which the cross-dressed character is both the object of desire (Juana Inés the page), and the obstruction to desire's fulfillment (Juana Inés the beautiful courtesan). This is all very commonplace in the conventions of Golden Age theatre, of course, where all ends well and gender confusion is put right. But Castellanos does not follow the model. When Celia realizes who the page really is, she also realizes that it is not him, but Juana Inés whom she desires: "Celia opens her arms . . . and Juana doubts a moment between flight and surrender" (314). At this juncture Celia understands what the audience and Juana Inés have all along: that their dialogue of seduction is subtextually homoerotic and that performance, play-acting, allows for what social practice prohibits or denies as a possibility. While at the end of the scene, after Juana Inés apparently has spurned Celia, bringing their play to an end, Castellanos opens it up again by having as a last image that of the two women being both attracted to and pulling away from each other. There is no closure; the *comedia de enredos* can go on, be repeated, and because of its very conventions—the transvestism of cross-dressing and gender confusion—it is an example of theatre that can work for and not against a feminist critique of gender stereotypes and sexual taboos.

In the more than fifteen years since its publication and staging, some of what *The Eternal Feminine* did and has to say may seem stale or obvious. But in 1973, when Castellanos finished writing *The Eternal Feminine*, it was farseeing in mapping out what would become major issues in feminism, and not only in Mexico. Although perhaps without such a clear or even a similar theoretical argument, Castellanos seems to have understood what Teresa de Lauretis has described as "the uncomfortable condition of being at once inside and outside gender" (*Technologies of Gender* 11), that gender is simultaneously representation and self-representation. Thus in *The Eternal Feminine* it is not just a question of the imposition but also of the assumption of gender constructs. In Castellanos's terms, this is to problematize gender by implicating women in their own engendering. At the same time, it is to suggest that because women are simultaneously in and out of this process, its disruption is no easy matter, and may require that women not so much change or modify it, but rather invent alternatives. As one of the characters says, "It isn't enough to discover who we are. We have to invent ourselves" (356).

III

And can you tell between them? —The Eternal Feminine, *Act II*

Exactly how women can invent themselves is never clearly articulated in *The Eternal Feminine*. Instead, there is implicitly the idea that whatever else might be involved, acting comes first, that building a new character is fundamental. Yet with the exception of the Sor Juana scene, a major obstacle to this process—the traditional sex-based opposition of male and female—remains stable in the Castellanos text. Once gender is posited as a construction, however, this binarism must be brought into question. If female is an artifice, then so must be male; if gender is enacted, then there must be various possibilities of how to act it. Judith Butler has argued that "gender cannot be understood as a *role* which either expresses or disguises an interior 'self,' whether that 'self' is conceived as sexed or not. As performance which is performative, gender is an 'act,' broadly construed, which constructs the social fiction of its own psychological interiority. . . . Genders, then, can be neither true nor false, neither real nor apparent" ("Performative Acts" 279). However, as Butler also points out, existing social structures are predicated on univocal, stable gendered signifiers. Thus gender is an effective policing mechanism for maintaining control of societies' members: "Performing one's gender wrong initiates a set of punishments both obvious and indirect, and performing it well provides the reassurance that there is an essentialism of gender identity after all" (279). While Butler is referring to societies in general, the phenomenon of extreme "machismo" in Mexico makes all the more dangerous and punishable any transgression of the heterosexual paradigm. By doing just this, the playwright Sabina Berman goes one step beyond Castellanos, putting in severe tension the *macho/ hembra* essentialism so fundamental to Mexican social and sexual practices.

In her short one-act play entitled *One* (*Uno,* 1978), Berman, like Castellanos, also refuses to tell a story in the traditional sense. Instead, she sketches a brief moment, a morning conversation between El and Ella (He and She). By freeing herself of narrative, Berman can dehistoricize the gendered sign to then show to what extent it is indeed a product of cultural practices and historical context. She does this with the help of a little physical adornment considered typically masculine: a moustache, that well-groomed growth of facial hair that on a woman connotes some kind of aberration, as with the moustachioed circus ladies, but that on a man's face is taken to be the quintessential sign of sexual prowess and masculine guile. Berman subverts such essentialist clichés by making this particular moustache a movable one. Although He wears it most of the time, it is on loan, for it really belongs to her. Most of the play's dialogue revolves around this extraordinary moustache, as the two characters discuss how She wears it when wanting to avoid being approached by other men, and how He dons it when seducing other women. He is wearing it as the play begins, the morning after the night of his encounter with *la morena* ("the brunette"). At the play's end, however, She puts it on, not to avoid a heterosexual liaison, but in order to seduce her husband in what is metaphorically a homoerotic encounter:

SHE: Tonight there is no other woman who tempts me. But if you want to take it off . . . Maybe there's a man that you like and if you want him to approach you you'll have to take off the moustache.
HE: No. There's no other man that I like as much as you. You're irresistible when you have your moustache on. Put it on.
He puts it on for her. He caresses her moustache. . . . They kiss on the lips.
(280; translation mine)

In the manner of Castellanos, Berman also elaborates on the theatrical metaphor, by highlighting to what extent gender is makeup and make-believe. She does this also through the convention of cross-dressing, which is summarized in the moustache. As costume and prop, as physical presence and linguistic referent, the moustache is emptied as a sign of masculinity associated with a particular body, and fills with meaning according to the context of the moment; or better said, according to the face to which it is attached. But even when He wears it, it is an unstable sign. According to Berman, He should be cast as "an effeminate man," who throughout almost all of the play behaves in ways commonly represented as female: he is insecure and timid; he has headaches and neuroses; he is always saying "excuse me" or "I'm sorry." In lovemaking He is the object of desire, the one who is acted upon; She pretends to be him, reenacting his seduction of the brunette, "caressing his back, his shoulders, his waist, his shoulders, his ass and finally between his legs. . . . He howls with pleasure" (274; translation mine). Here He is the seduced female, despite the moustache on his face.

The heterosexual setup is further imbalanced by having him be the one who suffers an "identity" crisis, in which he needs to have his presence affirmed in the gaze of an Other, thus subverting the patriarchal notion of women as invisible and only able to enter into representation as cultural male. He confesses to having no sense of existing as a man except as he is reflected in her eyes: "I can't see myself. I can't see myself with my own eyes. I can only see what I am in your look" (277; translation mine). He needs for her to tell him that she desires him as a man, and not as the woman that he might also be, something that She refuses to do, thereby denying him the comfort of a stable, unitary, male-gendered subjectivity. Berman has further unbalanced the situation by having her be played as "a masculine woman," producing yet another visual and semantic subversion: He is a man who looks and behaves like a woman, who depends on a woman's gaze for his sense of reality; She is a woman who both looks like and holds the supposedly superior power position of a man. So hers is a male gaze as well, which makes even more ambiguous who sees who through and reflected in what. A further displacement, one that would be immediately apparent to an audience, is that the two characters are meant to be almost mirror reflections of each other: they bear a surprising resemblance and both wear white pants and white silk shirts; they both are tall and slender, with short hair dyed a mahogany color. Obviously, Berman means to confuse, as well as fuse, where one begins and the other ends.

Her "masculinity" works on yet another level, in that as a woman throughout most of the play, she suffers a very significant lack. She is first of all without her moustache; as He says, "Now I know what's strange about you. You're not wearing your moustache" (269; translation mine). But in a metaphorical sense, the moustache stands for the almighty penis, or the "little bird," as He calls it, remembering his seduction of the brunette and the ecstasy, the reality he felt when she kissed it. But like the moustache, the penis is also a detachable item. Immediately after He has gone into ecstasy at the memory of his "little bird," she kneels down on the floor, looking for something she has lost:

SHE: (*Like a little girl*) Where is my nightingale? I'm tired of looking for it blindly.
HE: The shame . . .
SHE: Oh, so you have it? You have my nightingale, weeping willow? Oh, it's dead.
(279; translation mine)

He puts the moustache on her face so that She (as a he) can seduce him, and He (as a her), can be seduced. With moustache in place, She is once again complete, at least for that particular situation and moment. In another, the moustache might well be someplace else, or nowhere at all. As the play ends, there is such a purposeful confusion about which gender is which, that the moustache-*cum*-penis has become the locus of various and conflicting meanings, all of which are summarized in their final, gender-confused kiss, a parody of the kiss that closes the traditional heterosexual love story.

Confusion, of course, can breed ambiguity, and at times it is not altogether clear in *One* whether gender roles are being reversed rather than subverted. The "masculine" still seduces here, the "feminine" is seduced. Women (She as she) still suffers penis envy, and are metaphorically castrated. The manly moustache stands for the penis and the penis stands for power. Or rather it *stood* for power; now it is but a little dead nightingale, forever silenced. Total gender dismantling ultimately must start from this kind of zero point, where there is no noise, nothing present from the past. But to get there is not easy, for as Berman's play shows, notions of the masculine/feminine, or male/female, are so deeply engraved onto our cultural and mental maps that we must work with and through them in order to get rid of them. So while in *One* they keep surfacing as behavioral paradigms, the death of the penis seems to suggest that after the confusion, inversions, and reversals, a new beginning is indeed possible. And in a country like Mexico, where the heterosexual sex-gender connection is so powerful in sustaining the mystique of the "macho," to even suggest this possibility is to make quite a threatening statement.

I V

With the cherubins around her,
the angels sing and smile;
and the archangels rise above her,
to the highest throne they fly,
where the Holy Virgin Mother
ends the devil's power so vile.
— *"Ballads"* The Eternal Feminine

If the cult of machismo depends on clearly drawn heterosexual distinctions, it also desperately needs that the "woman" in that equation be boldly drawn. In her discussion of the master narrative of nationalism in Mexico, Jean Franco has underscored the important and ambiguous role that essentialized Woman has played in the symbolic field occupied by the Virgin of Guadalupe, patron saint of Mexico, and La Malinche, the much-vilified Indian woman who was Cortes's mistress and interpreter.[6] Although extremely complex in their development and equally complex in their manifestations, it does not oversimplify things too much to say that in Mexican cultural practice, the Virgin and La Malinche have worked and been worked to polarize Woman into two essences: the good and the bad, the self-sacrificing and the rebellious, the closed and the open, the safe and the dangerous, the asexual and the sexual. Not surprisingly, the discourse of *guadalupismo* and *malinchismo* are major obstacles to feminists in Mexico, who have worked to recuperate La Malinche, in particular, by retelling her story in ways that openly challenge official versions of it. For example, in her poem "Malinche," Castellanos does this by letting Malinche speak for herself, not as a woman who sold out to the foreigner, but as one who was sold into slavery by her own mother: "I advance toward destiny in chains / leaving behind all that I can still hear, / the funereal murmurs with which I am buried" (Ahern 97). In *The Eternal Feminine* La Malinche is one of the women who come back to life in the circus tent, to tell the untold story of how she was Cortes's equal, if not superior, in wit and intelligence.

While La Malinche has been given a voice, allowing for a serious feminist critique of her abuse by patriarchy, the Virgin as icon has not been so scrutinized, at least on the stage, although in every play that questions the role of mother and the "self-sacrificing little Mexican woman," there is implicit such a scrutiny. And while she is noticeably absent from *The Eternal Feminine*, Sandra Cypess has noted that the Virgin is ghosted in the main character Lupita, which is short for Guadalupe; a Lupita who before going to the beauty parlor, seemed destined to live the life of the virtuous Mexican

Woman. In Carmen Boullosa's *They Proposed Mary* (*Propusieron a María*, 1987), however, the Virgin is both a palimpsest and a character on stage, in a story that places her in a radically different context; or better said, in two texts that together destabilize the other powerful narrative of virginity, motherhood, modesty (*pudor*), self-sacrifice, and divinity. As in the other two plays discussed here, the question of narrative is fundamental in *They Proposed Mary*. Whereas Castellanos worked to break it up, and Berman really does not have one, Boullosa sets up the action on stage as something that actually happened, by claiming for herself the role of transcriber of some tapes recording the last night that Mary and Joseph spent together, before she ascended to the Heavens. These tapes were placed at the foot of their twin beds by someone with "an anthropological zeal," who activated them by remote control at 11 P.M., the couple's usual bedtime, in the hopes of getting their last words together. However, because of a bout of insomnia, Mary and Joseph spent a great deal of time talking, and therefore, the tape ran out just as she was ascending. What the audience supposedly witnesses, then, is an enaction of the transcription of the tapes, word for word. Boullosa, the transcriber, disclaims any responsibility, saying that "I leave it to the sociologists, the linguists, the anthropologists and theologians the considerations that can be gleaned from these transcriptions" (86; translation mine).

There is no question here that Boullosa expects anyone to believe in the veracity of this patently made-up dialogue, which she herself has subtitled an "impossible one." So the sense of authenticity that the tapes might have on one level (as ethnographic data) is immediately undercut by their content, which has no "real" referent to back it up. This warns against believing everything one hears just because it is communicated through a supposedly scientific and objective "medium": anthropology, tape recorders, the kind of "you are there" docudrama that cavalierly mixes fiction and fact, but passes itself off as what really happened. Yet if there is no proof otherwise, why could this dialogue *not* have taken place? Or at least something similar to it? These questions become more pressing as one hears what Mary and Joseph have to say to each other in the privacy of their bedroom. That is exactly the point, that they were a married couple, and therefore must have shared an intimate life. However, the notion of a virgin birth makes imagining that life problematic, although this is exactly what Boullosa does — imagine what one evening, one conversation in that life, with all of its contradictions, might have been like. Since Mary and Joseph sound very much like many other married couples, their dialogue is therefore not so impossible, after all; its very possibility is what makes strange the other narrative where it is seemingly impossible. Both narratives work with and against each other, for the Mary and Joseph of *They Proposed Mary* are, on one level, meant to be the biblical couple, as it is only the Mary of that version who is divine and capable of ascending to the heavens. But on another level, they are your average young couple whose life (text) repeats the textual paradigm of their historical/biblical/mythologized archetypes. This is what produces the absurdities in the play, for by repeating the archetype, Mary and Joseph engage in some rather pathological and sexually dysfunctional behavior.

They Proposed Mary was published in a collection of Boullosa's plays which she entitled *Heretical Theatre* (*Teatro herético*). The title is particularly apt when one considers that the playwright's purpose in writing this text was to offer an alternative fare during the Christmas season, when the *posadas,* which enact the birth of Christ, are traditionally staged in Mexico. Boullosa therefore had a clear sense of wanting to interrupt, to open a space in a theatrical tradition that reiterates a narrative with far-reaching effects on the daily life of women in Mexico. Just how heretical and unorthodox the play is can be summarized in Boullosa's depiction of the character Mary, who compares the sexual act with the taking of communion, the moment of penetration with receiving the host. Mary tells Joseph how she had anticipated that sex for the first time would transfigure her, just as she had thought her first communion would. But the wafer in her mouth melted, and nothing happened; then, after her first night with Joseph, she wondered if that was all there was to it. It would appear that Mary has fallen victim to the romanticism that links fireworks and sex, of sex with transcendental experiences. It soon becomes clear, however, that Mary has not "done it" with Joseph, that that first night she merely slept next to him, but not with him. She is married but still with hymen intact, a situation that allows Boullosa to poke fun at the very deep but obvious contradiction that the Woman as Virgin discourse tries to ignore or minimize: the fact that women, even the biblical Mary, are sexual beings.

Boullosa's Mary is, of course, frigid, a condition that has been prescribed by her identity in the sex/gender script operative in Mexico. As Evelyn P. Stevens has written, "The ideal dictates not only premarital chastity for all women, but postnuptial frigidity. 'Good' women do not enjoy coitus; they endure it when the duties of matrimony require it" (96). Mary has simply gone to the extreme of not doing it at all. Her Joseph admires this, but as Boullosa makes clear in the text, he is certainly not deprived, having gotten his sex on the side. That is, he enacts perfectly his macho identity: he worships wife and Virgin, but without any risk to his sexual needs and appetite. However, all is not perfect at home, as Mary does admit to being frustrated and wonders if there is something wrong with her. She cannot quite figure out what she is missing; she has touched Joseph with all her body parts and is still pure: "[I] touched you with my hands, with my thighs, with my toes, I passed your hand over my ears, I held your eyelashes still and softly to my lips, without letting you go . . . I reached the conclusion that it's not done with anything I have. What am I missing?" (91; translation mine).

Mary is like the sexual innocent who has done everything but the act, still technically virgin, experienced but with no sense of how her body works, or where her erogenous zones really are. As the venerated Mary, however, she cannot find the necessary part because in her codification as the pure woman, she has been desexed, her genitalia erased from her being and image. And yet the miracle of her pregnancy; for Boullosa's Mary is also expecting the arrival "of the savior, our son," whose due date of the twenty-fifth of an unnamed month makes him a real baby-on-the-way and an intertext with the Baby Jesus. Like most young parents-to-be, Mary and Joseph speak of how this new arrival will change their lives, of how the dynamics of three are very different from those of a family of two. But this will not be a normal change, because in giving birth, Mary the Mother will make the maximum self-sacrifice: she will literally disappear. Joseph understands that if she would only "do it" with him, she might be saved this fate. But considering herself different, even superior to other women, Mary refuses. When it is her time to go, however, and church bells ring and sacred music plays, Mary seems to change her mind: "It's that I don't want to anymore, it's that I don't want to anymore" (101), suggesting that maybe a little sex might have been worth it after all.

Because *They Proposed Mary* deals with the private world of marriage and of problems in the bedroom, represented as "a moment in the life of," it functions rather like realistic domestic drama, which makes it quite different from *The Eternal Feminine* and *One*. But it is realism very estranged by the particular way that Boullosa demystifies and confuses/collapses the story that her text tells with the other told and retold in the discourse of Virgin Worship. *They Proposed Mary* is both unbelievable (we know that the biblical Mary and Joseph never had this conversation), but believable, in that many couples are as sexually dysfunctional and for the same reasons. It is this pull between the two that makes the play seem so strange and yet familiar. Still, its total effect is the same as the plays by Castellanos and Berman: to disrupt, to fragment the tidy, third-person patriarchal narratives that have been passing themselves off as Truths about the nature and experience of gender. If Castellanos's particular target is the mythology of an essentialized Woman, and Berman's the heterosexual opposition male/female, Boullosa's is the absurd and crippling consequences of these supposed Truths on the lives people really live. Considering the stake in maintaining these Truths as self-evident, given their function and power in hegemonic discourse and official political projects, these plays are not only dangerous in what they say, but also in what they offer: a place to work out other possibilities for women in Mexico. To quote Sue-Ellen Case in the concluding remarks to her study *Feminism and Theatre,* "The feminist in theatre can create the laboratory in which the single most effective mode of repression — gender — can be exposed, dismantled and removed; the same laboratory may produce the representation of a subject who is liberated from the repressions of the past and capable of signalling a new age for both women and men" (132).

V

"I'm not talking to anyone. I'm speaking for."
"Isn't there a third way for those of us who belong to the Third World?"
— The Eternal Feminine, *Acts I, III*

Throughout this essay I have noted how narrative has become suspect in much feminist theatre because of the way it presents itself as self-evident, objective truth and irresistible — that is, as the only possible way of telling a given story. Sharing this mistrust to some degree, I cannot then turn around and present my narrative as transparent. Indeed, my relationship with the particular texts studied has very much to do with where and how I am positioned, as an Anglo-American woman and academic, and not a Mexican woman playwright or part of the feminist movement there; hence, the narrative voice changes here from the third to the first person (creating yet another fracture in this narrative). Although the problem of what constitutes subjectivity and how it is constituted is still very open to debate, the increasing conceptualization of subjectivity as positioning and experience has profound repercussions for any project which involves cultural differences such as those between me and the texts that I have analyzed here. While I am not convinced that experience alone automatically translates into more knowledge and a perfect understanding, the fact of difference and distance does have a considerable impact. I certainly cannot assume that I speak from *the* center or that I speak *for* these Mexican playwrights. But how off-center, in the sense of off the mark, does this make my reading of these plays? My answer is that they are not as far off as some might claim, but perhaps more so than I would like.

The fact that academic feminist criticism can, and is done without consideration of its implications for political praxis, or without considering it as political praxis, has brought charges from some of irrelevance, and of cultural insensitivity.[7] Our use of Continental and Anglo-American feminist theory has been criticized as a First World imposition on Third World cultural production, a kind of "information retrieval" approach, as Gayatri Spivak has called it, wherein texts of the Other are here and there collected to inscribe them into a project other than their own. The above quote from *The Eternal Feminine* — "Isn't there a third way for those of us who belong to the Third World?" — reflects what has been a real and understandable worry among Mexican feminists about being colonized by the movement in the United States, especially, and explains why in Mexico it is still controversial to use the term "feminist." As one reviews the literature on feminism written by Mexican, as well as Latin American writers and critics, a repeated question has been to what extent their particular positions in time and space mean that feminism for them must be different from that of their counterparts elsewhere, and if so, in what does that difference consist. Nonetheless, even in these discussions, there is reference to and use made of theory that comes from a wide variety of sources. Mexican feminism is not insular nor immune to "foreign" contact.

Nonetheless, there are consequences to using a particular theoretical construct on Mexican (and all Latin American) play texts that those of us in U.S. academic settings may not take enough into account. When first writing this essay, I used the verb "to deconstruct" with relative abandon, attributing to it the generalized meaning of showing conceptions and perceptions of phenomena to be constructions, rather than reflections of reality. At one point, however, when I fully faced its possible implications, I went back and changed it for words that are less loaded. Mary Poovey has warned that to "take deconstruction to its logical conclusion would be to argue that 'woman' is *only* a social construct that has no basis in nature, that 'woman,' in other words, is a term whose definition depends upon the context in which it is being discussed and not upon some set of sex organs or social experiences. This renders the experience women have of themselves and the meaning of their social relations problematic, to say the least" (52). I erased "deconstruction" as a critical term because I became uncomfortable with the thought that employing it could assume a purpose not implied by these texts, or embraced by Mexican feminists. While the three play texts obviously have aspects of gender construction as their theme, I am not sure they have deconstruction as their epistemology. While they put into crisis notions of essentialism, it is not so clear that what they advocate is abandoning altogether the concept of Woman as a distinct identity and a political tool. Indeed, there are special dangers to evacuating the semantic space occupied by Woman and the "feminine" in Latin America, where there are still a great many important battles to be won. Also, evacuating that space could mean losing some power already held. In her essay "Killing Priests, Nuns, Women, Children," Jean Franco has discussed how during the recent political terrorism in Latin America, many sacred female spaces have been violated; for example, the house. Without slighting the deleterious effect that the semiotic of the house and the cult of the family has had on Latin American women, Franco also points out that the house, nevertheless, had been a sanctuary, a place safe from outside violence. As Franco says, "Feminist criticism based on the critique of patriarchy . . . has rightly shed no tears for this liquidation of mother figures whose power was also servitude. Yet such criticism has perhaps underestimated the oppositional potentialities of these female territories whose importance as the only sanctuaries became obvious at the moment of their disappearance" (420).

This is not to waffle on issues, or to be apologetic for not being able to decide which way to go. In one sense, it is only to admit what much current theory emphasizes: that no reading is the only, true reading. But in another, it is to be caught in what some have called the "feminist impasse," and what others have seen as feminism's most dynamic aspect: the pull and tug between essentialism and materialism, or the simultaneous embracing of both, a willingness to accept contraction rather than resolving it, to challenge notions of fixed identity while at the same time, as Jane Gallop says, not want to escape them altogether. I personally opt for the double strategy and perhaps this is why texts like *The Eternal Feminine, One,* and *They Proposed Mary* are so appealing to me. They too do not seem willing, ready, or quite able to erase or ellide difficult contradictions in feminist, as well as in their own, discourse.

But how does what I think or say, as a U.S. academic, fit into debates among feminists in Mexico? Is my choice and appreciation of these texts more a reflexion of my position and priorities than of theirs? What, if any, importance do these texts have in relationship to feminist praxis there, as opposed to here? From what I have, clearly I attribute to *The Eternal Feminine, One,* and *They Proposed Mary* resonances that go well beyond the printed page or stage. I noted before that for many Latin American women writers and critics it has been important to distinguish what is different about feminism in their countries. One of the principle characteristics they have isolated is that feminism in Latin America is about oppression across gender, racial, and class lines. Sara Castro-Klarén, for example, has said that in Latin America there is not just a discourse on the eternal feminine, but also the colonial one of racial oppression, which has forcefully excluded Indians, mestizos, and mulattoes — male and female — from the hegemonic center, or the discourse of the noble savage, which has had an equivalent effect by trapping indigenous people within the limits of an idealized Western rhetoric, thereby effectively neutralizing the "savage" (41). One of Mexico's leading women writers, Elena Poniatowska, follows a similar line when she argues in her essay "La literatura de las mujeres es parte de la literatura de los oprimidos" ("Women's Literature is Part of the Literature of the Oppressed"), that Latin American women writers give voice to all the politically marginal, and therefore their mission is to help build solidarity with and among them. And Rosario Castellanos was clear and eloquent in her belief that women and indigenous people share a profound bond in being Mexico's most silenced groups.

This is to view feminism in terms of what Karen Offen has called a "relational feminism," wherein women's particular concerns are considered as part of larger projects of social reform, be they associated with official party platforms, as the liberal one of post-Independence, or with the utopias of leftist movements. However, since the 1960s in Mexico the efficacy of these alliances has come under close and heated scrutiny, because of the way "women's issues" have repeatedly been lost sight of or delayed; for example, women in Mexico did not get the vote until 1953, although agitation for it began as early as the 1880s. One of the noticeable differences with the new wave of feminism in Mexico is the formation and proliferation of autonomous, non-allied feminist groups whose purpose is to devise a politics that fits the needs of women of all classes, and not the other way around. An important aspect of this strategy has been to adapt the North American feminists' rallying cry of the "personal is the political" to local circumstances. This is not just to insist that what happens to women in private gets repeated in public, but also that the effects of power that women experience on a personal level *are* political acts, which is to significantly redefine the nature of the political. The three plays analyzed here implicitly make this connection as well. Although they all take place in private and so-called feminine spaces — the home and a beauty parlor — they are not about private "women's problems" as opposed to public, political ones; that particular binarism collapses here. The experience of gender articulation in these plays underscores its power to abuse, to oppress, to limit. The "real life" consequences of this were made quite clear, for example, during the earthquake of 1985, when the collapse of a building in Mexico City revealed the appalling, sweatshop working conditions of hundreds of *costureras* (seamstresses), who in addition to suffering gruesome hours, filthy facilities, low pay, minimum or no benefits, were also forced to endure verbal obscenities, threats, and sexual harassment which included episodes of forced intercourse, that is, rape. In the aftermath of the earthquake, owners of the factories were more intent on recovering their sewing machines than on rescuing workers who might still be alive or retrieving their dead bodies for burial. It was only then, with the support of feminists, in particular, that these seamstresses saw their plight as a really political one, not just as their lot as women, but their lot because of the way women, especially of their class, have been engendered in Mexico.[8]

Political theatre in Latin America has usually been construed as one dealing with public corruption; ideological struggles between the left and the right; specific occurrences, such as a massacre, a labor strike, the actions of a political figure or party; in fine, mostly what men do or make happen. By transgressing that particular artistic boundary, plays like *The Eternal Feminine, One,* and *They Proposed Mary* call into question the validity of such a limited definition of politics both on and off stage. These plays, however, not only make the connection between gender construction and political praxis; they also imply that that construction is representation, enactment. This in turn would suggest that the personal is to some degree individual or of the small group, the actor(s) doing, as Judith Butler says, his, her, or their gender, with the possibility of reinterpreting the script and choosing from a variety of acting methods. The question then becomes to what degree individual or "micro" politics can be effective in bringing about systemic change in Mexico, a question that has indeed been much debated by feminists there, who on the one hand seem to feel that they have not managed all their goals for being outside traditional structures, but on the other, are mistrustful of these structures for having failed them in the past; some see the need for alliances with these structures, others do not.

It is at this point that north and south can, and do dovetail. For although feminism here has been dominated by white middle-class women, the struggle over the past decade has been to be less exclusionary, to accept and respect diversity, to somehow allow for both coalitional and identity politics. It is not altogether true or fair, therefore, to insist on our extreme individualism, as opposed to the collective concerns of Latin American feminists. And if truth be told, the latter also have struggled to go beyond the rhetoric of inclusiveness and to break loose their solidly middle-class roots. Despite basic cultural differences, there is a commonality of challenges and purposes that allows for a dialogue in which voices from both sides are equally vital. My purpose in writing an essay as this one is to contribute something I believe to be of significance to this north-south dialogue. And yet I still must end on a tentative note. The plays I have discussed and their implied solutions to gender politics in Mexico are not the only ones to be considered. The selection of another three plays for analysis would certainly yield different results, which brings me finally to certain inescapable conclusions I have had to reach in the course of writing this essay: that it is unavoidably incomplete and that it is not innocent. The choices I have made and the angle from which I have viewed them neces-sarily intervene in my experience of the three play texts, as well as in the reader's experience of my text. This is not an apology but rather a friendly warning to beware of even fractured narratives, for in the end, they too are still narratives.

NOTES

This essay was written during a group research project sponsored by the University of Califor-nia Humanities Research Institute (Irvine, California). I want to thank the HRI, as well as the project directors, Professor Diana Taylor (Dartmouth College) and Professor Juan Villegas (UC/Irvine) for the privilege of that experience. My work there reflects a continuous and sometimes difficult process of rethinking ideas and beliefs; I consider it to be inconclusive and incomplete, only the first part of a long-term research commitment. Although I am indebted to all my colleagues there, I want especially to thank Sue-Ellen Case, whose presence and challenges have left a lasting impression.

1 Important contemporary women playwrights who began writing before then are, to name but a few, Luisa Josefina Hernández, Elena Garro, Maruxa Vilalta, and Marcela del Río. Their not being included here in no way reflects on their work or prestige; it is more a question of their not serving the purposes of this research as well as those playwrights who are discussed. Still, one has to underscore that whatever their importance, they remain numerically a reduced presence on the Mexican stage. The Mexican critic and playwright Guillermo Schmidhuber, in his valuable study *El teatro mexicano en cierne 1922–1938,* shows to what extent women in the 1920s and 1930s played a key role in the development of modern Mexican theatre — as actresses, playwrights, and patrons; for example, María Teresa Montoya, Virginia Fábregas, Teresa Farías de Issasi, Catalina D'Erzell, María Luisa Ocampo, Amalia de Castillo Ledón. He notes, however, that their influence was short-lived, and has not been repeated since.

2 Rosario Castellanos died tragically, by electrocution, in 1974. The other two playwrights selected for discussion here, Sabina Berman and Carmen Boullosa, are perhaps the bright-est stars among Mexican women playwrights who are continuing the kind of work Castel-lanos began. Other stars on the rise are Esther Krauze, Estela Leñero, and Leonor Azcárate. The director Jesusa Rodríguez is certainly a shining presence, having won international recognition for her directorial work in opera, and outstanding theatre experiments.

3 For further readings on Mexican feminism, refer to Anna Macías, *Against All Odds;* to

individual issues of the feminist magazine *Fem* (now defunct); as well as to the collection *Fem. 10 años de periodismo feminista*.

4 Although the bibliography on this topic is extensive, Diana Fuss, in *Essentially Speaking*, summarizes and critiques it quite thoroughly and convincingly. The bibliography offers ample sources for further consultation.

5 Translation of works by Castellanos are taken from Ahern, *A Rosario Castellanos Reader*. All other translations are mine.

6 See Franco, *Plotting Women*, 129–46. The now classic study of La Malinche, as cultural discourse and practice, is to be found in Octavio Paz, *The Labyrinth of Solitude* (*El laberinto de la soledad*), first written in 1950. Also see Sandra M. Cypess's *La Malinche in Mexican Literature*, which offers a comprehensive and very perceptive reading of this theme in writings by both men and women. The classic study of the religious and political cult to the Virgin of Guadalupe is Jacques Lafaye, *Quetzalcoatl et Guadalupe*.

7 See, for example, the comments of Hernán Vidal in "Introduction."

8 Two of Mexico's foremost contemporary "chroniclers" have recorded what those events were like: Elena Poniatowska in *Nada nadie*, and Carlos Monsiváis in *Entrada libre*. A recounting as told by feminists who participated (especially the Seminario Marxista-Leninista Feminista de Lesbianas) is in "Nosotras le entramos parejo con las costureras."

Jean Franco
A Touch of Evil: Jesusa Rodríguez's Subversive Church

❑

In September 1991 Jesusa Rodríguez and the singer/composer/pianist Lili-ana Felipe were about to open an independent theatre in Mexico City. The theatre on Calle Madrid in Coyoacán is named La Capilla, since the re-modeled building was formerly the private chapel of a vast old house. It would be hard to imagine a more evocative and provocative site for a the-atre directed by Jesusa Rodríguez, who has often targeted the Church with her irreverent and cutting satire. Furthermore, the house and its chapel once belonged to Salvador Novo, a major avant-garde and gay poet. After his death in 1975, Novo's heir rented the house to Jesusa and Felipe, who opened a bar, restaurant, and cabaret called El Hábito (a nice pun on the monastic "habit"). They decided to turn the chapel into an eighty-seat chamber theatre that would be independent of official funding, which is unusual for Mexico.

Independence is necessary for Jesusa, whose political and religious satire usually touched the raw nerves of nationalism and religious morality. De-spite a timid liberation movement in the sixties and the early seventies and an active if divided feminist movement, Mexico is still, on the surface at least, a very staid society. The Church, once persecuted by the State, is rapidly regaining its power and control over moral issues. Criticism of the government is still conducted within fairly narrow bounds. In 1991 a well-known journalist, Manu Dornbierer, was dismissed from the newspaper *Excelsior* for her overtly critical articles. The popular actor Hector Suárez was fired from Televisa, the television monopoly independent of the gov-ernment, for crossing the boundaries of the permissible. Meanwhile, Cath-olic bishops must have gained a great deal of confidence after the Pope's 1985 visit, which drew massive crowds to an open-air mass. After keeping a low profile for half a century, the bishops issued a declaration just before the 1991 elections saying that it would be a sin not to vote. This was rightly considered by more thoughtful observers to be motivated less by enthusiasm for democracy than by the promise of victory for the government and right-wing parties who would be trusted to keep abortion illegal and protect "Catholic" morality.

Satire is a minority opinion and this is precisely what gives Jesusa's performances their power. She plays devil to God. She countered the fantastic circus of the papal visit by protesting in the name of the Aztec mother of the gods, Coatlicue, whose terrifying statue stands in petrified and isolated splendor in the National Anthropological Museum. Coatlicue is one of many creations that embody the rejected, the excluded, the unmentionable. The Aztec "mother of the gods" looks anything but motherly. Her mouth is fanged and serpents are entwined around her body. For a long time, the statue seemed to epitomize the "inhuman" Aztec civilization, though in fact it was a symbolic map of a cosmogony and religion which it is difficult to personalize.

When Jesusa's Coatlicue speaks out, however, she mocks both cultural nationalism and the motives of the papal visit and even knocks the centenary celebration. Coatlicue, a neglected, nagging "mother of all Mexicans," demands to know why "nobody printed 500,000 posters to publicize me, why nobody ever built me a mammadrome and a mammarymobile; why they never invented machinery to allow me to kiss the ground at the airport [. . .] despite the fact that time is ripe for an ecological religion" (my translation, Rodríguez 402). Calling for a national crusade, Coatlicue summons the National Humanities and National Arts Councils (thus clearly indicating where the money comes from) to clarify whether the centennial celebrations are not-for-profit or for-profit and finally rallies her supporters with the untranslatable slogan: "*¡se ve, se siente,* Coatlicue *está presente! ¡se ve, se siente,* Coatlicue *es diferente!*" Or, in my rough translation, "Coatlicue, Coatlicue, goddess of the Freaky."

Jesusa takes national and universal icons and endows them with a life of their own; these icons include the devil, Don Giovanni, Coatlicue, and the Malinche (the indigenous woman who was the temporary mistress and permanent interpreter of Cortés and is widely regarded as the symbol not only of treachery but of the capitulation and degradation of the indigenous). These figures are clearly on the side of what has traditionally been considered as evil or sinister. When Jesusa presented *Donna Giovanni,* in which the entire (mostly female) cast played the Don, it was not intended as a feminist response to a macho figure but rather as a celebration of the

Figure 1. Jesusa Rodríguez, top, and Liliana Felipe in Rodríguez's adaptation of Oskar Panizza's *The Council of Love*. The play, published in Bavaria in 1894 and immediately banned, also caused an uproar in Mexico City in the 1980s. Photo courtesy of Jesusa Rodríguez.

Figure 2. Here Jesusa Rodríguez, left, depicts the devil in *The Council of Love*, appearing opposite an actor playing Christ. In her adaptation, the devil rails against the horrors of censorship. Photo courtesy of Jesusa Rodríguez.

libertine in all of us. In her adaptation of Oskar Panizza's *The Council of Love*, she plays the devil with such gusto that you suspect she is in love with him.

The Council of Love was originally written to mock Bavarian society, in which, despite or because of the Catholic religion, prostitution and syphilis flourished. In Jesusa's adaptation the play becomes both a comment on the AIDS crisis and on freedom of speech, with the many new forms of censorship and self-censorship.

Panizza's play is set in 1485 when syphilis first appeared in Europe. The drama was published in Zurich in 1894 and was immediately banned by the Bavarian government. The author was imprisoned. In Panizza's original, the beautiful young girl, Syphilis, is born of the union of Satan and Salomé. The devil, who is recruited by the Holy Family to help them regain their power and prestige, promises them that Syphilis is the solution. She spreads a poison so gruesome that people will "be able to pick one of their own bones right out of their bodies. They'll smell it and then they'll throw it, in horror, right across the room. That's when they'll start getting religious. Religious, religious, and more religious" (Panizza 129).

As Jesusa explains in the interview that follows, Panizza's play proved to be as unpalatable in the 1980s as it was in the 1890s. Censorship and prohibitions are still in place, despite the prevailing impression that we are living in a "free world." That is perhaps why Jesusa is never simply content with adaptation but allows her characters to develop and change according to particular audiences or environments. When she gave a solo performance in English for a New York audience at the Theatre for the New City (1987), the devil kept his horns, his bloodstained mouth, and wings covered with cobwebs and graffiti but at times he was also one of Macbeth's witches, and at times a trickster. Naked as only an archangel can be naked, the devil crouches at one point like Rodin's "Thinker" on top of a pedestal that later turns out to be a toilet. The toilet is surrounded by this devil's adepts, whom she names as (among others) Reagan, Pinochet, and, of all people, Grotowski, each represented as a paper dunce cap.

With scatological gusto, the witch devil drinks her own potion, shits powerfully, and produces an offspring — a blond doll that she immediately baptizes Barbie, as a tribute to Klaus Barbie. The devil as Mother nurses her child and slaves over a washboard, though Barbie turns out to be a nasty little creature, a true child of the age of mechanical reproduction who can mass-produce itself. When Barbie tries to strangle her maker, the devil turns executioner and tries to guillotine the doll, finally chopping her in pieces to begin the experiment anew.

The remarkable thing about these performances is not only their polymorphous nature, their infinite and baroque metamorphoses, not even the gusto with which Jesusa dances, moves, sings, speaks, mimes, but how she uses her body. She is not so much nude as naked, and it is a nakedness that gives the body a power of expression that we normally associate with the face alone. She plays the body like a virtuoso — dancing feet in tennis shoes suddenly imitate Chaplin's stuttering shuffle, hips undulate invitingly only to sag suddenly with age.

In the program notes for the 1987 Pepsico Summerfare, at which she and her company, the Divas, performed *Donna Giovanni,* Jesusa wrote, "We are constantly threatened by the vengeful thunderbolt of a world that prefers the sordid tranquility of boredom to the harrowing splendor of rebellion, of a society that prefers to be immobile rather than transgress." The words sound grandiloquent but they remind us that transgression is not an empty concept though pluralism may have changed the boundaries in ways which are not yet completely clear to us. In the interview that follows, which I recorded in August 1991, Jesusa reminds us that censorship is still something the theatre must confront and identify, whether it is the censorship exercised by majority "public opinion" polls on minorities or the careless sabotage of depoliticized bureaucracies. Far from feeling intimidated by the

reach of the self-censored media, she paradoxically sees this global extension as bearing the seeds of weakness and self-destruction.

In a country in which shame and decorum cement public life, Jesusa is
shameless and unafraid. When the presidents of Latin America met in 1992
in Guadalajara, Jesusa put on a presidential cabaret in El Hábito in which
some notoriously macho presidents sprang out of their closets and danced
cheek to cheek. The fearless mockery of politics and religion is her great
strength. Her cabaret, which adjoins her new theatre and helps support it,
celebrates eclecticism — whether sexual or cultural. You can hear contemporary music, jazz, rancheras, tango in her theatre, but most of all it is a place
to enjoy what elsewhere in Mexico may never be mentioned.

FRANCO: Could you tell us something of your career in the theatre and
also why you are so interested in the adaptation of classical texts?

JESUSA: The classics are a basic necessity like corn but they can also be
used as pre-texts or points of departure. Eleven years ago I staged and
directed my first work. My first work as a stage director was a version of
Macbeth in the Teatro de la Capilla in 1980. Although I had a very great
interest in theatre at that time, in those days I gave particular priority to the
visual aspects. I was more interested in painting and sculpture, that is, in the
visual image than in the text. So when I started my career in theatre it was
with this in mind. Afterwards, I got to know Julio Castillo, who was a
theatre director and was also greatly attracted to the image. During my first
five years in the theatre, working with him, my interest in the image grew.
Then when I directed my first play, *Macbeth,* in 1980, I realized that I was
absolutely unprepared to deal with the text and that, in fact, the text became
the support for the image and took second place to it.

Afterwards we began to work on other things, for instance the homage to
Frida Kahlo which we also put on in this theatre around 1983, before the
boom of interest in her work and which was based on her paintings. Then
we — that is a group known as Divas — did *Don Giovanni* (*Donna Giovanni*)
with an all-woman cast and we placed special emphasis on the visual aspect
of the work. [Particular scenes reproduced the composition of Mannerist
paintings. — ED.] What I tried to do with a text like this, which is familiar
to us all, an opera that everybody knows from memory, was to emphasize
the visual. That is why we used actresses and not singers, because the entire
emphasis was on the visual; of course it was also placed on acting but it was
still principally a theatre of the image. Afterwards, of course, I began to
realize that I needed to enlarge my aims in the theatre and around 1980 I
began to write satire for the cabaret.

I began to create sketches and as I began to write that kind of text, I became interested in the power of satire. And so I began to discover authors who influenced me greatly—for example, Jonathan Swift, because when you read of the reality of Ireland in the eighteenth century it seems identical to present-day Ireland. Perhaps there were fewer inhabitants but the poverty is still the same.

FRANCO: Although Swift was a misogynist.

JESUSA: But very strong and intelligent. His satire is very sharp. I also find it incredible that [Lucas] Cranach could create such bold images, such violent satires of the pope which would not be permissible today. It is as if we had lost some of our powers of expression.

FRANCO: It's surprising that the Church is recovering such a lot of strength in Mexico given the nineteenth-century reform movement and the Mexican Revolution which deprived the Church of much of its economic base.

JESUSA: When I referred to that kind of satire, I was thinking primarily of how it related to the development of our kind of theatre. For at first, we had a satiric theatre which was based primarily on the image. Now we are also trying to emphasize the text. I now feel that the theatre of images is incomplete just as the theatre that is purely textual is incomplete. There has to be a melding of the two. That is why now I am interested in working more with the text.

All this happened when *The Council of Love* fell into our hands. I considered it a classical text and indeed it is a classical satire, a work of genius. It was recommended to me in Paris in 1983 and it stuck in my mind, although I didn't read it until 1985. I came upon it accidentally when a friend of mine published it in Barcelona. When we read it we were fascinated. It seemed so extraordinary that we felt we had to make it known despite its religious emphasis — otherwise is would be like refusing to stage a work like *Macbeth* just because a usurper had seized the presidency. That would be terrible, wouldn't it? It was not the plot or the religion that were so important to us, but rather the manner in which the play represented the problem of corruption in the Church, in this case the Catholic Church. We were enthusiastic about the play but we reflected a great deal on when would be an appropriate time to stage it, and of course when we staged it we knew that for certain groups of fanatics, it was not an easy play to see. That is why we took so much care. We staged it in a very small theatre because we were not trying to upset any particular group, only to present a play that was unknown in Mexico. However, there was a terrible scandal because it happened to coincide with the Museum of Modern Art exhibition of a painting of the Virgin of Guadalupe with the face of Marilyn Monroe. That is when the scandal erupted. The people who censured the exhibition also threatened to close down the play.

FRANCO: Exactly what happened?

JESUSA: They [right-wing Church supporters] put pressure on us and made threats. Naturally we appealed to the Mexican Committee on Freedom of Expression. They organized a series of festivals and events. The theatre received support from all the intellectuals and even the government offered security guards. And it was never taken off the stage. But what does have repercussions is the history of such events.

Referring to what you asked about censorship, I believe that here in Mexico it is more a matter of self-censorship than censorship. You actually realize that unless you censor yourself you are not going to please everybody and they will put pressure on you. Also, there is the fear of taking risks, or risking one's economic position. I have observed that fundamentally people are more afraid of doing something, of taking risks and seeing what happens.

FRANCO: Do you think that inhibits criticism?

JESUSA: Yes, although it doesn't apply to me. I have no desire to censor myself at all, and cannot. However, what I would like to stress is that there is a path that is not being taken out of fear and that this path can take us a long way. Take Coatlicue for instance. Mesoamerican civilization exists but nobody touches it. It is like the exterminating angel. It is there and nobody deals with it because it is like a taboo; something prevents us from dealing with it. We can discuss the conquest. As everybody knows, we can go back that far. We can do plays, films, and write books on the conquest, but going further back is seen as too much of a challenge and seems impossible.

FRANCO: It is like a petrified myth.

JESUSA: I believe that if we take the difficult topics — religion and politics — to the limit, we encounter the same taboo. We don't deal with them, not because one could be attacked or censored but because there is a fear of following this particular path. I can assure you that it was very unpleasant when we were threatened in our own theatre. The actors were afraid of being beaten up on stage and that something horrible would happen to them; security guards at the door frisked the spectators as they came in. It is horrible, but in the end, considering *The Council of Love* as an artistic production, it was an extremely valuable experience for the actors. When they spoke their words, they did so with absolute conviction because in the morning paper you could read about the problem which Panizza discusses in that play — censorship. The devil has an extraordinary speech in which he says, "To think and not to be able to express our thoughts is the worst form of torture." And to say this on the stage when the problem was being discussed in the newspapers gave the work a much greater power than when it was staged before the threat.

FRANCO: There are, of course, taboo subjects in the United States and not only Mexico — the flag, the national anthem. My question is whether self-censorship takes different forms in subsidized theatre and in commercial theatre in Mexico?

JESUSA: The place where I believe there is the maximum amount of self-censorship is in television, in Televisa. Censorship feeds the work of those people. They even distribute lists of words that cannot be spoken on television, situations that cannot be shown, and of course ideas that cannot be conveyed. Television is the source. Panizza said that self-censorship is the syphilis of the brain; if we can indicate one virus that brutally contaminates freedom of expression it is effectively television. Television offers us a varnished life in which nothing happens, nothing is noticed, in which it is not possible to speak of politics or of human beings, or of welfare or of thousands of human problems because according to the people who run it, those are not human problems at all and therefore do not exist. I believe that this creates a huge reservoir of mental sickness which contaminates everything, including commercial theatre. Because commercial theatre attracts the same public as television it is television that sets the standards for these theatres. So they bring warmed-up Broadway shows or very harmless or stupid plays which are not at all permissive and which have the same list of censored words as television. And on the other hand there are subsidized theatres in which, unfortunately, the bureaucrat who accepts the projects will not take risks; for example, the Museum of Modern Art closed its doors during the Virgin of Guadalupe scandal. Afterwards it was clear that the bureaucrats were being very careful about certain exhibitions which had religious content. They didn't want problems. This is what censorship is about — it is about not getting involved, not getting into problems.

I believe there is a third type of censorship, a third violence that is just as terrible; that is censorship that comes from indifference and neglect. It is a form of censorship which makes people suddenly say that this can't be done because of the trade union rule, because the stagehands don't want to do it because they are not interested. And this too is a terrible limitation in our work. All the theatres in Mexico are run by that horrible organization called the Federation of Technical Workers. They have thousands of people who do nothing at all, and it is gradually killing theatre.

FRANCO: How do you avoid this problem?

JESUSA: Basically I have tried to work less and less in state-subsidized or commercial theatres. That is the idea behind my present project, to have a small chamber theatre which cannot easily survive on its own since there are only eighty seats. It is not a commercially viable theatre but we have a bar and the bar subsidizes the small theatre.

FRANCO: And is there a regular company?

JESUSA: There is a nucleus. I prefer people to do as they wish. I don't like to ask people to work only with me. I don't say, if you work here you can't work anywhere else, because on the contrary people ought to have difference experiences. Nevertheless, there is a working group, a production group of people who write for this theatre. And we also call on certain actors. But when as at the present moment I have to work for the City Theatre [Rodríguez was stage designer for *La sunamita,* an opera written by her sister, Marcela] I suffer because I have to put up with technicians who do not work, with bureaucracies who think they're doing a favor if they lend you a nail and who don't care about the work. I have reached the conclusion that the only way I can do what I want to do without making any compromises is to have a theatre of my own, and keep it going any way I can because anything else is just a lie; it means eating shit.

FRANCO: What do you see as the function of theatre at the present time, given the small public and the global reach of television?

JESUSA: I have had this question come from many people, people who ask what is the purpose of theatre, how far can it go. I feel all the time that working in the theatre is something like working in the kitchen; it is here and not in the living room where the salad is mixed. I would put cinema in the living room.

FRANCO: So theatre is a kind of laboratory or kitchen.

JESUSA: I see it as a small seed, a form of expression for a few people which afterward may grow into something bigger. For me, theatre resembles one of those laboratory experiments that people don't know about until it suddenly results in a really outstanding discovery. Nobody knows about the researcher who had worked on the discovery. For me this is what is attractive about the theatre. It is very human, a very organic form of life. I remember an example that made a deep impression on me: On the day that Jorge Negrete [a popular Mexican singer] died, Fleming, who discovered penicillin, also died. Jorge Negrete's death monopolized the headlines but there was only a tiny paragraph about the death of Fleming. This is amazing. Someone who managed to save the lives of millions with his invention is hardly mentioned in the newspaper. But this is the relationship between cinema, television, and the theatre. The theatre for me is that small paragraph that we all know represents something very strong, an achievement that has involved an enormous amount of effort before it reaches the newspapers.

FRANCO: In your work there is a lot of nudity. It's strange that in film nudity doesn't mean very much but in theatre it can still shock.

JESUSA: That is because the actor is there in person.

FRANCO: I'd like to hear more about your plans for an independent theatre, whether you intend to go on working in the same way, crossing the limits of what is permitted.

JESUSA: My great ambition is to be able to devote myself to this dream and inaugurate a small laboratory here, a chamber theatre in which I would begin to work more closely with the text. Liliana [Felipe] and I are going to begin with a show that we have been planning for some time which is a pre-Hispanic show and which will have its premiere in about a month and a half. What we would like is, on the one hand, to approach Mesoamerican aesthetics rather freely and fearlessly, rather as I did with Coatlicue. I have always wanted to get closer to that world and to that aesthetic, which is so different and yet which we see all the time. It is strange because Coatlicue is always on the entrance tickets to the museum, photographed in journals all over the place, but never becomes part of daily life. It is something that is already very distant from us.

FRANCO: A museum piece?

JESUSA: It occurred to me to construct a puppet Coatlicue and get inside her to make her dance. When I designed the puppet so that I could move the serpents all over the place and make her hearts beat, the response of the public astonished me very much because I never expected people to open up their hearts. They almost saw her as a Mother; they wanted to touch her and throw powder on her. That means there is a clear but repressed consciousness in those people. It is something that is in our roots and which we know but which we then leave in books and museums.

FRANCO: Something that is very mythified.

JESUSA: The first time I presented it was in front of a mass public. It was in the National Concert Hall during a festival, so people came in for free. They were ordinary people, people of every kind. What struck me right from the start was that the public watched it seriously but only gradually began to warm up, and at the end they were shouting. I have very seldom seen such a reaction from the public, who generally prefer to remain silent at this kind of performance. But on the contrary, the audience's enthusiasm was overwhelming. That is why I want very much to deal with this Mesoamerican world without being too solemn about it and without those attitudes that all this is sacred, all this is untouchable. I would like to see the humorous side of the forms, and the texts that are very funny — the playfulness, the sound of Nahuatl, which is so liquid, and things of this kind. We are not interested in exploring it from the archeological point of view or putting on a didactic show — that's why we call it a pre-Hispanic cabaret so that it will be less solemn. Coatlicue seems a little like a Mexican mother whose children have gone away. Nobody is left and she doesn't know what to do in the house. It is very difficult for a woman to go through this stage and so the idea was to use this situation but attach it to the mythology of Coatlicue. Of course her children are the 400 stars that have left her alone in the house which is the universe and the only thing she's thinking about is how to sell the house.

FRANCO: In the BBC film *Love and Power* you said that you were not that interested in gender differences, and I understand that by that you meant you weren't interested in the didactic aspects of feminism. At the same time you invite Chabela Vargas to your cabaret and give support to these women singers of another generation. Could you speak a little about women.

JESUSA: For me it has been almost a natural thing since I went to the preparatory school. My generation was one in which women began to be in the majority in many disciplines. I realized that we were three women and five men in the preparatory class and when I spoke to the boys most of them were there out of necessity whilst the women were there because they wanted to be. The boys had to have a career and the women were there because in defiance of their parents they had decided on a career.

I entered the *preparatoria* around 1980 and it was clear that women were pursuing careers and they were in the majority and were doing what they wanted to do. For me it was natural when I began my drama course to relate to the many women who were working in the theatre. At the same time I think there was an almost natural reaction to the fact that the theatre was very much a man's thing and this was the impression I had. I looked at the scenery and I asked myself why it was always made of cardboard or cloth. Why couldn't there be a scenery of rocks, or tree trunks or leaves? Why are they always made of paper or always of plastic? Years later I began to realize that this was a question that related to the education of girls and boys — that there are materials for boys and materials for girls and that this affects the stage designs.

I also think that Mexico has been a very gay country — gay directors, painters, actors, stage designers. I believe that our highest representatives of "machismo" are gay. Our grandmothers were lesbians. It's very striking but when you begin to think about it it's true. It would be interesting to know if the structure of Mexico has been a gay culture ever since the beginning — ever since pre-Hispanic times.

FRANCO: It has been taboo to mention this gay culture.

JESUSA: The absurdity of referring to it as a closet culture is that just the opposite seems to have been the case. The audience always loved gay singers. Juan Gabriel is a gay singer but that is no different from the past when gay singers were very much admired by the Mexican public. It is very natural but nobody says it and everybody knows it. Everyone knows who was gay and who wasn't and everyone knows about the grandmother of Mexican cinema and the great actresses that were formidable women and everyone knew they were gay. This is Mexico. It has always had a culture that was gay in many ways.

Another important change in recent years has been a strong reaction on the part of women against specialized division of labor. Perhaps this difference between the way men and women work existed before but went unnoticed. For instance, there is the relationship of Frida Kahlo and Diego Rivera. She was devalued and today, on the other hand, nobody would dare to compare their work. The work is not comparable. And nobody says that Diego is greater than Frida or vice versa, although I think at the time they did see her as a poor thing, an appendix to Diego.

But I feel that I belong to a different era. I found that working with women was a very different experience. For instance, if you and I go into the kitchen and start making a salad I am quite sure that you are not going to tell me you don't want to cut up the lettuce because your job is to wash the radishes and I am not going to tell you that I won't disinfect the vegetables because I came here to toss the salad and make the salad dressing.

When I came into the theatre I realized that the prevailing system was masculine. Everyone had their own job. "I am a stage designer so don't ask me to do anything that is not my job and I am an author and you're the director — so you solve the problem, you're the designer, so do it." That was not my way because I felt that the theatre was more like a kitchen.

FRANCO: And you do everything?

JESUSA: It's all the same to me whether I sweep the stage or direct the play. They are both necessary and if I can do what is necessary at any moment, I'll do it.

And I believe this is the kind of thing you find more among women's groups. It's natural. But not for a man. Because in a man there is the tendency to define responsibilities and not to trespass on someone else's terrain. This desire to change ways of working motivated me a great deal and naturally there developed a form of work which mostly involved women, though without excluding men or saying that they could not work in our group. Because naturally I believe that the ideas of a patriarchal society or of a feminine ideal have nothing to do with men and women. Margaret Yourcenar put it very well when she said that any woman who did not have masculine attributes and any man who did not have feminine ones would be useless. We all have those attributes. I have never accepted the idea that this is a man and so he doesn't interest me. And I understand the idea of what is feminine work or a feminine tendency in work in the sense that it follows different rules, just as masculine work does. I identify myself much more with feminine work and I believe that I feel this closeness to women but there is no direct relationship.

Underlying all this, there is the fact that art always comes up against conventional morals. That is art and without this liberation, art cannot advance. So I believe that as an artist one cannot spend one's time thinking of social canons and rules of conventional behavior. Art is always opposed to the establishment, and if the establishment is very revolutionary, the next day your own work will deny it. Art questions and overturns patterns of feeling, all the norms that regulate political, social, and everyday life behavior.

FRANCO: Actresses have often been marginalized in the societies of the past.

JESUSA: Because they don't conform to an ideal of womanhood. But in answer to your question, I find any form of sexual sectarianism difficult to take. I believe that artistic work cannot be governed by a single idea and that one is always questioning.

FRANCO: And this even applies to feminism?

JESUSA: Yes, because I think that any sectarianism—nationalism, for instance—is useful at a particular moment but the following day it might be useless and we have to jettison it. I think that we often fall in love with an idea and the idea is a dead one and we are still in love with it. If there is anything interesting about theatre it is that every single day one starts anew. It is not easy to repeat something or to put the tape back on the machine. So if you no longer adhere to something, it is difficult to go on representing it on stage. Every day you are obliged to rethink it. You cannot simply get away with saying, "I don't believe in the importance of this text but I'll do it anyway." You can tell when an actress really believes in the importance of what she is representing and when she doesn't. The same thing happens in everyday life. It is possible that some woman who has fought hard for feminism like Marta Acevedo [an editor of the feminist journal *Debate feminista*] who was a die-hard feminist, now says, I've had enough. I don't

Figure 3. The puppet of
Coatlicue — the Aztec
mother of the gods —
appears as the center-
piece of Jesusa
Rodríguez's pre-
Hispanic cabaret.
Photo courtesy of
Jesusa Rodríguez.

want to hear any more about feminism. And she is able to criticize it
without betraying its basic principles. That is the only way forward. I think
it horrible when people cling to what once fascinated them. That is why I
believe theatre is so interesting, because it can never stay in one place.

COATLICUE'S MAMMARY TOUR

The story of Coatlicue was recorded by Bernardino de Sahagún in the
sixteenth century. She was the mother of the warrior god Huichilopochtli
who sprang fully formed as a warrior from her womb. According to Sahagún's account, she was the mother of a tribe of Indians and was sweeping
one day in the hills of Coatepec when the hair of a feather floated down. She
put it under her clothes and as a result became pregnant which caused great
indignation among her children, one of whom led an expedition to kill her.
The plot failed, thanks to the embryo who guided the counterattack. The
statue of Coatlicue excavated from the Sacred Precinct of Tenochtitlán (the
site on which the conquerors built Mexico City) is an enormous stone piece
which writers such as Octavio Paz see as exemplifying the sacred horror and

"otherness" of Aztec civilization. The statue has nothing that we could identify as motherly. The divided head is fanged. There are claws, hands of flayed skin, and a skirt of serpents. It is precisely this "sacred terror" that Jesusa sets out to demystify.

Following the excerpt from Jesusa's piece *La gira mamal de la Coatlicue* (Coatlicue's Mammary Tour), published by *Debate feminista,* is my free translation. It is difficult to translate not only because of its inventive language but also because it refers to several topical events—the mysterious theft in 1985 of pre-Columbian antiquities from the Archaeological Museum, causing a major scandal, and the Pope's visit to Mexico which, in spite of the strict separation of religion and state, was an event of much pomp, attracting multitudes. Coatlicue's complaint is directed against many targets: it is an attack on the hype surrounding the Papal visit; an attack on the relegation of the indigenous past to the Museum; and against the celebration of the quincentenary of the "discovery." Finally, in her litany of place names, all of which come from Nahuatl, she changes the word endings from "masculine" to "feminine" and vice versa, satirizing the vagaries of translation and linguistic reappropriation.

¡Óiganme bien, mexicanos, mexiquenses, mejicones, mejidatarios y extranjenses! Yo soy el origen del origen, y a nadie se le ha ocurrido irme a recibir al aeropuerto. A diferencia de otros ídolos, nunca se me han hecho imprimir 500,000 carteles, jamás se me constuyó un mamódromo ni se me proporcionó un humilde mamamóvil, nunca me facilitaron la maquinaria adecuada para poder besar el piso del aeropuerto, nunca he hecho una gira, ya no se diga a Chalco, ni siquiera a Chapultepec, a Tlatelolco, nunca he realizado ese hermoso sueño de realizar una gira mamal con carácter puramente evangelizador, sobre todo ahora que tanta falta les hace una religion ecologista. Pero óiganlo bien hijos desagradecidos, a diferencia de otros yo los sigo queriendo porque una madre nunca olvida, porque aunque le soben la panza al Buda, o se vayan tras el Gurú, o se gasten la quincena en medallitas y rosarios, o anden todo el día de La Ceca a La Meca, seguirán siendo mis hijos. Además y los traje al mundo y ahí está la diferencia, porque madre sólo hay una y esa ¡ingratos!, soy yo, aquí y en China.

Y ya para finalizar hago un llamado a los demás dioses, que si bien se hallan devaluados teologicamente, van muy al alza en el mercado del arte:

¡A mí, Huichilopochtli, Coyolchauqui, Chalchiutlicue y Tescatlipoca! Iniciemos una Cruzada Nacional para que este pueblo recupere sus orígenes.

¡Unete Tlatelolca!, ¡únete Xochimilca!, ¡únete Iztapalapo!, ¡únete Oaxtepeco!, ¡únete Tlaxcalteca!

¡Unete Cato-lico!

Y por último exijo al Consejo Nacional para la Cultura y las Artes que defina de una vez por todas si el Quinto Centenario, es quinto, o es centernario.

¡Se ve, se siente, Coatlicue está presente!

¡Se ve, se siente, Coatlicue es diferente!

Listen to me carefully, Mexicans, Mexarians, Mexers, Mexants, and resident aliens! I am the origin of origins. But nobody has ever met me at the airport. Unlike the other idol, I can't get them to print 500,000 posters to advertise me. They haven't built my mammarydome; they have yet to come up with a machine which will allow me to kiss the floor of the airport arrival lounge. Nobody's organized an official visit to Chapultepec or Tlatelolco, let alone Chalco. I've never been able to realize my beautiful dream of a mammary tour—for the purpose of carrying on my evangelical mission, of course. And yet the time is ripe for an ecological religion. Listen, ungrateful offspring! Unlike these other idols I still love you. Even though you rub the Buddha's belly button, even though you spend your money on medals and rosaries and even though you'd search for Mecca from here to eternity, you'll always be my children. That's what makes me different. Because there's only one mother here or in China and that mother is me.

To conclude, I call on all the other gods because even though from my point of view they're worthless, the art market is bullish on them.

Huichilopochtli, Coyolchauqui, Chalchiutlicue, and Tescatlipoca! I call for a National Crusade to recover our national origins.

Tlatelolca, Xochimilca, Iztapalapo, Oaxtepeco, Tlaxcalteca unite!

Unite Cato Lico!

And as my last word, I demand that the National Humanities and Arts Councils issue a statement on the Quincentenary to tell us whether it is going to be worth a cent or a celebration.

Up with difference down with pluralism!

Coatlicue, Coatlicue, stands up for the Freaky!

Judith Bettelheim
*Ethnicity, Gender, and Power: Carnaval
in Santiago de Cuba*

❑

INTRODUCTION

My aim in this essay is to provide information relative to specific aspects of
Cuban history and to propose reciprocal associations within Carnaval culture that may clarify both Carnaval and other festival celebrations. How,
within the communal act of Carnaval, and its antecedents such as the parading of *cabildos* (a neighborhood mutual aid association), does power get
expressed either by ethnic groups or by ruling governments? The history of
Carnaval is a history of negotiations, of constant shifts and nuances. The
institution of Carnaval has created its own internal flow. During slavery,
when power discrepancies were greatest, reports describe "wild" celebrations of African Caribbeans. Today, control has been established, but does
ethnicity still play a major role in Carnaval? Carnaval is an expression of
shifting power negotiations among various aspects of Cuban society.

  25 July 1989, Santiago de Cuba. Again, as in 1987, I sat on a folding chair
in the bleachers next to the judges' section of the reviewing stand. The
Carnaval parade of 1989 had begun some three hours earlier. It was 11 P.M.
and a courtly entourage began approaching along the parade route lined by
cordoned-off spectators. The parade would end in the wee hours of July 26,
commemorating Castro's attack on the Moncada barracks on 26 July 1953.
As the costumed entourage slowly walked along, the twenty or so children
in front began to quicken their pace and smile at the jury. Some appeared
somewhat shy in front of so many spectators. I smiled and wondered if a
future queen and king in the royal lineage were among them. Behind the
children strolled a small musical ensemble, five drummers, a man playing a
hoe with an iron rod, two sets of *chekere* players, and a chorus of five elders.

They were followed by a queen and king and eight court members, all costumed in a vague nineteenth-century style complete with white gloves, crowns, and curly white wigs. The group walked along slowly, commanding attention without performing any particular choreographic routine. The crowd clapped and waved. A banner embellished with the name Carabalí Isuama proclaimed their identity and encoded their history to all who know about the African heritage in Oriente province. It was obvious that this group did not need to "perform"; their mere presence in the Carnaval parade commanded attention and respect.

I had seen the Cabildo Carabalí Isuama parade before, first in June 1986 during the Festival of Caribbean Culture, sponsored by the Casa del Caribe in Santiago de Cuba, and then again during Carnaval 1987. A smaller, similar group, the Cabildo Carabalí Olugo, also paraded in 1989, during the pre-Carnaval parade known as the *desfile corta,* held on July 23. Although on that occasion only seven out of the twenty *cabildo* members marched, they too regally strolled down the parade route, accompanied by a small musical ensemble and an entourage of children. The two pairs of queens and kings wore paper crowns atop stark white ringleted wigs and their coordinated yellow-and-white and red-and-white ruffled courtly costumes were cut from a satin cloth.

In Santiago de Cuba, the Cabildo Carabalí Isuama, although registered by the 1890s under the direction of the five Baracoa brothers,[1] is actually controlled by women, who are in charge of the altar and ritual activities. These women are *miembros propietos,* or members through lineage. In former times during Carnaval and special festivals, when two *cabildos* met on the street during public performances, they performed special rituals. The first section of the performance always referred in song to their lead dancer as "the dancingest black woman of the *cabildos*" (my translation) (Nancy Pérez 16).[2] The Cabildo Carabalí Isuama still maintains a seated royalty whose lineage descends through the female line.

Although I have previously written about the courtly entourage and fancy dress style in Caribbean festivals ("Jonkonnu," "Festivals"), these Afro-Cuban groups encompass a more detailed and deeper history than other performance ensembles I had researched. And the presence in Santiago de Cuba of more than one such courtly ensemble is particularly striking. It seems that today in Santiago de Cuba *cabildo* royal authority is still respected. Rank and authority were not being "imitated" in these Carnaval performances, but rather self-authority was being publicly displayed.

In July 1991, I returned to Santiago de Cuba for Carnaval, which unfortunately was canceled due to the cost and efforts given over to the hosting of the Pan American games that summer.[3] Although the Carnaval parade itself was canceled, Carnaval-time was celebrated quietly in designated neighbor-hoods; block parties were held; residents danced to recorded music; and limited quantities of beer were available. Certain Carnaval and *folklórico* groups (this is the official Cuban designation) performed in prescheduled locations for the international battery of journalists, television cameras, and tourists. At the televised opening ceremonies for the games, held at the newly completed sports arena, the largest Carnaval *paseo* La Placita per-formed a highly stylized and choreographed routine complete with acroba-tic stunts and synchronized dancing with hoops. Previous to these opening ceremonies, I attended a week-long series of cultural performances sup-ported by the Dirección Municipal de Cultura. Entitled "Noches de Folk-lor, Magia y Música en el Santiago Panamericano," these events were di-rected at tourists and entrance tickets were sold at hotels for U.S. dollars. Out of the seven scheduled events, three were held at Afro-Cuban Focos Culturales (government-sponsored meeting halls) and others at library pa-tios and downtown theatres.

Three Afro-Cuban cultural groups were permitted to perform at these events, including the revered Tumba Francesa, led by Queen Sara Quiala Venet, who inherited her position from her grandmother Consuela "Tecla" Venet Danget, the most cherished and well-known Tumba Queen in San-tiago, who was also known as "*la Reina cantadora.*" Tecla died in March 1988 when in her late nineties.

The *cabildo* queen, who often performed publicly during festivals and performed more selectively during religious ceremonies, plays an impor-tant role in cultural life today and has a long history among Afro/a-Cubans. For example, in April 1853, during the week following Easter, Fredrika Bremer was in Havana and visited a Lucumí Cabildo (Yoruba) (183–85).[4] There were seats for the king and queen under a canopy on one side of the room. "The customary dancing was going forward in front of this seat. One woman danced alone, under a canopy supported by four people." (This performance motif is still used to honor specific individuals during a festival or *Carnaval*. I have documented priestesses of the religious society Palo Monte walking beneath and holding up the corners of a white sheet during a Carnaval performance as they hoped their power would influence the jury's deliberations.[5]) Bremer continues:

Her dancing must have given great delight, for all kinds of hand-kerchiefs were hanging about her, and a hat even, had been placed upon her head. The women danced on this occasion with each other, and the men with the men . . . These Cabildos are governed by queens, one or two, who decide upon the amusements, give tone to the society, and determine its extention. (184)

Another cultural group closely associated with the Tumba Francesa is La Tajona, also led by a queen and also related to the history of Haitian French culture in eastern Cuba.[6] Tecla's mother, Nemecia Danget, was a dancer and later queen in a turn-of-the-century Tajona group, and her aunts, Yapé and Amalia Danget, also belonged to a Tumba group whose leader was Gaudiosa Venet. In the Tumba Francesa's Foco Cultural hangs an old photograph of Nemecia, who was born a free black of Haitian descent in El Caney, now a small village on the outskirts of Santiago. Today the leader of the Tajona society is Silvina Casamayor who presided along with Sara Quiala Venet at the performance I attended in July 1991. Three dancing couples were dressed in a "Haitian style," with white dresses trimmed in red and red headties for the women and white pants and shirts with red bandannas for the men. And the two queens, who did not dance, but reigned over the performance from the sidelines, were distinguished by their fancy ruffled dresses and their special accoutrements. One kept time with a *maruga*, a hollow cone with pebbles inside and decorated with colored ribbons, while the other blew a whistle which indicated that the couples, performing a version of the contradance, should change partners.

The special role of the royal entourage and female performers in Afro-Caribbean performance history and Cuban Carnaval culture merits particular attention. Carabalí Isuama and Carabalí Olugo as well as the Tumba Francesa and the Tajona are directed by women and this leadership is passed through the female line. In addition all four societies claim a royal ancestry and are distinguished by their evocation of a royal entourage. These groups parade during Carnaval, but do not compete against the other Carnaval *congas, comparsas, and paseos.* In their costumed appearances we may be looking at an Afro-Cuban appropriation, not imitation, of a royal European style that dates to at least the early 1700s. Are these contemporary *cabildo* and society members making a political statement by maintaining their distinctive courtly style? The history of black royalty and the royal entourage is often misinterpreted, although it is crucial to an understanding of Afro-Caribbean culture and performance history.

Plantation culture and urban society provided opportunities first for Africans in the Caribbean, and later for Afro-Caribbeans, to construct organizations which underscored national solidarity, like the *cabildos de nación* discussed below. At times this national solidarity actually reflected a common African heritage, and at other times "fictive" familial relationships or quasi-kin groups were constructed and acknowledged by members of various slave communities. For example, Africans who survived the Middle Passage on the same ship became "shipmates," a term connoting strong kinship ties. This term/concept extended to imply special relationships among members of a single plantation or a special society, such as the *cabildos* or the Tumba referred to above.[7]

Festive occasions, like the Carnaval performances, often provided the opportunity for public displays of national solidarity and social cohesion constructed through kinship networks. As such, actual coronations and the public performance of a courtly entourage should be regarded as more important and powerful performative mechanisms than their usual description as quaint "folkloric performances" implies. The historical evidence from other Caribbean locations verifies my suggestion that performances by contemporary *cabildo* members who, by retaining the regalia of the courtly entourage and parading during Carnaval, are asserting their continued presence and perhaps even subversive authority in Cuban society today.

A very public, well-documented coronation took place in Antigua on 3 October 1736,[8] when, before at least 2,000 spectators, a man named Court was crowned king of the Coromantees[9] of Antigua. As John Thornton explains in his discussion of Coromantee nations in the Americas, coronations often preceded revolts, and in fact African national groups often (re)formed for such festivities prior to actual rebellions. (There is ample evidence from the British Caribbean that at least 35 percent of the rebellions occurred around the Christmas season.) Although Court was elected king he was "of considerable family at home, but not of Royal Blood" (Thornton 6), thus underscoring the importance of constructed genealogies and kinship networks. Ample documentation exists of the festivities offered by Court and his Coromantee brethren. Court was eventually arrested by island authorities who contended that a particular celebration of his authority was actually a declaration of war.

This example from Antigua is replicated throughout the African Americas. Chroniclers continuously commented on the elaborate processions of Afro-Caribbean kings and queens during public festivals.[10] In Brazil analogous performance rituals developed during the festivities associated with the feast day for Our Lady of the Rosary (Nossa Senhora do Rosario) when the elections of the kings and queens of the religious brotherhoods were held and elaborate dance dramas, known as *congadas* or *cucumbys,* accompanied the coronations (Bastide 120–25).

Just as "fictive" kinship networks were established on plantations and in religious societies, Afro-Caribbeans established solidarity networks by electing a king and queen complete with courtly entourage. Most often these royal personages performed special dances which simultaneously established their aesthetic authority — by dancing well — and challenged their white masters by "imitating" the dances of the plantocracy. After studying such performances in Jamaica (see my comments on the Fancy Dress Jonkonnu royal entourage in "Jonkonnu" and "Festivals") and in Cuba, I am increasingly convinced that these dances and their accompanying singing contain satirical commentary on the position and comportment of the plantocracy. These performances, coronations, and accompanying dances are not mere "imitations" of a European form — the quadrille or the contradance or the waltz or the polka — but are also a concise and public way to display leadership, solidarity, and self-governing systems. It is not only, as Roger Abrahams and John Szwed suggest, an ironic, diasporic reversal, as many of "these dances began as peasant dances in Europe and spread to the upper classes, only to be changed; then they were carried to the West Indies by European planters, whose slaves took them up and again changed them" (227). As such coronations and concomitant performances are flexibly responsive to planter and subsequent colonial authority. After considered viewing of these performances within more elaborate and eclectic festivals and carnivals, I can suggest that published commentary seems to miss the point. These stylized performances of a royal entourage which exist side by side with "more contemporary" performances of elaborately feathered solo female dancers or intricately choreographed couples is not inconsistent with the social commentary embedded within the festival. These presentations are distinct yet complementary, and do not negate each other's validity. The performative genre of Carnavals is accommodating while still aesthetically and socially powerful, as evinced by the response of their own community. Carnaval in Santiago de Cuba is especially hybrid and complex (see below comments on the sexy dancing women of Santiago).

Contemporary Carnaval celebrations in Santiago de Cuba, Camaguey, and other Cuban cities derive from festivals honoring various Catholic saints, accompanied by the special public processions permitted the African slave population. Today, Carnaval organization also extends and perpetuates the organization of another historic Cuban festival, the Día de Reyes celebration (Day of the Kings, Epiphany, 6 January). The following late-nineteenth-century accounts of processions in Santiago underscore African Cuban participation and the importance of royal regalia in establishing authority during public processions.

An important *comparsa* [a special festival association] of Congo ne-groes of both sexes is passing in procession along the street. They have just been paying their respects to no less a personage than his Excel-lency the Governor of Santiago. . . . The troupe is headed by a brace of blacks, who carry banners with passing strange devices, and a dancing mace-bearer. These are followed by a battalion of colonels, generals, and field-marshals, in gold-braided coats and gilded cocked-hats. Each wears a broad sash of coloured silk, a sword and enormous spurs. These are not ordinary masqueraders be it known, but grave sub-jects of his sombre majesty King Congo, the oldest and blackest of all the blacks: lawfully appointed sovereign of the coloured community (Goodman 137).

Despite the colonialist and ironic tone of this description, it is obvious that the parade was an expression of power enacted in public and aesthetic terms. This is underscored by another account:

The black *cabildos* stand out because of the luxury of the colorful dec-orations and the luxurious outfits that the queens of the different na-tions wear. The slaves' masters participate in these parades to the rhythm of songs and drums, with sounds from *almirez, botijuelas, and maracas* [brass mortars, jugs, and rattles]. They liked to decorate the bodies of the pretty black women with gold bracelets, diadems of precious stones, diamond necklaces and earrings, and exotic embroi-dered shawls. The queens in their thrones were carried on palanquins (no original source given; Juan Jerez Villarreal 142).[11]

The institutional foundation of Carnaval today is rooted in urban history, in *cabildo* history.[12] As a type of corporate club, the *cabildo* owned its own land and buildings, administered the inheritance of the slave population, disciplined its members, and provided neighborhood police services. *Ca-bildo* power often rivaled civic authority and *cabildo* public processions pro-claimed ethnic and neighborhood solidarity. Today the *cabildo* maintains a powerful institutional and sociopsychological presence whose fluctuating public presence and power is reflected in the attitudes of Carnaval orga-nizers. As the artistic director of the Carnaval group, the *paseo* La Placita, explained, La Placita is like the "*gran cabildo*" (great cabildo): "Because during Carnaval we see, in our *barrio,* the *barrio* of La Placita, the coming together of grandparents, fathers, sons, nephews, etc. from different places. There are a few of us who stay here; we are the Santiagueros. There are others who have gone to work in different places, but when the time comes, they all come back here; we meet here. Its like finding the great *cabildo* family" (Pablo Estrada Pérez, Interview, 10 March 1990).

Today, three types of Carnaval groups exist in Santiago and each is rooted in the urban history of the *cabildo*. A *conga*, the most traditional and quintessentially Santiaguero of Carnaval groups, consists of a small group of musicians playing a special *conga* rhythm on drums and metal percussion instruments (fig. 1a). Santiago *congas* are accompanied by large circular drums called *congas*, brake drums, and lead by the *corneta china*, a double-reed horn played in a staccato wail (fig. 1b). *Congas* include some costumed performers, but they do not perform a choreographed routine and most *congas* are accompanied by neighborhood residents carrying identifying flags and banners. The second type of group, the *comparsa*, includes *conga* musicians and others playing well-known Cuban tunes. Santiago *comparsas* include the famous bands of *caperos* (figs. 2a and 2b), or male performers wearing elaborately decorated capes and hats. *Caperos* do not dance, but rather run in an undulating line while forming intricate figure eight patterns. The third and newest type of group is the *paseo*. Larger and more elaborately choreographed than the *comparsa*, the *paseo* can hire different groups of musicians and seems to have more flexibility in its costuming and routines. Although a *comparsa* may include male and female paired dancers, significant female participation in Carnaval is provided by the *paseo*. *Paseos* boast between 100 and 500 male and female costumed dancers and are known for their varied costumes.

Carnaval and its relation to power centers has changed over time. These changes are best understood when put in the perspective of *cabildo* history, a fluctuating history of recognition and underground activity. Eyewitness accounts of mid-nineteenth-century Día de Reyes celebrations stress the "fantastic" costumes worn by the black participants and the fact that each parading group was led by a solitary black masquerader, dressed either as a "*tambor mayor*" (a drum major) or in military fashion. These accounts also mention that each group elected a king and queen (who were actually of the royal lineage of given *cabildos*), who often paraded beneath a parasol. *Cabildo* hierarchy and authority is apparent in the use of courtly and military dress. These and other *cabildo* regalia, such as identifying flags and certain musical instruments,[13] publicly announce the *cabildos'* capacity for social commentary and activist behavior. In public performance the authority of the *cabildo* is demonstrated in visual terms, giving ritual activity both

Figure 1. In Santiago *congas* are accompanied by large circular drums (a) and lead by a *corneta china* (b), a double reed horn played in a staccato wail. Depicted are Conga Los Hoyos musicians, summer 1989, and Comparasa San Agustín children's section, Carnaval 1989. Photo by Judith Bettelheim.

aesthetic and social actuality, comprehensible to those who can read the language of its performance.

Cabildo performances in Santiago de Cuba were never prohibited, as they were in Havana after 1884[14] where private meetings and celebrations continued. But officially the *cabildo* began losing whatever power it had accumulated. It seems that by the turn of the century, in some areas, traditional African Cuban culture was already moving toward a folklorized public presence. In the Matanzas Carnaval of 1875 the big hit was the *comparsa* called "Los Negros Congos," organized by the mulatto Andrés Solís, and composed of twenty couples performing a choreographed routine (Moliner Castañeda, *Las Comparsas*). By 1900 *comparsa* groups had also added small floats, with decorated messages from their commercial sponsors, to their public processions.

However, in Santiago some of the most African (*"el más negro"*) of the Carnaval groups, those today that are known as *congas*, continued to come into direct conflict with the authorities. On 19 June 1919 the main newspaper in Santiago printed an announcement, known as the Edict of Mayor Camacho Padro, prohibiting *"comparsas carabalies"* with African style danc-

Figure 2. In Santiago *comparsas* include the famous band of *caperos,* or male performers wearing elaborately decorated capes and hats. Shown is Comparasa Paso Franco, Carnaval 1989. Photo by Judith Bettelheim.

ing and drumming" from appearing in Carnaval (Brea and Millet 111). As a result of public outcry, journalists and others began a campaign against the Edict. For example, one of the most "African" of the Carnaval groups from the barrio of Los Hoyos dared to come out and perform, singing the following: "Camaco doesn't want African *congas;* but I am coming with my trombon; until they give me the prize . . . bon! bon! bon!" (Brea and Millet 112). This expressive popular outcry contributed to the rescinding of the edict.

By the mid-twentieth century many *cabildos* developed into and integrated with other social groups to form *comparsas.* These *comparsas,* especially those incorporating masquerades and processional street dancing, were relegated to the neighborhoods where they originated, and at times were banned.[15] After a period of sporadic outings, during the period of increased tourism in the 1930s and 1940s, they were allowed to function again. For example, in Havana in 1937 the mayor's office authorized the resurgence of *comparsas* in that year's Carnaval, since in the previous few years they had been forbidden "for the fear that their patriots would use them to . . . disturb the order" (Administración del Beruff Mendieta 6). Still, official newspapers carried sensationalistic and derogatory stories about "cult activity" and the harmful presence of African-derived societies, often accompanied by related stories of the kidnapping of white Cuban children for these activities. (The implication being that these African Cuban organizations were "cults" in the pejorative sense is maintained today.)

Many scholars and informants from Havana credit the influence of Fernando Ortiz[16] with the diminished restrictions against pre-Lenten *comparsa* outings in the capital during the 1930s. In fact, Ortiz's influence around Havana may have helped promote the continuation of African Cuban *comparsas* and the related Abakuá brotherhoods there.[17]

Today in Havana, neighboring Matanzas, and Santiago de Cuba Carnaval is celebrated from 18 to 27 July, in honor of the Revolution, with the final complete Carnaval parade held on 26 July. This date commemorates Castro's assault on the Moncada barracks in Santiago de Cuba, on 26 July 1953, which was specifically planned to coincide with traditional Carnaval in that city. It is not unusual for governments to officially change the date of carnival celebrations. In Bermuda the traditional Gombey festival used to take place between Christmas and New Year's, but today most Gombeys come out in August during the national holiday for Cup Match. Nassau's Junkanoo parade is held on Boxing Day so as to not compete with Trinidad Carnival in February. And in Luanda, Angola, carnival has been moved to 27 March, celebrating the date of South African withdrawal from Angola during the second war of liberation, 1975–76 (Birmingham 96). Breaking away from the Christian calendar and establishing a political date for carnival celebrations, in order to institute a more contemporary nationalistic and/or political caste to these celebrations, is becoming more and more common. But Cuban Carnaval history is a little more complicated, especially in Santiago de Cuba, Cuba's second largest city and the city with the largest African Cuban population.

Carnaval today does not meet stereotypical expectations of parading agit-prop-style street performances. The themes are rich, eclectic, and even raunchy. In Santiago de Cuba in both the 1987 and 1989 Carnavals, the five-year-old *paseo* Textilera, composed of factory workers and their friends, included 250 dancers whose performances of choreographed cabaret routines were accompanied by a live drum ensemble and recorded popular music. Other groups included the *paseo* La Kimona, with kimona-clad dancers and men dancing as *ninja* spirits.

During my 1989 fieldwork in Santiago de Cuba I was aware of growing controversy regarding the degree of government support given to the various Carnaval groups.[18] The newly formed *paseo* Textilera has an entire textile factory and its workers at its disposal. They have ample rehearsal space. During Carnaval 1989 I noticed that all the female dancers, perhaps more than 100, wore matching leather shoes, quite an accomplishment in Cuba where it is often difficult to find a supply of shoes at all! Why does such a new Carnaval group merit such strong government support? The position of this particular textile factory in government hierarchy most certainly affected patronage. As with *cabildo* history, the official support and recognition given to various festival groups influences not only their public visibility, but their aesthetic demeanor. Government support and recognition is as much a power issue today as it was in the nineteenth century.

Prior to the Revolution the thematic organization of each group's Carnaval performance was characterized by eclectic internationalism. Since the Revolution this international flavor has been highlighted by homages to socialist equality and subcultures within Caribbean/Latin American unity.[19]

A brief history of the *paseo* La Placita, Textilera's constant rival, will suffice as a capsule of Carnaval history. Celebrating its fiftieth anniversary in 1988, La Placita is also substantially supported. Many credit this to the neighborhood's political history. La Placita's history is rooted in Santiago's history and the *paseo's* development can be used as a case study in twentieth-century Carnaval. La Placita is located in a neighborhood famous for its revolutionary fighters and subsequent political leaders, and a neighborhood adjacent to the infamous Afro-Cuban barrio of Los Hoyos which supports its own Carnaval *conga*. In fact, *paseo* La Placita was born out of Los Hoyos as a breakaway group in 1938. During the dictatorship of Governor Gerardo Machado (1924–33) activists from barrio La Placita worked to overthrow the government and by 1931 many had affiliated with the Communist Party. General Antonio Maceo, a leader during the Ten Years War (1868–78)[20] and the Independence War of 1895, known as "Cuba Libre," was born in this barrio and his home became the meeting place for subsequent political leaders.[21] Again in 1952 two famous *placiteros,* people from the neighborhood of La Placita, Lester Rodriguez and Pedro Miret, joined Fidel Castro in storming the Moncada barracks in Santiago. The barrio became an arena of armed rebellion and today it is known as "Placita de las Martyres" in honor of its history of activism for a free Cuba.

During the political turmoil of the 1930s, Carnaval was suspended although a few groups came out in 1934 and 1935. When La Placita marched in the Carnaval parade of 1938 it was sponsored by the Eden Cigar Company, the soap company Crusellas, and the Cuban branch of Colgate-Palmolive. During this period La Placita directly competed with its neighbor *conga* Los Hoyos. On its parade route La Placita often took a detour to perform in front of the central office building of Eden cigars.

By July 1948 La Placita was fully organized as a *paseo* and paraded during Carnaval as "El Paseo Los Sultanes" which presented a panorama of "Arabic culture." The women on the float all wore face scarves and long flowing skirts, while the men wore turbans, scarves, and baggy pants. The fact that by the 1940s female participation in certain Carnaval groups was publicized as a welcome innovation underscores another aspect of Carnaval history. Integral to the category of *paseo* is the organization of groups with sections of couple dancers or a chorus of female dancers. And concomitantly, these dancers are costumed according to a generalized theme, rather than as individual characters. While many Santiago Carnaval enthusiasts bemoan the popularity of the *paseo*, with its recorded music and contemporary choreography, it is through the *paseo* that female participation in Carnaval has become guaranteed. (A parallel historical development is evident in Trinidad Carnival where 70 percent of the performers are women.)[22]

Aside from the women who belonged to the lineage of the historical *cabildos*, with their established courtly entourage, in the twentieth century only a few women have been able to achieve solo recognition and penetrate the performing aspect of Carnaval. (Almost all the costume designers and seamstresses are women.) The most famous of these, Gladys Linares Acuña, died in about 1986. Her participation as a *campanera*, playing the *campana macho*, the by now pan-Caribbean percussion instrument made from the brake drum of a car, is legendary in Santiago de Cuba. Beginning at about the age of 15, she displayed so much talent and determination that she was permitted to apprentice to Conga Los Hoyos, the oldest, blackest, and most famous *conga* in Santiago. She played with them until her death at the age of 49. Known affectionately as La Niña or Ma-Fi-Fa, she achieved such special status that Los Hoyos created a *bandera*[23] in her honor (fig. 3), which hangs permanently in their Foco Cultural.[24] Anyone who asks will hear the by now standard story about Ma-Fi-Fa: "She was a delicate woman, very short, thin, in other words, tiny, slender. It was inconceivable that among all those black men, that a woman that delicate and feminine, a woman who had no masculine characteristics . . . Astonishingly, when she died the two men who performed the autopsy reported that she was a virgin. [This] is really hard to believe, that among so many men . . ." (González Bueño, Interview 21 July 1991).

Gladys Linares Acuña's participation as a *campanera* was inspirational. In the early 1980s an all-women *conga* was founded by the cultural worker

Figure 3. Conga los
Hoyos created a banner,
or *bandera,* in honor of
solo performer Gladys
Linares Acuña, who died
in 1986. Photo by Judith
Bettelheim.

Gladys González Bueño and functioned for about two years, although they
never competed in Carnaval. González Bueño contends that the participants were mostly *paleras* or *santeras* (priestesses of the religions Palo and
Santería), but that community pressure forced the group to disband despite its special status. Other Carnaval groups permit young girls to train as
musicians and perform during Carnaval, but they stop playing when they
begin an active social life in their mid-teens. Of course, women can always
participate as singers. Certainly the corollary between Acuña's reputation
and her virginity (real or imagined) and the status of young girl musicians
is parallel to women's participation in ritual activity world over, when the
"contamination" of menstruation and childbearing restricts participation.[25]
It is not important if Ma Fi Fa was a virgin or not; what is important is that
the story has become an accepted text on female participation in Carnaval.

Female authority in Santiago cultural and religious life is not at first apparent. Following a pattern reported by fieldworkers throughout Africa and the Caribbean, initially I was introduced to male Carnaval leaders and male spiritual leaders. But consistently after repeated interviews and visits with certain cultural groups, I would meet the women in charge. This is especially true in my research with artists working with religious groups or with performers whose affiliation was with "folkloric" groups. As Gladys González Bueño explains (and certainly this is nothing new to students of Africa and the African Diaspora):

> They [men in *congas*] accept or reject women based on a special and unique socio-cultural phenomenon that exists here in Santiago, and especially here in this neighborhood of Los Hoyos. There is matriarchy. I'm the boss here; he is not the boss here, and I'm not even from Santiago. It is a unique phenomenon that exists in the homes of Santiago. Men in this neighborhood are known for being somewhat tough, macho, goodlooking . . . but as soon as they step through the door the one in charge is the woman. (González Bueño, Interview 25 July 1991)[26]

This story of male public authority and female private authority is reflected in the most famous *cabildos,* Tumba Francesa and Isuama, as well as in many *casa-templos,* or private religious societies throughout Santiago.

During Carnaval 1989 a group of Swiss and Germans had come to Santiago to apprentice with musicians at the Teatro Cabildo, a contemporary folkloric theatre company. At least half were women. They participated as special European (white) *conga* drummers in Carnaval. The Santiagueros reaction during Carnaval was one of surprise and amusement and I overheard many comments and debates about talent and appropriateness. But women have slowly begun to infiltrate male-dominated Carnaval throughout the Caribbean. In the realm of music there are female pan players in Trinidad, especially with the smaller pan bands that travel on wheeled platforms along the carnival route, and in Martinique women are now included in the marching bands as percussionists, often playing gongs or sticks.

Both in Cuba and in Trinidad the structure of carnival groups has had to change to accommodate the many women who want to participate as dancers. For example, one of Santiago's Carnaval groups most known for its sumptuously costumed female dancers, La Placita, first acquired that reputation in the 1940s when local commercial companies, such as Crusellas soap, began to give substantial monetary donations to major groups. La Placita created a character "Panchita jabon Condado," a laundress, who had a solo dance role and danced a narrative about getting clothes clean.[27] (In my research on Santiago Carnaval history I have noted an unspoken distinction being made between women who participate in Carnaval by posing or dancing on floats and women who actually march and dance in the streets during a parade. In the first instance they are showcased and away from contact with onlookers, in the second the women's aura is considered more immediate and more powerful.) It was not until 1950 that La Placita established an entire section which featured about fifty dancing women. The theme was "Los Turistas" modeled after a "typical North American tourist." The men wore baseball caps, flowered shirts, white pants, and sunglasses. The women wore circle skirts and flowered blouses, with straw hats. As a special feature, the float was a new American automobile with a *corneta china* player on the hood. During the 1950s, despite the profound political turmoil created by Batista's coup d'etat and Castro's attack on the Moncada barracks, La Placita continued to establish sections with choreography that supported female participation. Each year's theme was structured around a different "Fantasía": Cubana in 1951; Guajira (*campesinos*) in 1952; Gitano-Húngara in 1953 and Escocesa (Scotland) in 1955. La Placita did not compete in 1954 as too many young men from the barrio had left to join the freedom fighters. In 1956 the theme was "Fantasía Brasilera" and the women were costumed with Carmen Miranda–style outfits complete with fruit salad headdresses, and the float was decorated with palm trees and oversized pineapples. Again in 1957 and 1958 the *paseo* didn't parade because of increased political tensions in the city. With the Triumph of the Revolution in 1959, Carnaval began again and La Placita's theme was "Fantasía de Cuba." Their float was decorated with sugar cane and fruit and received a $200 prize from La Reforma Agraria.

Each year since the Revolution La Placita dedicates its theme and concomitant aesthetic overview to various aspects of pan-Caribbean or pan-socialist culture, from "Fantasía Staliana" in 1960 to "Fantasía Czechoslovak" of 1964 to "Fantasía Indochina" of 1970 to "Fantasía de Cuba en el CAME" (Council for Mutual Economic Assistance) of 1976 and "Fantasía en el Cosmos" of 1984. Since 1967 each La Placita Carnaval parade has included a special section of costumed paired male and female dancers who lead the *paseo* and have become its special trademark. In the 1960s they were directed by two local, well-known dance instructors, Gloria and María Rodríguez. By the mid-1980s the artistic director and choreographer were both men. Beginning with only about ten dancing couples, the 1989 outing that I witnessed included about seventy-five couples and at least 100 solo female dancers, in addition to the hundreds of other participants. The entire *paseo* performed a summary of their previous themes, from the homage to Hungary in 1949 to the present. To lead off this eclectic 1989 melange a section of about 100 female dancers performed, costumed in white cabaret-style leotards and colored wings: blue, green, black, and white. This particular section was lead by a couple performing a pas de deux in complete cabaret-style (fig. 4). All other sections of the Carnaval performance were highlighted by scantily clad cabaret-style dancers bumping and grinding in front of a banner announcing each section. (These female performers were initially frowned upon by post-Revolutionary authorities, but since the rise of tourism in the 1980s they are once again a popular part of Carnaval parades.)

As I reread my fieldnotes from this particular performance, I realize that I imposed my own sense of North American irony on the performance as I noted the rich juxtaposition between the semi-nude dancers performing an impeccable bump and grind beneath a billowing Soviet flag in the section "Fantasía Sovietica."

My own confused reaction to these luscious Cuban dancers has prompted another avenue of research and self-reflection. When I started working in Cuba in 1985, something started nagging at me. I finally knew I had to confront an aspect of Cuban culture that was not only perplexing, but that I was ill-equipped to deal with: the sexy lady, the Tropicana dancer, the bumping and grinding dancers on the Carnaval floats . . . As Jeannie Forte has written: "Women performance artists expose their bodies to reclaim them, to assert their own pleasure and sexuality, thus denying the fetishistic pursuit to the point of creating a genuine threat to male hegemonic structures of women" (252). Although the particular Cuban situation I am describing does not dovetail with all of Forte's remarks, the gist of her argument merits serious consideration.

Given the cultural conditions which repress not only woman's sexuality, but prohibit her from *being sexual,* because being sexual is always defined in terms of the patriarchy, how have female performers dealt with sexuality as an active agent, to be used positively against suppression, rather than as a negative attribute?[28] This question has direct bearing on some African material, and the Afra-Cuban examples in this essay. Let me introduce the eastern Nigerian "Women's War" of 1929 from the point of view of a feminist performance piece.[29] The widespread rebellion was led by women whose behavior was described by male witnesses as "shocking," "obscene," "hostile," and "disrespectful."

The following was described in the official Commission of Inquiry Reports, 1929:

Figure 4. Cabaret-style dancers, Paseo la Placita, Carnaval, Santiago de Cuba, July 1989. Photo by Judith Bettelheim.

Many women were dressed in sack cloth and wore *nkpatat* (green creeper) in their hair, carried sticks and appeared to have been seized by some evil spirit. . . . the women were led by an old and nude woman of some bulk. They acted in a strange manner, some lying on the ground and kicking their legs in the air, and others making obscene gestures . . . Some were nearly naked wearing only wreaths of grass around their heads, waists and knees, and some wearing tails made of grass. Some of the [reinforcements of women] were carrying machetes . . . the women, speaking their native language, were calling the soldiers pigs . . . (Philippi 40).[30]

There have been a number of diverse commentaries on this action. Much of the European commentary represents the Igbo women as out of control, exemplifying the stereotype of the black, sexualized female, an icon of deviant sexuality. Desa Philippi's commentary elucidates this action differently:

By choosing to represent themselves the way they did, the Igbo women were not simply parodying an imposed stereotype but asserting concrete difference in the face of racial and sexual domination. . . . their use of bodily symbolism and genital display mocks and dislocates the colonial representations of them . . . By radically adopting their position of exteriority, the Igbo women forced the symbolic order to teeter on the edge of the social void which it itself created. (Philippi 41)[31]

The Igbo women chose a very powerful weapon, self-presentation. The sexual black female is no longer a fantasy, but a reality that can only be controlled through destruction. She is no longer the fantasized Other.

Other studies underscore the importance of this self-(re)positioning of the female body in performative modes. Among the Balong, who live at the base of the Cameroon mountains, "the women too are prepared to come out in defense of their sex" (Ardener 35).

When a man insults his wife and says 'Your ass de smell' it is like insulting all women, and all women will be angry . . . The women will tell other women and in the evening they will go to that man and demand a fine of £5 and one pig and soap for all to wash their bodies because he has said that women smell. If the man refuses, the women will send a young woman round the village with a bell to warn men to stay indoors. They [the women] will be angry and they will take all their clothes off. They will shame him and sing songs. (Ardener 35)

Shirley Ardener also reports an even more aggressive and dramatically performance-oriented female practice among the Kom of the west Cameroon grassland plateau. *Anlu* is a disciplinary technique used against those who, for example, beat or insult a parent, beat a pregnant woman, or abuse an old woman. "*Anlu* is started off by a woman who doubles up in an awful position and gives out a high-pitched shrill, breaking it by beating on the lips with the four fingers. Any woman recognizing the sound does the same and leaves whatever she is doing and runs in the direction of the first sound. The crowd quickly swells" (37). As Francis Nkwain, a Kom, explained to Ardener, song and dance follow as the nature of the offense and the provocateur are identified. Then a troupe of women, who have gone to the bush, return "donned in vines, bits of men's clothing and with painted faces . . . No person looks human in that wild crowd, nor do their actions suggest sane thinking. Vulgar parts of the body are exhibited as the chant rises in weird depth" (37). As Ardener indicates, "Revenge is taken on an offender by corporate action, and typically he is disgraced by a display of vulgarity on the part of the women."

What I am proposing is that rather than assuming the role of victim, some African and African American women have asserted their sexuality in performance as an oppositional practice. They manipulate a colonial or racist or patriarchal authority by means of that which is often used to subjugate them: their sexuality. These women use the sexual woman, sexy women, as an emblem of liberation, challenging notions of female sexuality and behavior. We must take another look at commentary on sexuality, victimization, or fetishism.

Recent writing on the politics of feminism makes it quite clear that much feminist theory has been the province of privileged white women and that women of color may have slightly different feminist objectives.[32] A politically puritanical feminist stance against explicit sexuality or even against sex workers is the product of a particular cultural and class bias. As such, we must be able to integrate examples like the following into discussions of feminism. While walking the market women's trail across southern Haiti, Karen McCarthy Brown had the following conversation. Brown encountered a market woman and asked her what she had to sell. The woman replied, "Beans, tomatoes, and my land." Brown responded rather incredulously, "You're going to sell your land?" The woman grabbed her own crotch.[33]

Women are usually socialized either as good girls or bad girls, but as Paula Webster writes: "The good girl/bad girl distinction will fail to terrorize us and control our access to pleasure only if we set out to destroy the double standard" (Tamblyn 18). As an icon of deviant sexuality, atavistic and lascivious, the stereotype of the black female is reproduced across a wide range of discourses. To return to the example of the Women's War of

1929 for a moment, Desa Philippi reminds us that "At the point of conflict the women appear to enact the stereotype of the sexualized, erotic, black female, but in fact they were doing something else . . . For a short moment positionality is shifted from the silent bearer of colonial meaning to power-ful self-representation (41).

How can we interpret these actions — these acts of self-(re)presentation in Africa and their continuities in Afra-Caribbean history as part of a gen-dered history? The literature on women's role in slave rebellions and re-bellions against colonial authority is growing every day. What specifically interests me is the role of women as leaders or intermediaries in these rebellions. For I see a parallel in perceptions of their militant roles and perceptions about their performance roles in both religious and secular events. Often certain slave women were characterized as verbally aggres-sive, indolent, troublesome, badly behaved, etc. These women chose as their form of rebellion that which they had control over, their own be-havior. The "historical invisibility" of women's role in uprisings does not mean that they did not take part. These women were punished for their behavior; they were "bad girls!" The arena for their rebellion was in "cul-tural resistance." Thus women participated in and became leaders in tradi-tional African-based religions. When the priestesses from Los Hoyos, dis-cussed above, attempted to come out with their own Carnaval group the male Los Hoyos leadership and the "rules" of the Carnaval Committee basically made it impossible for them to officially enter the Carnaval parade. Consequently they participated on the sidelines, yet directly demanded attention and respect as priestesses as they performed beneath their special canopy.[34] Remember, the legendary Jamaican Maroon leader and warrior Nanny was an Obeah woman. The British refused to negotiate with her and demanded to speak with the "headman" instead. Thus the colonial docu-ments distorted the role of women in all genres of rebellion (Bush 24). Slowly, much evidence is beginning to surface regarding the way in which black women in slavery were able to "act out" their defiance. Such a woman, Sukie, was displayed for sale on the block in Virginia, and as the prospective buyers were forcing her mouth open to check her teeth, she pulled up her dress and challenged the men to see if they "could find teeth down there." Many other slave women participated in these everyday acts of resistance by performing defiantly, often with sexual aggression.[35] These female roles: the priestess, the bad girl, and the entertainer all may be approached from the point of view of recent feminist theory dealing with performance and transgressive daily behavior. In these roles woman is agent, not carrier of meaning, but producer of meaning. She is active, not passive.

During a trip to Santiago de Cuba I was able to interview some of the dancers I had photographed during Carnaval 1989. These dancers performed in cabaret style and two were featured on the Cubanacan float, organized by the recently established Cuban Tourist Association. Moraima, 22 years old in summer 1991, had been dancing for three and a half years at a local hotel show and was delighted that I had photographed her. "I was eager to learn to be a show dancer . . . My parents are proud of it . . . They never stopped me. I see this as a normal job; it's my job and I perform it. It is my profession" (Interview, 10 March 1990). As I continued this interview I attempted, tentatively and sometimes awkwardly, to ask my own inelegant questions, as much to clarify my own misgivings as to understand Moraima's position. During Carnaval 1987 and 1989 I had noticed that European male visitors, especially the Soviet men who had special front-row seats, gloated and gawked at the dancers and insisted on taking many photographs of themselves posed with the dancers. Although the dancers obliged, I also noted side comments and negative facial expressions passed among them. These men were behaving very differently from the Cuban men at Carnaval, who were enthusiastic and appreciative, and yet simultaneously distant. After all, semi-nude dancing women in Carnaval were ordinary, exciting but not exotic. So I phrased an awkward question to Moraima:

J.B.: Foreigners seem to react to you as something strange. How do you feel about this, as a woman?

MORAIMA: We don't feel offended. You can't feel bad about that. It's a natural thing that comes from them and you can't judge them as bad or feel bad.

J.B.: Many feminists in the U.S. feel that women shouldn't dance for men as you do. As a Cuban woman, what do you think about women in my country who say that this kind of dancing is all mixed up with machismo?

MORAIMA: As long as there is respect toward us as dancers, even if we dance semi-nude. I think it is natural that it might be like this . . . If you are asking me I'll tell you not to take it as something bad. It's a natural thing that occurs only when we dance; it's not forever. At the moment that we dance we respect ourselves.

It seems obvious from the above exchange that Moraima, as well as the other dancers I spoke with, viewed their performed sexuality as just that, a performance. For them, the sexual black female is a part of their cultural heritage that they are proud of. Sexuality, and its use in performance, is inherent in and vital to many African and African-based performance traditions. For example, the Cuban rumba is derived from the dance the Yuka, which is often described as a 'courtship' dance during which the male dancer gives the female the *golpe de frente;* in the rumba this is called the *vacuno,* or vaccination. It actually consists of a kick toward the female's genital area. In the dance, sometimes the woman covers her genital area with the corner of her skirt and turns away from the *vacuno,* and sometimes she does not. The decision is hers. Sex is the performance topic. In other dances the male/female couples touch and slap each other's thighs or grind suggestively. Sexuality is performed publicly and everyone joins in. For the Cuban cabaret-style Carnaval dancers, they are enjoying their performance. Especially in the *paseos* that have expanded their structure and choreography to include more and more female dancers, the women finally have an opportunity to perform during Carnaval, for historically their roles were restricted to "folkloric presentations."

In addition to the hundreds of women who perform in "modern" dances during Carnaval, there are those for whom the pull of traditional, or "folkloric," African Cuban culture is still very strong in Cuba today. Many Carnaval participants appreciate this heritage in a personal way that goes beyond folklore. For example, the 1989 performance of *paseo* La Placita discussed above was organized like a play with various acts and scenes, including a section "Fiestas de America" with a tribute to Mexico with a Mexican "hat dance" and a tribute to Afro-Cuba with a dance honoring five Santería *orichás*[36], Changó, Babalú Ayé, Ochún, Yemayá, and Eleguá. The Ochún was particularly well performed, very convincing. I suspect that for the last section of her dance, Ochún was possessed. The choreographer ran out to support her and embrace her as he accompanied her to the sidelines. Was I watching an actor or a practitioner, or a combination of both? As the director of La Placita, Manuel Fernando Quincosis, commented: "There are people who still have these beliefs, but the dancers do it from a cultural point of view. More than anything, it's maintaining the culture. . . . There are a few, always, who believe" (Interview, 10 March 1990). It is these believers who each year perform with the more traditional Afro-Cuban sections of the large *paseos.* One dancer, Carlos Cavado (fig. 5), admits that although he has been asked to dance in cabarets, he doesn't like them. "I've never liked cabaret because it's a whole other thing. The branch I like is folklore, strong stuff. Cabaret is . . . it's very nice and beautiful, some really beautiful dances. But I like folklore, the black branch, as we call it here . . . Since that's what I like, that's what I do" (Interview, 10 March 1990). Most of the dancers performing in these folkloric presentations are confident that

Figure 5. Carlos Cavado dances the deity Changó, *paseo* La Placita. Carnaval, Santiago de Cuba, July 1989. Photo by Judith Bettelheim.

their participation is helping to keep that aspect of African Cuban culture vibrant. These are cultural performances, supported by centuries of practice and belief.

Carnaval organizers (especially Poder Popular, a branch of city government which is officially responsible for the organization of Carnaval[37]) claim an emphasis on unity, like the subtitle of the important journal *Del Caribe* published in Santiago, *El Caribe Que Nos Une* (*The Caribbean That Unites Us*). For them, the performed reality is equality. Carnaval subthemes emphasize folklore and ethnicity, and all components are treated equally. Distinctions within the community of the Caribbean are expressed through performance, but the performances emphasize that no one sector is more important than another. In Carnaval, at least, the officially intended message of equality is successfully portrayed. For example, during the July 1989 Carnaval parade the crowds in the stands responded enthusiastically to the float sponsored by Cubanacan. Complete with live pop music and scantily dressed gyrating women, the crowd rose to their feet and applauded as the dancers threw paper serpentinas. And this same crowd applauded equally heartily when the *orichá* Babalú Ayé, from the *paseo* La Placita, was held aloft by three other male dancers. The Babalú Ayé was especially convincing, with a limp, a deformed arm, drools, and trance-like dancing.

La Placita's artistic director, Pablo Estrada Pérez, who started dancing with La Placita at ten and who is now in his forties, emphatically explains the *paseo*'s commitment to a two-sided reality, a reality which he claims correctly reflects contemporary Cuba and the Caribbean/Latin America as well as Cuba's African heritage.

> In our themes we bring out our cultural ancestry as well as the modern side of Cuba. We pay attention to the *rescuing* [emphasis mine] of folkloric values; that is why there are religious, ritual, elements within the *paseo*. There are people in our *paseo* who belong to folkloric groups and know these dances; so we learn from these people. All these kinds of groups have been created by our government in order to *preserve* [emphasis mine] the Afro-Cuban culture. So any way, there is always the modern, the Tropicana-style as you call it, and there is the folkloric. (Interview, 10 March 1990)

Most Carnaval organizers agree with this assessment that African Cuban culture needed or needs "rescuing" and that in post-revolutionary Cuba this rescuing process is part of the official work of cultural institutions. (This attitude and cultural agenda are shared by most Caribbean nations.)[38] Indeed, since the Revolution, the foregrounding of African Cuban culture has been official cultural policy. Argeliers León, a noted scholar and senior researcher at Casa de las Américas in Havana, was named director of the Folklore Department of the National Theatre after the Revolution and three African Cuban "religions," Palo Monte, Santeriá, and Abakuá, have all been presented in dramatic productions. León and the current choreographer for the Conjunto Folklórico, Rogelio Martínez Furé, both conduct extensive fieldwork in preparation for these productions and include explanatory notes in their programs. The same is true for Rex Nettleford and Fradique Lizardo, directors of the National Dance Theatre of Jamaica and the Ballet Folklórico Dominicano respectively. These institutions, and their parallel organizations in other Caribbean countries, emphasize this "rescuing" process in their artistic productions.

The same might be said of the frequent appearance of Yoruba-based costumed *orichás* in festivals, *Carnavals,* and dance presentations all over Cuba. For example, a 1988 ballet I attended, sponsored by the Dirección Provincial de Cultura, Santiago de Cuba, was entitled "Ercili."[39] The main characters were Ercili (Erzulie) and Ogun Guerrero (Ogun the Warrior). (Ironically the Ercili was danced by a blond female lead dancer from Belgium, who was part of an official collaborative program.) The narrative was loosely based on the stories told in the Haitian Cuban communities[40] located in the mountains above Santiago de Cuba and research conducted by scholars at the cultural organization, the Casa del Caribe, in Santiago.

In Santiago de Cuba during Carnaval 1989 eight out of nineteen groups included tributes to traditional African Caribbean culture in their repertoires. Some recreated the courtly entourage; others included choreographed routines paying homage to the *orichás* of the Santeriá religion, and still others incorporated songs and dances learned from the Haitian Cuban communities of Oriente Province. A song performed by Cabildo Carabalí Isuama included the chorus "Africa, Africa, we cannot forget you," and a section of the *paseo* Sueño sang "My Mother, my Father came from Haiti. I dream of Haiti."

The *paseo* Los Pinos also included a Haitian Cuban section. The performers were dressed in white with red kerchiefs and headties, and the Ogun "impersonator" wore a blue kerchief and carried a machete. As he danced in the center of a circle created by the other performers, he directed attacks on the other dancers and then turned the machete on himself. Although the *paseo* did not announce the title of this sequence, its homage to the Haitian Ogou is obvious from the following description from Haiti:

The vacillation of Ogou's anger, its tendency to switch targets from his enemies to his followers, has historical precedent. This is a facet of his character which is present in the Yoruba tradition, which the slaves no doubt brought to the island of Hispaniola. . . . Ogou's anger comes full circle and ultimately is directed against himself. This is the dimension of Ogou's character that reveals itself in the final movement of his ritual sword dance, when he points the weapon at his own body. (Karen McCarthy Brown 76–77)

The performance of this Cuban Ogun and of a dancer from the *paseo* El Tivoli[41] who performed a possession ritual often associated with the very traditional Afro-Haitian Cuban Tumba Francesa groups, are both additional evidence of the vitality associated with traditional African Cuban culture.

As Victor Turner suggests, a cultural performance is part of an ongoing social process when people themselves are conscious of—through participating themselves or witnessing—the nature, texture, style, and given meanings of their own lives. I reject an abstract structuralist model of culture which claims to approach meaning without attending to the relevance and importance of the action of a cultural performance; the structuralist model tends also to deny the real activist aesthetics that are embedded in such performances. Most conventional analyses of carnival celebrations worldwide stress the importance of what is usually called "rites of reversal" when there is a suspension of all hierarchical ranks, privileges, norms, and prohibitions during the carnival celebrations. The commoner plays king; the folk take over the streets, and as Mikhail Bakhtin (*Rabelais*) so eloquently points out, festive laughter is directed at everyone, even the carnival participants themselves. But this overused formula does not apply to Cuban Carnaval today.[42] In Santiago the actual Carnaval parade is quite distinct from Carnaval celebrations, and the costumed performers, although having fun, are serious and highly competitive. The street celebrations do not include costumed performers, but rather are dancing and eating/drinking street parties held in specially designated areas of the city. It is a common "joke" in Santiago (where food shortages are frequent) that one cannot buy chicken in the market during Carnaval because it is being reserved for the special street vendors.

In European carnival there is often a thin line between the spectator and the participant, for carnival performances occur in public, in the open, in a town square or along a main street. Frequently the spectator is swept up into the narrative of the action. This is basically still the case in Port of Spain, Trinidad, where the *mas* bands may end up parading across the Savannah stage in front of the footlights and television cameras, but they have marched from their respective neighborhoods to Frederick Street and up the length of the street to the Savannah. Street interaction happens not only on Mardi Gras, but during the three days before. The Carnival Roadmarch of Monday and Tuesday includes thousands and thousands of revelers.

But that is not the case in Havana or Santiago de Cuba today. In Santiago the Carnaval groups do not dance together in the streets. Their parade is limited to a four- to five-block area of the Alameda, which is cordoned off by bleachers and grandstand. There is no street intermingling of the Carnaval groups where costuming (disguise, transformation) and concomitant characters permit a genre of interaction reserved for this occasion in other countries. In Santiago de Cuba even the audience is restricted (and I use the word audience very deliberately), for tickets for the Carnaval parade are hard to come by and certain sections of the grandstand are reserved by invitation only. It is in front of a reserved section, where the jury also sits, that the various groups actually perform for their awards. Bakhtin warns that carnival must not be confused with what he terms the self-serving festivities fostered by governments, secular or theocratic. For Bakhtin, carnival is revolution itself, while others regard carnival as a safety valve for the passions of the folk, who might otherwise lead a revolutionary uprising. But, I believe, by the late twentieth century, that the definition of carnival itself is changing. In most celebrations that I am aware of, competitions restricted to special cordoned-off areas are the norm. More and more, authorities are restricting street interactions, and carnival parades resemble theatrical performances structured by a proscenium arch.[43]

Before the Revolution in Santiago de Cuba, all day long costumed Carnaval groups would mingle with people on the major streets in town. The streets would be lined with what Santiagueros refer to as kiosks, or stalls selling food, drink, etc. As *conga* musicians marched down the street, people would pour out of their houses and join the procession. Or cars with loudspeakers would play a favorite tune, and instruct the people to come out in the streets and dance. Eventually the entire street would be packed with dancing people. Today, the stalls which sell food and drink and the music are restricted to certain hours, and the recorded or live music is limited to a stage area built in designated streets in certain neighborhoods. There are no costumed characters on the street. The intermingling is restricted to social dancing in special public areas.

In 1988 I attended Carnival in Port of Spain, Trinidad, while living with a family in the Belmont section, the home of Jason Griffith's famous "Sailor bands." One day as we were resting from the previous night's activities, a section of a *mas* band from the neighborhood marched by. Soon the entire block was following behind the musicians. I have been told that all neighborhoods in Port of Spain support these spontaneous parades. This genre of street interaction is extremely limited in Santiago de Cuba.[44] A few times I have seen members of a theatre group, Cabildo Teatral Santiago, borrow costumes and go house to house in certain neighborhoods, singing, in character, and asking for donations. Today, this is a deliberate nostalgic activity designed to help recall traditions and provide amusement.

Carnaval embraces heterogeneous traditions. It includes religions, class structure, ancestral city identities, and popular culture. Carnaval is multivalent; impersonation is balanced by self presentation; people play others and people play themselves. The entire performance is organic, as each segment, of history or of the performing group, competes for recognition. Often history is played as a living text. As the festivals of the French revolution used the model of antiquity to visually and psychologically create a new order, Cuban Carnaval stresses Caribbean and Socialist unity expressed through performances that pay tribute to the folklore of individual nations.

The construction/reconstruction of certain performance elements can be looked at as the use of unfamiliar things in familiar settings or familiar things in unusual settings. In either case the leaders of each Carnaval group have deliberately chosen to, or agreed to, incorporate a specific cultural genre into a larger performance. The use of the familiar allows for a broad-based appreciation and understanding, such as the Tropicana style of dancing and undress. Remember, after Castro closed the Tropicana, popular pressure forced its reopening. Carnaval's insistent emphasis on ethnic heritage is more problematic.

Ethnic or national heritage is still important in Cuba, although much of its public presentation is reserved for folkloric presentations. These folkloric elements have a long history in public performances. While Yoruba de-rived religion, and concomitant *orichá* worship is widespread in the Americas, there is national recognition that only in Cuba did a Cross River tradition from Nigeria, known as the Abakuá society in Cuba, implant, survive, and flourish. Not only does the Abakuá *ireme* (the costumed spirit-dancer) play a major role in cultural performances, but the use of the *ireme* as a national emblem is a deliberate, self-conscious statement on the part of official cultural institutions (figs. 6a, 6b, and 6c). The Abakuá society has developed a reputation as the most socially dangerous and potentially sub-

Figure 6. *Ireme* dancers wear
costumes designed in 1987 for
Paseo Seuño. Carnaval, Santiago
de Cuba. July 1989. Designer Yupy
Prat is shown at right. Photo by
Judith Bettelheim.

versive of all African Cuban groups. Yet the *ireme* is depicted on airline posters, meeting hall banners, designer fabrics, etc. *Ireme* dolls are sold at all tourist hotels.

How does an emblem of a powerful and extant African Cuban brother-hood publicly function in contemporary Cuba? Fernando Ortiz's publications have, in post-revolutionary Cuba, reinspired a new generation of festival artists. Today in Cuba ethnic dance theatre or *danza folklórico* is often used as a restoring device for national pride. Do these tourist items and the folkloric performances violate African Cuban cultural values? Is there a disparity between the beliefs of this minority and national cultural values? Used as a case study, does the persistent image of the *ireme* point to the existence of multiple realities which are mediated by a common symbol, the *ireme*? Official Cuban cultural policy claims that public aesthetic display is important in resurrecting, preserving, and/or rejuvenating African Cuban culture, especially when that culture was so deprecated in pre-revolutionary society. But I wonder.

Public display often can diffuse the power of an image, especially if that image was once restricted in its use and symbolic interpretive potential. The Abakuá society used to have a secret language. In 1975 Lydia Cabrera published a book which decoded that language, and today these same, once-private ideograms are used to decorate banners in conference halls and are displayed with translations.

Have national cultural institutions appropriated imagery from a power-ful African-based Cuban brotherhood and thus perpetuated the continued demise of that social force? Certainly by incorporating the performance of Abakuá *ireme* dancers or performances by a costumed Changó or Ochún into Carnaval, expressions of ethnicity get aired publicly. Where does one draw the line between public expressions of ethnicity accomplished with pride and "folkloric propaganda"? Cuban Carnaval performances present common emblems which can be interpreted in multiple ways, reflecting the existence of multiple realities which are mediated through performance and exhibition, often employed against their original intent. One must carefully appreciate the simultaneous Carnaval performances of "characters" from Afro-Cuban life with beautiful dancing women. In both cases a prideful heritage and personal power is being performed in public. At this particu-lar point in my research I believe that these images, these Carnaval per-formances — the royal entourage, the *orichá*, the sexy dancer — are double coded. For African Cubans they are powerful messages, reminders of an ongoing rich and powerful reality. According to official culture they are indicators of the new status, an elevated status, of the African Cuban in post-revolutionary society.

NOTES

1   In Santiago the Carabalízona (*sic.*) de Santa Lucia was registered by 1884 and in 1894 the Baracoa Brothers officially named the new organization Cabildo Carabalí Isuama (Nancy Pérez 12). The Carabalí Isuama, like the other important twentieth-century Santiago *cabildo*, the Carabalí Olugo, pays homage to ancestry from the Igbo area of Nigeria where the Isuama live next to the Elugo (Olugo?), north of the area of the Kalabari Ijaw. To-day in Nigeria, Isuama is an Igbo group living inland and upriver from the Kalabari Ijaw (Ijo). Carabalí Isuama operated on two levels: as a public *cabildo* that danced and marched during street festivals, and as a private *cabildo* that supported the *mambises* against the Spanish in the Wars of Independence (1868–95) and that held private religious ceremonies. Although there are discrepancies in the historical sources, it seems that Carabalí Isuama was not given permission to perform publicly from the 1920s until after the Triumph of the Revolution. That does not mean that the *cabildo* did not meet or carry on their activities. That they appear regularly during Carnaval demonstrates their strength and explains some of the enthusiasm among Santiago spectators. (In Cuba Carabalí generically refers to the many groups arriving from the Bight of Biafra.)

2   The first dance they performed is called the Bata Armarilla, after their costume, a yellow and white long dress with full arms. I think it is important to note that yellow and white are the colors of Ochún who is associated with the Virgin of Caridad del Cobre and whose basilica is located a twenty-minute drive from Santiago.

3   Due to Cuba's severe financial crisis, Carnaval celebrations were canceled in 1992. But in honor of the fortieth anniversary of the storming of the Moncada barracks in Santiago in July 1953, in 1993 a very small version of a Carnaval parade was held in the central square. At this writing I have not been able to obtain a list of the performing groups.

4   Bremer identifies this particular *cabildo* as Cabildo de Señora Santa Barbara [Changó] de la nacíon Alagua.

5   In a discussion of the initiation of an *iyawó* into the Regla de Ocha religious society David Brown remarks: "When the *iyawó* must leave the throne for daily ritual cleansing baths . . . at least one initiated person . . . suspends a piece of symbolically pure white cloth, canopy-like, over the *iyawó's* head on the way to the bathroom" (392).

6   In my 1993 publication, *Cuban Festivals: An Illustrated Anthology,* I detail the history of Haitian French culture in eastern Cuba and include an expanded section on the Tumba Francesa and Tajona.

7   Even in religious societies special kinship networks have been created. For the practitioners of Palo in Santiago de Cuba *carabela* refers to certain Kongo spirits of deceased ancestors who were victims of the Middle Passage. A comparable kinship term among the Suriname Maroons is *sippi*, among Haitians it is *batiment* and in Brazil it is *malungo*.

8   I would like to thank John Thornton for allowing me to paraphrase his work on Court and the Coromantees in colonial America. Thornton and I participated in an NEH seminar and the material was included in his presentation (see Thornton).

9   Coromantee was the name of a port in the small state of Fante on the Gold Coast, but it

has become the English-language term for Akan people from the nation now known as Ghana.

10   See Abrahams and Szwed.

11   This and other translations are by me with the assistance of Sergio Waisman and Alina del Pino. In many cases I have been unable to find an exact translation of the Cuban, especially when phrases are part of an Afro-Cuban vocabulary or are particular to Santiago. In this case the *almirez* must be a type of percussion instrument, probably similar to the brake drum so popular today. The *botijuela* is a wind instrument created from an earthen jug with holes cut on one side. Fernando Ortiz indicates that it is known as a *bunga* by older Afro-Cubans (*Nuevo catauro de Cubanismos* 89).

12   In Cuba the *cabildo* is a mutual aid society, organized by neighborhood and ethnicity. Historically membership was structured by descent, although today other factors are influential.

13   The Carnaval Museum in Santiago has in its collection a Tumba Francesa drum which is decorated with the national crest and the date 10 October 1868, the date of the beginning of the Wars for Independence. The Tumba Francesas of Oriente Province developed from *cabildos de nación* and with the law of 2 January 1887 all Tumba groups received the name of a saint to parade behind and their king and queen became known as president and presidenta (Castillo 27).

14   On 19 December 1884 by official decree both public processions of *cabildos* and Día de Reyes celebrations, which officially lasted from 1823–84 in Havana, were prohibited.

15   *Comparsas* also encompassed the neighborhood *parranda,* or groups of musicians and singers, and the *charanga,* a small neighborhood party group.

16   Fernando Ortiz (1881–1969) is one of Cuba's most prolific and revered scholars. His first publication on African Cuban society appeared in 1906, *Hampa Afrocubana: Los Negros brujos,* and he published continually until his death. A pioneer of modern sociology and anthropology in Latin America, Ortiz originated the concept of "transculturation" which emphasizes a horizontal lending and borrowing of cultural constructs, in opposition to 'acculturation' which posits the enveloping of one cultural mode by a more dominant mode.

17   In the early 1920s Ortiz published a series of *ireme* images in a major early work on African Cuban culture. Most of my fieldwork has been in Santiago de Cuba, and to the best of my knowledge there is no organized Abakuá brotherhood in Oriente Province. Although it is evident, from the interviews I have conducted, that Abakuá-based knowledge is still important for many individual Cubans there. (Ortiz, "La fiesta afrocubana del 'Día de Reyes'"). Today in Cuba the costumed dancers representing members of the Abakuá society are called *ireme.* Traditionally these same dancers were known as *diablitos* or *ñáñigos,* the individual members of Abakuá. Ortiz's publication included the by now often-reproduced mid-nineteenth-century engraving by Pierre Toussaint Frederic Mialhe, who was born 14 April 1810 in Bordeaux and was professor at the Academy of Painting in Havana, 1831–34 and 1857–61, and the 1870s and 1880s paintings of the Andalucian-born Cuban costumbrista Victor Patricio Landaluce, who died in Havana in 1890. Lydia Cabrera, who did most of her research in the 1940s and 1950s, published her first work on this subject in 1958, *La sociedad secreta Abakuá,* which, as it turns out, was the last book she published in Cuba before leaving. Both this publication and her *El monte* of 1954 include photographs of Abakuá *ireme.*

18   Historically, before and after the Revolution, patronage and wealth has correlated with

the race and class of a given Carnaval group's members. The variability of government patronage merits a much deeper analysis than I can provide here, although it is relevant to remember that in Cuba all means of production is owned by the state.

19   In 1989 the *paseo* Sueño included a danced narrative about Jamaican police harassment and the Rastafarian lifestyle in their performance.

20   The Ten Years War began in October 1868 with the "Grito de Yara" in Oriente Province and remained a struggle restricted to the eastern part of the island.

21   Oriente Province and its capital Santiago de Cuba has consistently produced leaders and supporters in revolutionary struggles. In 1878–80 a new separatist war broke out in Oriente, but after nine months the rebellion was crushed. During the War for Independence Antonio Maceo and Maximo Gomez launched their campaign on the western provinces from the east. Maceo was killed in 1896.

22   In the late 1940s after the war, some women who were professional hairdressers and seamstresses brought out their own small female bands. Everyone dressed the same and the most popular costumes were the Barbajan cooks or the Martinique dancers, dressed in long skirts with layers of lace trim, off-the-shoulder blouses, headties, and hoop earrings. By the early 1960s younger male band leaders began to divide their bands into sections which permitted the increased female participation. Each section consisted of female solo dancers costumed identically. By the 1980s female participation exploded. I thank Pamela Franco, a graduate student at Emory University and a scholar of carnival, for helping to verify this information.

23   When I visited the Foco Cultural of Los Hoyos in 1986 I first saw and photographed this *bandera*. It wasn't until subsequent trips that I was able to collect her history.

24   Since 1980 when the Ministry of Culture in Santiago first began funding the Foco Culturales, or buildings which are for the exclusive use of a cultural group in their neighborhood barrio, eight have been established.

25   See, among many works on this subject, Mary Douglas.

26   For an important discussion of woman power behind male authority and more visible performance presence see Anita J. Glaze.

27   This and subsequent data about La Placita's performance history is from an unpublished Trabajo de Diploma written by Violeta del Rosario Fernández de la Uz.

28   The following remarks were originally written as part of a paper "Deconstructing the Mythologies: From Priestess to Red Hot Mama in African and African American/Caribbean Performances," presented at the 1990 national African Studies Association meeting, Baltimore.

29   The following information is from statements by witnesses translated into English by male interpreters, and selected for final recording by the all-male Commission of Inquiry (Ifeka-Moller 128).

30   There is a precedent among Igbo women for this action. "Sitting upon a man" has been described as follows: "if a woman, or several women, think that their customary rights or economic interests are being subverted by careless men (or women) they get together outside the offender's hut, shouting scurrilous gossip, abusing the man, who cowers in his hut, and dancing in sexually loaded, obscene fashion" (Ifeka-Moller 132). She continues: "Militant women everywhere in the oil-palm belt practiced sexual insult" (143).

31   In *Anthills of the Savannah*, Chinua Achebe also uses the Women's War as a pivotal motif in developing the character of Beatrice Okoh. Prompted by a discussion with her friend Ikem, "who has written a full-length novel and a play on the Women's War of 1929 which

stopped the British administration cold in its tracks, being [Ikem is accused] accused of giving no clear political role to women." Beatrice thinks: "But the way I see it giving women today the same role which traditional society gave them of intervening only when everything else has failed is not enough, you know, like the women in the Sembene film who pick up the spears abandoned by their defeated menfolk. It is not enough that women should be the court of the last resort because the last resort is a damn sight too far too late" (Achebe 84).

32   To note some recent important examples, among many, see bell hooks, *Talking Back;* and Chandra Talpade Mohanty, Ann Russo, and Lourdes Torres, eds.

33   From a conversation with Karen McCarthy Brown, August 1990.

34   In an analogous gesture of performing power, a group of female dancers celebrating pre-Carnaval activities at Casa del Caribe in July 1991 danced beneath a white sheet and "captured" the assistant director of Casa beneath the sheet, forcing him to dance with them, rather than remain on the sidelines watching.

35   I thank Syadia Hartman for this reference which was included in a lecture at a panel "Art and the Forbidden: Images of Female Aggression" at San Francisco State University on December 4, 1991. The story is from *The Slave Narratives: Virginia,* ed. George Rawick.

36   The Santería religion is in part derived from a Yoruba religious base, *orichás* being Yoruba dieties.

37   In existence since the mid-1970s, Poder Popular is based on an electoral system for local, regional, and national assemblies of its members.

38   See Rex Nettleford.

39   This production was a joint project of the Conjuntos Folklóricos Santiago and principal dancers from the Ballet Royal de Wallonie, Belgium.

40   I am currently writing an article exploring the influence of these Haitian-Cuban communities on cultural life in Oriente.

41   Tivoli is the original French-Haitian neighborhood in Santiago.

42   The appropriateness of applying this formula to Brazil also is disputed hotly today.

43   It is interesting to note that in French revolutionary festivals the emphasis was on open, horizontal space, stressing lack of boundaries, while in Cuba, festival space is delineated by parallel barriers which create vertical lines of closed performance.

44   Sometimes *conga* musicians may celebrate the opening of Carnaval week by parading in their own neighborhoods around their Foco Cultural, but I have only heard of this happening in two special neighborhoods, Los Hoyos and San Pedrito.

Donald H. Frischmann
New Mayan Theatre in Chiapas: Anthropology, Literacy, and Social Drama

❑

Sna Jtz'ibajom, Cultura de los Indios Mayas A.C. (The Writers' House, Mayan Indian Culture, Inc.) is a Tzotzil and Tzeltal Mayan-language writers' cooperative and theatre company[1] based in San Cristóbal de las Casas, Chiapas, in the center of Mexico's southernmost state and Mayan area. This creative cultural venture has now weathered over ten years in one of Mexico's most interethnically conflictive areas. How did The Writers' House come into existence? What survival strategies has it employed? Who are its protagonists and supporters? What are its objectives, artistic models, and its relationship to the social, political, and historical milieu of the Chiapas Highlands? In this essay I shall address these and related questions.[2]

Chiapas is Mexico's southernmost state, bordered by Guatemala to the east, the Mexican states of Oaxaca and Veracruz to the west, Tabasco to the north, and the Pacific Ocean to the south. Capital Tuxtla Gutiérrez (pop. 300,000) is located in the tropical, coffee-producing lowlands. San Cristóbal de las Casas (pop. 110,000), cultural center and former Spanish capital, is nestled in a valley amongst the Highlands rainforests. It is accessible via a ninety-minute bus trip from Tuxtla. The fifty-mile stretch of two-lane highway climbs through some 5,000 feet of the Sierra Madre del Sur. Forty-five years ago, this was still a twelve-hour journey by mule. Paved roads are a recent phenomenon, and air service to Tuxtla even more recent.

Despite this relative inaccessibility, the classic Mayan civilization flourished here, as evidenced by the silent stone monuments left behind. Palenque, Bonampak, Yaxchilán, Toniná, and other former ceremonial and population centers attract archaeologists and visitors from around the world. Highlands townships of Zinacantán and San Juan Chamula are in the immediate vicinity of San Cristóbal, although each constitutes a highly distinct ethnic and cultural zone: San Cristóbal is generally the *Ladino*'s territory—those of Spanish, or even mixed-blood or indigenous descent who dress in Western clothing and speak Spanish as their primary tongue.[3] Surrounding San Cristóbal is a multitude of Mayan townships, each distinguished by its own dress style and language or dialect. The two principal Highlands indigenous groups are the Tzeltales and the Tzotziles; the two are very closely related—linguistically and culturally—though each speaks its own Mayan language.[4]

POST-CONQUEST CHIAPAS AND INTERETHNIC CONFLICT

Since the 1524 arrival of the Spaniards in what is present-day Chiapas, relations between Spaniards, or Ladinos, and indigenous peoples have been difficult, at best. Violence has frequently erupted, particularly when demands upon the native population have become unbearable. One of the geographic loci of this essay, the Tzotzil township of Zinacantán, continued to be the indigenous "capital" of the Highlands in 1572, when a native government was instated by the Spaniards. However, all native towns of Highland Chiapas were quickly apportioned out to individual Spaniards who were free to exact tribute from the inhabitants via the *encomienda* system. After the abolition of the *encomienda* in 1720 indigenous peoples saw their rights continually diminished and their communal lands taken over by Ladinos despite laws to the contrary. Until the early nineteenth century economic exploitation by landowners, political officials, and even priests was the order of the day. These excesses led to nativistic, messianic movements such as the Tzeltal Rebellion (1712–13) and the Chamulan "Caste War" or War of St. Rose (1867–70). While Ladinos managed to put down the uprisings, there was much bloodshed on both sides (Laughlin, *Of Cabbages* 10–11; Bricker, *The Indian Christ* 43–69, 119–25).

But the exploitation did not cease. Until recently, a wide-spread system of indentured labor on lowland coffee plantations kept the Highland Maya and other indigenous peoples at the mercy of Ladinos. At the time of the Mexican Revolution of 1910, the plight of the Chiapas peons was "probably the worst of all in the nation" (Cosío 227; Laughlin, *Of Cabbages* 11).[5] The land reform policy inaugurated by the revolution reached the Highlands only in the 1940s, benefiting however only the wealthier Indian families (Laughlin, *Of Cabbages* 11–12).

Anthropologist Robert Laughlin, whose research and friendship with the Highland Maya date from 1959, describes the difficult social climate which still existed not long ago:

> In 1951, when the National Indian Institute arrived in San Cristóbal to set up education, medical, and agricultural programs for the Indians, the directors of the institute were accused [by the Ladino oligarchy] of being communists. At that time Indians were not allowed on the sidewalks and were jailed if found in town after sunset. Ten years later *Ladinas* [non-Indian women] still stationed themselves at the entrances to San Cristóbal at dawn to waylay the incoming Indians, grabbing their chickens and vegetables and giving them a few centavos in return. To see Indians kicked into the backs of second-class buses was not unusual. ("Tzotzil and Tzeltal" 21)

Changes have slowly taken place. Collier points out that debt-indentured slavery on the haciendas has been replaced by a community that has retained and reemphasized its Indian identity, vesting its political power in the leadership of a few energetic and forceful men. Through them, Chiapan Indians deal with the outside world not as a dominated case, but as a collectivity negotiating with a state government that mediates among society's elements (Collier, *Fields of the Tzotzil* 150).

Laughlin describes other types of change:

> No longer today do Indians travel to San Cristóbal with fear in their hearts; no longer do they expect that any surprise encounter with a Ladino will lead to their death. They are more worldly wise, more willing to seek work in distant places, eager to strike up conversations with Ladinos and to stare into the eyes of Ladina girls. Now they dare to challenge the authorities of church and state. But though all would agree that their fathers and grandfathers suffered greater hardships, they are not at peace with the present. "Everything is changing, nothing is the same now," they say. "The schools knock down our culture. The young people have learned to speak Spanish. They read and write, but they are forgetting our customs. Some men are rich, they own trucks, they travel to Mexico City, but they refuse to serve our gods. Punishment will come. We will all die in the year 2000" (*Of Cabbages* 21).

Within this context the founding members of The Writers' House grew up, were educated, and eventually became political and cultural activists in the Highlands. Their local grass-roots work has been assisted and nourished through friendships and alliances with outsiders. Some of these individuals have come from far beyond the sacred mountains which surround and still protect the township centers; in fact, many have come from other countries. Some have found lasting friendship, which has brought them back again and again. Our story begins here — the story of others who have traveled to the Chiapas Highlands, and of my own journey. This essay belongs to us all, but particularly to the writers, actors, and teachers of The Writers' House.

ANTHROPOLOGISTS, LITERACY, AND MAYAN CULTURAL ACTIVISM: THE FOUNDATION OF THE WRITERS' HOUSE

In order to trace the steps leading to the creation of The Writers' House, we must begin with the arrival of the Harvard Chiapas Project directed by Professor Evon Z. Vogt. From 1957 to 1975, undergraduate and graduate students steadily traveled to the Chiapas Highlands to carry out field-data collection, particularly in the townships of Zinacantán and San Juan Chamula. As a result, a large number of books and articles have appeared — and continue to do so — making this, along with Yucatán, the most minutely studied ethnic area in all of Mexico.[6]

Locally, the project hired a number of men, and a few women, as translators, transcribers, and informants, resulting in one of its most important by-products: a renewed sense of pride and interest among local project participants in their own culture. The incentive of working for Vogt also resulted in literacy for many a Tzotzil, laying part of the groundwork for The Writers' House. Founding member Anselmo Pérez Pérez from Zinacantán learned to read and write from his *compadre* Domingo de la Torre in order to accompany him to work at Harvard. De la Torre was afraid to come alone since he had heard stories of North American cannibalism (Laughlin, "As For Me" 57–59). Both men *did* come to Harvard and collaborated with Robert Laughlin intermittently from 1963–75 on *The Great Tzotzil Dictionary of San Lorenzo Zinacantán*. De la Torre's eldest son Juan would eventually join Anselmo Pérez Pérez as cofounder of The Writers' House, along with Mariano López Méndez from neighboring Chamula. Mariano's father had also worked for Vogt beginning in 1966; Mariano would eventually work with anthropologist Gary Gossen in Chamula.

Let us assume the Tzotzil perspective for a moment: During the years of the project (and until the present day) we would have witnessed a steady stream of enthusiastic outsiders coming to learn how *we* live, think, worship, talk, and work. They would then go on to publish numerous books and essays about even the most commonplace aspects of our lives. In time, several of us would decide to pose a logical question: Why should *just* outsiders be involved in writing down our native folktales, and learning to read and write in our language?

In 1981, Pérez Pérez, López Méndez, and De la Torre López asked themselves precisely that question, and as a result formed the Sociedad Cultural Indígena de Chiapas (Chiapas Indigenous Cultural Society). Prior to then, the men had "all worked separately at home, writing stories," according to De la Torre López. That same year they obtained financial backing from Chiapas Governor Juan Sabines (brother of prominent poet Jaime Sabines) and were able to publish their first books: *La primera cartilla Tzotzil* (*The First Tzotzil Primer*) and a bilingual edition of three Tzotzil folktales. Eight months later the Sabines administration ended and the project stalled, so the men turned to a friend for advice: Dr. Robert Laughlin — Harvard Project alumnus, Curator of Middle American Ethnography at the Smithsonian Institution, San Cristóbal part-time resident — and most importantly — close friend to the De la Torre family.[7] He suggested that they make a personal plea for help at the upcoming conference "Forty Years of Anthropological Research in Chiapas" (San Cristóbal, 1982). The result was a modest grant from Cultural Survival, Inc.[8] In Vogt's words:

> Our former informants were telling us that we anthropologists had aroused their interest and self-consciousness about their own culture, but that while we had presumably made good studies, we had taken our knowledge away with us. They added that the younger generation of Tzotzil-Tzeltal Mayas are now widely literate in Spanish, but increasingly ignorant about their own culture which is rapidly slipping away. The informants expressed a deep desire to at least record their customs on paper before they disappear entirely. The Writers' Cooperative was launched soon thereafter. (Vogt, "The Chiapas Writers' Cooperative" 46)

In 1983 the men obtained legal, nonprofit organization status under the name Sna Jtz'ibajom, Cultura de los Indios Mayas A.C. (The Writers' House, Mayan Indian Culture, Inc.). Their stated objectives were — and continue to be — as follows:

> Reinforce the maternal language, in both oral and written form, and the written manifestations of the Tzeltal and Tzotzil cultures.
>
> Promote bilingual education giving preference to the mother tongue, with adequate learning materials.
>
> Make known the essential aspects of autochthonous culture to the

Spanish-speaking Mexicans so that they may appreciate and not denigrate it.

Support the literary, dramatic, and audiovisual creations of the Indians — who have a great treasure of histories, traditions, and legends — through literary workshops and adequate translations. (Sna Jtz'ibajom promotional materials)

The 1982 appeal to the anthropologists contained an element of alarm regarding acculturative processes in the Chiapas Highlands. Juan de la Torre López explains: "In the primary schools they teach us about other cultures and use another language: Spanish. The relative distance between our knowledge of Spanish and Tzotzil thus increases, with Tzotzil assuming an increasingly subordinate position." Indeed, the contact with Ladino culture is generally seen by the Maya as the most destructive of cultural forces. This deeply felt situation is expressed through folktales in which "the Ladino almost without exception, is an evil character, whether layman or priest — 'the spawn of an Indigenous woman and a white dog.' Running through the folktales is an ever-recurring refrain: 'Once the town had wealth, now it's penniless; if what had happened had not happened, we would be on top, the Ladino face up'" (Laughlin, *Of Cabbages* 12).

This sentiment also surfaces in The Writers' House puppet version of the timeless Zinacantec folktale "El cura diablo" ("The Devil Priest"). This tale recounts how a village priest once made use of trickery to seduce local women. The priest is presented as an incarnation of the devil, and by no means as a mere human gone astray. This characterization thus provides the outsider with a perspective on the Maya's ever-vigilant attitudes toward the ministers of the Roman Catholic church, particularly since the majority are Ladinos.

CULTURAL CONTROL AND THE WRITERS' HOUSE PROJECTS

The writers' appeal — and the work which they have carried out to date in literacy, writing, publishing, and theatre — constitute an attempt to (re)-gain a decisive degree of *cultural control*[9] over the written and oral expressions of their own cultural elements. On one hand, they seek to *reassume control* of that which is theirs (autonomous cultural elements); and on the other hand, to *appropriate* for their own use those elements/practices which are not part of their present-day culture due to historical processes of deculturation and domination. And unlike most of the anthropological literature which their culture has inspired, their writings are destined for Tzotzil and Tzeltal audiences. The goal then is to form homegrown producers and consumers of Mayan cultural narratives (written and dramatized), and also to control the circuits of distribution of these products.

The Writers' House work in theatre began with the 1985 creation of the Lo'il Maxil (Monkey Business) traveling puppet theatre.[10] The group began to present dramatized versions of folktales which they had written down and published locally. The puppet shows, performed mainly in Tzotzil and Tzeltal Mayan languages, were intended to inspire audiences to learn to read their brightly colored, bilingual (Tzotzil-Spanish) booklets. The puppet troupe has since carried out frequent tours through the Tzotzil and Tzeltal townships of Zinacantán, Chamula, Tenejapa, and San Andrés Larráinzar. They have also performed in Zoque (Chiapas) and Yucatec Mayan communities, and have taken part in the Fiesta Nacional de Teatro Comunidad (National Community Theatre Festival).[11] The demand for such performances has been great, although the group's arrival in certain hamlets has been frustrated at times by poor roads and failing vehicles.

In 1988 The Writers' House literacy project La Escuela Tzotzil (The Tzotzil School) initiated classes thanks to Smithsonian Institution grants (1988–90). It continued to function in 1991 thanks to a one-year W. K. Kellogg Foundation grant, yet ceased to operate in February, 1992 when further funding could not be secured. Other international sources of support for The Writers' House (besides Cultural Survival, 1983–85) have been CEBEMO (Holland), the Merck Family Fund, and the Inter American Foundation (1986–89). The Writers' House projects have also received some assistance locally, and nationally, within Mexico.[12]

The Tzotzil School had been coordinated by Writers' House member Antonio de la Torre López and former member Manuel Pérez Hernández.[13] In all twenty-three hamlets of Zinacantán and Chamula townships, Tzotzil teachers were contracted to hold four hours of classes weekly in their houses for individuals of all ages. The Writers' House provided notebooks, pencils, blackboards, benches and tables, as well as monthly stipends for teachers (U.S. $30) and students (U.S. $0.80). At the time of its closure, the school boasted a total 1,600 graduates. The six-month course, which was completed by 90 percent of enrollees, included semi-monthly exams. Didactic materials included The Writers' House publications (the *Primer* and folktales). By the end of the course, students had to prove their ability by writing a short story. The diploma awarded to graduates states "*La lengua materna es cultura*" ("The mother tongue is culture"). Those graduates who have shown the greatest promise as writers have been invited to join The

Writers' House as full-time fellows.[14] 1991 stipends for the writers were U.S. $230–80 per month.

On a typical day, the eleven writers/actors arrive at 9 A.M. for a four-to-five-hour work day at the San Cristóbal headquarters. Most of this time is spent creating (writing, editing, and drawing), rehearsing, and performing — as part of the puppet theatre and/or the live actors' group. (The literacy project coordinators would spend every other day at a separate office handling paperwork, or supervising classes in both nearby and distant hamlets.) The main offices are equipped with a few typewriters and Kaypro computers, Beta and VHS video decks, files, storage and rehearsal space. The core group commutes daily from Zinacantán and Chamula, while a few have left more distant towns to live in San Cristóbal.[15] Accomplished writer Francisco Alvarez Quiñones is the only non-Mayan member; his main task within the group is Spanish-language script writing.

1993 full-time Writers' House members were: cofounders Mariano López Méndez (Chamula), Anselmo Pérez Pérez (Zinacantán), and Juan de la Torre López (Zinacantán, Secretary); also, the latter's brother and former Tzotzil School coordinator Antonio de la Torre López (Zinacantán, Treasurer), Diego Méndez Guzmán (Tenejapa — Tzeltal, President), and newer (1992–93) members Domingo Gómez Castellanos and María Santis Gómez (Chamula), Francisco Javier Hernández Pérez, Margarita de la Cruz López, and Mariano López de la Cruz (Zinacantán), Cristóbal Guzmán Meza and Hermenegildo Sánchez Guzmán (Tenejapa–Tzeltal), and part-time actress Celia Serrano Rodríguez (San Cristóbal). Additionally, former members Petrona de la Cruz Cruz (Zinacantán) and Isabel Juárez Espinosa (Aguacatenango) are both very promising dramatists and talented actresses. Their work has been presented at the Second International Women's Playwrights Conference (Montreal 1991) and at Texas Christian University's Fourth Festival of Mayan Culture (1992). While they most likely are Mexico's first indigenous women playwrights, their society has not yet exempted them from traditional gender expectations; their response has been an aggressive defense of their chosen paths.[16]

LIVE THEATRE: INFLUENCES, CHALLENGES, CONTRADICTIONS

Sna Jtz'ibajom's writing abilities and experience in traditional narrative laid the foundations for new dramaturgy, upon which the writers embarked in 1989. Five of the group's seven plays have been directed by Ralph Lee, artistic director of New York State's Mettawee River Company. Lee's work

has some essential parallels with that of the Mayan group. During summer months, the Mettawee is an itinerant troupe performing in rural up-
state New York and New England. The Writers' House is also an itinerant
group, touring monthly to different communities in the Highlands, and
beyond. Mettawee also organizes periodic pageants and parades, including
the Greenwich Village Halloween Parade, incorporating numerous masks
and giant puppets. (Lee is a recognized theatrical mask maker and is commissioned by the best-known of U.S. theatres.) Through the Monkey Business Puppet Theatre, The Writers' House had already created masks for all
of its many characters.[17]

Mettawee's productions revolve around "spirits, gods, and demons" (Allen 10–11), drawing upon Native North American, East Indian, African,
European, and Mayan cultural traditions (including a 1982 *Popol vuh* adaptation). The Writers' House actors' and puppet theatre themes derive from
well-known folktales which still form part of the local oral tradition: *El
haragán y el zopilote* (*The Loafer and The Buzzard*) and *¿A poco hay cimarrones?* (*Who Believes in Spooks?*); also, from more recent incidents which may
be undergoing gestation as potential folktales: *Herencia fatal, drama Tzotzil*
(*Fatal Inheritance, A Tzotzil Drama*), and episodes from the more remote
past: *Dinastía de jaguares* (*Dynasty of Jaguars*).

The paths of Lee and The Writers' House began to converge in 1988 as
Lee was searching for Central American material. Someone suggested he
contact Laughlin, a prominent researcher of Tzotzil oral tradition. Laughlin
had himself received a tip on Lee from Alfred Bush of the Princeton University Library, who had seen Lee's shows and thought he would be an interesting match for the Mayan group (Lee, Interview).

In retrospect, both Lee and The Writers' House members feel positive
regarding the yearly (1989–93) two-to-four-week experiences together
in San Cristóbal, although there have been tense moments. Some physical exercises initially caused a bit of cross-cultural trauma, especially for
the women members: Lee dared ask a mixed-sex group of Tzotziles and
Tzeltales — including a prominent shaman (Anselmo Pérez) and ex-mayor
(Mariano López) — to line up, open their mouths, stick out their tongues,
and make strange sounds. Nevertheless, the actors eventually came to appreciate their increased physical and vocal agility. Juan de la Torre states:
"We had no idea how to move around on stage."[18] Lee helped with stage
movements, blocking scenes, and fine tuning the group's script. Given the
writers' "shyness," Lee states that he chose to use a "light touch" in directing
the Mayan group, inducing them to provide suggestions and solutions. He
wanted the results to be "their work" (Interview).

Choice of performance language is a complex, and somewhat contradictory issue. As previously stated, one of the writers' objectives is to "reinforce the maternal language, in both oral and written form." While the
puppet theatre works mainly in Tzotzil and Tzeltal, the live actors' plays
have been predominantly in Spanish. There are several reasons. First of all,
The Writers' House has deliberately brought together both Tzeltal and
Tzotzil speakers, the two major Highlands ethnic groups. None, however,
are fluent speakers of the others' tongue; as a result, their lingua franca is
Spanish, in which all are highly fluent. Also, the puppet performances
required the participation of just a few of the writers at any one time, and all
of the voices could therefore be either Tzeltal or Tzotzil. The live actors'
pieces, on the other hand, have been premiered in Spanish; a few have been
subsequently translated and presented in Tzotzil. The group comments that
if their budget were greater, they would hire enough writers-actors to have
two groups, one performing in Tzotzil, the other in Tzeltal. Lee's work with
the group was possible only through Francisco Alvarez and Robert Laughlin who are fluent in Spanish, Tzotzil, and English.

The use of Spanish, however, makes performances linguistically accessible to other indigenous and nonindigenous peoples. This includes both the
neighboring Zoques, as well as important, potential supporters: Patricia
Ortiz Mena de González Garrido (the past Chiapas governor's wife) and
Cecilia Ocheli de Salinas (the wife of President Salinas de Gortari) were
impressed by a performance in San Cristóbal. This led to an invitation to
represent Chiapas in the November 1989 Muestra Nacional de Teatro,
Mexico's prestigious National Theatre Showing. Their rendition of *The
Loafer and The Buzzard* placed *sixth* among fifty-six performances by theatre
companies from all of Mexico! January 1993 performances for a group of
visitors from northern Mexico and Texas also led to sorely needed financial
support for creative projects and a Museum of Tzotzil Culture in Zinacantán. Also, performances held at Gertrude Duby de Blom's Na Bolom Mu-
seum/Guest House in San Cristóbal are meant to attract the attention of
Mexican and international visitors.

On the other hand, performing in Spanish in an indigenous community
such as San Juan Chamula remains contradictory to the stated goals of the
Writers' House; it also linguistically excludes most indigenous women and
older men who are overwhelmingly monolingual. Laughlin observes that
familiarity with the tales portrayed usually overrides such linguistic difficulties. Nevertheless, *The Loafer and The Buzzard* is now routinely and
spontaneously performed in Tzotzil in indigenous communities to the fascination of audiences.[19]

I was present at a Spanish-language performance of *Fatal Inheritance, A Tzotzil Drama* at the Casa de la Cultura in San Juan Chamula on 24 June 1991, during the culmination of the three-day Fiesta de San Juan. The audience, mainly men with some women and children, was truly fascinated with the live theatre performance. There were no seats, and a continuous pushing match ensued throughout the performance: Everyone's goal was to earn a place at the foot of the small, elevated stage. To my initial surprise, particularly *dramatic* moments elicited great excitement and laughter! Several times, a physical wave of emotion swept through the entire crowd, from left to right, nearly bringing us all down onto the floor!

That day at Chamula any neat dividing line between *stage drama* and *social drama*[20] seemed to be nonexistent for the indigenous audience. This was particularly striking during a scene where a confession is flogged out of two accused murderers. By this point in the play, the stage itself was full of curious and excited onlookers — children and men, surrounding the actors in an attempt to get a closer look at the stage events, which so curiously resembled episodes of *real life* out in the central plaza. That day I became fully aware, for perhaps the first time, of the power that live theatre can achieve to truly *move* an audience — emotionally as well as physically! It was wonderful to experience this rare and special moment off to one side of the dusty Chamula plaza, far from the luxuries, comforts, and conventions which most people associate with theatre.

FROM FOLKTALES TO HISTORY: FIVE MAJOR PRODUCTIONS

The Writers' House five major actors' theatre productions to date are: *El haragán y el zopilote* (*The Loafer and The Buzzard*, 1989), *¿A poco hay cimarrones?* (*Who Believes in Spooks?*, 1990), *Herencia fatal, drama Tzotzil* (*Fatal Inheritance, A Tzotzil Drama*, 1991), *Dinastía de jaguares* (*Dynasty of Jaguars*, 1992), and *¡Vámonos al paraíso!* (*Let's Go to Paradise!*, 1993). The first three are based on elements of the Tzotzil and Tzeltal oral traditions; the fourth, on written sources (Mayan and non-Mayan); and the most recent, on both oral and written sources.

The writers first discovered their potential for acting during a 1987 puppet tour to Antigua, Guatemala; two anthropologists approached them, and asked if they could dramatize a Chol Mayan folktale the following day. Back at their hotel the group listened intently as member Francisco Alvarez began to read the text, and soon everyone was acting out the piece, "paddling canoes" on the floor. A quick rehearsal the next morning was

Figure 1. The Writers' House in *Herencia fatal*. Left to right: Mariano López Mendez, Manuel Pérez Hernández, Isabel Juárez Espinosa, and Albina López Gómez. Photo by Marcey Jacobson.

followed by the group's first live performance. Improvised as it was, the experience opened new horizons for the writers (Laughlin, Personal Communication).

Later that same year, members of the puppet troupe were able to observe contemporary live drama for the first time at the Fiesta Nacional de Teatro Comunidad (Coxquihui, Veracruz, November 1987). These two experiences inspired the group to set their next artistic goal: They would take their own actors' theatre piece to the Fiesta Regional de Teatro Comunidad (Tlaxiaco, Oaxaca, September 1989). Despite their lack of experience, coupled with the typical Tzotzil avoidance of verbal display, the budding actors found encouragement in the elegant simplicity of the folktale *The Loafer and The Buzzard* and went to work on the script.

The Loafer and The Buzzard (1989)
The Loafer and The Buzzard is based on a role-switching motif: The Loafer who aspires to switch places with the seemingly easy-going Buzzard gets his wish through divine intervention. By the time he realizes that the Buzzard's life is not so easy either, the Buzzard has already impressed the Loafer's wife

through hard work. Soon, the now desperate Loafer-turned-Buzzard returns home to beg for food, but crash-lands in his wife's patio and dies. Upon discovering the switch, she accepts the Buzzard as husband: Despite his odor, he is not a loafer. In the end, she rewards his dedication to the cornfield by inviting him to bed.

This piece reflects the moralistic, fable-like quality of much of traditional Mayan narrative and drama.[21] Indeed, Laughlin observes that "on several occasions the raconteur would explicitly state that he had been told a certain tale 'so he would not grow up to be lazy like the buzzard man' " (Laughlin, *Of Cabbages* 5). An outstanding feature of the stage version is the Buzzard's costume, particularly an enormous, beaked head mask created with Ralph Lee's inspiration.

Who Believes in Spooks? (1990)

But I find ¿*A poco hay cimarrones?—Who Believes in Spooks?*[22] to be much more fascinating, given its supernatural protagonist (Hikal, phonetically j'ik'al) and the complex historical processes which have led to his multilayered persona. To begin with, the Spanish word *cimarrón* (Chiapan Spanish equivalent of Tzotzil and Tzeltal *hikal*) immediately suggests the historical phenomenon of the *negro cimarrón,* the runaway black slave. But locally, *cimarrón* has other meanings: It is used in reference to someone who is bad or evil (*malo*), mean (*cabrón,* literally: "a bastard"), stubborn (*terco*), and hard to catch (*difícil de agarrar*). And while the character portrayed is indeed of black coloring, the group is quick to point out that *cimarrón* "has nothing to do with African people, but rather the demon who lives in the mountain caves," i.e., the Hikal.

This play is a dramatized composite of Tzotzil and Tzeltal folktales from Zinacantán, Chamula, and Tenejapa which recount the evil deeds of this nocturnal creature.[23] But there is also an element of firsthand experience! Member—and prominent Zinacantec shaman—Anselmo Pérez Pérez has *seen* the Hikal. In fact, the stage Hikal was costumed from a drawing based on Pérez's experience: He is about a meter tall, is black and curly-haired, has a white chest, wears black shoes, wide-brimmed hat, and cape. Sarah Blaffer, who has studied the Hikal complex in detail, summarizes the essential characteristics of this prominent protagonist of the oral tradition:

He lives in caves and comes out at dusk to steal chickens and to molest people. A thief and a murderer, he also carries lone women off to his cave and keeps them there. Hikal's most striking feature is his sexuality; he has a six-foot long, death-dealing penis. Women raped by Black-man become superimpregnated. In some cases the woman swells up and dies; in others, her children begin to appear within three days of conception and then keep coming, one child a night. A common complaint concerning *Hikaletik* [plural form] is that they "breed too fast." Despite this potency, Zinacantecos are convinced that there used to be many more Black-men than there are today. Formerly, they could not leave their houses for fear of Black-men. One Zinacanteco narrates: "The spooks have gotten fewer. Long ago we couldn't go outside until nine o'clock [A.M.]. At three o'clock [A.M.] you close up the house, close the door . . . Supplies of wood and water must be stored ahead of time; all needs must be attended to inside the house." (20)

Hikal tales generally revolve around four situations, as identified by Blaffer (all four are included in *Who Believes in Spooks?*):

1. Hikal comes to the house of a woman cooking corn and murders her or carries her off, or both. He grabs her while she is asleep by the fire or when she goes to pour out the *nixtamal* (lime water in which the corn is boiled before it is ground). Each time, the woman's neighbor hears the corn boiling over onto the fire, making the sound *pululu;* actually, this sound is the blood of Hikal's victim.

2. Hikal accosts either a man alone or two [Zinacantec] travelers, and they fight. Except in one case, the men are unconscious, asleep, drunk, or in a faint. The outcome will be the death of Hikal and either a trip to Black-man's home or the rescue of one of his victims.

3. Hikal longs for company and beseeches Saint Sebastian the Martyr and San Lorenzo [Saint Lawrence] to give him one of their children. These tales describe his quest. The fact that the saints do not really give him one of their children suggests that pious people who comply with Zinacanteco norms are protected from Hikal.

4. The travelers [as in 2 above] rescue a girl wrapped up in a straw mat. [Or] the girl who is stolen while throwing out her *nixtamal* or while kneading clay is rescued from the spook's cave by being pulled out with a rope. (21–23)

In these tales — Blaffer observes — women tend to be raped or murdered, whereas men, the brave ones at least, are rewarded with money, meals, or marriage (23). When women are so punished, it may be because of an underdose of care in their female responsibilities. The Hikal himself represents the ideal type of masculinity (hardness and potency) carried to a dangerous extreme: He punishes those men in myths who are not hard enough and rewards those who live up to the ideal type. The ideal type, concludes Blaffer, might be called "hardness in moderation," neither too soft and womanlike, nor as hard as the Hikal. Therefore, "by his own example and by the retributions he enacts, Hikal clarifies normative roles for men and women in Zinacantán" (120–21).

The Writers' House prefers to view the message embodied in their version somewhat differently. For them, the play "speaks of the way to overcome the demons: men and women uniting for this purpose, with the help of the patron saints of Chamula and Zinacantán." However, neither The Writers' House version nor the folktales contains any scene in which men and women actually unite. Brave men and the (male) Saints deal some blows to the Hikal, while brave women deal others, but always separately. In the final scene of *Who Believes in Spooks?* the Hikal is finally killed (impaled) by an old woman defending her granddaughters whom he has trapped in the family *temazcal* (steam bath). Just prior to the fatal blow, the old woman's response to the Hikal's request for one of her girls contains a sharp social commentary: "A girl? Just so that you can eat her up? Who do you think you are, that you can take my girls away — a Ladino [*jkaxlan*] or a boss [*cacique*]?" As the men and women discover the dead Spook, each sex group (men and saints together, then the women) proclaims separately: "We men/women beat the *Cimarrón!*" Finally, in unison they proclaim "We all beat the *Cimarrón!*"[24] Perhaps this constitutes a message of "unity" in a society still very bound by traditional sex roles. However, it becomes obvious that The Writers' House decision to do this play had more to do with the predominance of the Hikal in the oral tradition, and the dramatic potential of a stage version.

The masks and costuming, created by The Writers' House, with the collaboration of Lee and Robert and Miriam Laughlin, reveal transcultured aspects of several of the characters: The Hikal himself is costumed as described by eyewitness Anselmo Pérez Pérez; he also wears an anthropomorphic, bat-like mask. Since no one else in the group has *seen* the Hikal, the other members were largely guided by their imagination, fueled by folktales which they first heard as small children. Francisco Alvarez pointed out to the actors that the Hikal may be related to the bat which decapitates and (temporarily) kills Hero Twin Hunapú in the *Popol vuh* (also depicted in ancient Mayan iconography). There is indeed ample evidence for this cited in anthropological literature.[25] When the group examined photos of Chiapan bats, they decided that they really were frightening enough to be part of the Hikal's costume; and as always, this protagonist of the oral tradition dresses more like a Ladino than a Maya (wide-brimmed Andalusian hat, cape, sword) while he also looks like a bat (scalloped cape, mask, winglets on hat). As traditional dress in Highlands Chiapas is highly codified along sex and township lines, the Hikal is easily recognized not just as an outsider, but as the enemy.

Given his dark coloring and kinky hair, another of Hikal's ancestors would seem to be African. Nevertheless, there are practically no blacks living today in San Cristóbal nor in the outlying indigenous towns, nor is there any widespread, popular historical memory of blacks having ever lived there. Through association with the Hikal, however, Tzotziles and Tzeltales are terrified of blacks and will do anything to avoid contact with one (Laughlin, Personal Communication). Regarding the Hikal's historical ties to Africans, Laughlin observes that:

> In a sixteenth-century Tzotzil dictionary compiled in Zinacantán, *hical* is given as "negro de guinea" [a black from Guinea]. The Spook's negroid features may derive from a memory of the African slaves. Although Negroes are no longer native to the region, as late as 1778 there were 723 living in San Cristóbal. They were treated more as confidants than as slaves, for they were permitted to wear daggers and to dress in European clothing. As such, they served the role of majordomos and foremen who most likely were entrusted with the task of inflicting physical punishment on their master's Indian serfs (Favre 81–82). It is not farfetched to assume that the Spaniards increased their authority by spreading stories of the Africans' former cannibalistic appetites. The Spook's cave-dwelling habits may possibly be traced to a memory of African slaves who escaped from the lowlands and sought temporary refuge in the wildest mountain areas. This is supported by the Spanish name for the Spook, "Negro Cimarrón," "Black Runaway Slave." (*Of Cabbages* 348)

Blacks were also strongly represented in invading Spanish armies and punitive missions during the Tzeltal Rebellion of 1712–13 (Bricker, *The Indian Christ* 63–64), thus adding additional historical fuel to the Maya's fears which are still alive today. However, the African branch of Hikal's ancestry turned out to be more problematic than useful to the group. In fact, one of the reasons for emphasizing his relation to *bats* was precisely to de-emphasize the connection with *blacks*. Why? The group's previous use of a black puppet had drawn accusations of racism from Ladino and foreign spectators in San Cristóbal and in the United States. In order to avoid new misunderstandings with nonindigenous audiences it was decided that the

Hikal should not look *too* African. While the dark coloring and kinky hair remained, the stage Spook definitely looks more like a bat.

The painted, papier-mâché masks worn by other characters also reveal interesting insights into Tzotzil beliefs. In the play's folktale sources, three locally venerated saints appear as antagonists to the Hikal:[26] San Sebastián (a prominent saint in Zinacantán), San Lorenzo (Zinacantán's patron saint), and San Juan (patron of Chamula). In *Who Believes in Spooks?*, however, they appear simply as "Sebas," "Lencho" (familiar, "nickname" forms of Sebastián and Lorenzo), and "Juan." While it is perfectly acceptable to make direct reference to the saints in oral narrative, the group members were unable to directly portray them upon the stage, or even refer to them as "saints." (The saints, they explain, are the images kept in the churches, and no one may impersonate them.) They were instead characterized as "old men" and given corresponding masks: Soldier San Sebastián wears a military-style cap and long Ladino-style pants, topped off with a Zinacantec tunic; San Lorenzo dresses as a native Zinacantec, including cotton short pants (the only one of the three who somewhat resembles the local church icon); and San Juan wears an old-fashioned Chamulan hat, traditional woolen poncho, and carries an old-fashioned tobacco horn. Finally, the old Chamulan woman who kills the Hikal wears a round, white face mask representing the Virgin of the Moon, syncretic night protectress of women.

In summary, the Hikal-Cimarrón brings together characteristics of ancient supernatural bats, as well as black soldiers and overseers, Spaniards and Ladinos — the Maya's historical enemies, and his behavior is censurable. On the other hand, the saints and the old woman display syncretic characteristics — part Tzotzil, and part European Christian; they are also identified with the magical, amuletic forces which protect the communities in exchange for the latter's adherence to prescribed moral values. Between these two poles we have brave women and men who become the saints' "field soldiers," dealing crippling, and finally, deadly blows to the unwelcome predator. This play thus joins *The Loafer and The Buzzard* in setting forth archetypal, normative examples for human behavior.

Fatal Inheritance, A Tzotzil Drama (1991)
Fatal Inheritance, A Tzotzil Drama (*Herencia Fatal, Drama Tzotzil*) — The Writers' House 1991 production — also demonstrates great concern for the behavior of Highlands men and women. As in the case of the Hikal, men are chastised for violent behavior against women sparked by greed, alcohol, and disrespect for family ties. On the other hand, the women characters

Figure 2. Petrona de la Cruz Cruz, left, Antonio de la Torre López, center, and Isabel Juárez Espinosa, right, in *Herencia fatal*. Photo by Marcey Jacobson.

stand as positive role models who not only respect the elders, but also, in the face of men's violence, demonstrate self-sufficiency and stand firm in their demand that justice be done. This is ultimately made possible by an exemplary *presidente municipal* who makes every effort that the guilty be punished, and the aggrieved women protected.

Having previously written several *comedias*,[27] the writers decided to attempt something different: a *drama*. The writers relate how this was a great challenge, since none except Francisco Alvarez was fully familiar with the genre. The breakthrough came as a result of discussions which led them to realize that indigenous communities are *full* of dramas! Everyone then brought to the workshop a true story of social drama: family conflicts, land disputes, killings, thefts, etc. The incident portrayed was chosen because it represents a common situation: Orphaned women frequently are robbed of their inheritances by other family members. Also, local officials too often defend abusive individuals (out of fear, bribes, etc.) rather than punishing them; as a result, the aggrieved are left without protection or legal recourse.

The story line for *Fatal Inheritance* was thus adapted from a real-life occurrence of domestic violence (circa 1987) in the Tzeltal township of Tenejapa.[28] Member Diego Méndez Guzmán was personally touched by this incident, which he retold to the group: Following their parents' death, two brothers apparently killed one of their two sisters and hid her body in order to obtain her share of the inheritance. The body was never located, however, and the accused assassins were soon released from jail. The writers — dissatisfied with this turn-of-events — decided to institute some radical changes in their stage version: The *presidente municipal* who hears a witness's and the surviving sister's pleas for justice, orders the accused brothers arrested. He believes the women's accusations against these known troublemakers, which are strengthened by inconsistencies in the brothers' alibis. His decision is to publicly flog a confession out of them, even though Ladino law prohibits this practice. The weaker brother succumbs, and the witness's cowardly husband also finally talks. The *presidente* sends all three men off to prison, thus protecting the aggrieved and punishing the guilty.

Herencia Fatal thus presents an *ideal* version of how violent crime should be dealt with. The tension between this *stage drama* and the underlying — yet different — *social drama* is underlined in comments made by the *presidente municipal* to the inept and dopey town judge: He repeatedly warns him not to "pull any tricks, or cover for the guilty," particularly "bosses [*caciques*] and abusive individuals." The judge is uneasy about seeing true justice done, and suggests that they bring in the authorities from Jobel (San Cristóbal). The *presidente municipal* insists, however, that justice can be done without going outside the community: "What do you think *we* are here for? What will people say if they think that we aren't able to take care of our town's problems?" And once the confessions have been obtained: "We didn't need for the outside authorities to come in, just to complicate everything, as always. . . . They just spend their time making dirty deals." Finally, the *presidente* praises the women's courage: "Well, it's all over now, thanks to Paxku's coming to accuse them. God! I wish that everyone were so brave as you! Now you know — if you have problems, come and see me."

Diego Méndez Guzmán comments that this play "is meant to educate people, to show that killing people is not to be taken lightly." He also points out that since performing the play in numerous towns, the group has discovered that such killings are common, as is the legal trickery which allows the guilty to go free. Many spectators have praised the group for presenting such positive examples, thus recognizing the need for change. It remains to be seen whether this specific stage drama will help reduce the frequency or influence the nature of similar social dramas. One thing is for sure: People are not likely to forget the positive images presented by The Writers' House theatre. Laughlin has observed that "the depth of moral concern of Spanish oral literature is equaled in Zinacantec tales, but in Zinacantán it is expressed with somberness; righteousness vindictively triumphant, or injustice unhappily endured" (*Of Cabbages* 9). The Writers' House version of the Tenejapa incident definitely contributes consciously to the former variant of local lore.

Dynasty of Jaguars (1992)

Dinastía de jaguares (*Dynasty of Jaguars*), was premiered at the Southern States' Theatre Festival held in March 1992 at Mérida, Yucatán. Billed as "epic drama," this three-act piece spans a vast time period, beginning with the mythical times of origin, through the Classic Mayan period, and up until the Spanish Conquest. Lee was again guest director, and Francisco Alvarez's Spanish-language script was again modified and enriched through group discussions and experiences.

The play unfolds as a Mayan shaman magically transports his apprentice back in time to witness three historic episodes deemed as essential knowledge for the present-day Maya: the Conquest of Chiapas (act I); the *Popol vuh* episodes of the birth of the Hero Twins Junapú and Xbalamké, their defeat of the Lords of Death, and the creation of the four Jaguar Lords, founders of the "all of the World's tribes" (act II); and finally, the story of how King Pakal Balam (Shield Jaguar) of Yaxchilán maintained intertribal

Figure 3. *Dinastía de jaguares*. Indigenous leader Sanguieme being tortured.
Photo by Macduff Everton.

unity by choosing as his A.D. 752 successor K'uk Balam (Bird Jaguar) — his
son by a recent wife — rather than his incompetent firstborn (act III).[29]

Data was once again obtained from anthropological sources. Jan de Vos's
recent study *La batalla del sumidero* informs act I. In his controversial
study, de Vos revises popular belief that thousands of indigenous peoples of
present-day Chiapa de Corzo leaped to their death in the Sumidero Canyon, rather than surrendering to the Spanish. Instead, through a methodic
presentation of previously uncovered documents, de Vos demonstrates that
a smaller number of Chiapanecs fell into the canyon not as a collective
suicide, but after having being fired upon by a Spanish arquebus. Act III
was inspired by a trip to Copán, Honduras, and on-site consultation with
Mayan hieroglyphic expert Linda Schele (as well as by Schele & David
Friedel's joint study). The group learned that recent anthropological work
has identified intertribal warfare as a significant contributing factor in the
decline and demise of ancient Mayan civilization.

This theory was translated by the group into a message which stresses
unity and peaceful coexistence as the keys to strength and survival. The
latter are closely linked to the perpetuation of key cultural elements: cus-

toms, language, and rituals. While these vary from people to people, the shaman concludes that "only the names change; the Great Creator Spirit remains constant." Just as the Hero Twins of the *Popol vuh* triumphed over death — not through brute force, but through ingenuity and wisdom — so must all oppressed people "resist," and in so doing, be "worthy and prudent" in their demands for justice. In the end, only education and peaceful solutions will prevent "severe punishment" from Mother Earth. The shaman's apprentice, moved by his teacher's words, ends the play with the optimistic words: "We shall never die!"

Former writer-actress Petrona de la Cruz Cruz, who participated in the creation of *Dynasty of Jaguars,* best expresses the significance of this play for Sna Jtz'ibajom:

> This play has made me think, and has made me dream about our ancestors, about what they were like. There have been so many generations which have since passed through this world, that we need to recover the culture of our first ancestors, and show it to people who have forgotten. I cannot go from person to person, or from house to house explaining what our ancestors were like, how they passed through this world, how they used to live. Through *Dynasty of Jaguars* we can now show people how things were, and what the Conquest was like. This play is very important for the people of Chiapas. (Interview, 1992)

Let's Go to Paradise! (1993)

The script of *¡Vámonos al paraíso! (Let's Go to Paradise!)*, The Writers' House 1993 *tragicomedia* focuses upon the extreme abuses committed by lowlands coffee growers against indigenous peons: indentured labor, machete blows for "laziness," double hours, and filthy living conditions. Sick peons are left to die, and are buried in the coffee fields as "fertilizer" for the plants.

Divided into two acts, we observe how a contract peon leads an undercover government inspector into a German-owned coffee plantation ironically named El Paraíso: "Paradise." Both men witness firsthand the abuses ordered by the owner, and carried out by his foremen; however, the peon employs magic to gain mischievous revenge against an overseer, introducing the comic element so necessary in this otherwise tragic play. While the events portrayed are identified in an epilogue as being from the 1930s, it is suggested that the present status quo has not significantly changed; the surviving peon briefly informs us that reforms instituted as a result of such investigations have since dissolved through bribery, and that: "Everything became covered up again so that we Maya remained the same or worse off than before, just as occurs with the Guatemalan refugees, who practically work for nothing. That is what is happening to today's Maya, on the very lands where our ancestors lived as this Continent's most civilized people."

And closing comments by the German coffee grower make the spectator reflect on the nature of Chiapas' number one cash crop: "As I was saying, my dear friends, our plantation El Paraíso exports the world's best coffee. And the best thing is that it allows us to make lots of money! Come on, try some! Wouldn't you like a cup of the best export-quality coffee? Mayan coffee? Really — there are no more cadavers!"

Thus, what is "paradise" for a very few outsiders, is hell for the majority, the indigenous peoples who continue to struggle to maintain moral and physical integrity in a still neocolonial economic system. *Let's Go to Paradise!* was again directed by Ralph Lee, whose February 1993 residency was made possible by a grant from the Bancomer/Rockefeller-supported Fondo Para la Cultura (Fund for Culture).

FINAL THOUGHTS

In mid-1993, Year of Indigenous Peoples, The Writers' House continues its search for the financial means by which to carry forth the array of cultural activities outlined in this essay. The achievements have already been impressive: They have publicly addressed Mayan social norms, mythology, social conflict, economic exploitation, the Spanish Conquest, and the pre-Hispanic past through puppetry and stage drama — in the Mayan townships, in the Ladino stronghold of San Cristóbal, and beyond; and they have made native-language literacy a reality for 1,600 Tzotzil Maya. They have, in short, increased their degree of cultural control, recovering lost cultural practices, and strategically incorporating useful elements from other cultural traditions.

The daily hard work has been squarely on the shoulders of the writers-actors; nevertheless, their success has also resulted in part from friendships and alliances with outsiders — both Mexican and foreign, including influential members of the anthropological community. Perhaps the long-term satisfaction and nonthreatening nature of many of these relationships have contributed to The Writers' House vision of mutual respect and peaceful coexistence as set forth by the shaman in *Dynasty of Jaguars*. I have learned much through my relationship with these artists, actors, and teachers, and hope that others — both Maya and non-Maya — may also find inspiration in their work.

NOTES

I express my appreciation to Sna Jtz'ibajom, Robert Laughlin, and Ralph Lee for their time and patience in answering my many questions. *Kolaval!* Thank you!

1 While the Writers' Cooperative works in both languages, the theatre presentations have been in both Tzotzil and Spanish; and prior to its closure in 1992, the Literacy Project's focus was exclusively Tzotzil.

2 I have collected my data since 1986 through both informal and structured interaction with authors, actors, and project advisors: conversations, interviews, correspondence, attendance at performances, and home stays in Chiapas and Texas. Summer 1991 fieldwork in Highlands Chiapas was carried out thanks to a Texas Christian University Research Fund Grant; Winter 1993 fieldwork was facilitated by TCU sabbatical support. For additional background information on Sna Jtz'ibajom see my articles "Active Ethnicity" and "El Nuevo Teatro Maya;" also, Breslin, and Miriam Laughlin.

3 While the term *indio* [Indian] has been accepted as valid nomenclature by many indigenous peoples, it traditionally carries colonial or neocolonial connotations of inferiority. The Writers' House ambiguously rejects the term while also using it as part of their legal name, possibly as a reflection of the generally benevolent usage of the word by anthropologist allies. I prefer to break with the use of the imposed/assimilated Western term in favor of *indigenous* or *indigenous peoples*. However, *Indian* and *indio* have so permeated Mayan-area scholarship that when quoting directly or indirectly from such sources, it is impossible to avoid its usage all together.

4 The Tzeltal Maya are the nation's sixth largest ethnic group, numbering 258,835; the Tzotzil Maya rank seventh at 232,423. Instituto Nacional de Estadística.

5 For a succinct, literary treatment of this situation, see Pozas, and Wilson.

6 Essays by a number of the participants, including reflections on their collaboration, may be found in Bricker and Gossen; see also Vogt, *Bibliography*.

7 Laughlin began fieldwork in Chiapas in 1959 and learned Tzotzil from Domingo de la Torre. Laughlin has maintained a long-term personal relationship with (ex-)informants and their families. He refers to himself as a "facilitator," spending great time and energies to assist Sna Jtz'ibajom through his contacts in the larger world. While in Zinacantán, Laughlin speaks only in Tzotzil, dresses as a Zinacantec, and closely adheres to local cultural tradition.

8 From Cultural Survival promotional material: "Cultural Survival, founded in 1972 by social scientists at Harvard University, is a non-profit organization concerned with the fate of tribal peoples and ethnic minorities around the world. The organization responds to requests for aid from grass-root groups and supports projects which help indigenous peoples cope with situations which threaten their basic human rights."

9 Occasionally in this essay I shall utilize elements of Guillermo Bonfil Batalla's model of *control cultural* (cultural control). This consists of "the system by which the social capacity for decision is exercised over cultural elements" (material, organizational, knowledge-related, symbolic, emotive). The satisfactory realization of social actions depends upon an ethnic group's ability to put these cultural elements into play through the power of decision ("La Teoría" 27). The basic building blocks of this model are four "areas" of culture, in which the cultural elements and the power of decision may correspond to one's own ethnic group or to an extraneous group: *autonomous* culture (own decisions and elements), *appropriated* culture (own decisions, extraneous elements), *alienated* culture

(extraneous decisions, own elements), *imposed* culture (extraneous decisions and elements). See "La teoría del control cultural." A briefer discussion of the model may be found in "Lo propio y lo ajeno."

10 The puppet theatre grew out of a special workshop given to Sna Jtz'ibajom members by former Bread and Puppet Theater member Amy Trompetter. A previous yet apparently unrelated puppetry experience in Chiapas was the 1950s' Teatro Petul in which Domingo de la Torre participated; one of Teatro Petul's most renowned collaborators was writer Rosario Castellanos; see Mendoza and Herrera.

11 The Asociación Nacional de Teatro Comunidad (TECOM) is an umbrella organization which united rural and some urban community theatre groups in yearly national and regional showings, and offers summer workshops in popular theatre techniques. For more on TECOM, see my articles "Mexico: VII Fiesta Nacional" and "Misiones culturales"; and Navarro Sada.

12 Sna Jtz'ibajom has also received the support of Mexican State cultural agencies: The General Office for Popular Cultures in Mexico City (Dirección General de Culturas Populares) and the Chiapas State Department of Culture and Recreation have collaborated, in part, with the publishing program. The Chiapas Institute of Culture has at times sponsored state-wide tours for the theatre group, and in 1992 sponsored the publication of two books. Office space for the coordination of the literacy project has been provided by the National Indigenist Institute (INI). The actors' theatre group has also "sold" a good number of performances. Donations are greatly appreciated and may be arranged through this writer.

13 Pérez Hernández left the group in mid-1992 to assume the directorship of the Casa de la Cultura at Zinacantán.

14 The group took first-, second-, and third-place literary prizes for stories on ecological themes by Juan de la Torre López and now former member Isabel Juárez Espinosa at the Segundo Encuentro de Indios Mayas y Zoques (Second Gathering of Mayan and Zoque Indians), Tila, October 1991. Former member Petrona de la Cruz Cruz was awarded the prestigious Rosario Castellanos Literary Prize in 1992 by the State Government of Chiapas for her original work.

15 Mariano López Méndez's daily commute to San Cristóbal from Chamulan Petej hamlet is via bicycle or foot, depending upon the weather. Each one-way trip lasts from one to two and a half hours (Vogt, "The Chiapas Writers'" 46).

16 For further information on the lives and work of these two women, see Miriam Laughlin.

17 Masks are not as common in present-day Tzotzil dance dramas and rituals as they are in some other areas of Mexico. Costuming *is* generally quite elaborate, and more than compensates for the lack of face covering. On Mexican dance masks and costuming, see Cordry, Esser.

18 The group is quick to point out that they themselves have staged two plays without the help of maestro or teacher: *Entre menos burros, más elotes* (*Fewer Donkeys Mean More Corn*) and *El burro y la mariposa* (*The Donkey and The Moth*), both family-planning pieces commissioned by state agency MEXFAM. A total of 100 Tzotzil-language performances resulted.

19 A June 1993 Tzotzil-language performance in the remote hamlet of Romerillo so captivated the audience that no one budged despite being soaked in a torrential downpour! The audience's stamina inspired the actors to forge ahead: The magic and novelty of the theatrical experience was more powerful than this formidable obstacle set forth by nature!

20 Categories proposed by Victor Turner; one of Turner's most interesting proposals is that "there is an independent, perhaps dialectic, relationship between social dramas and genres of cultural performance in perhaps all societies." While in this essay I do not systematically pursue Turner's proposals, I believe his observations to be valid for much of Indian and *campesino* theatre which I have witnessed in Mexico.

21 Much of traditional Mayan drama as observed and recorded by the first Spanish chroniclers, and recorded in Mayan sources such as the books of *Chilám Balám*, was indeed *moralistic*, setting forth positive examples for behavior, while chastising negative role models; and *fable-like*, in that it many times employed animal characters or other allegorical figures. See Acuña, and Edmonson, *Heaven Born* and "Quiché Literature."

22 A "loose" translation suggested by Laughlin.

23 There are at least seventy local versions; some are recorded in Laughlin, *Of Cabbages*.

24 English translations of the plays are mine.

25 See: Blaffer 57–67, & Laughlin, *Of Cabbages* 65, 348 for a discussion of this point and additional references.

26 Former member Manuel Pérez Hernández points out that for the Tzotzil Maya, a community's positive values — "good customs and ways of speaking, acting, and behaving" — are believed to have originated with that community's founding, patron saint. Human adherence to these norms is therefore pleasing to the saint, and ultimately attracts good fortune. Pérez Hernández goes on to state: "This is the origin of our sense of indigenous identity" (Pérez Hernández, "Como nos identificamos" 6).

27 *The Lazy Man and The Buzzard* and *Who Believes in Spooks?* are both considered "comedies" by the group. Despite the macabre nature of the Hikal and his deeds, the "Spook" is in many parts of the play a pitiful, laughable creature. This is particularly true when he negotiates with the saints and with the old Chamulan woman. These characters are superior and more powerful than the Hikal, and he shrinks to a whining beggar in their presence.

28 In the play, the place of the events portrayed has been fictitiously transferred to the Tzotzil township of Zinacantán; this locus is not identified through dialogue, however, but by the actors' clothing.

29 Coe points out that "perhaps the most complete documents we have for the temporal dynasties which ran the ancient Maya centres are carved on the many stone lintels of Yaxchilán; from these Proskouriakoff has reconstructed the history of the extremely militant 'Jaguar' dynasty, which ruled the site in the eighth century A.D." (172).

Cynthia Steele
"A Woman Fell into the River": Negotiating Female Subjects in Contemporary Mayan Theatre

❏

Había una mujer que era muy noble ni siquiera peleaba con su marido, y entonces estaban contentos en su casa . . . [Un día fue al río a lavar la ropa.] Pero desgraciadamente no fue allá adonde llegaba siempre, sino que se fue donde estaba muy hondo; y ella bajó sus cosas que traía y cuando iba a sacar una cubeta de agua, se resbaló con una piedrita y se cayó al río, la mujer ya no podía salir, como no sabía nadar. Lástima la señora se murió allí porque no tenía compañía, nadie la ayudó a salir.

There was once a woman who was very noble; she didn't even fight with her husband, so they were happy at home . . . [One day she went to the river to do the laundry.] But unfortunately she didn't go to the same place she usually did; rather, she went where it was very deep. And she put down the things she was carrying, and when she was about to take out a water bucket, she slipped on a little rock and fell into the river. The woman couldn't get out again, since she didn't know how to swim. What a shame that the woman died there because she didn't have any company; no one helped her get out. — "Una mujer cayó al río," traditional Tzeltal tale told by an elderly woman in Aguacatenango to Isabel Juárez Espinosa, 1983

In contemporary Mayan society, it is considered extremely dangerous for a woman to venture out by herself, to "strike out on her own." Her sexuality invites male aggression (whether by a human rapist or by the water god who inhabits rivers and lakes); and her lack of escorts (male relatives or older, "asexual" female relatives) renders her helpless to defend herself against such attacks. Safety resides within the four walls of the home; yet even there, a woman left in a room by herself runs the risk of being slain by the "Cimarrón" or spook. "Stay where we can see you," her culture tells her, "don't go too far."

The late 1980s and early 1990s have witnessed a flourishing of native political and cultural movements in Latin America dedicated to the preservation of indigenous cultures and the establishment or preservation of some degree of political and cultural autonomy from the national states. What happens, though, when the defense of indigenous "traditionalism" conflicts with other human rights, including freedom of religious and political affiliation and women's rights? Gender struggles within ethnic nationalism have been apparent, for instance, in the African American and Chicano movements in this country since the 1970s. Recently similar conflicts are emerging in the context of movements for indigenous self-definition in Mexico. In Chiapas, a Southeastern state with a large Mayan population, such issues have become increasingly intertwined with heated political and religious struggles, which are in turn related to national politics and are influenced by the presence of both U.S. and Mexican anthropologists.

In 1988 a Mayan theatre collective emerged out of an indigenous writers' workshop based in San Cristóbal de las Casas, the economic and political capital of the Chiapas Highlands. This collective, Sna Jtz'ibajom, was founded by several Tzotzil- and Tzeltal-speakers from indigenous communities surrounding San Cristóbal. Prime among these were the two communities that have been made internationally famous by U.S. anthropologists, Zinacantán and San Juan Chamula. Mirroring Mayan power relations, the language that is dominant in the theatre troupe is Tzotzil, the language spoken in these two communities; moreover, the largest number of participants is drawn from Zinacantán, the primary site of the influential Harvard Project since the 1960s. In fact, most of the founding members of the collective either have been themselves informants for the Harvard anthropologists or are sons of informants. Most of the funding for Sna during the first few years derived from U.S. foundations, through the efforts of the troupe's intellectual patron, Smithsonian anthropologist Robert Laughlin. More recently these funds have been supplemented by generous support from the state government of Chiapas, which, in collaboration with the Mexican state and the governments of four Central American countries, is aggressively seeking to promote "ethnic tourism" to the Mayan region.[1]

Over the three decades in which the Harvard and Stanford Projects have been active in Zinacantán, this Mayan peasant society has changed rather dramatically. As Frank Cancian has documented in *The Decline of Community in Zinacantán,* the town has evolved, in response to local and global changes, from a tight-knit, fairly insular community of peasant corn farmers into a society of increasing class divisions and inequalities, in which a few men form an elite of truckers, merchants, and government employees, and the majority are wage workers and semi-proletarians who merely supplement their incomes with farming. Greenhouse flower farming now takes precedence over the traditional corn crops; chemical-intensive agriculture takes precedence over labor-intensive (Collier, "Changing Inequality," 112). During this period women's work has continued to be fundamentally domestic but has become somewhat easier, due to the widespread use of corn-grinding mills, the practice of purchasing rather than gathering firewood, and men's widespread adoption of Western-style clothing, which is purchased rather than woven (Cancian 79). George Collier has traced the radical change in marriage practices during this period, from bride-wealth-based marriages (in which the newlyweds indebted and subordinated themselves to their parents for several years following their marriage) to elopement as normative. As a result, women now play a significant role in choosing their marriage partners, and young adults have greater independence from their parents ("Changing Inequality" 119).

In this context of incipient capitalism and increasing inequality, it is not surprising that deep political divisions and conflicts have emerged. Lynn Stephens has analyzed a similar process among the Zapotecs of Teotitlán del Valle, Oaxaca, and the challenge that these changes posed to the village's unified community-based ethnic identity (28). Like the Zapotecs, the Mayas of Zinacantán are striving to maintain and continue projecting just such a cohesive, harmonious image of themselves. On the one hand, they are at the center of the contemporary Mayanist culture movement in Mexico, striving to preserve and stimulate pride in "traditional" Mayan culture.[2] These efforts are being heartily encouraged by the federal and state governments, which are interested in promoting "La Ruta Maya," which is increasingly drawing U.S., Canadian, Western European, and Mexican tourists to Southeastern Mexico, Guatemala, Belize, Honduras, and El Salvador.

This popularized image of Zinacantán is apparent in an article which appears in the current issue of a Mexican magazine devoted to promoting "ethnic tourism" among Mexicans, *México Desconocido* (*Unknown Mexico*):

Unlike what is happening with the majority of Mexico's ethnic groups, which live consumed by poverty and acculturation, there coexists in Zinacantán a past rich in tradition and a present prosperous in economic outlook. The Zinacantecs are a good example of what can be achieved when the heart is divided between work and the conservation of original customs. This village is a product of crop diversification and the desire to be better without losing ancestral values. Five hundred years after the Conquest, Zinacantán is like a ray of light, a guiding light in the deep, dark tunnel that our race is passing through. (Díaz Gómez 68)

The article goes on to celebrate Mayan women as the last repository of ancient traditions:

> Unlike the men, who have gone from sandals to cowboy boots, the Zinacantec ladies still go barefoot and are the iron-willed repositories of many myths and customs which the gentlemen no longer respect. They are the shield against acculturation and the umbilical cord connecting these Mayas with their past. (68)

Hispanic and Anglo cultures have traditionally idealized pre-Columbian Mayan civilization, in contrast to Aztec culture; for most of this century, the former have been portrayed as peace-loving scholars and priests, the latter as warriors and cannibals. It wasn't until the 1980s that these stereotypes began to be seriously challenged. For instance, new epigraphical research by Linda Schele and Mary Ellen Miller demonstrated that the classical Mayas, like the Aztecs, systematically sacrificed war captives, drawing the blood of their victims and sometimes decapitating them. The authors go so far as to call blood "the mortar of ancient Maya ritual life."[3] Nevertheless, in the popular imagination, both in Mexico and abroad, the competing images of peaceful, scholarly Maya and bloodthirsty Aztec, 'good' and 'bad' Indian, tend to persist.

Five hundred years after the conquest, Highlands Chiapas, which was long the government's showcase for Indian policy intent on assimilating Indians into national society, is now offered as proof of the Mexican state's respect for cultural diversity. On a small scale, the same noble savage/ignoble savage dichotomy exists with regard to the two largest Mayan groups, the Zinacantecs and the Chamulas. Zinacantecs are frequently characterized by the press as hard-working, harmonious, elegant, and proud, while the neighboring Chamula Mayas are portrayed as aggressive, violent, drunken, and dirty. As Jan Rus has demonstrated, this barbarous image derives partly from a false historical account of the Tzotzil rebellion of 1869–71, in which the Chamulas allegedly crucified an Indian child in order to have their own savior. It also derives from a real history of rebellion and independence that sets the Chamulas apart from the Zinacantecs (who helped the Spaniards conquer Chamula). Moreover, in recent decades they have become much more impoverished than their neighbors. While the reasons are largely economic and political, in popular accounts Zinacantecs' relative prosperity is usually explained in psychological terms: their work ethic has led to prosperity and social stability, while the Chamulas' laziness and unruliness explains their poverty and social ills. Furthermore, Chamula, like several other Mayan communities and like many ethnic communities in the U.S., has a high internal rate of murder and other violent crimes; again, the explanations are socioeconomic and political in nature, but each media account of Chamula violence feeds the paranoia of conservative Mexicans.

As I mentioned above, while Sna is run as a collective, the members who have acquired the most influence within the troupe are primarily men from Zinacantán, especially three brothers of a key Harvard ethnographic informant. (The other influential members of Sna are a former informant from Chamula and a young Tzeltal-speaking man from Tenejapa.) Because Zinacantecs are dominant, in the troupe as in the Highlands community, it is in their interest to promote the popular image of themselves as the true inheritors of the noble classical Mayans, a sort of "civilized" version of the Lacandón Indians of the rain forest. (The Lacandóns are popularly — and erroneously — thought to be "the last lords of Palenque," direct descendants of the builders of that magnificent pre-Hispanic city.[4]) Moreover, the Zinacantecs' interest coincides with that of the federal and state governments in promoting ethnic tourism.

As one example, earlier this year the three brothers from Zinacantán opened a museum in their family compound, aimed at international and Mexican tourists, and featuring a display of Zinacantec clothing in a traditional conical, thatched-roof house. (Ironically, since such houses are no longer built in Zinacantán, a carpenter had to be brought from Chamula to construct the museum.) When my students toured the museum immediately after it opened in April 1993, the brothers' introductory speech stressed the need to preserve appropriate gender roles in contemporary Mayan society, with men taking their place in the fields and women remaining at the cooking fire and loom. This speech seemed ironic, since the men in this family have themselves deviated from these traditional roles by devoting themselves to anthropological research, theatre, and now museumography. (Needless to say, their wives have not deviated.)

The options available to women in traditional peasant society are extremely limited. One of the original female members of Sna, Petrona de la Cruz Cruz, argued as much in a recent essay:

In the indigenous communities of Chiapas, women have many problems: tradition demands that women stay in their houses, because people think that only men can and should work in the fields or in other non-domestic activities. People believe that a woman's duty is to clean the house, cook, have and take care of the children, fetch water and firewood, and constantly weave, because the family should wear new clothes at each religious festival, and since there are many festivals, women have to be forever at the loom, weaving new clothes for each celebration. (See Appendix I for the complete text.)

The issue of women's rights within the contemporary Mayan (or other indigenous) community may be seen, to a certain extent, as parallel to the issue of religious freedom. As Carlos Monsiváis has noted, the vast majority of leftist critics have viewed the mass conversions of Chiapas Indians to evangelical Protestant religions with alarm, and they have been slow to criticize the Indian elites who have expelled more than 30,000 Mayans from their homes and communities in recent years. Rather, Mexican leftists, like the Indian leaders, tend to view conversion as assimilation and thus betrayal of their "traditional identity." Moreover, the Indian leaders' motivations are by no means strictly religious or cultural; they are also protecting their economic interests and their fifty-year political alliance with the hegemonic national party, the PRI, against incursions by opposition parties of both the right and the left. (The Protestant converts tend to affiliate with opposition parties.) Since the 1950s, Mexican writers and intellectuals have assumed that the evangelical missionaries in the region are mere instruments of the CIA. (For instance, see Rosario Castellanos's short story, "Arthur Smith salva su alma," included in the collection *Ciudad real*.) The evangelicals' remarkable success in acquiring new converts in the Mayan region over the past two decades demonstrates that such explanations are insufficient. Rather, it seems clear that both traditional Catholicism and liberation theology (Chiapas is the home of Mexico's leading liberation theologian, Archbishop Samuel Ruiz) have failed the Mayan community.

As Carlos Monsiváis persuasively argues, people's freedom to choose their own religious and political affiliations must be defended, along with their other human rights, which have been systematically violated by the Indian governments during this crisis. Most frequently these violations have been limited to expulsion from the community and confiscation of property, but they have sometimes also involved violence, including torture and murder.[5] As Monsiváis sees the problem, "That's how things are: In a secularized society like Mexico's, conversion to other beliefs becomes a serious political problem. And an overarching goal becomes clear: the immobility (the Loyalty to Idiosyncrasy) of the indigenous communities, which we try to preserve solely through religious unanimity, ignoring the inroads of modernity and the laws of the Republic" (8). This is the politically charged climate, then, in which the recent gender conflicts have emerged within Sna Jtz'ibajom.

Since 1988 the collective has produced a new play every year. The works have progressed over the past six years from comedies representing contemporary Mayan folktales, often with didactic intent, to dramas addressing contemporary social problems in the Indian communities, to a historical epic in 1992, commemorating Mayan resistance to the conquest. Moreover, prior to 1992 the feminist content of these works became increasingly pronounced, even as the two initial female members of the troupe began to author individual works addressing women's issues.

Sna's first play, *Entre menos burros, más elotes* (*Fewer Donkeys Mean More Corn*, 1988), which was partially funded by Mexico's family planning institute, addresses the destructive consequences, for both the mother and her family, of having too many children too close together. The husband is initially portrayed as insensitive and demanding of his sickly wife, who has become anemic after having eight children in as many years; the children are also malnourished and ill. When the wife explains to the husband that she can't cook his dinner because he hasn't brought home any food, he responds by trying to place the blame on her: "Well, that's what you're here for, to make my dinner. If you don't, why did I marry you, anyhow?" (1, my translation).

Because he realizes, however, that his fields are no longer yielding enough food to feed his family, he travels to the city to look for work; there he is exploited and robbed, and is persuaded that he's better off in his hamlet. He receives advice, first from a friend (who also informs him about the availability of free government medical clinics for his sick children), and then from a village elder who appears to him in a dream, convincing him that his family's economic and health problems are largely due to poor "resource" management:

What you should do is carefully cultivate your land; turn the earth, fertilize it with compost, plant orchards. That way it can produce for you. Because if every year you try to plant only corn, it gets worn out and then doesn't want to yield anything. It's the same with your wife. She's tired and sick because of all the kids she's had. When you go home, you should take good care of them, if you really love them: both your land and your wife. If you take care of them, you'll see how things will work out. Go on, go home now. (7)

This comparison echoes a long-standing characterization of the land in Latin America as the female principle waiting to be improved and fertilized by the male farmer. Woman is the earth in which the male seed is planted. Here, however, the comparison between the male as producer or actor, and the female as vessel for the male seed, is made explicit.

Meanwhile, an angel has stopped the desperate wife, transformed into a moth, from succumbing to the temptation of self-immolation in the flame of a candle. She must not neglect her responsibility to her eight children. In this scene, female subjectivity is explored to some extent, and the woman's plight is portrayed sympathetically.

At the end of the play, the village elder reappears to the woman and her husband and educates them about birth control, reassuring them that they don't have to forsake pleasure (more specifically, the husband doesn't have to forsake it, since he is portrayed as the sexual partner) in order to avoid exhausting their financial and physiological resources with more children. Birth-control pills and injections are suggested as contraceptive methods. No mention is made of the possible side effects of these methods for the women who use them, or of the possibility of the men's participating in birth control, with condoms or vasectomies.

In short, this play has a clear didactic intent encouraged by the Mexican government: to promote birth control (for women), crop rotation, use of government clinics, and paternal responsibility in the indigenous community; and to discourage rural-urban immigration. This, in short, is the least traditional of Sna's productions, preaching the official government line ("The small family lives better"), which promotes a progressive, pro-choice position, even if for the wrong reasons (pressure from the IMF to control birth rates).

On the other hand, the collective's next two plays, *El haragán y el zopilote* (*The Loafer and The Buzzard*, 1989) and *¿A poco hay cimarrones?* (*Who Believes in Spooks?*, 1990), both seek to reinforce 'appropriate,' 'traditional' gender roles in the Mayan community.

In *The Loafer and The Buzzard*, the protagonist's wife is the personification of the ideal Mayan woman, a good cook and weaver who uses her charm to keep the debtors at bay. However, she is saddled with an irresponsible husband who fails to meet his male obligations as bread-winner (or, more precisely, corn-grower). Although he pretends to be working the fields, he actually spends his days sleeping, and as a result the couple gets further and further in debt. The play's humor derives from the lazy man's foolish scheme — of trading places with a buzzard so he won't have to work at all; his pathetic demise when he flies too close to a cooking fire while desperately searching for something to eat; and the wife's ironic satisfaction with her new, hard-working husband, whose only drawback is his stench. The lowly buzzard, the play implies, is "more of a man" than her man. Traditional sex roles are thus reinforced and the work ethic validated for both genders.

In ¿A poco hay cimarrones?, it is the woman who pays the price of not adequately carrying out her wifely duties. If the negligent buzzard-husband was punished by being "cooked" (and thus becoming food for either buzzards or humans), in this play and the popular Mayan folktale that it is based on, the negligent or oversexed wife is raped, subjected to a monstrous pregnancy (shades of Bosnia), and/or murdered by her kidnapper, the "Cimarrón," or "spook."

In her book The Black-man of Zinacantan, Sarah C. Blaffer studies this bogeyman figure central to contemporary Mayan mythology. She traces the roots of both the turkey-buzzard of the first play and the black spook of the second (as well as the hummingbird) to the bat-demon of classical Mesoamerica, which was associated with blood, sacrifice, and eroticism. The quality of punishment has been added to these characteristics in contemporary manifestations of the bat-demon. As she mentions in passing, the character in the recent folktales and the play is also related to the escaped black slaves who took refuge in the Highlands during the colonial period; the use of the term negro cimarrón — black runaway slave — in the play makes this connection clear.[6] In a broader sense, the "spook" is associated with Ladinos, or Spanish-speaking Mexicans, and with non-Indians in general.

Blaffer analyzes the folktales that served as the basis of Spooks in terms of reinforcing appropriate male and female behavior. The spook "attacks both sexes, but he is rarely successful against males, at least not against the brave ones" (106). Rather, brave men are rewarded with food, land, money, and/or a beautiful wife (107), while cowardly men are humiliated (as when they urinate on themselves out of fright). The spook's female victims, on the other hand, are punished most violently. An excess of masculine sexuality (the spook's six-foot penis) counters a perceived excess of female sexuality, resulting in the woman's monstrous pregnancy and death. In addition to cowards, Zinacantec folktales chastise men who are negligent cargo-holders. Thus, men are seen as evading their responsibility in the political sphere, while women are portrayed as doing so in the sexual realm.

The woman in the tale is punished for not being careful in her female responsibilities (often represented by tasks associated with cooking corn), which Blaffer interprets as interchangeable with being careless with her sexuality (120). "Women in Zinacantan are considered dangerous," as Blaffer explains, especially in certain "ambiguous" conditions, notably when they are pregnant or menstruating and are believed to have the power to cause soul-loss. At such times (or when dealing with *nixtamal,* or lime water for cooking corn, which is symbolically associated with body waste and therefore with menstruation), a woman needs to take extraordinary precautions to safeguard her sexuality. Similarly, when a *cargo*-holder neglects his duties, his wife is often accused of being "too strong or distractingly oversexed" (133). The tale admonishes women to behave "as women": to perform household work diligently, to not venture out alone, to not be "independent to the point of masculinity." Writing in 1972, Blaffer notes that a Zinacantec woman who violates these norms "runs the risk of being gangraped by a group of young men from the village" (132).

Sna's 1991 production is entitled *Herencia fatal, drama Tzotzil (Fatal Inheritance, A Tzotzil Drama),* although some members of the troupe preferred the more poetic *Cuando nuestras almas lloran (When Our Souls Weep).* The members of the troupe, including the women, insist that this is not a feminist text, but rather a play about injustice in the broadest sense. Nevertheless, it clearly addresses gender roles in contemporary Mayan society, condemning the male characters' irresponsibility, drunkenness, greed, cowardice, and violence toward women, as contrasted with the female characters' integrity, valor, and solidarity with one another. In this work, a dying father deeds his house to his two single daughters and decrees that his farm land be divided equally among his daughters and sons. This is not a traditional arrangement; typically all property would be left to the sons, since it would be taken for granted that the women would marry, move into their husbands' houses, and live off of their husbands' land. The explanation given by the sisters for preferring to remain single is that, in contemporary Mayan society, women want more out of life than motherhood, and men are no longer dependable husbands and fathers:

> LOXA: If we were married, we wouldn't have time for anything. Just look at your wives: loaded down with children, without getting anything out of it.
>
> TINIK: No; married women work too hard, and for what? So the husband can come home drunk, and after spending all his salary, mistreat his wife and children, like all the men we know?
>
> LOXA: That's right. Men aren't any good anymore. As our mother used to say, "You're better off alone than with bad partners."
>
> TINIK: If there were only respectful, hardworking, good men like our

father. But there aren't any more men like that. You'd think the devil had gotten into them all. (6–7)

Loxa and Tinik's two brothers, angry that they haven't inherited the house and all the land, try to persuade their sisters that it isn't appropriate for women to live alone, that they will invite gossip, particularly sexual gossip, and will humiliate their brothers. When the sisters accuse them of merely using these arguments as a pretext to steal their land, the brothers hatch a plot for getting Tinik, the more assertive sister, out of the way, so they can persuade Loxa to submit to their authority. They lie in wait when Tinik leaves for the fields, and kill her with a machete. In walking alone to the fields she is violating two aspects of the gender code: women who venture out alone are seen to be inviting harm, and those who insist on doing "men's work" like farming are considered "*marimachas*" or "dykes," unnatural women who deserve to be punished for "acting like men." During the trial the murderers once again try to turn a political, gender issue into a sexual, moral accusation: they argue that no harm has befallen their missing sister but that, true to her promiscuous nature, she has surely run off with some man.

The subplot of the play is also feminist. A female neighbor, Paxt'u, insists that she and her husband go see that Tinik reaches the fields safely, since she doesn't trust Tinik's brothers. She and her husband, Akuxtin, witness the murder, but the husband is cowardly, "like a woman," and refuses to testify against the brothers. Paxt'u, on the other hand, proves to be a forceful and persuasive witness, and impresses the municipal president with her courage. (It is torture, rather than her appeal to ethics, which eventually persuades all three men to confess — the brothers to the murder and Akuxtin to refusing to tell what he had witnessed.) The brothers are sent to prison in San Cristóbal de las Casas, and Akuxtin is sentenced to eight days of hard labor as punishment for his cowardice. Paxt'u then takes her children and moves in with the surviving sister, Loxa, indignantly proclaiming that she doesn't want to raise her children around such a poor role model as her husband.

Thus, the play focuses on female subjectivity, featuring strong, assertive, independent female characters. It validates an array of nontraditional options for women, including remaining single, living in female communities, owning property, and farming. *Fatal Inheritance* was based on an actual murder trial in the Tzeltal community of Tenejapa; in real life the brothers' punishment for the murder was far less severe than in the play.

In 1992, the troupe's mestizo director, Francisco Alvarez, wrote a play commemorating the modern Maya's classical ancestors, entitled *Dinastía de jaguares* (*Dynasty of Jaguars*). The principal female character is a Mayan queen who accepts her husband's polygamy; then reluctantly allows the other wife's son to succeed her husband to the throne, although Mayan tradition dictates that her own son should be king; and finally agrees to ritually sacrifice herself at the ceremony recognizing the illegitimate heir, in order to ensure the dynasty's survival. It is impossible to imagine a more literal celebration of female self-sacrifice.

As I will discuss below, life imitated art in late 1992 and 1993, when the two original women members of the troupe departed, under varying degrees of duress. The new play which Sna staged, *¡Vámonos al Paraíso!* (*Let's Go to "Paradise"*), focuses on the exploitation of Indian laborers on the plantations by Ladino (European and Hispanic Mexican) bosses. In this play the troupe's original actresses have been replaced by two new Mayan women, who are relegated to extremely minor, nonspeaking roles. The principal female character, the plantation-owner's daughter, is a homely, vulgar, man-hungry German girl, who is played in slapstick by an Indian man in drag. While it is obviously poking fun at foreign women, this characterization might also be interpreted as chastising "undesirable" female behavior within the Indian community, like the male clowns who cross-dress during Zinacantec religious celebrations (Blaffer 49).

Most of the humor in the play is based either on these ethnic and gender stereotypes (of Europeans and women) or on scatological elements. For instance, the mistreated Indian laborers ultimately take revenge on their tyrannical Ladino foreman by convincing him to follow the "traditional" Mayan cure for dysentery, by eating his own feces. The concept of "tradition" is thus used as a weapon for cultural self-defense and self-assertion. According to the play's stereotypes, Ladino men are greedy and cruel, yet gullible; Ladino women are repulsive, aggressive, and oversexed; and Indian women are demure and submissive to their Indian men, who are crafty and astute.

Isabel Juárez Espinosa, a Tzeltal-speaker from Aguacatenango, and Petrona de la Cruz Cruz, a Tzotzil-speaker from Zinacantán, were the first two women members of Sna. Over the four or five years of their collaboration with the troupe, they developed into quite talented actresses and assumed increasingly important roles in Sna's productions. In 1991, as a result of an invitation to participate in the International Women's Playwrights Conference in Toronto during the summer of 1991, Juárez Espinosa and de la Cruz Cruz became Mexico's first indigenous women playwrights. Both women's first plays interrogate female roles in the contemporary Mayan societies of Highlands Chiapas. Petrona de la Cruz Cruz's first play, *Una mujer desesperada* (*A Desperate Woman*, 1991), is particularly interesting to feminist critics because of its relentless examination of domestic violence, as it relates to rural poverty; male authoritarianism, alcoholism, incest, and domestic violence; and female economic and psychological dependency.

Fatal Inheritance ends by validating the Indian justice system and arguing that the Ladino system, which has been restricted to trying murderers in the Mayan community, is not even necessary in these cases. However, *A Desperate Woman* involves a more global critique. The young woman referred to in the title kills her stepfather, who has repeatedly abused, then killed, her mother and has attempted to assault her sexually; she then goes on to commit suicide, since she trusts neither the Indian nor the Ladino system to understand her actions and treat her justly.

The two women's work with Sna has entailed great personal risk. Most pointedly, they have aroused suspicion among their townspeople regarding their sexual virtue. Many people, including some of their family members, assume that actresses are prostitutes. Both women reached the theatre as a result of traumatic personal histories involving considerable hardship and suffering, which took them out of their traditional societies and roles, to the city and roles as single mothers and servants. Juárez Espinosa's Chol husband was assassinated in the agrarian struggles of northern Chiapas while she was pregnant. She initially supported her child by working as a servant and cashier in San Cristóbal. De la Cruz Cruz survived an abusive home life during her childhood only to be kidnapped, repeatedly raped, and impregnated by a man from her community. She also supported her son, along with her sister, following their mother's death, by working as a servant in San Cristóbal.

It was this ambiguous status as single mothers from fractured primary families that made it possible for them to become actors and playwrights; a woman who had never been married, or whose primary family was intact, or who was currently married, would probably have encountered great resistance to entering such an unconventional and independent career. Ironically, as we shall see, it was precisely the independence fostered by the theatre and travel which eventually forced the women out of the collective.

In order to protect the actors' privacy as much as possible, I will refrain from using their names in the following relation of events leading to the women's severance from the troupe.

In mid-1992, one of the women became pregnant by a married member of Sna. Because the women had repeatedly been warned by the men that they could not continue participating in Sna if they ever became pregnant,

and because she was embarrassed, she abruptly stopped attending rehears-
als. A male member of the troupe sought her out to find out why she had
disappeared, and the troupe subsequently accepted her decision to leave.
Also, at that time the baby's father voluntarily left Sna.

In December of 1992 the other female member of Sna, along with a male
Mayan anthropologist, was awarded the Premio Chiapas, a prestigious
annual prize given by the state government to a leading artist or writer. It
was the first time that an indigenous person had received this honor. Later
that month the woman was informed by the male members of Sna that the
collective had run out of funding and would have to disband; therefore, she
should not come to rehearsal anymore. Later she learned that, contrary to
what she had been told, the troupe did still have funding and was continuing its activities without her. They hired two new female actresses, to replace the original women.

It seems probable that professional jealousy was one motive for this
action, and that the jealousy was exacerbated by gender issues. In addition
to the prize, the two women had been receiving attention in U.S. journals
and invitations to attend international conferences. Moreover, some male
members of the collective may have felt uncomfortable with the increasing
feminist content of Sna's productions, and with *A Desperate Woman*'s scathing critique of the Mayan patriarchal family structure and justice system.
However, the male members of the troupe give other reasons for their
decision. The woman in question, they claim, did not offer to share her
monetary prize with the other members of the troupe, although she had
written her works while collaborating with and receiving financial support
from the collective. She counters that she was waiting for the January arrival
of the group's mentor, Robert Laughlin, in order to turn the prize money
over to him.

Most importantly, the men claim, the actress in question had aggressively
pursued a married man in the troupe, against his wishes, and she had
deviated from Mayan tradition by being sexually active outside of marriage,
by using Western rather than traditional clothing, and by living in San
Cristóbal rather than in her indigenous community. She denies the sexual
allegations and defends her right to choose where she lives and how she
dresses. As for the alleged adultery, she says that she has merely been a close
friend and confidante of the man whom she allegedly seduced, and that
Mayan men can't understand such platonic friendships between men and
women. While she was expelled from the troupe, her alleged partner in
adultery was recently chosen by the men in Sna to be their new president.

The double sexual standard regarding adultery, which John Haviland observed in Zinacantán in the 1970s, clearly persists in the 1990s.[7] At the same time that this man has accepted the leadership of Sna, he has continued to defend the expelled actress before their colleagues, and to collaborate with her and the other woman who left the troupe in staging selected scenes from Petrona de la Cruz Cruz's play *Una mujer desesperada* (*A Desperate Woman*). Although de la Cruz Cruz wrote the play more than a year before she left the collective, Sna had never staged it in Mexico. The current productions are sponsored by the Grupo de Mujeres, a feminist collective of professional Ladino women in San Cristóbal. At present de la Cruz Cruz is at work on a second play, regarding the gender conflicts that have plagued Sna, and suggestively entitled *El desprecio de los hombres* (*The Contempt of Men*).

In converting a personal and political conflict into an accusation of female sexual excess, the men in Sna are participating in a time-honored tradition in patriarchal societies, both Mayan and Ladino. This situation highlights the contradictions that can arise when a defense of "tradition," even in the context of anticolonial struggles, ignores intersecting issues involving human rights and freedoms, including feminism. With the expulsion of the two women, a dramatic trajectory that was increasingly feminist, addressing an array of women's issues, ranging from birth control, to domestic violence, to challenges to patriarchal patterns of property ownership and family structure, has reverted to the traditional feminine ideals of silence and self-sacrifice. Women who dare to venture out on their own, like the courageous sister in *Fatal Inheritance,* are once again sucked into the depths of the river.

APPENDIX I
Theatre and the Problems of
Women in Highlands Chiapas (1991)
Petrona de la Cruz Cruz

I am from Zinacantán and belong to the Tzotzil ethnic group, which means The Place of the Bat; I am a descendant of the Mayas. For several centuries before the conquest, my ancestors did theatre, which still survives in the community festivals, in which many characters put on costumes and perform: they dress up as animals, or personify ancestral beings in order to observe traditional ceremonies dedicated to God and the sacred ones. In keeping with tradition, women have had very little participation in these ceremonies, although we know that in the past they achieved important *cargos* (religious offices). At present women participate only as wives of the civil and religious authorities, or as ceremonial cooks, with passive roles; when the participation of a female character is called for, it is the men who dress up as women; a woman has never been asked to play the part of Shinolan, or the Mestiza woman.

In the indigenous communities of Chiapas, women have many problems: Tradition demands that women stay in their houses, because people think that only men can and should work in the fields or in other non-domestic activities. People believe that a woman's duty is to clean the house, cook, have and take care of the children, fetch water and firewood, and constantly weave, because the family should wear new clothes at each religious festival, and since there are many festivals, women have to be forever at the loom, weaving new clothes for each celebration.

But that's not all. Distrust is also common, and many husbands are jealous; they don't like women to talk to other men, unless it is absolutely necessary. This is how male children are also brought up, so not even single women have the freedom to speak or express their ideas or feelings, since the whole family is watching to see that the girls don't talk to or smile at the boys. For these reasons, most indigenous women grow up to be very shy; they are embarrassed to say what they think, they can't openly express their emotions, their needs, their suffering or happiness, because there is so much criticism. Any conduct that isn't in keeping with tradition makes people have a low opinion of women and criticize them.

Beyond these limitations, indigenous women receive a very poor education. Many of them don't manage to finish elementary school, because their parents send them out to watch over the sheep, or to fetch firewood or learn to weave. Although many of them would like to continue their studies, their parents put all sorts of obstacles in their way: they claim that they don't have money to support their studies, that they're only wasting their time in school, and that they're not going to reap any benefit from it, since they'll soon marry, so it's better for them to learn how to be good wives and mothers. Almost all young women resign themselves to cutting their education short and staying home, waiting to get married. The few girls who dare contradict their parents and insist on continuing their studies have to go to the city to work as servants in order to pay for their education. While 2 or 3 percent are fortunate and their parents are willing to pay for them to complete their schooling, we ourselves have a wrong way of thinking, because when they do give us that opportunity, we almost never follow through on it, preferring to fall in love and get married instead.

As for the theatre, while all women enjoy seeing it, it is very daring for a woman to become an actress; women who have done so are considered crazy or shameless. In Highlands Chiapas no more than five indigenous women, including us, have acted. Now attitudes are starting to change; today there are women broadcasters in indigenous languages, and now it is possible to see our plays on videos screened in the communities, thanks to the vans of the Chiapas Institute of Culture. Still, it is an activity that can only be engaged in by widows or single mothers, like us; because right now it is very difficult for an unmarried woman to think about studying acting or drama. In our case, the theatre has helped us to better ourselves; it has allowed us to develop confidence in ourselves, and it makes us feel useful, because we realize how influential it is in improving our communities' way of life. Through drama we can explore family and social problems that couldn't be expressed any other way. People learn to value their mother tongues and the virtues of their culture, and they are made aware of the vices and defects of our society, all the while being entertained, not feeling attacked or scolded. This makes it possible for people to seek solutions to their problems, or to satisfy the need to express their feelings. The theatre has also helped the Mestizo audience, which has looked down on our language and culture for so long, to familiarize themselves with our ways of thinking and living, and we have observed that they now regard us with more respect, and in many cases even with admiration, since people realize how difficult it is to do theatre in the countryside, especially in indigenous villages. In the beginning we presented amusing plays, puppet theatre and comedies based on our legends; then plays reflecting on and posing solutions for everyday problems, like family planning, alcoholism, and education, through tragicomedies; now we have moved on to producing plays of social criticism, and dramatic and historical works based on life in our communities.

We know that in the past our Mayan ancestors developed a grandiose theatre, full of art and content. We are studying how to motivate our people to reclaim the great theatrical expressions of the past, and thus sow the seeds of our cultural renaissance.

(Translated from the Spanish original by Cynthia Steele.)

NOTES

I would like to acknowledge the Latin American Committee of the Social Science Research Council, as well as the Latin American Studies Committee and the Department of Romance Languages and Literature at the University of Washington, for their generous research support.

All English translations of Spanish texts are mine.

1   The Mexican government is now publishing an attractive magazine, *Mundo Maya,* intended to promote the region to potential tourists. In addition, there have been numerous recent U.S. documentaries, a special issue of *National Geographic,* and a tourist guide devoted to the topic.

2   In the wake of centuries of colonialism and internal colonialism, the problem of defining "traditional" Mayan culture obviously becomes very problematic.

3   "Blood was the mortar of ancient Maya ritual life. The Maya let blood on every important occasion in the life of the individual and in the life of the community. It was the substance offered by kings and other nobility to seal ceremonial events . . . Although Maya warfare fulfilled several needs, the primary ritual role was to provide the state sacrificial victims, whose blood was then drawn and offered to the gods . . . The heretofore popular view of the Classic Maya has never taken into account such preoccupations as blood and bloodlines, nor has it emphasized the individual rulers prominent in Maya history . . . In Mesoamerican studies, a propensity for gore had always been attributed to the Aztecs. In contrast, the Maya were always assumed to be a superior race, thoroughly removed in time, space and culture from such behavior. In the new view presented here, however, the Maya have fallen from their pedestal; in doing so, they become a part of the community of man, the builders of a civilization that included both the darkest and the most brilliant possibilities of human behavior" (Schele and Miller 15).

4   See Jan de Vos, *No Queremos,* pp. 35–37, on the historical roots of this misconception.

5   See Gary Gossen on the torture and murder of Manuel Caxlán, the first leader of the Protestants in Chamula.

6   Robert Laughlin explains: "The Spook's negroid features may derive from a memory of African slaves. Although Blacks are no longer native to the region, as late as 1778 there were seven hundred living in San Cristóbal. They were treated more as confidants than as slaves, for they were permitted to wear daggers and to dress in European clothing. As such, they served the role of majordomos and foremen who most likely were entrusted with the task of inflicting physical punishment on their masters' Indian serfs (Favre, 81–82). It is not farfetched to assume that the Spaniards increased their authority by spreading stories of the Africans' former cannibalistic appetites. The Spook's cave-dwelling habits may possibly be traced to a memory of African slaves who escaped from the lowlands and sought temporary refuge in the wildest mountain areas. This is supported by the Spanish surname for the Spook, "Negro Cimarrón," "Black Runaway Slave" (Laughlin, *Of Cabbages* 348).

7   In his 1977 study of the role of gossip in Zinacantán, Haviland notes, "there is no doubt about the bias in men's gossip about adultery: a cuckold is made foolish by his adulterous wife; a man committing adultery is simply following his natural (if excessive) impulses (Can you blame him if he is a man?), even if he wrongs his wife in the process" (80). Haviland also reports Zinacantecs' perception that sexual mores are degenerating, and the extreme frequency of illicit sexual relations as a theme of gossip in the community (76). The centrality of gossip to everyday life is apparent in Zinacantecs' unusually high interest in the doings of their neighbors, and their concomitant obsession with secrecy within the household (27).

Jorge Salessi & Patrick O'Connor

For Carnival, Clinic, and Camera: Argentina's Turn-of-the-Century Drag Culture Performs "Woman"

❏

INTRODUCTION

The oppressed and marginalized have as much right to irony as the subtlest defenders of civilization. Indeed they have more need of duplicity: to appear at all in public discourse requires strategic compromises with an alien, if privileged, discourse; to negotiate public space often requires that the public spaces themselves be doubled back, folded into the utopian no-space of theatre or carnival. At some point we realize that we have a taste for double talk, a knack for it. Let other discourses ask whether this taste for duplicity, for irony, is "congenital" or "acquired." When we look into the past for our "congeners" and find that they have fashioned themselves into vivid images despite all odds, how do we preserve the inner doubledness of each voice, each performance, as we put their images and voices once again into circulation for their admirers?

This essay forms part of a larger project to broaden our notions of the crossings between sex, gender, self, and nation in Argentina from the turn of the century to the present. Here we turn to a subculture in which men dressed up as women, threw parties, exchanged photographs, and flamboyantly paraded themselves through the streets during carnival — and, less securely, on other evenings. We find their stories where Michel Foucault, if no one else, enjoined us to look: in the archives of the criminologists, public hygienists, and medical theorists who generated the discourses around marginal sexualities. Foucault knew that both the surveiller and the surveyed were altered by the act of surveillance, but focused his attention on the surveiller's discourse. As we focus on those surveyed, we note the diversity of their understanding of themselves which forced the clinicians to contradict their own taxonomies or angrily wrench apart the signs that their patients had made a life of juxtaposing. And we reproduce some of the photographs taken by them, taken from them by the medico-legal establishment, as each level of discourse (but surely not also our own) attempts to fix meaning into an image of reality, or what the black and Latino gay voguers of the movie *Paris Is Burning* would call Realness.

"DE ALLÍ SE LANZÓ AL PÚBLICO":
BUENOS AIRES, CARNIVAL OF MEN

The 1880 declaration of Buenos Aires as capital city and federal district of the Argentine republic marks the end of the domestic quarrels between local chieftains and the beginning of the great immigration that, between 1880 and 1914, transformed Argentina and created a new culture. Although smaller in numbers than the immigration reaching the United States earlier in the century, relative to the native population the immigration to Argentina was far larger. Most of these immigrants, unable to become small-farm owners due to the *latifundia* system of land tenure, established themselves in one of two coastal cities, Buenos Aires or Rosario, to work in the growing urban industries and commercial ventures. By 1900 the suburban and white, preferably Anglo-Saxon, immigration that had been imagined by the Argentine ideologues of the mid-nineteenth century had in reality become an immigration of large and visible groups of foreigners, mainly Italians and Spaniards, many young males without traditional family ties and often from the poorest areas of their home countries.

The concentration of most workers in Buenos Aires, during the first decade of the twentieth century, allowed a new Argentine labor movement to develop and challenge the hegemony of the patrician landowning class that had until then kept a tight grip on power. Thus the immigration that provided the labor necessary for the integration of Argentina to the Euro-centric blueprint of "progress," "modernization," and "internationalism" was now a foreign force living within national borders and capable of striking against and paralyzing the meat and grain exporting economy that kept enriching the landowning class.

At the turn of the century Buenos Aires became a good example of the phenomenon of unplanned urban growth and the consequent clashes between old and new social formations and cultural groups. Maneuvering among and between these groups, a gay subculture arose with strategies analogous to other local "simulators" in the bourgeois and patriarchal hegemonic culture. Various authors have suggested that the theatre is one of the

Figure 1. Cocoliche.
Photo courtesy of Ana
Cara Walker.

most paradigmatic spaces of turn-of-the-century Buenos Aires.[1] Ana Cara
Walker, in an article entitled "Cocoliche: The Art of Assimilation and Dissimulation Among Italians and Argentines," speaks of that curious dramatic
character the *cocoliche*. Emerging first as a dramatic persona and then as a
linguistic phenomenon improvised under the circus tent during the last
decades of the nineteenth century, Cocoliche is a native urban Argentine's
parody of an Italian immigrant's imitation of a rural gaucho; as a favorite
carnival costume character, he is once again reappropriated by the city's new
immigrants of every ethnicity (see fig. 1). Cocoliche facilitated an, at times,
uneasy dialogue between natives and foreigners, and the Cocoliche phenomenon underlines the importance of folk and popular expressive forms
in precipitating social change and cultural redefinition.

 With the rise of new cultural groups and social classes that erased the
clear-cut definitions among the social formations previous to immigration,

it is not surprising that José María Ramos Mejía, a representative of the ruling liberal elite and founder of forensic psychiatry in Argentina, in his work *Los simuladores del talento en las luchas por la personalidad y la vida* (*The Simulators of Talent in the Struggles for Personality and Life*), first published in 1903, found it necessary to invent a new psychiatric category, that of simulators. Predictably the term simulator includes all outsiders who, becoming a part of a new upwardly mobile population, seek to integrate themselves into the mainstream culture. Ramos Mejía's ideas, disseminated through a prolific written production and from key positions in the state bureaucracy of the time, became models for sociopolitical analyses and for the official ideology of the modern Argentine state. This psychiatrist, hygienist, and pedagogue is a crucial example of a functionary who, in the words of Hugo Vezzetti, represents "the modern incarnation of the moralist and a paradigm of a governor" in post-immigration Argentina (14).[2] José Ingenieros, a medical doctor and psychiatrist, criminologist, sociologist, literary critic, and faithful disciple of Ramos Mejía, in his "Psicología de los simuladores" ("The Psychology of Simulators") further developed a classification and described an etiology of simulation.

These studies and medico-legal treatises on simulation, or "passing," reflect the longing for stricter border controls around the definitions of class and nationality. During this historical period characterized by a pervading cultural, political, and economic insecurity created by the process of immigration and "modernization," these longings became especially intense regarding issues of sex and gender. The changing gender structure of the economy precipitated by the increasing number of women working for a salary, the noticeable demographic imbalance between the number of male and female inhabitants of Buenos Aires, and the growth of a new urban gay subculture, raised major concerns about gender roles and the changing mores of a city with a large majority of young foreign males.

In Alberto Sábato's words, "Toward the end of the century Buenos Aires was a gigantic multitude of single men" ("Estudio preliminar 15). Censuses of the period suggest that two-thirds of all foreign immigrants were males, and nearly four-fifths of the adult males of Buenos Aires were foreigners.[3] Such already astonishing figures are underestimates which do not include immigrants who returned to the city between stints as seasonal laborers in the interior, or the "swallow workers" (*trabajadores golondrinas*) passing through Buenos Aires twice a year back and forth on cheap trans-Atlantic fares from the Argentine interior to their countries of origin. Manuel Bejarano concludes that toward 1910 "increasingly there existed a great mass of nomadic men without ties of any kind" (Bejarano 138).[4] Most of these *trabajadores golondrinas* arrived alone or in groups and did not have families — but if they did have them, these families often remained in Europe waiting for them to return or establish themselves in the new country. All these men escape the statistics by only staying briefly in Buenos Aires during the first decade of the twentieth century.

It is not difficult to find evidence of the prevailing anxieties about a population hard to define in terms of social class, sex, or gender. As male-male sex increased in a city with an overwhelming majority of men, for example, some doctors suspected the growth of a hidden population of hermaphrodites. In 1904, Carlos Roche, a medical doctor, in an article entitled "El pseudo-hermafrodismo masculino y los androginoides" ("Masculine Pseudo-Hermaphrodism and the Androgynoids") argues that "pseudo-hermaphrodites," or men with a diverse exterior conformation of the genitals, "are numerous . . . At birth they are usually classified as women, and are raised and educated as such until puberty, when with the development of the sexual instinct at puberty they reveal their true nature" (421). The doctor goes on to allege that "unfortunately, the large majority of these cases go undetected at birth, because the examination of newborn infants is usually performed by nonprofessionals" (430). According to Roche, after puberty these men "avoid the presence of a medical doctor for fear of being detected, enjoying the sexual advantages of living as and with women" (434).

"Living as . . . women": the taxonomic response of Dr. Roche has shifted onto the question of performance, of producing recognizable signs for an audience. The brief but intense history in gender studies of the term "performance" stems from deconstruction and its assault on J. L. Austin's concept of the performative speech act.[5] Deconstruction retains Austin's focus on the first person singular utterance, but characteristically emphasizes the discrepancy between self and speech when I sing that I am what I am. In her ground-breaking synthesis of Foucault, Lacanian psychoanalysis, and gender studies, *Gender Trouble,* Judith Butler argues that *all* genders are performed, enacted in discourse or even in the private discourse between myself and my self-image. This is equally true of the "pseudo-hermaphrodite" who lives as a woman, the biological woman whose boyfriend makes her "feel like a natural woman," and the lip-synching drag queen who milks the same song for laughs on stage and then hums it to himself when his boyfriend arrives with roses. Butler makes broad claims for "the subversion of identity" when people of marginal sexuality perform gender; without challenging Butler directly, Marjorie Garber in the recent book *Vested Interests: Cross-Dressing and Cultural Anxiety* shifts the focus of performance, through a dazzling array of examples, onto the diversity of intentions and uses that cross-dressers hope to achieve with reference to already existing identities within their societies. Subversion may always be the effect, but some transvestites declare by word or deed their intent to assimilate.

In any case they had better be watched. To control the presumably hidden population of hermaphrodites "who satisfy their sexual instincts by more or less natural means, therefore creating considerable moral disorders in the social environment" (430), the doctor proposes "a modification of the article of the civil code regarding the sex of newborns. This modification would add the category of 'of dubious sex,' establishing that all individuals declared 'of dubious sex' at birth should be examined at the age of 15 or 16, when the matter of sex can best be settled" (433). The doctor's concern with taxonomizing bodies in the hope of fixing identity reflects, we suggest, the preoccupation of a turn-of-the-century Argentine medico-legal establishment bent on identifying and controlling a new population in the "*público*" of the almost all-male carnival of Buenos Aires, a new population always perceived to be simulating or adopting different models of performance, impersonation, acting, or passing as a strategy for assimilation into and subversion of the traditional patriarchal culture.

"EN ESTE TEATRO . . . LA PROMISCUIDAD DE SEXOS SE REALIZA EN GRANDE ESCALA": DRAG AS THEATRE

The doctors' pursuit of some almost invisible populations is a symptom of cultural anxiety; on the other hand, some people will do almost anything to get noticed. Beyond attempting to control all men and women who break the cultural, economic, and social models proposed as "national" by the Argentine state ideology of the turn of the century, the homosexual panic disseminated by means of the texts we will now explore aims to regulate and control a subculture that thrives on visibility, the homosexuals and transvestites in Buenos Aires. We must not draw our boundaries too narrowly; let us remember that homosexual panic enacts, as Eve Kosofsky Sedgwick explains, "the regulation of the male homosocial bonds that structure *all* culture," as well as a control over "a nascent minority population of distinctly homosexual men" (184).

This new minority of homosexuals in turn-of-the-century Buenos Aires is studied and described in great detail by Francisco de Veyga in a series of clinical histories published between 1902 and 1904. This criminologist doctor, specialist in the study of homosexuality, is an intimate friend—together with José Ingenieros—and one of two favorite disciples of J. M. Ramos Mejía. Veyga studies and documents a homosexual subculture that seems to acquire a subversive visibility during carnival. In an article published in 1902, for example, Veyga constructs the life history of a heterosexual married man who begins by wearing costumes during carnival, continues throughout the year, and ends up dedicated to his newly acquired fame as a star among homosexual transvestites. In the following passage, which for its interest we shall quote at length, the doctor's use of theatrical imagery and vocabulary reflects his concern with the public visibility of this homosexual subculture. This concern in turn expresses the anxiety that the "truth" of gender, as Butler argues, "is a fantasy instituted and inscribed on the surfaces of bodies" (*Gender Trouble* 136). Finding previous proclivities in the past of his patients, Veyga writes:

Before getting married, and for some time afterwards, the diversion to which he devoted the greatest enthusiasm was dressing up for carnival. He had a weakness for performing in carnival song and dance groups and in parties with stage designs. The adjoining photograph represents him in showy dress, cutting a good figure. In this theater, where promiscuity of sexes is achieved on a grand scale, homo-sexual relations are not difficult to start up. In carnivalesque associations there is a purpose other than the aesthetic: the exhibition of forms, the intentionality of the musical airs and the decidedly erotic character these people give to their meetings, all boldly proclaim the goal to which they tend. And indeed it is there, in those parties, receiving loaded compliments on his physical endowments, and mixing with Uranists[12] of every species, that he began to perceive the first intimations of his change. One day he met a subject who approached him head-on—the usual seducer, the initial agent of these deviations which seem to be exclusively the work of nature—and he did not hesitate to yield. The man says that "they had spoken to him so often of the matter," and that he saw around him so many scenes of this type, without understanding that they might be reprehensible, that "it seemed to him his duty to try it."

From there he threw himself into *el público* (in Spanish meaning both the public and the audience). His appearance in the world in which he figures "was a smashing success," just as it had been predicted to him, and as he himself supposed, he took the name of "Rosita de la

Plata," celebrating an *écuyère* who at the time cut a considerable figure
in the demimondaine society, and took little time to surpass her in
fame. He still preserves said fame, although his star is already fading
from the ravages of time and the rude competition presented by so
many newcomers in the market, more or less gifted than he. To what
does he owe his fame? To very little, to be sure. To his care in always
lying in wait for parties and to his indefatigable activity in the labor of
feminine imitation. "Rosita" follows fashion, and sets the fashion for
his peers. Here, he is portrayed in the photograph, in a dress, inciting
envy in many for his gracious air and arrogance at the same time. *She*
has imposed the fashion of several costumes and of these outrageous
portraits which seem to be a specialty of these people, so idiosyncratic
are they. ("Inversión adquirida" 203, parentheses and italics in the
original)

The narration documenting the path out of the closet and the subsequent
life of "Rosita de la Plata" (see fig. 2) follows a stereotypical pattern of the
life and career of a theatre diva; moved by an original "great passion for
performing in song and dance groups" she first "surrenders herself to the
scene," "throws herself into the public," "has a smashing success," and "sur-
passes her rivals in fame," until "her star fades from the ravages of time."

Notwithstanding the exaggeration with which Veyga here seeks to implant and disseminate homosexual panic in this fragment, as well as in the
rest of his articles on sexual inversion, he uses tropes and metaphors of the
theatre to depict a large, visible, and well-defined subculture of homosexual
transvestites who share habits, dress, language, and meeting places, both at
carnival time and the rest of the year. Among these men there are role
models who jockey for fame; "fashionable dress" and styles which can be
"set," and which other people "follow"; and fashionable habits, such as "the
fashion . . . of these outrageous portraits which seem to be a specialty of
these people." Dresses, styles, fashions, and photographs circulate within
this subculture in a profusion of "so many scenes of this class," in which
"homosexual relations are not difficult to start up" because "mixing with
Uranists of every species" there is an always renewed variety of "so many
newcomers." More profoundly than with the crossings of ethnicity and class
in the Cocoliche figure, this drag theatre becomes a subversive and popular
public parody. Butler explains that drag is a

perpetual displacement [which] constitutes a fluidity of identities that
suggests an openness to resignification and recontextualization; parodic proliferation deprives hegemonic culture and its critics of the

Figure 2. Rosita de la
Plata. Photo courtesy of
Jorge Salessi.

claim to naturalized or essentialist gender identities. Although the gender meanings taken up in these parodic styles are clearly part of hegemonic, misogynist culture, they are nevertheless denaturalized and
mobilized through their parodic recontextualization. (*Gender Trouble*
138)

The creation of a new space in which these men are able to distance themselves from the humiliation they endure as sexual outcasts while creating an
alternative moral order and culture in which they are in control, begins with

the adoption of a new naming system with which these men, by taking female names, reinvent their gender. Rosita "took the name of Rosita de la Plata," a name like Aida, "with which another subject became distinguished in the very special world in which she moves" ("Invertido sexual imitando la mujer honesta" 368). Luis D. "has adopted the name '*La Bella Otero*,' the celebrated Parisian cocotte of whom she presumes to be the rival" ("Inversión profesional" 493). "Aurora is a thirty-year-old man" ("Inversión adquirida" 195), while "Manon, for such is her *nom de guerre*, was a healthy boy until the age of fifteen" ("Inversión congénita" 44). And the selection of clothing is as telling of one's "true gender" as the selection of a name: "An adolescent recently abandoned to inversion has adorned himself with the name 'Darclée' and cannot give himself to the scene without his wig and a woman's blouse" ("El amor" 337). Let us notice that most of these men adopt the names of fashionable characters and divas of the glittering turn-of-the-century world of the opera, the theatre, the circus, or the cafe-concert: Rosita after "an *écuyère* who at that time cut a considerable figure"; Aida after Verdi's opera; Manon after Massenet and Puccini's operas; la bella Otero after "the celebrated Parisian cocotte"; and Darclée after Hericléa Darclée, the Rumanian soprano who sang her world-famous Tosca in Buenos Aires in 1897, 1903, and 1907. Veyga, exasperated with the dramatic visibility — and pride — of the men creating these parodic repetitions, concludes: "Finally given entirely to the life of these people, with a new name which they have given themselves, they end up becoming characters of a public show, without being troubled by their sad reputation, indeed often proud of it" ("El sentido moral" 26–27). After coming out and renaming themselves "these people give themselves entirely to" a parallel, parodic reality.

Veyga describes a homosexual subculture gathering in balls, parties, and social events all year round. These gatherings fulfill a number of social functions that strengthen the sexual identity of the members of this subculture. Emphasizing the importance that one of these reunions has in re-affirming the sexual identity of a forty-year-old man, the doctor writes:

> the occasion, a friend's celebration, required that his companions take him to a party of homo-sexuals, enthusiastically telling him about the novelties that he would encounter there. That party decided his situation forever. The interest that the "ladies" provoked in him was immense, to the point that he "felt crazed by their grace and attractions; but to tell the truth" (according to him), he was not experiencing a purely casual interest, but one of "affectionate sympathy and compan-

ionship" . . . The fact is that from that night, having made friends with many of the partygoers, his medium and his field of action became those that had just been revealed to him. ("Inversión adquirida" 207, parentheses and quotation marks in the original)

This feeling that it was "not . . . a purely casual interest, but one of 'affectionate sympathy' and 'companionship,'" suggests that this man was encountering a developed social network that encouraged the assertion of his newly found identity.

"ESTOS RETRATOS DISPARATADOS QUE PARECEN SER UNA ESPECIALIDAD DE ESTA GENTE": FIXING THE DOUBLE IMAGE

The evidence of this rich marginal world in early twentieth-century Buenos Aires is an important antecedent in the history of homosexual subcultures. As Jeffrey Weeks notes, "Until comparatively recently, very few people found it either possible or desirable to incorporate sexual mores, social activities and public identity into a full-time homosexual 'way of life'" (202). However, in the homosexual subculture of Buenos Aires at the turn of the century we see precisely this incorporation of sexual mores and social activities into a "homosexual 'way of life.'" While some of these men come out, find their peers, and assert their sexual identities, others are like Manon, who "in feminine clothes gives free rein to her inverted feelings, attending invited soires and dances in which, together with others, she acts out the role of grande dame" (Veyga, "Inversión congénita" 46). Incorporating sexual mores with a public identity, some of these men take their parody of the "truth of gender" to the streets. La bella Otero creates "disorders and scandals, motivated by her habit of going out into the streets dressed as a woman" (Veyga, "Inversión profesional" 493). To public visibility, to the disorder and scandal of drag outside in the streets or inside ballrooms and private homes—these men add the parodic repetitions of ceremonies and rites that are parodies of traditional sex/gender systems. The incredulity in Veyga's tone shows that even the exceptions reinforce the rule for him: Aida, who is discreet (in male clothing) at work, "imitates an honest woman" in drag, is serially monogamous, prudish in conversation, and—the best proof that she is a "*mujer honesta*"—claims to get no pleasure out of the sexual act with her "husband." Explaining that "the marriage of sexual inverts is not a rare occurrence, to be sure, but this ceremony ordinarily happens only as an act of scandalous ostentation," Veyga nevertheless is

shocked as he describes the marriage of Aida "with the conventional apparatus of a real wedding: *she* dressed in white, her head adorned with orange
blossoms, he in tuxedo and white gloves" (Invertido imitando a la mujer
honesta" 371, emphasis in the original) (see fig. 3). Here Aida's own ideas
of decorum are ignored by the doctor; for him the parody calls into question the "naturalness" of the "conventional [heterosexual] apparatus," and
thus it too becomes an "act of scandalous ostentation," "makes public" the
"dramatic and contingent construction of meaning" that Judith Butler calls
"gender as a corporeal style, an 'act,' as it were, which is both intentional and
performative" (*Gender Trouble* 139).

Aside from their concern with these parodic repetitions, Veyga's histories
convey a serious preoccupation with the photographs of these men in drag.
Along with each case history, Veyga publishes a series of photographs that
fascinate but baffle him. At the beginning of the long fragment of Rosita's
history quoted earlier, Veyga calls special attention to "the adjoining photograph representing Rosita in showy dress, cutting a good figure"; later he
points out "that phogoraph in a matinee dress." Furthermore, "these outrageous portraits," the doctor proclaims, "seem to be a specialty of these people" ("Inversión adquirida," 203). This means that these men made a habit
of dressing in drag and having their picture taken, to be kept, copied, shown,
given, or passed around and commented upon. La bella Otero writes, know-
ingly, that s/he had "the honor of giving Dr. Veyga some portraits with a
dedication" ("Invertido profesional" 496), and did not, according to the
doctor, "hide very well his desire to figure as a case history in the book on
sexual inversion that we are preparing" ("Invertido profesional" 494).[7]

Veyga's concern with these photographs exemplifies the subversive possibilities Walter Benjamin sees in photography: the mechanical reproduction
of photographs has the possibility of disseminating ad infinitum the parodic
repetition of drag with its challenge to the "authenticity" of gender. Furthermore, this dissemination of photographs subverts the traditional homoge-
nizing function of mass media. Susan Buck-Morss writing about Benjamin's
interest in photography explains that "photography democratized the reception of visual images by bringing even art masterpieces to a mass audience"
(133). But in Veyga's history, the masterpieces spread among a "mass audience" are images that, erasing the gap between sign (woman) and referent
(man), make clear that gender is a mere inscription on the surface of the body.

Pointing out the explosive potential of this erasure, Benjamin explains
that photographs "acquire a hidden political significance. They demand a
special kind of approach; free-floating contemplation is not appropriate to
them. They stir the viewer; he feels challenged by them in a new way . . . For

Figure 3. Aida. Photo courtesy of Jorge Salessi.

the first time captions become obligatory" (226). So, below each photograph our doctor adds captions such as "Manon — Congenital Sexual Invert in Dance Costume" (Veyga, "Inversión congénita" 18–19) (see fig. 4), "Rosita de la Plata — Inverted by Suggestion" ("Inversión adquirida" 200–201), etc. But the tension between captions (describing men: *invertido* having in Spanish the masculine adjective ending) and images (of women) subsists, creating an ironic hybrid discourse and making visible drag's "fluidity of identities that suggests an openness to resignification." Veyga not only makes obvious this fluidity of identities in the pages of his texts, he contributes to the reproduction and dissemination of these images of wo/men.

Stirred, Veyga writes of Manon's photographs, "The photographs we publish suffice to give an idea of correct yet suggestive carriage" ("Inversión congénita" 46), while in a photo of Aurora he points out "the illusion that he must have offered that night can be measured by the demeanor in the adjoining photograph of Aurora in drag" ("Inversión adquirida" 195, parentheses in the original) (see fig. 5). Challenged, Veyga then tries to reorganize, fix the "right" construction of gender. Of course this operation was first performed on Aurora's own body. "When they brought him to the observation clinic of the Police Department he was still dressed as a woman, and I may be excused from speaking of the deprivations he underwent to become accommodated to the locale." ("Inversión adquirida" 194). Afterward, the police took a mug shot of Aurora required to portray a man, which Veyga also publishes, next to Aurora's photo in drag, in an effort to shatter "the illusion," writing, "The art which he uses to arrange himself can also be valued, comparing the face that he has in said portrait" ("Inversión adquirida" 195) (see fig. 6). In language such as the above, Veyga aims for a higher humanist style of writing than that of his colleagues (Carlos Roche's analysis of "pseudo-hermaphrodites" takes place in blunt one-sentence paragraphs of brutish vulgarity, for instance). Veyga's wit is seldom better than jocose; it is predicated on assuming "knowledge of the world" ("I may be excused from speaking of"; "the usual seducer, the initial agents of these deviations which seem to be exclusively the work of nature"). The closer he gets to individual case histories, the more agitated with such tics his prose becomes; his prose only "straightens out" in the summary essays of 1903 and 1904 on love and the moral sense among inverts, which contain no photographs. The shifts of fashion have been kind to Aurora's photograph: even stripped by the police of formal drag attire, s/he is a model of contemporary androgynous allure.

Roland Barthes explains that "photography . . . began historically as an art of the Person, of civil status, of what we might call, in all senses of the

Figure 4. Manon. Photo courtesy of Jorge Salessi.

Figure 5. Aurora. Photo courtesy of Jorge Salessi.

Figure 6. Aurora. Photo
courtesy of Jorge Salessi.

term, the body's formality" (79). Veyga of course has the last word in 1904,
although the words seem contaminated by his subject's double speech,
producing a knowing tone of voice that knows too much of the wrong
thing; the photographs that illustrate his words complete the subversion of
medico-legal enterprise. Some of these subjects want to assimilate; some
want the fame "a gracious air and arrogance" can produce. One had her
woman's face taken away from her, yet still performs woman for those with
eyes to see her. In spite of the doctor's effort to (re)construct the gender of
Aida, Rosita, or Aurora, their published photographs are indeed documentation of an "identity and civil status . . . the *body's formality*" forever deconstructed by image of fe/males of "correct yet suggestive carriage." Whether
in carnival, at the clinic, or especially in front of the camera, these individuals of a drag subculture engage in a "correct yet suggestive," rigorous yet
subtle, double discourse.

NOTES

1   See for example María Cecilia Graña.

2   Ramos Mejía was the founder and first president of the Círculo Médico Argentina in 1875, founder and first director of the Asistencia Pública in 1882, founder and first titled professor of the chair for nervous and mental illness of the University of Buenos Aires in 1887, president of the national Department of Hygiene in 1892, and president of the National Council of Education in 1908.

3   In the *Segundo censo de la República Argentina* we read, "As can be seen, it is the foreign population that constitutes the difference favoring men . . . ; that foreign immigration is made up of two thirds men explains the difference" (xxxv). Studying statistics from 1914, Carl Solberg notes that of all "males of age 20 or over, 77.2 percent (in 1914) were foreign born. Thus nearly four-fifths of Buenos Aires' adult males were foreigners" (96–97).

4   Comparing the number of people in 1910 working on farms the entire year (82,368 men and 30,202 women), with the number of people farming only during the harvest months (226,328 men and 11,647 women), Bejarano observes: "Just the mention of these figures is sufficient to demonstrate without further commentary that family units represented a very low percentage, and that the majority of workers migrated to rural areas without their women and children, or was constituted by people who had none as yet" (123).

5   Paul de Man's "Semiology and Rhetoric" (in *Allegories of Reading*), a general deconstructive turn on Austin, engendered essays by Shoshana Felman, Barbara Johnson, and some of Eve Kosofsky Sedgwick's recent public lectures on the positionality of shaming.

6   Devotees of Uranian Venus, the classical goddess of homosexual love. For comments on Veyga's attempts at a "literary" style, see "La inversión sexual adquirida" 18.

7   To our knowledge Veyga's book on sexual inversion was never published. For a full description of the dynamics that can be involved in the doctor-patient relationship of the sexual case history, see Wayne Koestenbaum on the collaboration between Havelock Ellis and J. A. Symonds in Ellis's *Sexual Inversion*.

D i a n a   T a y l o r

Performing Gender: Las Madres
de la Plaza de Mayo

❑

Theatre is an Oedipal affair, the scene of the cut or the wound, of the crown that burns its
wearer. Theatre enacts the costs of assuming the displacing image returned back to society —
the mask that alienates as it procures entry into society. — Barbara Freedman, "Feminism,
Psychoanalysis and Theatre"

This essay explores conflicting gender roles and their representation in
the performance of authoritarian politics during Argentina's recent "Dirty
War" (1976–83). I will limit my inquiry to the two principal spectacles of
the period. The first: the military Junta's representation of its heroic (implicitly masculine) mission of rescuing Argentina, conceived as a wounded,
bleeding, maternal body or *Madre Patria* (Motherland), from its subversive "children." The second: the Madres' of the Plaza de Mayo public demonstrations in the name of those same "children," the 30,000 Argentines
who were abducted, raped, tortured, and permanently "disappeared" by
military forces.

The staging of Argentina's "tragedy" is instructive to those concerned
with performance studies and its relationship to gender and civil conflict.
For one thing, the entire scenario of "national reorganization" or *Proceso*
set in motion by the military was highly theatrical. By this, I am referring
not only to the obvious spectacularity of the confrontations, the public
marches, the struggle to control public space and attention, the display of
instruments, images, and icons. I am also referring to the subtext or master
narrative used by the military which "explained" and energized the public
battle of images and which worked to transform the "infirm" social "body"
into a passive (i.e., "feminine") one. The Argentine scenario, then, like all
scenarios, involved both narrative and spectacle. For another thing, the

Madres, a group of nonpolitical women, organized one of the most visible and original resistance movements to a brutal dictatorship in the twentieth century. Theirs was very much a performance, designed to focus national and international attention on the Junta's violation of human rights. The terrifying scenario in which the Madres felt compelled to insert themselves was organized and maintained around a highly coercive definition of the feminine and motherhood which the women simultaneously exploited and attempted to subvert. The spectacular nature of their movement, which cast the "Mother" in a central role, inspired and influenced numerous other political women's groups throughout Latin America, the Middle East, and Eastern Europe.[1]

Before engaging in this inquiry, I want to clarify the critical assumptions under which I am operating. *Performance,* as I use it in this context, is not antithetical to "reality" nor does it suggest artificiality. More in keeping with its etymological origins, performance suggests a *carrying through,* actualizing, making something happen. My use of *fantasy,* likewise, is not opposed to "reality." Rather, I am proposing that the "Dirty War" was a national mise-en-scène of collective and individual fears and anxieties triggered by economic and political crisis. The notion of gender — both masculine and feminine — as a representation, similarly, does not mean that individuals have free and easy access to a repertoire of roles nor that the roles chosen or imposed do "not have concrete or real implications, both social and subjective, for the material life of individuals" (de Lauretis, *Technologies* 3).[2] Rather the opposite. I am following the lines of reasoning worked out by feminists thinkers from Simone de Beauvoir to Judith Butler who posit that one is not born a woman but becomes a woman due to socialization into patriarchal societies. As Butler notes, "[w]hen Beauvoir claims that 'woman is a historical idea and not a natural fact, she clearly underscores the distinction between sex, as biological facticity, and gender, as the cultural interpretation of significance of that facticity. To be female is, according to that distinction, a facticity which has no meaning, but to be a woman is to have *become* a woman, to compel the body to conform to an historical idea of woman,' to induce the body to become a cultural sign, to materialize oneself in obedience to an historically delimited possibility, and to do this as a sustained and repeated cultural project" ("Performative Acts" 273). I will argue that the strength and the limitation of the Madres's movement lies in the conscious use of the socially sanctioned role of motherhood for political ends. Finally, it is not enough to point out that certain roles and representations have negative or limiting implications for social subjects. Rather, the challenge lies in understanding and, conceivably *modi-*

Figure 1. The first military junta. From left, Admiral Emilio Massera (navy), General Jorge Videla (army), Brigadier Orlando Agosti (air force). Photo by Guillermo Loiacono.

fying, the production of subjectivity through those roles and representations, through their ability to highlight modes of visibility or invisibility, their construction of positionality and, hence, "destiny."

II

The gendered representation of the Argentine social "body" played a key role in the rhetorical and operational workings of the "Dirty War." In its first pronouncement, published in *La Nación* on the day of the military overthrow or *golpe* (literally *blow*) on 24 March 1976, the Junta declared itself the "supreme organ of the Nation" ready to "fill the void of power" embodied by Perón's widow, María Estela Martínez de Perón (commonly known as "Isabelita"), Argentina's constitutional president.[3] With a show of muscle, the Junta undertook its exercise in national bodybuilding, determined to transform the "infirm," inert Argentine masses into an authentic "national being." The military heralded its ascension to power as the "dawning of a fecund epoch," although the generative process was not, strictly speaking, as it recognized, "natural." María Estela Martínez de Perón's govern-

Figure 2. The military on parade. Photo by Guillermo Loiacono.

ment was sick; its "productive apparatus" was exhausted; "natural" solutions were no longer sufficient to insure a full "recuperation." As President Videla of the Junta declared a few months later, the Patria was "bleeding to death. When it most urgently needs her children, more and more of them are submerged in her blood" (Troncoso 59). The war was being fought in the interstices of the Mother Patria, in her bleeding entrails; it was thus transgressive, hidden, dangerous. The "Dirty War" manifested itself in dirty images — the menstrual blood, maternal blood, the blood associated with female sexuality and internal (civil) violence — as opposed to the images of the Gulf War, for example, that was represented as a clean, bloodless war of specialized "surgical strikes." As Argentina's military leaders made clear in this first blueprint to a national project, social violence would be fought in interior spaces — both "open and hidden subversion would be eradicated." In practice, as the testimony of thousands of victims and witnesses attest, the raid on interiority was carried out in homes, torture chambers, and other private parts traditionally associated with the female body. In order to save the Patria, the social body would be turned inside out and upside down.

Opposed to the interiority associated with subversion, danger, blood, and femininity, the military represented itself as unequivocally masculine, aggressively visible, all surface, identifiable by their uniforms, ubiquitous, on parade for all the world to see. Staging order was perceived as a way of making order happen. The display of the military leaders in church or with the Catholic archbishops aligned military and sacred power, stabilizing the former through identification with the latter. Simultaneously, this display reenacted and constituted the new social order: all male, Catholic, and strictly hierarchical. The unholy trinity — Army, Navy, and Air Force — were depicted as one entity, set apart as in religious iconography, the embodiment of national aspirations of grandeur. They spoke as one central, unified subject; their "we" supposedly included everyone.[4] Visually, the spectacle affirmed their centrality by emphasizing the distance and tension between the great leaders and the undifferentiated followers. As opposed to the highlighted images of the Junta in isolation, their subordinates were presented in linear formations of seemingly identical bodies in military attire. The military body was a whole body, contained, always ready for action, always under control. But it also presented itself, conspicuously and perhaps even consciously, as a threateningly sexualized phallic body/machine. The military male's insistent display of hardware was not only a form of generalized torture, a showing of the instruments. It also affirmed the

Figure 3. Pro-military ad that appeared in the major centrist newspaper, *La Nación*, the day before the coup (March 1976). "You're not alone . . . / Your country is behind you. / Yes, your fight isn't easy. / But knowing that truth is on your side / makes it easier. / Your war is a clean war. / Because you didn't betray. / Because you didn't swear in vain. / You didn't sell out your *patria*. / You didn't think about running away. / Because you clutch the truth in / your hand, you're not alone." Courtesy of Diana Taylor.

explicitly masculine and directed nature of power, unstoppable in the face of any possible resistance.

From a perspective of narrativity, political authoritarianism was represented as an oedipal drama of male individuation which offered scenarios of individual heroism, of secret danger and self-sacrifice to elucidate what it promoted as Argentina's structural need to rid itself of pollution, which the Junta expressed in terms of "plunging in dissolution" (*La Nación*, 24 March 1976). The struggle, according to the Junta, was a shared one, "all the representative sectors of the country should feel themselves clearly identified with the project: In this new stage there is a combat role for each citizen. The task is hard and urgent. It is not without sacrifice, but one takes it on with the absolute conviction that the example will be set from the top." The combat role that the military envisioned for the population, it soon became clear, was not an active one. Rather, the desired attitude was one of blind belief in the narrative and mimetic identification with the military endeavor. The heroic soldier male was depicted as descending into the dark, dangerous underground to overcome evil and reemerge victorious, individuated, his own man and the uncontested ruler/savior of the ailing land.[5] The enemy or obstacle was implicitly feminine — the *other,* the site of blood and internal conflict — which in the illustration of the soldier is associated with all that is dark and threatening, unformulated and unknowable. The eyes of the population (condemned to spectatorship) were fixed on the male hero. They were encouraged to identify with him and see the conflict from his perspective, to stand behind him: "you're not alone." Not with him, certainly not participating, but behind him, legitimating the struggle. Even at this date, before the "Dirty War" was fully underway, the combat was declared "clean": "*tu guerra es limpia.*" The image of the young warrior male, in a manner typical of fascist iconography, worked to neutralize its violent and sinister quality by "binding" innocence with danger, idealism with brutality. The soldier looks innocent and vulnerable; the caption says he clutches "truth" in his hand. If we look closely, we notice his rifle is barely visible. Is this the face that murdered 30,000 individuals?

In the Junta's mythic narrative/spectacle, females were both the obstacle to and the image of harmony, both the cause (*putas, locas*) and the justification (Patria) of violent politics. The Junta represented its undertaking as procreative, ostensibly continuing in the Latin American tradition of foundational fictions (Sommer 24). However, the coupling of what Doris Sommer calls "Eros and Polis" in the nineteenth century now ceased to be envisioned as a romance predicated on mutual desire and agreement: it signaled rather a failed romance, an act of rape. The idea of consent vanished entirely from the fantasy as well as from the political practice. As it was dismantling Argentina's democratic and judicial systems, the Junta spoke of interjecting itself forcefully into the political vacuum to create a new social body.[6] While not altogether "natural" (the Junta conceded) it still served "Nature's" more urgent reproductive goals. The legitimation of the use of political force for "necessary" ends follows the same logic as Freud's position on aggression and sadism, which he sees as "normal" and biologically justified in that they serve the "need for overcoming the re- sistance of the sexual object by means other than the process of wooing" (*Three Essays* 48). The military not only suspended the need for political consent but rationalized and even promoted violence against women. Rape and sadism, after all, were ultimately in the service of "Nature." The ends (placed above question) justified the means. Having overcome women metaphorically, the Junta appropriated birthing capabilities. The geneal- ogy of the military male was depicted as entirely patrilinear, handed down "through the blood of our heroes" (Troncoso 40). "*La ley de la sangre*" (blood ties) which from Greek tragedy onward differentiated between family (private) and political (social) duties was written by the military to appropriate once again the interior, familial space traditionally closed to it. In this new family, each member's first obligation was toward their father (the Junta) and their mother (the Patria). Children, potential Oedipuses, became highly suspect. Real women were written out of the narrative. Even traditional notions of a woman's domestic "sphere," a nonpolitical space, "disappeared." As the Junta had warned, all the interior/private spaces were turned inside out.

The Junta's mythic construction had concrete, practical repercussions for women. The image of the *female* body, reduced exclusively in this narrative to a *maternal* body, sustained the entire discourse. But that maternal image was fractured — on one side, the bleeding, virginal, abstract Patria, a fixed and controlled figure who legitimated the Junta's actions; on the other the whore, the bitch, the madwoman, the mother of bad children, the woman who wouldn't stay put and, hence, deserved all the suffering that befell her. The first was the very image of harmony, an ideal seemingly abstracted somewhere above the narrative structure. The Patria constituted a thor- oughly patriarchal invention of femininity, as illustrated by the word *Patria* itself — a feminine term for nationhood derived from *patriarchy*.[7] The bad woman — as historical subject — on the other hand was conceived as the obstacle to harmony; she (according to the master narrative) activated the narrative by being uncontrollable, by incarnating the birthplace of evil. The hero was forced to overcome her and all she represented. He, embod-

ied in the torturer, had to beat her, violate her and, ideally, eliminate her altogether — all in the name of the Patria (Woman).

The gendering of the enemy on a metaphoric level played itself out on the
physical bodies of those detained during the Junta's seven years in power.
The negative image of the "public" or active woman provoked the attack on
women — who made up 30 percent of the "disappeared" — and enabled the
systematic assault on the reproductive organs of all female-sexed prisoners
held in captivity.[8] Women were annihilated through a metonymic reduction
to their sexual "parts." Abducted women were raped as a matter of course.
Testimonies repeatedly allude to guns shot into vaginas and wombs, to
breast being pounded, to buttocks and mouths being ripped open. Pregnant women, who made up 3 percent of all the disappeared, were often
abducted, raped, and tortured simply because they were pregnant.[9] If and
when they gave birth they were beaten, humiliated, and often killed. Children born in prison were killed or given away to military families.[10] In a
concentration camp known as Olimpo (Olympus), the distinction between
embodied and disembodied "womanhood" (women/Woman) was made
brutally evident as military soldiers tortured female prisoners in front of the
image of the Virgin Mary (Bunster-Burotto 299). Nor was the attack on the
feminine exclusively reserved for women. All those abducted, regardless of
their sex, were gendered feminine. Before being killed, men were routinely
raped and sodomized with the *picana electrica* (electric cattle prod) as a
means of transforming them into the penetrable, disposable bodies of misogynist fantasies.

The profound ambivalence underlying the image of the feminine was
(and is) the source of its efficacy and appeal. The mythic version of events
offered up by the military made sense, at least to a part of the population
educated in a tradition that explains male individuation in terms of female
submission. Thus it would be facetious to argue that gender issues are
incidental to what happened in Argentina during the "Dirty War." The
misogyny of the fantasies was vital to its efficacy. It not only motivated the
scenario by engendering an obstacle; it also made sense of the urge to
overcome the "feminine" other. "In its 'making sense' of the world," as
Teresa de Lauretis points out in "Desire in Narrative," "narrative endlessly
reconstructs it as a two character drama in which the human person creates
and recreates himself out of an abstract or purely symbolic other" (121) —
for my purposes here, the Patria. The work of narrative, de Lauretis continues, "is the mapping out of differences, and specifically, first and foremost, of sexual difference" (121). The Patria, imagined as a purely symbolic, virginal mother figure, united Argentina's good children, the soldier

males, who were expected to identify with and model themselves on the national father-figures. The "subversives," the incarnation of non-cohesion or nonparticipation, were the bad children who threatened to destroy the father and claim the Patria for themselves. They were configured as something deadly *inside* the social body rather than as the external enemy of traditional warfare. They were the sons of bitches and *locas*, flesh and blood mothers who had to be eliminated from the social body. Nationhood, for the Junta, was built by blows to the female/feminized body, both literally and rhetorically. This Motherland, to paraphrase from Joan Landes's study of the French Republic, was "constructed against women, not just without them" (12).

The visual and narrative strategies evident in this staging of power were, perhaps not surprisingly, consistent with other totalitarian spectacles of power. Leo Bersani and Ulysse Dutoit note that the "occupation of our visual field by identical forms is the esthetic order which celebrates a secure political hegemony" (6). Everywhere the state displaced civil society. The manifest world order was presented as logical, rational, and self-evident. This grandiose kind of representation offered a heroic narrative with a linear progression in which the "climactic moment or goal . . . is an image of perfect immobility" (6). The spectacle of power aimed, thus, to mask the historical-ideological-gendered specificity of hegemony with the picture of eternal, universal, immutable stability and values (embodied in Argentina by the image of the Patria). The past was appealed to in order to divert attention from a present that would no longer bear examination. The Junta's staging placed the sacred needs of the Patria above discussion and attempted to reduce violence to an element of plot, where it could "be isolated, understood, perhaps mastered and eliminated. And, having been conditioned to think of violence within narrative frameworks, we expect this mastery to take place as a result of the pacifying power of narrative conventions as beginnings, explanatory middles, and climactic endings" (Bersani and Dutoit 51). The fascination with the spectacle that mesmerizes the audience into conformity was inextricable from the narrative structure of the drama — the participant's mimetic identification with the hero, the longing for control and order, the desire for narrative resolution. The identification with the lone, male hero also enabled a very selective view of events. As the anthropologist Marcelo Suárez-Orozco observes, "the great majority of Argentines, not unlike other peoples facing similar extreme circumstances, developed conscious and unconscious strategies of knowing what not to know about events in their immediate environment" (492). The audience's resistance to the spectacle, however, should not suggest that important portions of it did not participate in, or facilitate, the events. On the contrary, the general public's reaction was somewhat analogous to covering one's eyes during the terrifying parts of a horror show—a term that was soon applied to the *Proceso*. The majority of the public reacted exactly as it was meant to react; it played its part beautifully.

The Junta's display was performative and communicative, involving both visual and narrative components: *performative* because it was not only theatrically orchestrated but because its function was "obviously performative in that its pronouncements are not only assertive but have practical consequences" (Sarlo 38)[11]; *communicative* in the Artaudian sense of inciting a far-reaching, "contagious" delirium capable of affecting entire collectivities. As Beatriz Sarlo observes in "Política, ideología y figuración literaria," Argentines experienced a profoundly altered sense of daily life: "fantasies of persecution, death and loss marked the general tone of the period" (32). Suárez-Orozco uses similar terminology from George de Vos ("instrumental" and "expressive") to describe the behavioral modes of political actors in the master narrative. "Instrumental behavior is seen as behavior motivated in pursuit of some specific goal: A torturer may discharge an electric current on his prisoner's penis in order to 'extract' a confession and to spread terror in the population. Expressive behavior, on the other hand, is action which can be seen as an end in itself: A torturer may discharge electrical current on his prisoner, not even pretending to extract any information, but because of the sadistic sensuality involved in the act" (487). Thus, individual and collective fantasy of control and domination, played out against castrated, feminized, and penetrable bodies (literally and/or metaphorically), meshed into a highly organized system of terror in which hatred of the feminine was not only the consequence but, simultaneously, its very reason for being.

The misogynist, ahistorical narrative was useful in obscuring the fact that the economic crisis and political chaos that precipitated the military coup of 1976 were a result, in part, of conflicting economic interests specific to the mid- to late twentieth century: international capitalism had the effect of eroding Argentina's social institutions and programs and it clashed with the interests of Argentina's strong labor unions that had gained power during the period of post–World War II prosperity under Perón. It is not coincidental that the Junta's dismantling of a constitutional system of collective decision-making (such as the dissolution of Parliament and the Supreme Court in the days following the coup) should have been represented in terms of the lone male, situated in a dark vacuum beyond the boundaries of communal life, with only the stars to guide him. Nor should it surprise us that the emphasis on the solitary hero coincided with Argentina's economic drive toward privatization, consumerism, and international capitalism. As civil society "disappeared," members of society were pushed into the "individual" and "private" sphere. The home, then, became the target for repressive tactics. The criminal politics of the authoritarian dictatorship got people where they lived. Myth, as Dominick LaCapra and Teresa de Lauretis observe, is used to make sense of the world — to reduce structural changes to a level of plot. The Junta's epic had a beginning and an end; it declared the initiation of a fecund era and tried (ultimately successfully) to legislate a *punto final* (full stop) to accusations of human rights violations. History, as invoked by the Junta, was idealized as a founding myth and placed outside, or at the beginning, of what we would traditionally call the historical process.[12] All opposing representations or interpretations of Argentina's national drama were prohibited by the military leaders. Theirs, after all, was the ultimate performance. Declaring an end to conflict and decreeing resolution, they claimed to have put an end to drama. "History," as one of the Junta leaders proclaimed, "belongs to me."[13]

III

And in the midst of this brutal political climate, the Madres went to the Plaza de Mayo to publically protest against the military leaders who were "disappearing" their children.

The Madres' strategy was also performative and communicative. Their aim was to insert themselves into the public sphere and make visible another version of events. For those unfamiliar with the Madres, I will include a brief overview of their movement. At 11 A.M. on Saturday, 30 April 1977, fourteen Madres first took to the plaza to collectively demand information concerning the whereabouts of their loved ones. The women had met in government offices, prisons, and courts looking for their missing children. As soon as they got to the square, the women knew they had miscalculated — while the Plaza de Mayo is the political, financial, and symbolic center of Buenos Aires, it was empty on Saturday mornings. They realized immediately that they had to make a spectacle. Only by being visible could they be politically effective. Only by being visible could they stay alive. Visibility was both a refuge and a trap — a trap because the military knew who their opponents were, but a refuge insofar as the women were only safe when they were demonstrating. Attacks on them usually took place as they were going home from the plaza.

So the Madres started meeting on Thursday afternoons at 3:30. They walked counterclockwise around the obelisk in the Plaza right in front of the Casa Rosada. They started wearing white kerchiefs to identify themselves publicly as a group. They turned their bodies into walking billboards, carrying banners, placards and photographs of their children. Gradually, the number of women grew. They belonged to different social classes (54 percent working class), religious groups, and came from different parts of Argentina. Most of the disappeared were in their early twenties, 30 percent were working class and 21 percent were students. By July there were 150 Madres. Public response to their activities was mixed. Most Argentines tried to ignore them, crossing the street to distance themselves as much as possible from the women. Some passersby insulted them; others whispered support and solidarity. On 5 October 1977 they placed an ad in La Prensa demanding the "truth" about 237 disappeared persons, accompanied by pictures of the victims and the signatures and identity card numbers of the Madres. They got no reply. Ten days later, hundreds of women delivered a petition with 24,000 signatures demanding an investigation into the disappearances. The police tried to disperse them—spraying tear gas at the women, shooting bullets into the air, and detaining over 300 of them for questioning. Foreign correspondents, the only ones to cover the event, were also arrested. News of the Madres and their anti-Junta activities soon spread internationally. The battle for visibility commanded more and more spectators. Largely due to the public recognition and financial support from human rights groups from the Netherlands, Sweden, France, and Italy, the Madres were able to survive politically and financially. Amnesty International sent a mission to Argentina in 1976 and reported on the disappeared. In 1977, President Carter sent Patricia Derian, U.S. Assistant Secretary of State, to investigate the accusations of human rights abuses; she estimated that 3,000 people had been executed and 5,000 disappeared.[14] The United States cut military aid to Argentina and canceled $270 million in loans (Marysa Navarro 254). Although the Junta tried to dismiss the Madres as "madwomen" or "*locas,*" they realized they had to get rid of them. So in December of that year, they infiltrated the Madres' organization and kidnapped and disappeared twelve women, including the leader of the Madres, Azucena de Vicenti and two French nuns. But the Madres continued to return to the plaza. During 1978, the military intensified its harassment and detentions of the Madres. In 1979, it became impossible for them to enter the plaza which was cordoned off by heavily armed police. The women would stand around the plaza and raid it—dashing across the square before the police could stop them, only to remind the world and themselves that this was still their space.

Figure 4. The Mothers of the Plaza de Mayo. Photo by Cristina de Fraire.

In 1979, the Organization of American States (OAS) sent the Inter-American Human Rights Commission to Argentina. The Madres organized to bring mothers from all over the country to testify before the commission in Buenos Aires. As many as 3,000 people lined up at a time to testify before the commission (Marysa Navarro 253). The Junta, unable to block the investigation, launched its own counterattack of inscribing slogans on people, mimicking the visual strategies the Madres used. They made up posters and used their bodies too as walking billboards marked with a pun on human rights: "*Somos derechos y humanos*" ("We are right and human"). In that year, practically banished from the plaza, the Madres formed the Association of the Madres de Plaza de Mayo. In January 1980, the Madres returned to the plaza, ready to face death before relinquishing it again.

Over the years, the Madres' notion of motherhood had gradually become political rather than biological. They came to consider themselves the mothers of all the disappeared, not just their own offspring. Their spectacles became larger and increasingly dramatic — they organized massive manifestations and marches, some of them involving up to 200,000 people: the March of Resistance in 1981, and again the following year; in 1982 the March for Life and the March for Democracy; in 1983, at the end of the last military Junta, they plastered Buenos Aires with the names and silhouettes of the disappeared. In 1986, when it became clear that Alfonsín's government would do nothing meaningful to punish those responsible for the atrocities, they staged the March for Human Rights as a procession of masks. However, redefining motherhood has also been problematic for the Madres. Individually, many Madres admitted that they had lost hope of finding their children alive: "We know we're not going to find our children by going to the square, but it's an obligation we have to all the *desaparecidos*" (Jo Fisher 153). The tension between the biological death of their children and the living political issue of disappearance and criminal politics placed them in a conflicted situation. Were they now simply the mothers of dead children? If so, should they claim the dead bodies offered up by forensic specialists, accept compensation and get on with their lives? Did they need to hold onto the missing bodies in order to bring the military to justice and continue their political movement? Could the Madres, now a political organization, survive the death of their children? By 1986, the dilemma had split the group in two.[15] The group that now calls itself the Madres de la Plaza de Mayo, headed by Hebe de Bonafini (as opposed to the "Linea Fundadora" headed by Renee Epelbaum) felt committed to keeping the "*desaparecidos*" alive. They demanded "*Aparición con vida*" ("Back Alive") for all the disap-

Figure 5. "Marcha por los derechos humanos," March 1986.
Photo by Rafael Wollmann.

peared. However, their list of the disappeared no longer includes the children of the Linea Fundadora. The Linea Fundadora, nevertheless, also continues to work to bring the perpetrators to justice. They too travel, lecture abroad, and document their history with the names of both the victims and victimizers left off other lists or written out of other histories. Both groups, made up mainly by women in their sixties and seventies, continue to march around the Plaza de Mayo.

IV

The Madres' movement, most scholars would agree, is full of contradictions. Their conscious political aim was to incriminate the Argentine Junta and bring their children's torturers and murderers to trial. They succeeded in seriously damaging the Junta's legitimacy and credibility — aided by Argentina's failing economy and the military's own gross errors in judgment, particularly in the Falklands/Malvinas War. They also saw nine leaders from the three successive juntas face the most publicized trial in the country's history.[16] The Madres staged one of the most powerful, courageous and influential resistance movements of our times. In Suárez-Orozco's words, they "turned an interrupted mourning process (no bodies, hope, uncertainty) around and articulated out of their maternal pain and rage (their words), and survivor's guilt one of the most visible political discourses of resistance to terror in recent Latin American history. The mothers, by coming together to find out what was done to their children, subverted the silence and the centrifugal isolationism imposed during the years of terror by forcing public debate over the years of terror" (491).

Without diminishing the importance of the Madres' "politics of resistance" (Ruddick 227), commentators interested in the Madres and other women's political groups in and outside Latin America have pointed out the many contradictions posed by their movement — a movement that destabilized the military but left a restrictive patriarchal system basically unchallenged. The Madres won significant political power, but they claim not to want that power, at least not for themselves but only for their children. The women's shared struggle for missing children bridged class and religious barriers in Argentina, but the Madres have not politicized those issues. They recognize that "women are doubly oppressed, especially in Catholic-Hispanic countries" (Jo Fisher 155) and they have formed alliances with women's coalitions in Nicaragua, El Salvador, Uruguay, Colombia, Chile, and other Latin American countries. But they are not feminists, if by feminism one refers to the politicization of the female-sexed person's subordinate status.[17] The Madres left the confines of their homes, physically and politically, but they have not altered the politics of the home — for example, the gendered division of labor. After coming home from their demonstrations most of them still cook and do housework for their remaining family, even in those cases in which the husbands are at home full-time. The Madres took to the streets in order to protect their children and families; nonetheless, their political activity has estranged many of them from the surviving members of their families who were not prepared to accept the women's new roles: "They say if you stop going to the square, you're one of us again. My family now are the Mothers of the Plaza de Mayo," says one Madre (Jo Fisher 156). Having left home, they have established a new *casa*, or home, for their new family. There they continue their unpaid labor, their political activity. There, too, they nurture the young people who come to talk to them: "We cook for them, we worry about their problems, we look out for them much as we did for our children" (Diago 187).

How to explain these contradictions? Some commentators, such as Beatriz Schmukler and Laura Rossi, both from Argentina, gloss over the contradictions; they "are not interested" in examining them (Rossi 146). Rather, they focus on the positive aspects of the movement and dismiss its limitations. Other commentators stress the importance of gender in regard to the women's political activism. "The Madres are notable in that they are strictly a woman's movement," writes the Argentine sociologist María del Carmen Feijoó (Jaquette 77). Elsewhere, María del Carmen Feijoó and Mónica Gogna stress that it was the women's idea to go to the square and that their men had little faith in the strategy (Jelin 91). Suárez-Orozco notes "the very important gender bifurcation" evident in the fact that the Madres "turned private pain, rage and terror into a *collective* project of resistance, while fathers of the disappeared turned inward, often isolating themselves from any collective projects, often going into major narcissistic depressive states and developing high morbidity and death rates" (497). The question, for some Argentine commentators, was merely *which* gender identity the Madres were performing. One Argentine journalist put it simply: the Madres were the only ones who had balls. Hebe de Bonafini herself refers to having balls (Diago 82), suggesting perhaps that by rejecting their legitimate roles as domestic mothers, the Madres had crossed the gender line. Laura Rossi disagrees. It's not that the Madres had "balls." "Rather it is precisely this lack that constitutes the Madres of the Plaza de Mayo. Their access to politics is a product of this lack. Absence of the son. . . . The Madres perform (literally *make*) politics starting from the empty void simultaneously covered over and revealed by the nostalgic and grotesque metaphor — having balls. Their power lies in not having them but, rather, in their lack. Theirs is not the power of force but the power of weakness — the strength," and here Rossi quotes an unidentified Spanish feminist, "that generates from that hole within . . . the power of the cunt" (152). Rossi concludes her study on the Madres noting that with "the power of the cunt the Madres ignited the wick of powerlessness. Through powerlessness, they changed reality in a way that power itself was not able to achieve" (153). Others scoffed at the Madres' "weakness" as a "female luxury."[18]

V

Some of the contradictions can be understood, I believe, by distinguishing between the Madres' performance of motherhood and the essentialist notions of motherhood sometimes attributed to them and which, in all fairness, the Madres themselves often accentuate. Although much has been written about the Madres' strategy of politicizing motherhood, little has been said about their underlying concept of gender as performance and the impact of that concept on authoritarian discourse and politics. Once they decided to march, the Madres' self-representation was as theatrical as the military's. The Madres' movement did not begin when the individual mothers became acquainted in their search for their children. It originated when the women consciously decided to protest and agitate *as* mothers. That *as* marks the conceptual distance between the essentialist notion of motherhood attributed to the Madres and the self-conscious manipulation of the maternal role—understood as performative—that makes the movement the powerful and intensely dramatic spectacle that it has been.[19] María del Rosario, a Madre, wrote a poem in August 1977 (quoted by Fisher 89) that conveys the women's consciousness of their participation as *role* in the Argentine tragedy:

> With our wounds exposed to the sun, Plaza de Mayo,
> We show you these Argentine mothers. . . .
> historical witnesses to the nation,
> in silence, like beaten dogs,
> we walk across your paving stones

The women, most of whom had no political background or experience, realized that they were a part of a national spectacle and decided to actively play the role that had traditionally been assigned to them—the beaten dogs watching in silence, the underdogs, the powerless who cannot speak yet nonetheless witness and testify to the crimes. Yet they shifted the site of their enactment from the private sphere—where it could be construed as essentialist—to the public—where it became a bid for political recognition by means of what U.S. scholars would call "identity politics." The Madres' decision to make their presence visible in the plaza, stage center so to speak, was a brilliant and courageous move. While the plaza had been the locus of Argentina's community-building, no one had ever used it as the Madres did, much less during a state of siege in which public space was heavily policed. They perceived and literally acted out the difference between motherhood as an individual identity (which for many of them it was) and motherhood as a collective, political performance that would allow women to protest in the face of a criminal dictatorship. "We show you these Argentine Mothers" writes María del Rosario, a motherhood somewhat different from the "we" who performs it because it is mediated through the public space of the "you" (the plaza) that transforms their identity from an individual to a political one. María del Rosario speaks, but the Madres are silent. The role of mother was attractive, not because of its "natural" or essentialist qualities but because it was viable and practical. It offered the women a certain legitimacy and authority in a society that values mothers almost to the exclusion of all other women. It offered them, they believed, a certain protection against retribution — for a military that sustained itself on Christian and family values could hardly attack a group of defenseless mothers inquiring after their missing children. It offered them visibility in a representational system that rendered most women invisible for, among the few roles open to Argentine women, the suffering mother is the most popular and certainly the most socially rewarding. As the dramatist Diana Raznovich observes in *Casa Matriz,* her play about a "substitute" mother rented from an agency that specializes in fulfilling its client's fantasies, "You can't ask for a more tragic effect . . . I am the suffering mother *par excellence.* Dressed in black, scrubbing, weeping. . . . I am the Great Suffering Mother, the Mother immortalized by the tango. Literature is full of me. I'm the biblical mother, 'in sorrow thou shalt bring forth children.' I'm the holy Mother. Just look at these big fat tears!" (in Rais 179). As the Madres recount how they dressed down as dowdy old women and became quick change artists — slipping on less traditionally "motherly" attire such as wigs, high heels, and brightly colored clothing to escape arrest — playing the role of mother was also fun and empowering. For once, they manipulated the images which had previously controlled them.

Unfortunately for women generally, and Latin American women particularly, there are few good roles.[20] The Madres attempted the seemingly impossible — a public demonstration of maternal protest — in itself a contradiction in terms. From a representational point of view, the image nullified itself even as it came into being. "Public" women in Latin America, as Jean Franco notes, are considered prostitutes or madwomen — that is, nonmothers, even anti-mothers.[21] As one non-Argentine commentator (consciously or unconsciously reproducing the patriarchal discourse) stated, "There have been only two important women in Argentina, Evita and Isabelita, and they were both whores."[22] Evita, Perón's popular first wife, was very aware that she could augment her political efficacy by downplaying her visibility. Perón was "the figure," she said, and "I the shadow" (Eva Perón, *Mission* 81). *Good* mothers are invisible. They do not gather in groups; they stay home with their children. And as the childless Evita had once said, "the home is the sanctuary of motherhood and the pivot of society. It is the appropriate sphere in which women, for the good of their country and for their own children, fulfill their patriotic duty daily." She resolved the contradiction by declaring herself "the mother of my people" working in the "great home of the Motherland."[23]

The Madres tried to overcome the limitations intrinsic to the role of motherhood by modeling themselves on the Virgin Mary, the ultimate mother who transcends the public/private bind by carrying her privacy with her even in public. In "Her," the boundary is simultaneously inside and outside. Thus, Christian and Jewish women alike initially played the Mater Dolorosa and exploited a system of representations and stereotypes that had so effectively limited most forms of visibility and expression: "At first they marched as if in ritual procession: faces serious, eyes turned upward in supplication, heads covered . . . peaceful, rapt, pleading" (Diago 29). For the Madres, the boundaries of domesticity were also inside and outside. Hebe de Bonafini, for example, has been known to demonstrate in her bedroom slippers to underline the hominess, and thus nonthreatening aspect, of their movement. The women may have stepped outside the home momentarily, the slippers suggest, but they take their home with them wherever they go. The virginal role allows the women to perform traditionally acceptable "feminine" qualities — self-sacrifice, suffering, irrationality. Again, reading the different statements from various mothers indicates that the choice of the qualities was based more on accessibility and viability than on their political or ideological commitment to traditional values.[24] Even as they took one of the most daring steps imaginable in their particular political arena, they affirmed their passivity and powerlessness. They, as the poem makes clear, exposed their wounds. They were both Christ and Mary, victim and witness. As Feijoó notes, they incorporated a "feminine logic based on respect for the traditional role of women, who are thought to be altruistic and vicarious. This made it possible for women to reject a conventional political model of participation based on the 'rational calculation of costs and benefits' and to substitute another one based on 'sacrifice.' Despite its sex role conventionality, traditionalism became a daring gesture, an indictment of its original meaning of passivity and submission" (in Jaquette 77). Yet even that virginal role — sanctified by Argentine society though it was — did not protect the women for long. The women's public exposure resulted in their being ostracized from the Church. They had gone beyond the representational constraints of the role: pain was permissible, perhaps, but not anger. Silence, maybe, but not protest. As Monsignor Quarracino commented: "I can't imagine the Virgin Mary yelling, protesting and planting the seeds of hate when her son, our Lord, was torn from her hands" (Rossi 149).

Similarly, the Madres attempted to manipulate the maternal image that was already overdetermined by the state. The "motherhood" performed by the Madres was, after all, designed by the patriarchal system they lived in. The military, attempting to capitalize on women's traditional duties and exploit them further, pressured mothers to police their children. Through the media, they reminded the women repeatedly that it was their patriotic responsibility to know where their children were, who they kept company with and what they were doing. The Madres turned that reasoning around claiming that it was precisely their maternal responsibilities that took them to the plaza in search of their children. This was, the Madres made believe, a *private* matter, a *family* matter. If the personal had become political, and Madres had to take to the streets, it was not because they were feminists but because the military had blurred private/public distinctions by raiding homes and snatching children in the dead of night. One of the most interesting political conflicts of the period, then, was the struggle to define and control "motherhood." In opposition to the church and the state who attempted to lock women in passive, domestic roles, Hebe de Bonafini came to identify the Madres as those who had left their patriarchal home behind and "who have broken with many of the aspects of this system we live in" (Fisher 157).

The Madres, unaccommodating Jocastas, threatened the all-male narrative in part because they refused to comply with the military's version of events and forget about their children, in part because they embodied the birthing capabilities that the Junta had claimed for itself. Moreover, they spoiled the Junta's parade by destabilizing the visible field and re-semanticizing the terms of the struggle. They responded to the military spectacle with a spectacle that inverted the focus. What had been invisible before — from domestic women to "subversives" — was now visible for the world to see. The women too sought to expose themselves, but they showed their wounds rather than their instruments. Or, rather, the Madres' wounds were their instruments. By exposing themselves, sacrificing themselves, they sought to expose the violent politics the military tried to cover up. Through their bodies, they wanted to show the absence/presence of all those who had disappeared without a trace, without leaving a body. Clearly, the confrontation between the Madres and the military centered on the physical and semantic location of the missing body — object of exchange in this battle of images. While the military attempted to make their victims invisible and anonymous by burying them in unmarked graves, dumping their bodies into the sea or cutting them up and burning them in ovens, the Madres insisted that the disappeared had names and faces. They were people; people did not simply disappear; their bodies, dead or alive, were somewhere; someone had done something to them. Instead of the military's ahistorical forgetting, the Madres inscribed the time and dates of the disappearances. Instead of dismembering, remembering. The Madres challenged the generals' claim to history by writing themselves and the "disappeared" into the narrative, literally as well as figuratively. Their bodies, inscribed with names, dates, and faces were "written into the message" to borrow a phrase from Ross Chambers.[25] Opposed to the image projected by the Junta of a lone, heroic male leaving family and community behind, the Madres emphasized community and family ties. Instead of the military's performance of hierarchy, represented by means of rigid, straight rows, the Madres' circular movements around the Plaza, characterized by their informal talk and pace, bespoke values based on egalitarianism and communication. While the soldiers' uniforms, paraphernalia, and body language emphasized the performative aspects of gender, the Madres too were highly conscious of the importance of their gender role, specifically their maternal role, and manipulated it accordingly. The Madres also had their "uniforms," though these may not have been immediately identifiable as such. They presented themselves as elderly, physically weak, and sexually nonactive women. Yet they resisted even the most brutal treatment. When the military tried to force the women from the plaza, they marked their presence indelibly by painting white kerchiefs around the circle where they usually walked. Instead of the empty streets and public spaces mandated by the military curfew, the Madres orchestrated the return of the repressed. Buenos Aires was once again filled with images of the missing people; spectacular bodies, ghostly, looming figures who refused to stay invisible. The public spaces overflowed with demonstrators as the terrorized population gradually followed the Madres' example and took to the streets.

The narrative and spectacular elements underlying the Madres' performance relied as much on myth-making as the military's did. They too had to justify their actions by appealing to "Nature." Hebe de Bonafini expresses the Madres' belief that "our movement stems from our identity as mothers. Mothers are the ones that breast-feed, raise and look after their children. This is historically true. If the child (son) is in trouble, it is the mother that comes to his help. It he's taken prisoner, it is she who defends him and visits him in jail. The mother-lion is a very central figure" (Diago 121). This rhetoric, which sounds as suspect as the military discourse, is not, I would claim, an expression of the Madres' belief in woman's place in the "natural" order but, rather, an attempt to ground their identity politics and legitimate their struggle. So too, their use of spectacle looked "natural" and simple; they, like the military, also stressed universal, immutable, and eternal values. They represented motherhood as something forever fixed. They seemingly adhere to the tradition of women's lamentations which dates back more than 2,500 years to Greek drama in which women express protest through public demonstrations of pain and sorrow. In Argentina's tragic scenario, the Madres embodied "pity" while the military males staged "terror." But pity and terror are inextricably linked. As the Greek theatre scholar Gilbert Murray notes in his foreword to *Euripides: The Trojan Women,* "pity is a rebel passion. Its hand is against the strong, against the organised force of society, against conventional sanctions and accepted Gods. . . . it is apt to have those qualities of unreason, of contempt for the counting of costs and the balancing of sacrifices, of recklessness, and even, in the last resort, of ruthlessness. . . . It brings not peace, but a sword" (7). The military, quick to pick up the threatening quality of the Madres' pitiful display of their wounds-as-weapons branded the rebellious women *emotional terrorists.*

The short- and long-term effects of the Madres' activism has been the subject of much debate. Some commentators stress that the Madres changed little in Argentina. There were fewer women voted into positions of power after the "Dirty War" than before it; the Madres "had a weak institution with minimal functional differentiation; they rely heavily on strong personal leadership and are held together by gender solidarity, not organizational sophistication" (Jaquette 78). Others maintain that the movement, "without being concerned about changing the ideology of femininity, in fact caused a transformation in women's consciousness and the female role" (Jelin 91).

Questions as to the Madres' movement efficacy in the political realm, however, are locked into two, interconnected positions — their use of identity politics and their use of performance.

How can identity politics effectively liberate political actors from stereotypes and systems of representation that have previously precluded political activism? Ross Chambers posits a double hypothesis pertaining to identity politics: "(1) to have a cultural identity (in the sense of an 'individual' 's being subsumed into a categorized group on the assumption of self-sameness) is tantamount to being appropriated into the position of cultural mediator or mediating other, with respect to a community of differentiating communicating subjects — a community whose own cultural status is 'forgotten' by its members while it is in fact constituted by the construction of the cultural other that mediates it — then (2) that other who is inscribed, however facelessly and namelessly, in the community's messages as the object of an appropriating gesture is also, inevitably, included in that community's affairs, and forms part of its culture, by virtue of the very gesture that seeks to distance it" (*No Montagues* 9–10). In my reading of the Madres' use of identity politics and their bid for political visibility demonstrates the limitations of identity politics outlined by Chambers in that the women are drawn into (appropriated by) the discourse and logic from which they are trying to differentiate. They are sucked into a battle of images that is played through them, and around them, which allows for the communication of individuated subjects (politicians) while they themselves remain faceless and nameless (the Madres).

This same problem faces their performance. The Madres seemed to see little choice but to assume the role they deemed safest and which they knew best. Nonetheless that role played into a national fantasy predicated on sexual difference — specifically the castration fantasy that "explains" male potency and dominance and the female's lack thereof. Thus, they were contained and positioned by this oedipal narrative. Much as the military's performance was a display of virility, the Madres' spectacle was a public display of *lack*. They made it evident that had no previous political identity or background, no expertise — they were just housewives; they had no power, no weapons — just absence, missing children, sons who were no longer there. The Madres were positioned as mediators between warring fathers and sons. While consciously performing "motherhood," the Madres were trapped in a bad script: They perpetuated the oedipal narrative by repeatedly asserting that they had been made pregnant by their children (Diago 79). The potential for equality and power, the women claimed, could only be regained by means of the restitution of the missing member. They represented themselves as the furrow in which the seed of the future was planted (Diago 169). The implication, then is that the phallus (penis) must pass through them to produce the new "Man": "the day will come when one of our sons, whoever he might be, will cross the Plaza de Mayo and enter the Government Building; and that young man, that man will be our son" (Diago 169). I agree with Laura Rossi's statement that "the missing body of the son represents the dismembered body of the mother" (149–50), but she fails to recognize the woman's dismemberment as part of the castration scenario. Hence, we disagree on its meaning and efficacy. For me, the castration scenario is violent and disempowering rather than liberating. It seems imperative to envision a different scenario in which political conflict in the social "body" will not automatically be justified in terms of sexual difference to be played out through an attack on the "feminine."

The political denouement of this national fantasy of castration was predictable, built into the fantasy itself. The son, according to the Freudian scenario, cannot afford to ally himself with the weak, castrated mother. He must identify with the father and bypass her to join the ranks of power. Like the lone soldier male, he may cast one nostalgic look behind. National reconciliation leaves women on the sidelines, somehow marginal to the happy ending. As one Madre describes: "We helped the political parties . . . thanks to us marching at the front, they were able to open a way to elections. If not, they wouldn't be where they are today, in Congress" (Jo Fisher 112). Another adds: "We knocked on their doors many times and they wouldn't let us in" (Jo Fisher 113). The negotiations between the fathers and sons were hammered out on the women's backs in a move that Chambers has called "the back-grounding of the mediating instance" (*No Montagues* 10). The Madres have also been ignored by the Argentine media: "There is a conspiracy of silence. They never publish our communiques and they don't mention our participation in events or cover our demonstrations . . . The police filmed us, but the media, no" (Fisher 144). And because they know that publicity is essential to their group's survival, they realize that "if they don't write about us, we don't exist" (144).

The Madres, the women seem to be saying, exist only in representation. I would go further and say that, to a degree, they were framed by a system of representations through which they sought to claim visibility. It seems clear to me that the maternal role they chose to unite them was highly problematic. When the Madres decided to go beyond their individual search for their children and politicize motherhood, that decision was a conscious political choice—they could have (for example) performed as women, wives, sisters, or human rights activists. The Women in Black, from the Gaza Strip, for example, include but do not focus on motherhood. Motherhood, however, seemed a logical and powerful choice for identity politics. The maternal image appears to be endlessly generous and expandable; it has a long and noble tradition in Argentina; many could identify with the mother-figure and a whole group of women could share her suffering. Yet, the assumption of sameness obscured real political, class, and social differences of Argentine women and limited the arena of confrontation. By the very fact that the maternal image subsumes boundaries, it also subsumes difference. What happens to other Argentine women who want to speak and act for themselves rather than for or through their children? What happens to the other issues (in addition to human rights violations), and other roles (in addition to motherhood) that need to be publicized and politicized? By taking on that one role to the exclusion of others (as one does in theatrical performance) the Madres were unable to maximize their political options in order to modify the environment that had proved so damaging not only to their children, but to women in general. It is not, I believe, that they did not want to include these other issues. Their individual statements attest to their concern with many social and political issues. However, the role did not allow for their politicization. Rather, the maternal role once again relegated the women to the subordinate position of mediators between fathers and sons. Communication took place through and around them, yet they were dismissed and ignored as background noise. Once again, much as in the military discourse, the historical and material conditions of real women are eclipsed behind the image of Woman. As the women marched around the plaza, as they were harassed, arrested, tortured, and disappeared, the battle continued to be fought on the female body.

On one level, then, I have to conclude that the military and the Madres reenacted a collective fantasy that reaffirmed the negativity of the female-sexed partner and made it difficult for her to extricate herself. The performances staged by each reconstituted the stereotypical binaries: the military acted, the Madres reacted; the Junta's narrative had a linear progression while the circular, repetitive nature of the Madres' demonstrations suggested — from a representational point of view — that they weren't going anywhere. The Madres challenged the military but played into the narrative. The Junta might be performing the authoritarian father while the Madres took the role of the castrated mother, but both parties were reenacting the same old story. Their positions were, in a sense, already there as *pre*text or script. Their participation in the national tragedy depended little on their individual position as subjects. On the contrary: their very subjectivity was a product of their position in the drama.

Looking beyond the maternal role, however, and looking at the individual women who walked away from the plaza, we see a group of women who redefined the meaning of "mothers," "family," and "home" in a patriarchal society. Mothers, flesh and blood women, are now more free to act and take to the streets. They can be bold, independent, political, and outraged even as they take on the role of the submissive, domestic creature. Their new "home" is a negotiated space; their new "family" founded on political rather than biological ties. What has been accepted as the Madres' traditionalism in fact has more to do with the negotiated alliances of radical feminists. Their new family reminds me of what Cherríe Moraga, in *Giving Up the Ghost*, calls "making familia from scratch / each time all over again . . . with strangers / if I must. / If I must, I will" (58). The Madres, thus, made the transition from identity politics to coalition politics. The women may choose to adhere to their old ways, cooking for the younger members of the group, but that is now a choice they exercise. Their political activism, explicitly designed to empower the new "Man," in fact made new people out of the Madres, people with options. As de Bonafini says, "For me cooking for twenty is the same as cooking for one, and we like to eat together because this is also a part of our struggle and our militancy. I want to continue being the person I've always been. Sometimes I'm criticized for wearing a housecoat and slippers in public but I'm not going to change. Of course my life is different" (Fisher 158). The performance of motherhood has created a distance between "I" and the "person I've always been." It is as if the women's conscious performance of motherhood — restrictive and problematic though it was — freed them from the socially restrictive institution of motherhood that had previously kept them in their place. The performance offered that disruptive space, that moment of transition between the "I" who was a mother and the "I" who chooses to perform motherhood.

In closing, I would like to remark that the phenomenon I have discussed here holds true in general of various other spectacles of the period. It's not that there was no opposition — far from it — but the opposition was by and large caught up in the narrative offered by the Junta. While opponents to the Junta may have tried to resist or challenge acts of terror, they could not overthrow the dictatorship. Insofar as they could not control the discourse, those involved in oppositional movements, like the Madres, had no choice but to manipulate its grammar, logic, and vocabulary.

Being caught within an ideological web of signification, extremely limiting though it is, however, need not imply that there is no "outside" ideology. One way of imagining an "outside" is perhaps implicit in the performance model itself. Performance, as a carrying through, needs the audience to complete its meaning, tie the pieces together and give them coherence. The Madres relied for their efficacy and survival on capturing the attention of spectators — Argentines who might dare to reinterpret the Junta's version of events as well as the foreign spectators who might feel compelled to bring pressure to bear on their governments. Alternate "readings" of the military narrative have been offered. Clearly, we can advocate for better scripts. But for that to happen, it seems to me, we have to be a more critical audience, an audience that refuses to suspend disbelief and withholds applause. Only by interrupting these particular performances of power can the underlying narratives be rendered ineffectual. Social actors can modify their actions and their alliances to enhance their life-chances. Fantasies can change — at least that's my fantasy.

NOTES

1   Mothers' movements inspired by the Madres of the Plaza sprang up in Chile, Brazil, Nicaragua, El Salvador, Guatemala, and other Latin American countries. Women's groups such as the "Women in Black" from the Gaza strip, the Kenyan Mothers, and the Yu-

goslavian Mothers are recent examples of the political mobilization organized around motherhood.

2   See also Judith Butler's *Gender Trouble.*

3   All translations from Jo Fisher's *Mothers of the Disappeared* are hers. All other translations from Spanish are mine unless otherwise noted.

4   See Francine Masiello, Beatriz Sarlo, and Balderson et al. for discussions of the representation of the military as a unified subject.

5   Teresa de Lauretis suggests that the hero of oedipal narratives "must be male, regardless of the gender of the text-image, because the obstacle, whatever its personification, is morphologically female" (*Alice Doesn't* 118–19).

6   The desire to formulate a "new," implicitly masculine social body is not new — the Junta merely presented it as such while, in fact, tapping into a gendered fantasy of origin that dates back to the "discovery" of the Americas. Since the conquest and colonization of the New World, from Columbus and Amerigo Vespucci onward, the conquest and post-Independence narratives (Sarmiento's *Facundo*, for example) have the conqueror/colonist/Argentine male striving to impose order and define himself in opposition to the empty, dangerous, chaotic, implicitly feminine geography.

7   I want to thank Elizabeth Garrels for helping me clarify this connection.

8   While almost all the women were raped, there are numerous accounts of violence directed at the womb: "they had shot open her womb" (Jo Fisher 104); and of battered breasts and bleeding vaginas (*Testimonios* 30), etc.

9   As Rita Arditti and M. Brinton Lykes write in "'Recovering Identity,'" "the level of cruelty aimed at pregnant women and children suggests that special gratification was obtained by attacking the most vulnerable individuals" (463).

10   General Ramón Camps explained the rationale for disappearing babies: "It wasn't people that disappeared, but subversives. Personally I never killed a child; what I did was to hand over some of them to charitable organizations so that they could be given new parents. Subversive parents educate their children for subversion. This has to be stopped" (quoted in Jo Fisher 102).

11   See too Shoshana Felman's definition of performative enunciations in *The Literary Speech Act*, "not to inform or to describe, but to carry out a 'performance,' to accomplish an act through the very process of their enunciation" (15).

12   It is impossible to develop the implications of the Junta's displacement of Argentina's critical sociopolitical conflict onto the mythic, ahistoric realm in this paper. However a few fundamental reasons must be given for this strategy. The displacement drew public attention (or at least discussion) away from a profound political shift against Argentina's working class, which had, historically, dominated twentieth-century politics. This was a part of the Junta's economic plan, developed by Martinéz de Hoz, to enter into international capitalism.

13   Eduardo Massera, quoted by Marguerite Feitlowitz (30).

14   Figures from John Simpson and Jana Bennett (279).

15   I disagree with Ann Snitow's assessment in "A Gender Diary" that the Madres split "along the feminist divide" (49). Both groups, as I see it, have an ambivalent relationship to feminism. According to the Madres de la Plaza faction, tensions started in the group after Alfonsín came to office at the end of 1983. The "Linea Fundadora," they maintain, wanted to negotiate with Alfonsín and take a more pacifist line. There was also an election in the

movement in January 1986, which intensified the suspicion and resentment among the women and provoked the final rupture. See Diago (193–95).

16 Only five of the leaders were convicted. Videla, president of the first junta, received the most severe punishment — life imprisonment. His sentence was lifted in December 1990 by President Menem after repeated uprisings from the right-wing in the military. Everyone else has been acquitted.

17 Laura Rossi states that, without being feminists, the Madres have actually come to the same realization that underlines feminism, that the personal is political (152). I think that the Madres have become increasingly feminist, except that feminism is largely misunderstood in Argentina (and Latin America as a whole) to mean radical separatists, men-haters. The word feminism, moreover, is too loaded with imperialist, "First World" connotations to be considered useful to the Madres. Hebe de Bonafini, the leader of the Madres, states the following: "I don't think the Mothers are feminists, but we point a way forward for the liberation of women. We support the struggle of women against this *machista* world and sometimes this means that we have to fight against men. But we also have to work together with men to change this society. We aren't feminists because I think feminism, when it's taken too far, is the same as *machismo.* So yes, we want to say that we agree women should have the same place as men, not above or below, but equal, and we have pointed a very clear way forward to this. I think we have also raised some new possibilities for women, the most important of which is the possibility of the socialization of motherhood. This is something very new" (Jo Fisher 158).

18 J. Colotto in a homage to former chief of the Federal Police Alberto Villar, quoted in footnote 18 by María del Carmen Feijoó and Mónica Gogna (Jelin 111).

19 I am indebted to Marianne Hirsch for helping me through this part of the essay.

20 Women in Argentina today are legal minors; they are bound by law to show "reverential fear" for their husbands (Graciela Maglie and Gloria Bonder in Giberti and Fernández, eds.). Universities are considered a "factory for spinsters" (Jo Fisher 37). There is little or no justice or recourse for battered women. These conditions indicate that socioeconomic and historical conditions, rather than "natural" or "biological" ones, keep women fixed in their subservient roles, onstage and off. Both in social and theatrical representations, women are defined primarily in relation to male needs and desires.

21 Franco writes ("Self-Destructing Heroines" 105): "to describe someone as a 'public woman' in Latin America is simply not the same as describing someone as a public man. . . . The public woman is a prostitute, the public man a prominent citizen. When a woman goes public, she leaves the protected spaces of home and convent and exposes her body."

22 Conversation with Marshall Meyer (Dartmouth, December 1991), the politically active rabbi who served on the Argentine National Commission on the Disappeared.

23 From *My Mission in Life.* Also quoted in Chaney (21).

24 Graciela de Jeger, who is a Madre, makes the statement that they believe in the "liberation of men and women. Clearly, women are doubly oppressed, especially in Catholic-Hispanic countries. We are oppressed as workers in a dependent capitalist country, because women work in the lowest paid, least qualified work and we also have housework to do. This makes it more difficult for women to take part in the struggle" (Jo Fisher 155). It is a fact that the Madres support divorce and there are members who have gone as far as to discourage women from marrying in the first place.

25   This particular phrase is from Ross Chambers and is given in his lecture titled *No Montagues Without Capulets: Some Thoughts on Cultural Identity*. Later, I offer a discussion on "identity politics" and "cultural politics" and my work is based in part on Chamber's observations.

Juan Villegas
Closing Remarks

❑

Strategies for reading Latin American cultures or "Hispanic" or "Latino" cultures in the United States vary according to the interpreting subjects and their historical contextuality. One of the most important aspects of cultural and literary analysis brought by anthropological studies is the belief that the description or interpretation of a specific culture is always mediated by the historian's social imaginary, her/his system of values and degree of cultural competence in reading the signs and the context in which the signs were produced. From this perspective, what is defined as a culture is actually the product of the anthropologist or historian's discursive practices. As such it is a discourse caught in a continuous process of being defined, redefined, and adjusted by the defining subjects according to new historical, economic, and social conditions in which the defining subjects are immersed, the specific discursive practice itself, and the potential reader. Hence defining or framing Latin American and Chicano/Latino cultures should be understood as a discursive practice mediated by the cultural historian's ideological and cultural position, and by the perception of Latin American and Chicano/Latino cultures in the cultural system in which the historian is inserted. To write about Latin American or Latino cultures in the United States therefore is always mediated by the writer's perception of the real as well as the construction of these fields by the legitimized cultural systems in the United States.

Any reading of Latin American or Chicano/Latino cultures in the United States has to take into consideration the dominant modes of representation of those cultures in their country of origin, and the different factors contributing to their perception by the general audience. For many Americans, for example, the visual perception of Latin America is mainly represented by the image of a dictator, dressed as a general with a large number of medals. Chicanos or Latinos, on the other hand, are often depicted as *"pachucos,"* or individuals dressed with bandannas. Most TV news, an important mediating factor in the representation of cultures in this country, emphasizes the barrio's social problems and continually portray "Latino" gangs in various studies or news items. These images have been the product of an interested selection of the real events reinforced by the media. The Chicano or Latino artist cannot free herself or himself from those images and has to struggle with them, and is inclined to represent the group with the traits imposed by the dominant cultural discourses. The academic discourses sometimes tend to take the images as reality. In Latin America the representations of Chicanos or Latinos in the United States are even more stereotyped.

In the specific case of the main topic of this book—Latino and Latin American performance—the hegemonic cultural discourse in the United States has silenced the existence of Chicano/Latino or Latin American culture or theatre. The exclusion of Latin American theatrical discourses or Latin American cultural products from most histories of Western theatre or Western culture, however, is not a given, but rather, a historical condition.[1] This exclusion is mainly due to a misinterpretation of Latin American cultural texts—which is usually founded on the historian's assumptions—the theoretical model employed, and the cultural context of the historian. On the other hand, the Latin American texts themselves—their mode of production, aesthetic codes, and contextuality—do not reveal their own specificity and significance in relation to the models being used by the dominant critical discourses within Western cultures.

Most studies on Latin American cultures and Chicano/Latino cultures in the United States prefer some canonical texts or search for unifying issues. There is a tendency to understand Latin America as a homogeneous whole. Historians emphasize problems related to certain groups, and literary critics tend to privilege texts easy to insert within European texts and traditions. The issue of the relationship between the various Latin American cultures and the Chicano/Latino cultures most of the time is not discussed. On the other hand, traditional studies on theatre—Latin American or Chicano/Latino—tend to neglect the "theatrical" and "performance" side of "theatre" and privilege "dramatic texts." *Negotiating Performance: Gender, Sexuality, and Theatricality in Latin/o America* departs from this approach and it pays more attention to non-canonical texts from Latin America, those usually not included as part of the dominant culture such as carnival and "performance." It devotes a great deal of space and interest to a diversity of cultural forms associated with "Hispanics" in the United States. In the latter, the emphasis is on cultural manifestations traditionally considered marginal. It also attempts to apply some recent theoretical strategies to alternative cultural products.

On the surface the book does not seem to have a thematic unity. The unity, however, emerges from the purpose of offering to the reader the diversity of cultural manifestations without proposing a single issue or topic as the defining factor. The editors wanted to call attention to a series of fields and cultural manifestations which must first be studied by themselves, and only later studied in their relationship to other fields. The search for a unifying theme may have lead to a misrepresentation of the diversity. This goal also implied highlighting a different concept of "theatre" and some theatrical manifestations from nondominant cultures. Unfortunately, the purpose also inevitably lead to selection and exclusion: exclusion of issues and fields which should be studied in order to reach a better understanding of the diversity of cultures in Latin America and in the United States.

SITUATING THE CRITICAL DISCOURSES

It has been pointed out that "Professions may not be tools of hegemonic social classes, but neither do they operate in isolation from the discourse of their environment with its hegemonic assumptions about society and the world. The validity of learning produced by professionals is judged according to its resonance with these assumptions of the broader social discourse" (Dirlik 31).

Most writers in this book are associated with U.S. universities. This fact necessarily leads to a privileging of issues and strategies which have been emerging or becoming significant options in that context. Critical discourses focusing on performance, cultural diversity, gender, and the deconstruction of colonial discourses are some that form the critical horizon of this book. From this perspective, the book brings to the U.S. scenario the issue of multiculturalism and diversity of cultures historically named "Hispanic." These lines of research are highly attractive fields for new innovative critical discourses in U.S. universities. This insertion explains some of the topics discussed and also justifies some of the exclusions.

My contention is that most strategies and many of the concepts used in the book are dependent on a process of cultural legitimation within U.S. academic institutions, and as such imply the exclusion of potential significant voices, mostly from Latin American critics or theorists, for whom the range of issues raised in a book like this would probably have been different.

The dominant academic and administrative discourses at most universities in the United States have been described as ethnocentric, Eurocentric, and patriarchal by those scholars who specialize in minority discourses. The speaking voices in this book should be heard in the context of the dialectics of traditional or dominant critical positions with emerging critical and administrative attitudes. The support for understanding the other's culture sometimes has been questioned even by those who support cultural diversity. For some critics, acceptance and support of cultural diversity may be construed as a cultural self-serving inquiry on the other and otherness by the dominant ideological discourse, which would interpret the other from its point of view and for its own benefits. According to this interpretation, the academic discourses in U.S. universities become the subject, and as such, a believer in its own merits and the definer of the "other" culture. For others the trend toward multiculturalism is a politically and economically self-serving device by which the superpower attempts to know and understand the other/others in order to appropriate them. Edward Said, for example, has suggested the disturbing theory that the trend toward multicultural studies and understanding otherness in anthropology is related to the dominant culture's imperialist needs: "To practice anthropology in the United States is therefore not just to be doing scholarly work investigating "otherness" and "difference" in a large country; it is to be discussing them in an enormously influential and powerful state whose global role is that of a superpower" ("Representing" 213). For others, multiculturalism may be understood as a rejection of the ethnocentric tradition and as a sign of the independence of academic institutions with regard to society.

From this optimistic perspective, the trend toward multiculturalism will indicate the sign of a new beginning for "American" culture, which is interested in understanding society as the coexistence of a plurality of cultural systems, each one recognized as valid, independent, and self-evolving. From this perspective, this book may be understood as a contribution to the understanding of the plurality of cultures commonly subsumed under the sign "Hispanic" in order to avoid the simplification and stereotyping of individuals and social groups.

The current multiculturalist trend should hopefully be construed as one step in the slow transformation toward a multicultural society which is feeling the presence and active participation of diverse groups. The continuous pressure by groups characterized by ethnic, gender, or cultural factors, and their growing economic and political importance, are contributing to the creation of a social consciousness oriented toward diversity and multiculturalism. The implied utopia is a society in which all individuals are "subjects" because the "other" will be free to be himself or herself without impositions by a dominant culture. This is not the "Golden Age" of Don Quijote, in which there is neither mine nor yours; it is neither the socialist nor the "communitarian" utopia. This new utopia could be construed as the utopia of "freedom to be different."

This is neither the time nor the place to analyze the historical factors leading to this utopia. It is important to note, however, that the leading philosophical and academic discourses in the West support this utopia. In the United States, these trends are evident in academic practices that privilege those critical and philosophical discourses emphasizing the so-called "other" and multiculturalism. Administratively, the establishment of recent programs such as ethnic or women's studies is a clear sign of this orientation. With regard to teaching, new courses and requirements have been established. New journals have appeared that emphasize minority discourses, explore alternative strategies for reading literary texts, and that attempt to diversify the canon by rejecting or supplementing the traditional canonical texts.

The realization of the utopia, within a general trend of actions and reactions, is not without conflicts. Within the society of the United States, for example, there is a backlash caused by these trends. The efforts made toward reaching this ideal induce some groups from the dominant cultures to react with measures limiting changes or nullifying the marginal cultures' efforts for recognition. The state of California increased tuition for out-of-state students, therefore reducing the possibilities for foreign students to study in and graduate from the UC system. Tuition hikes also make it more difficult for minority students to participate in it. There are organizations that want to establish English as the legally mandated official language, and in some California cities, some groups have even attempted to prohibit commercial signs in a foreign language on the streets.

Negotiating Performance identifies with those post-structuralist trends which tend to reject totalitarian views of culture and with those practitioners in social theory who search for alternative models capable of doing justice to historical specificity. The question, however, is the potential misunderstanding of marginal cultures when the strategies are mediated by the need of legitimation by the institution and the hegemonic cultures in the institution. Does the need for legitimation lead toward a selection of issues which may be more important to the strategy and the institution than to the culture or cultures being described? Is there a potential misinterpretation of "Hispanic" cultures in the United States and Latin American cultures when the writers choose to highlight some concerns according to the emerging critical trends in the United States?

I have questioned the legitimacy or the authority of representatives of dominant cultures to adequately interpret the Other's cultures. I have argued that the dominant cultures' models and assumptions usually contribute to a misinterpretation of marginal cultures. I have stated that Latin American cultural objects are usually distorted or, at least, misinterpreted when they are read using European cultural models. In general terms, I am inclined to support those who believe that hegemonic cultural discourses impose their own codes on the other's culture.[2] As Edward Said asserts: "Contemporary criticism is an institution for publicly affirming the values of our, that is, European, dominant elite culture, and for privately setting loose the unrestrained interpretation of a universe defined in advance as the endless misreading of a misinterpretation" (*The World* 25).

Gayatri Chakravorty Spivak, in her essay "Can the Subaltern Speak?," comments on some contemporary writings which in one way or another deal with the topic of otherness. She questions the ability of some European contemporary thinkers to represent the Third World subject within the Western discourse. If we accept the pertinence of Spivak's assertion and reinforce it with other quotations from well-known writers,[3] the participants in this collection of essays face at least two series of problems of which I am a part. If I pretend that this "I" is a collective one, the question is what or who does the "I" represent? Latin Americans? Latinos? University professors? Professors teaching in U.S. universities? University professors teaching Latin American Literature in the United States? A University of California professor? A Latino professor living in the United States or Southern California? What is the common denominator of all these labels? Which one has more power to validate my discourse? What or who gives me the authority to speak for any of these or other groups? What or who legitimates my authority? If I or any participant in this volume uses the "we," the same question appears again: who is the collective entity represented by "we" and what is the legitimating factor of this speaking for the collective? What is the defining and unifying component, if one exists, of this group? What gives the group authority to make statements on the subject or the other in Latin American, Chicano, Latino cultures? If I say that my "I" represents University of California professors, does this "I" represent the dominant cultural and political discourse of this university? If it does not, what will it take for this I's discourse to be considered as such?

The association between the writers and United States critical discourses is important in order to understand the present form and content of this volume. These discourses, however, are not monolithic nor ahistorical. On the contrary, the dominance of some discourses is associated with political and social changes. As Diana Taylor explained in the introduction, the research for this volume began with a proposal for a collective research in the University of California Humanities Research Institute. The present collection of essays, therefore, does not represent the original intention of Diana Taylor and myself when we proposed the project of "transcultura- tion" to the University of California Humanities Research Institute. Diana Taylor explained some of the factors leading to the departure from the original intention during the period we were together at Irvine. I would like to add to her comments that the project kept changing even after the closing of the collective meetings and that reasons for the changes are as important as the changes themselves. In the initial proposal the issue of "transculturation" implied both the reutilization or appropriation of cul- ture and the political factors leading to the selection and reutilization of cultural products, which at the time were important issues discussed in Latin American and to lesser degree in some Spanish departments in U.S. universities. The fall of the Eastern bloc and new trends in the studies in Humanities led to significant changes in the project. The devaluation of utopias of social revolution led to the exclusion of some of the topics dis- cussed in the meetings, and which were important for some of the partici- pants. The topic of the political significance of theatre in Latin America, for example, became less attractive. The question of the options of the political left in Latin America after the fall of the Soviet Union was discussed many times in the meetings and finally disappeared from the volume. The project changed with the displacements in U.S. universities. The group became more interested in cultural diversity in the United States and Latin Amer- ica than the initial proposal. The new project also placed more emphasis on feminist issues or gender issues, some of which (such as lesbian and gay cultures) have not yet become acceptable in Latin American academic discourses.

I believe that the major differences between this book and one on a similar topic produced in Latin America would be that a Latin American book would place less importance on cultural diversity, would emphasize the political use of culture, and would relate the issues with the political and social conditions in Latin America and the United States. The insertion of cultural products within the national projects would also have been a signif- icant topic. A Latin American reader interested in cultural studies will be surprised to see the lack of references to Antonio Gramsci, Pierre Bourdieu, and some British cultural historians, who have emphasized the relationship between culture and power. He or she may also be surprised to see that some dominant trends in cultural studies in Latin America are not mentioned, such as the books and essays by José Joaquín Brunner, Pedro Morandé, and, especially, Néstor García Canclini, who has integrated anthropological studies and Bourdieu's theories and his practical cultural analysis in order to describe cultural events in Latin America.[4]

WHAT DO WE MEAN BY?

I have already discussed the "we" and its representativity. Diana Taylor questions "Whom were we referring to when we used the term "Latino" and "Latin American"? What did we mean by "culture" and "theatre" and whom, and what, did those categories leave out? Later, she asked "What did we mean by *performance* — given that the term not only designates diverse phenomena in English but, to complicate matters, has no equivalent in Spanish." These are important questions and their potential answers do represent adopting cultural and political positions regarding Latin American cultures and Latino cultures in the United States. In the following pages I would like to argue that the use of words or defining terms is also an intellectual process affected by historical circumstances and the context of the defining subjects.

The Term "Latino"
Ethnic definitions or definitions of social groups deserve some consideration from the point of view of the defined, the definer, and the context of the definition. The context of the process of defining is a key to understanding the definition. Once more, the question is who gives authority to somebody to describe or define or, put more simply, just to assign a name to a group of persons. In *performing,* Latino or Latina, Chicano and Chicana, are words used with different meanings and connotations. And these meanings are related to the political position of the writer in relation to some institutions' positions within the U.S. society.

Some years ago I founded the Irvine Chicano Literary Contest. At that time (1974), I invited several scholars working on topics related to "Hispanics" in the United States to discuss the name of the contest. They all were professors at the University of California, Irvine. After extensive discussions the conclusion was that "Chicano" was the only term available at the time to describe the contest's potential audience and, from their point of view, the only politically correct means of labeling the contest. At the time, according to those I consulted, "Latino" was considered a derogatory term. Following their advice, the call for entries included the restriction that the participant should be of a "Mexican descent." As a reaction to this description I received two angry letters strongly complaining that I was trying to disunite the Hispanic groups by privileging one of the groups. One of the letters was written by a Guatemalan. Three years ago a Chicano professor renamed the Chicano Literary Contest and it became a Chicano/Latino Literary Contest. At the University of California, the term "Latino" has recently been included in official documents, courses, and programs. At the University of California, Irvine, a new program was created in 1992: "Chicano/Latino Studies Program." Some of the scholars who participated in the 1974 discussion are now members of this program.

It is interesting to note also that "Latino" was not a word included in the original proposal to the University of California Humanities Research Institute for the conference we hosted in conjunction with the research residency on the "Representation of Otherness in Chicano and Latin American Theatre and Film." Because the HRI is a California institution, the proposal used the word "Chicano," which was the term officially accepted to describe Americans of Mexican descent. This exclusivity has mainly been due to the traditional dominance of Mexican culture and Mexican descendants in the state. The numbers regarding "Hispanics" in California has considerably changed in the last ten years. Political, economic factors have attracted a large number of Latinos from Central America to Los Angeles and Southern California, changing the composition of the Hispanic population in the state.

"Chicano" is a word that in California twenty-five or thirty years ago represented a political and social stand and as such was adopted by some groups and rejected by others. The term rejected by "Chicano" intellectuals and "Chicano" leaders at that time was "Mexican American." The new meaning for "Latino" — which has to be differentiated from "Latin" as an adjective — I would like to believe represents today a recognition of the multiplicity of cultures within the traditional totalizing umbrella of "Hispanics." It is also an attempt to overcome the restrictions implied in the word "Chicano" which did not include other national groups in the country. This implied recognition, however, may undermine the political connotations that "Chicano" had some years ago. The word "Latino" may be loaded with negative connotations when used by non-Latinos in American culture because of its association with the sign "Latin" which may imply a stereotyped character partially imposed by Hollywood. Latino is a sign that needs to be deconstructed and redefined. Its use should be contextualized. It may bring some groups together, but it also may contribute to depoliticize a movement and to stereotype a diversity of social groups and cultures. A quick glance at the *Los Angeles Times* on Sunday, 18 September 1993 suggests some of the problems I have referred to: "Latino students are the largest ethnic group, representing 34% of the student body countywide . . ." (p. A-1, written by Matt Lait, *Times* staff writer). On page A-28 the headline states: "Police Action at Protest Enrages Latino Leaders." In this story the writers (Eric Young and David A. Avila, also *Times* staff writers) distinguish between Latino and Chicano: "300 students were demanding more Latino educators and more Chicano studies in schools." Do these quotations mean that "Latino" is currently being used in the non-Latino media as a term with political connotations and "Chicano" only as an academic discipline? This struggle for redefining terms related to "Hispanics" in the United States and the present efforts by intellectuals or producers of academic and artistic discourses for appropriation is evident in the essays included in this volume. Some of the issues are precisely the contextualization of the resemantized signs, their insertion in the process of institutionalization, and the social and political position of the writers.

The Term "Performance"
The term "performance" and its use by some of the writers in this book opens up an interesting theoretical issue; that is, the use of terms born of a need to describe a phenomenon in one culture and their application to what seems to be a similar phenomenon in another culture. One approach may argue that it is proper to use words or concepts from European culture or Latin American culture in order to describe similar phenomena in other cultures. For some, this approach allows them to perceive or to highlight facts or processes which the local vocabulary did not allow them to see. For others, the strategy may lead to the imposition of codes of one culture into the reading of other cultures. The issue here again has to do with both a potentially "better" description of a phenomenon and the legitimation of the description and the object by using legitimizing words by the dominant culture.

With regard to "performance," the fact that the term does not exist in Spanish may mean that this form of art is specific of the Latino or alternative cultures in the United States, and that the form was produced or was born out of necessity in the United States, but it does not exist in the other culture. It may signify too that it is a product of specific circumstances in the United States. To reuse the term may deform some other cultural or theatrical expressions which may seem similar if attention is not paid to the differences.

Does "performance art" imply a protest by a marginal group, for example? What is the term's specific connotation? Is "performance" a cultural and theatrical product often used by Latinos in the United States? Does the term carry these connotations when describing Latin American theatrical activities? Does the Spanish language have a specific term to describe the specificity of "performance" in Latin America?

The Concise Oxford Companion to the Theater when speaking of "Performance group" refers to "collective creation." Under this heading it describes it as a theatrical move started in the sixties in which a "group of persons working together develop a production from the initial concept to the finished performance through research, discussion, improvisation, writing and rehearsal" (97). It points out that it became the "typical ·method of alternative theater movement of the 1960s and early 1970s" (97). It mentions the "Performance Group" founded and directed by Richard Schechner. In Latin America the expression "collective creation" implies the substitution of the individual author by the theatrical group as "authors." It is loaded with political undertones and it is predominantly associated with leftist political groups. It apparently does not include some of the connotations being used to describe a "performance" in the United States scenario.[5]

I believe that it is less authoritarian and perhaps it would be less of an imposition of one culture over another if we were to find or redefine a Spanish term or expression, which may be able to describe the Latin American theatrical modes. This I believe is a better alternative rather than using the loaded and untranslatable term "performance." This difficulty leads to the core of several related issues: the understanding of the sign "theatre" and the large number of attempts to find alternative modes to its canonical mode of understanding the term.

Redefining "Theatre"

When writing on theatre most scholars and historians tend to restrict the object to one modality, which mainly defines the dominant culture's traditional view of "theatre." Some of the theatrical activities studied in this volume — such as carnivals, religious festivals, popular rituals, or political demonstrations — do not fit this definition.

In order to accommodate or include such activities in a legitimized "history of theatre" I would suggest the terms "theatricality" or "theatrical discourses" be used instead of "theatre." I propose that a theatrical discourse or "theatricality" be understood as a means of communicating a message by integrating verbal, visual, auditive, body, gestural signs to be performed in front of an audience. The perception of the message is intended to be received visually. The message is ciphered according to codes established by the producer's or receiver's cultural systems. My assumption here is that a given theatricality implies a system of "theatrical" codes which are integrated in the cultural system and the social and political context. This concept denotes that in a specific historical period there is a multiplicity of "theatrical systems," each one with different theatrical codes, and different levels of legitimation. Each theatrical system constitutes a sub-system related to a sub-cultural-system.

In Latin America and in the West, for example, the expression "theatre" has mainly been reserved for one mode of theatricality, the one limited to actors performing on stage, usually in a theatre. To renovate or modernize "theatre" has mainly implied secondary changes within this description, such as a plurality of stage spaces, on destroying the fourth wall, inciting the audience to participate in the action, and so forth. Acting schools in Latin America teach European or international techniques such as those of Stanislavsky and, more recently, Barba. Augusto Boal's theories have addressed the need to change the theatrical stage, the modes of performing, the kind of theatrical characters, and the audience's attitudes. Boal's theories, however, do not substantially change the concept of "theatre."[6] In his characterization, he still insists in the essential elements of the Renaissance idea of theatre: staging a "play" in front of an audience. Boal's most significant change is the displacement from a "closed" stage to an open stage, such as streets, factories, villages.

Redefining "theatre" as theatrical discourses or theatricality will allow the inclusion as part of the "history of theatre" a large number of "popular" or nondominant theatrical discourses such as those associated with, for example, political, religious, social, political, sexual, bourgeois, feudal, Japanese, Chinese, British, or Victorian stagings.[7] It may contribute to the legitimation of other forms of theatrical discourses. It may also lead to the study of different forms of theatricality. This is to say that historically it is possible to relate some forms of gestural and linguistic performances to specific periods or world views. It will also permit the examination of the relations between coexistent systems in a discrete historical period or space, and to deconstruct those factors leading to their inclusion or exclusion from the cultural system legitimized or validated by the dominant cultural group or canonized by histories of theatre.[8] A theatrical discourse is a mode of visual perception related to historical conditions.[9] Accepting the term as it has been redefined, allows the assertion that traditional "theatre" is just one mode of theatricality, limited to a cultural tradition.

In Latin America during the last twenty-five years, for example, changes in religious "theatricality" have been relevant to both social and political mutations as well as changes in religion and theatre. The political and pragmatic foundations for the religious transformations have been some of the most important political moves in Latin America. A brief comment on some visual perceptions of the Catholic mass as spectacle may signal the significance of the changes. In the traditional — before Vatican Council — Catholic mass, theatricality implied a great distance between the priest and the parishioners. The priest was the main actor and the key persona on stage, the only one with access to God. Most of the time he turned his back to the audience, who followed his movements with respect. When the priest finally faced the audience, he was invested by the power of God: showing the sacred host or pardoning the audience's sins. Even the language used by the priest and his assistants — Latin — contributed to distancing the audience and established a feeling of dependency, respect, and fear. The old Church theatricality was a distancing one — like the traditional European theatre — reinforcing the psychological and physical distance between the actor on the stage and the audience.

The emergence of new social demands and the strong competition with Protestant churches — who are reaching popular and marginal sectors with a more earthly and optimistic world view and a more open theatricality — have influenced the canonized Church theatricality. The new theatrical codes — such as the language used, the priest facing the believers, use of guitars instead of an organ, or the use of folk music instead of Gregorian chants, lay women or lay men leading prayer, etc. — communicates a different message from a different Church for a different potential audience in a new historical context. In the new mass, the priest seems to indicate that he is sharing his access to God with the audience. The new Church theatricality is a community-oriented performance, in which the people have become involved and an active participant. Similar to this is the theatricality of some new plays in Latin America, which attempt to utilize theatrical codes from popular cultures, which were previously excluded from bourgeois theatre.

Reinscribing a new meaning to "theatre" or "theatricality" makes it possible to understand the search for legitimation in the history of "theatre" and the use of dominant theatrical texts and codes for self-legitimation by dominant social formations. This expanded concept of "theatrical discourse" or "theatricality" will call attention to the emergence of different theatrical modes produced by new historical contexts. The studies on U.S. Latino theatrical discourses in this volume, for example, may contribute to the understanding of Latino theatricality in the United States and its relationship to social forms and behaviors such as a search for ethnic identity within the national imaginary. It may also make evident how the dominant discourses have contributed to the imposition of theatrical modes of social behaviors, such as dressing codes, hairstyles, language expressions, and their presence in "ethnic" theatrical discourses. From this perspective, I would argue that "performance" is a mode of theatricality preferred by some alternative discourses in the United States, whose codes implied a reaction to the established mode of theatricality in this country as was perceived by some theatrical innovators in the sixties and seventies. The performance mode implied a position of political or social protest. In comparison *"teatro colectivo"* in Latin America was mainly a strategy of theatrical production in which the "author" or "individual creator" was substituted by the group. It usually implied a political and social message of social revolution, but the theatrical codes did not necessarily imply a break with traditional theatre techniques or structures.

I feel that *Negotiating Performance* is a significant step toward the necessary awareness of cultural diversity in the United States and toward the recognition of the multiplicity of cultures in Latin America and in the United States regarding groups traditionally described as "Hispanics." Theatrical discourses produced by these groups are deictic of their theatricalities, and these are signs of their social behavior in specific social and political contexts. *Negotiating Performance*'s critical discourses are also deictic: signs of the need to use the tools legitimized by the institution in order to read nondominant cultures, and also signs of the diversity of theatrical modes within the broad fields of Latin America and of Latinos/as in the United States. The critical discourses are loaded with the cultural assumptions brought by the emergence of new trends and new attitudes in United States universities. New trends which are creating an awareness of cultural diversity, and new efforts by others of silencing diversity and reinforcing a dominant culture.

NOTES

1   In *The Concise Oxford Companion to the Theater* edited by Phyllis Hartnoll and Peter Found, for example, there are no references to Latin American playwrights, groups, or theatrical movements.

2   I attempted to deconstruct the critical discourse on Latin American theatre in *Ideología y discurso crítico sobre el teatro de España y América latina.*

3   See, for instance, Jean Franco, "Beyond Ethnocentrism: Gender, Power and the Third-World Intelligentsia" in Nelson and Grossberg; Giles Gunn, *The Culture of Criticism and the Criticism of Culture* and *The Interpretation of Otherness;* Neil Larsen, *The Discourse of Power.*

4   See especially: Néstor García Canclini, *Las culturas híbridas* and *Arte popular y sociedad en America Latina;* and by José Joaquín Brunner, *Un espejo trizado.*

5   On "teatro colectivo" see Francisco Garzón Céspedes, ed., *El teatro colectivo de creación colectiva,* a collection of essays and documents.

6   See Augusto Boal, *Técnicas latinoamericanas de teatro popular* and *Teatro del Oprimido.*

7   Hernán Vidal comments on theatricality and human rights in Latin America in "Political Theatricality and the Dissolution of the Theater as Institution."

8   An expanded concept of theatricality is being used in several essays and books on English literature and culture, especially of the Middle Ages and Renaissance. See, for example, John M. Ganim and Christopher Pye. A similar concept is used by Jenaro Talens in *La escritura como teatralidad* in interpreting some Spanish medieval and Golden Age writers.

9   See for example the cultural analysis of photography by Bourdieu.

Tiffany Ana López & Jacqueline Lazú
Bibliography

❏

Abrahams, Roger and John Szwed. *After Africa: Extracts from British Travel Accounts and Journals of the Seventeenth, Eighteenth, and Nineteenth Centuries concerning the Slaves, their Manners, and Customs in the British West Indies*. New Haven: Yale UP, 1983.

Achebe, Chinua. *Anthills of the Savannah*. New York: Anchor/Doubleday, 1987.

Acosta, Oscar Zeta. "The Revolt of the Cockroach People." *Los Angeles in Fiction*. Ed. David Fine. Albuquerque: U of New Mexico P, 1984.

Acuña, René. *Farsas y representaciones escénicas de los Mayas antiguos*. Mexico City: UNAM, 1978.

Administración del Alcade Dr. Antonio Beruff Mendieta. *Las comparsas del Carnaval habanero, cuestión resulta*. La Habana: Molina y Cia, 1937.

Adarga. Supplement of the *Revista del Consejo* 5 (September 1992): Special Issue: Indian Literatures of Chiapas. Centro Chiapaneco de Escritores, Instituto Chiapaneco de Cultura.

Agosín, Marjorie. "Literature." *Latinas of the Americas*. Ed. K. Lynn Stoner. Westport: Greenwood Press, 1990.

Aguilar Penagos, Mario. *La celebración de nuestro juego. El Carnaval chamula, un sincretismo religioso*. Tuxtla: Gobierno del Estado de Chiapas, 1990.

Ahern, Maureen, ed. *A Rosario Castellanos Reader*. Austin: U of Texas P, 1988.

Alarcón, Norma. "The Theoretical Subject(s) of *This Bridge Called My Back* and Anglo-American Feminism." *Making Face, Making Soul/Haciendo Caras: Creative and Critical Perspectives by Women of Color*. Ed. Gloria Anzaldúa. San Francisco: Spinsters/Aunt Lute Foundation Book, 1990.

Alexander, William. "Clearing Space: AIDS Theatre in Atlanta." *The Drama Review* 34.3 (1990): 109–28.

Allen, Paula Gunn. "Some Like Indians Endure." *Making Faces, Making Soul/Haciendo Caras: Creative and Critical Perspectives by Women of Color*. Ed. Gloria Anzaldúa. San Francisco: Spinsters/Aunt Lute Foundation Book, 1990.

Allen, Terry Y. "Ralph Lee's Halloween Casserole." *Amherst* (Spring 1989): 9–11, 22.

Almaguer, Tomás. "Chicano Men: A Cartography of Homosexual Identity and Behavior." *differences: A Journal of Feminist Cultural Studies* 3.2 Special Issue: Queer Theory. (1991): 75–100.

Alonso, Ana María, and María Teresa Koreck. "Silences: 'Hispanics,' AIDS, and Sexual Practices." *differences: A Journal of Feminist Cultural Studies* 1 (1989): 101–24.

Anderson, Benedict. *Imagined Communities: Reflections on the Origin and Spread of National-ism.* London: Verso, 1983.

Anzaldúa, Gloria. *Borderlands/La Frontera: The New Mestiza.* San Francisco: Spinsters/Aunt Lute, 1987.

——, ed. *Making Face, Making Soul/Haciendo Caras: Creative and Critical Perspectives by Women of Color.* San Francisco: Spinsters/Aunt Lute Foundation Book, 1990.

Aponte-Parés, Luis. "Casitas As Metaphor: Place and Culture." Unpublished manuscript, 1991.

Apple, Jacki. "Politics, Performance and the Los Angeles Festival." *Visions* (Spring 1991): 14–17.

Ardener, Shirley. "Sexual Insult and Female Military." *Perceiving Women.* Ed. Shirley Ardener. London: J. M. Dent and Sons, 1975.

Ardiles, Arturo, et al. *Hacia una filosofía de la liberación latinoamericana.* Buenos Aires: Editorial BONUM, 1974.

Arditti, Rita and M. Brinton Lykes. " 'Recovering Identity': The Work of the Grandmothers of the Plaza de Mayo." *Women's Studies International Forum* 15.4 (1992): 461–71.

Arias, Jaci. "El amanecer de un proyecto cultural Maya-Zoque Chiapaneco que se entreteje en la diversidad." *Revista del Consejo* 8 (March 1993): 29–34.

——. "Mucha semilla desparramada: Del indiocidio al consumo de las indianidades o '¿indio-fagia?' " *Ojarasca* 8 (May 1992): 24–34.

Arnold, Matthew. *Culture and Anarchy.* New York: Cambridge UP, 1966.

Arroyo, Rane. *Wet Dream with Cameo by Fidel Castro.* Unpublished manuscript, n.d.

Augenbraum and Ilan Stavans, eds. *Growing Up Latino: Memoirs and Stories.* Boston: Houghton Mifflin Co., 1993.

Austin, Gayle. *Feminist Theories for Dramatic Criticism.* Ann Arbor: U of Michigan P, 1990.

Bakhtin, Mikhail. *Rabelais and His World.* Bloomington: Indiana UP, 1984.

——. *The Dialogic Imagination.* Austin: U of Texas P, 1981.

Balderston, Daniel, et al. "El signo latente on *Respiración artificial* de Ricardo Piglia y *En el corazón de junio* de Luis Gusman." *Ficción y política: La narrativa Argentina durante el proceso Militar.* Ed. Hernán Vidal. Madrid: Alianza Editorial; Minnesota: Institute for the Study of Ideologies and Literature, 1987.

Barros-Lemez, Alvaro. *Paralaje y circo: Ensayos sobre sociedad, cultura y comunicación.* Uruguay: Monte Sexto, 1987.

Bash, Harry H. *Sociology, Race, and Ethnicity: A Critique of American Ideological Intrusions upon Sociological Theory.* New York: Gordon and Breach, 1979.

Barthes, Roland. *Camera Lucida.* Trans. Richard Howard. New York: Hill & Wang, 1981.

Bastide, Roger. *The African Religions of Brazil.* Baltimore: Johns Hopkins UP, 1978.

Béhague, Gerard. "Popular Music in Latin America." *Studies in Latin American Popular Culture* 5 (1986).

Bejarano, Manuel. "Inmigración y estructuras tradicionales en Buenos Aires (1854–1930)." *Los fragmentos del poder.* Ed. Tulio Halperín Donghi. Buenos Aires: Sudamericana, 1987.

Bennet, Tony. *Outside Literature.* New York: Routledge, 1990.

Benjamin, Walter. *Illuminations.* New York: Schocken Books, 1968.

Bergman, David. *Gaiety Transfigured: Gay Self-Representation in American Literature.* Wisconsin: U of Wisconsin P, 1991.

Bergmann, Emilie, et al. *Women, Culture, and Politics in Latin America.* Berkeley: U of California P, 1990.

Berman, Sabina. *Uno. Teatro de Sabina Berman.* Mexico City: Editores Mexicanos Unidos, 1985. 268–80.

Bernheimer, Martin. "An Ignorable *Dents* Plays Downtown." *Los Angeles Times Calendar* 10 Sept. 1990: F1, F7.

Bersani, Leo, and Ulysse Dutoit. *The Forms of Violence.* New York: Schocken Books, 1985.

Bettelheim, Judith. "Jonkonnu 2nd Other Christmas Masquerades." *The Journal of Ethnic Studies* 13.3, 1985.

———. "Festivals in Cuba, Haiti, and New Orleans." *Caribbean Festival Arts.* Eds. John Nunley and Judith Bettelheim. Seattle: U of Washington P, 1988.

———, ed. *Cuban Festivals: An Illustrated Anthology.* New York: Garland Press, 1993.

Birmingham, David. "Carnival at Luanda." *The Journal of African History* 29 (1988).

Birringer, Johannes. "Invisible Cities/Transcultural Images." *Performing Arts Journal* 33 and 34 (11.3, 12.1): 120–38.

Blaffer, Sarah C. *The Black-man of Zinacantan: A Central American Legend.* Austin: U of Texas P, 1972.

Blonsky, Marshall, ed. *On Signs.* Baltimore: Johns Hopkins UP, 1985.

Boal, Augusto. *Teatro del oprimido.* Mexico: Editorial Nueva Imagen, 1980.

———. *Técnicas latinoamericanas de teatro popular.* Mexico: Editorial Nueva Imagen, 1982.

Boffin, Tessa, and Sunil Gupta, eds. *Ecstatic Antibodies: Resisting The AIS Mythology.* London: Rivers Oram Press, 1990.

Bonfil Batalla, Guillermo. "La teoría del control cultural en el estudio de procesos etnicos." *Revista Papeles de la Casa Chata* (Mexico City) 2.3 (1987): 23–43.

———. "Lo propio y lo ajeno: Una aproximación al control cultural." *La cultura popular.* Ed. Adolfo Colombres. Mexico City: SEP/Premiá, 1982. 79–86.

Boullosa, Carmen. *Propusieron a María. Teatro herético.* Puebla: Universidad Autónoma de Puebla, 1987.

Bourdieu, Pierre. *Sociología y cultura.* México: Grijalbo, 1990.

———. *La distintion.* Paris: Ed. de Minuit, 1979.

———. *Reproduction in Education, Society and Culture.* London: New Berry, 1990.

Bowne, Alan. *Beirut.* New York: Broadway Play Publishing Inc., 1988.

Brantlinger, Patrick. *Crusoe's Footprints: Cultural Studies in Britain and America.* New York: Routledge, 1990.

Brea, Rafael and José Millet. "Acerca de la presencia africana en los carnavales de Santiago de Cuba." *Revista de la Biblioteca Nacional José Martí* 3 (Sept.–Dec. 1987).

Bremer, Fredrika. *The Homes of the New World: Impressions of America.* London: Arthur Hall, Virtue & Co., 1853.

Brenkman, John. *Culture and Domination.* Ithaca: Cornell UP, 1987.

Breslauer, Jan, and Sean Mitchell. "Fear of the M Word: Multiculturalism and the Arts – Can a Culture Clash Be Avoided in L.A.? The Good News: No." *Los Angeles Times Calendar* 2 June 1991: Cover story.

Breslin, Patrick. "Coping with Change, the Maya Discover the Play's the Thing." *Smithsonian* 23.5 (August 1992): 78–87.

Bricker, Victoria Reifler. *Ritual Humor in Highland Chiapas.* Austin: U of Texas P, 1975.

———. *The Indian Christ, The Indian King.* Austin: U of Texas P, 1981.

Bricker, Victoria Reifler, and Gary H. Gossen, eds. *Ethnographic Encounters in Southern Mesoamerica.* Albany: State U of New York; Austin: U of Texas P, 1989.

Brody, Janet Esser, ed. *Behind the Mask in Mexico.* Santa Fe: Museum of New Mexico, 1988.

Bronfen, Elisabeth. *Over Her Dead Body: Death, Femininity and the Aesthetic.* New York: Routledge, 1992.

Brown, David H. *Garden in the Machine: Afro-Cuban Sacred Art and Performance in Urban New Jersey and New York.* Diss., Yale U, 1989.

Brown, Karen McCarthy. "Systematic Remembering, Systematic Forgetting: Ogou in Haiti." *Africa's Ogun: Old World and New.* Ed. Sandra T. Barnes, Bloomington: Indiana UP, 1989.

Brunner, José Joaquín. *Un espejo trizado: Ensayos sobre cultura y políticas culturales.* Santiago, Chile: Facultad Latinoamericana de Ciencias Sociales, 1988.

Buck-Morss, Susan. *The Dialectics of Seeing: Walter Benjamin and the Arcades Project.* Cambridge: MIT Press, 1989.

Bugeja, Michael. "Culture and Anarchy in the War of the Worlds." *North Dakota Quarterly* 54.2 (Spring 1986): 79–83.

Bumbalo, Victor. *Adam and the Experts.* New York: Broadway Play Publishing Inc., 1990.

Bunster-Burotto, Ximena. "Surviving Beyond Fear: Women and Torture in Latin America." *Women and Change in Latin America.* Boston: Bergin & Garvey, 1986.

Burgin, Victor, James Donald, and Cora Kaplan, eds. *Formation of Fantasy.* London and New York: Methuen, 1989.

Butler, Judith. *Gender Trouble: Feminism and the Subversion of Identity.* New York: Routledge, 1990.

———. "Performative Acts and Gender Constitution: An Essay in Phenomenology and Feminist Theory." *Performing Feminisms: Feminist Critical Theory and Theatre.* Ed. Sue-Ellen Case. Baltimore: Johns Hopkins UP, 1990.

Cabrera, Lydia. *Anaforuana: Ritual y símbolos de la iniciación en la Sociedad Secreta Abakuá.* Madrid: Ediciones C.R., 1975.

Cady, Joseph. "AIDS on the National Stage." Rev. of *The Way We Live Now: American Plays and the AIDS Crisis. Medical Humanities Review* 6.1 (1992): 20–26.

Cady, Joseph, and Kathryn Montogomery Hunter. "Making Contact: The AIDS Plays." *The Meaning of AIDS: Implications for Medical Science, Clinical Practice, and Public Health Policy.* Eds. Eric T. Juengst and Barbara A. Koenig. New York: Praeger, 1989. 42–49.

Cancian, Frank. *The Decline of Community in Zinacantan.* Stanford: Stanford UP, 1992.

Carby, Hazel V. "The Politics of Difference." *Ms.* Sept.–Oct. 1990: 84–85.

Carter, Erica, and Simon Watney, eds. *Taking Liberties: AIDS and Cultural Politics.* London: Serpent's Tail, 1989.

Case, Sue-Ellen, ed. *Performing Feminisms: Feminist Critical Theory and Theatre.* Baltimore: Johns Hopkins UP, 1990.

———. *Feminism and Theatre.* New York: Methuen, 1988.

Castellanos, Rosario. "Arthur Smith salva su alma." *Cuidad real.* Xalapa: Universidad Veracruzana y La Letra Editores, 1982 (1960).

———. *The Eternal Feminine.* Trans. Diane E. Marting and Betty Osiek. *A Rosario Castellanos Reader.* Ed. Maureen Ahern. Austin: U of Texas P, 1988.

———. "Malinche." Trans. and ed. Maureen Ahern. *A Rosario Castellanos Reader.* Austin: U of Texas P, 1988.

———. *El uso de la palabra.* Ed. José Emilio Pacheco. Mexico City: Excélsior, 1974.

Castillo, Teresa Toranzo. "La Tumba Francesca 'los Maceo-Bandera-Moncada' como exponente de la cultura popular tradicional." Trabajo de diploma, Facultad de Artes y Letras, Universidad de Oriente, June 1988.

Caro Baroja, Julio. *El Carnaval. (Anánlisis histórico-cultural)*. Madrid: Taurus, 1979.

Carvalho-Neto, Paulo de. *El Carnaval de Montevideo. Folklore, historia, sociología*. Sevilla: Universidad de Sevilla, 1967.

Castoriadis, Cornelius. *The Imaginary Institution of Society*. Cambridge: Polity Press, 1987.

Castro, Carlo Antonio, ed. *Sk'oplal te Mejijolum/La palabra de México*. Tuxtla Gutiérrez: Gobierno del Estado de Chiapas, 1986 (Colección Fascimilar del Periódico Tzeltal-Tzotzil de 1956–1957).

Castro, Guillermo. *Política y cultura en Nuestra América, 1880–1930*. Panamá: CELA "JustoArosemana," 1985.

Castro-Klarén, Sara. "La crítica literaria feminista y la escritora en Latina América." *La sartén por el Mango*. Eds. Patricia E. González and Eliana Ortega. Río Piedras, Puerto Rico: Edición Huracán, 1985. 27–46.

——, Sylvia Molloy, and Beatriz Sarlo eds. *Women's Writing in Latin America: An Anthology*. Boulder: Westview Press, 1991.

Cembalest, Robin. "Goodbye, Columbus?" *ARTnews* October 1991: 104–09.

Certeau, Michel de. *Heterologies. Discourse on the Other*. Minneapolis: U of Minnesota P, 1986.

——. *The Practice of Everyday Life*. Berkeley: U of California P, 1984.

Chambers, Ian. "Contamination, Coincidence, and Collusion: Pop Music, Urban Culture, and the Avante Garde." *Marxism and the Interpretation of Culture*. Eds. Gary Nelson and Lawrence Grossberg. Urbana: U of Illinois P, 1988.

Chambers, Ross. *No Montagues Without Capulets: Some Thoughts on 'Cultural Identity.'* Lecture, Dartmouth College, 1992.

——. *Room for Maneuver: Reading (the) Oppositional (in) Narrative*. Chicago: U of Chicago P, 1991.

Chaney, Elsa M. *Supermadre: Women in Politics in Latin America*. Austin: U of Texas P, 1979.

Chesley, Robert. *Hard Plays: Stiff Parts*. San Francisco: Alamo Square Press, 1990.

Christense, Judith. "Las Comadres, Border Boda." *High Performance: A Quarterly Magazine for the New Arts*. 12 (Spring 1991): 44.

Clifford, James, and G. Marcus, eds. *Writing Culture: The Poetics and the Politics of Ethnography*. Berkeley: U of California P, 1986.

Clum, John M. *Acting Gay: Male Homosexuality in Modern Drama*. New York: Columbia UP, 1992.

Coe, Michael D. *The Maya*. New York and Washington: Praeger, 1966.

Collier, George A. "Changing Inequality in Zinacantan: The Generations of 1918 and 1942." *Ethnographic Encounters in Southern Mesoamerica*. Eds. Victoria Bricker and Gary Gossen. Albany: State U of New York; Austin: U of Texas P, 1989. 111–23.

——. *Fields of the Tzotzil*. Austin: U of Texas P, 1975.

Colombres, Adolfo. *Sobre la cultura y el arte popular*. Buenos Aires: Ediciones del Sol, 1987.

Comunicación y culturas populares en Latinoámerica. Seminario del Consejo Latinoamericano de Ciencias Sociales. México, 1987.

Cordry, Donald. *Mexican Masks*. Austin: U of Texas P, 1980.

Cosío Villegas, Daniel, ed. *Historia moderna de México*. Mexico City Editorial Hermes 1956. Vol. 4. (of 6).

Crimp, Douglas, ed. *AIDS: Cultural Analysis/Cultural Activism*. Cambridge: MIT Press, 1988.

Crimp, Douglas and Adam Rolston, eds. *AIDS Demographics*. Seattle: Bay Press, 1990.

Cruikshand, Jeffrey L., and Pam Korza. *Going Public: A Field Guide to Developments in Art in Public Places*. Amherst: U of Massachusetts P, 1988.

Cruz, Migdalia. *Telling Tales. Telling Tales and Other One Act Plays.* Ed. Eric Lane. New York: Penguin, 1993.

———. *Miriam's Flowers. Shattering the Myth: Plays by Hispanic Women.* Ed. Linda Feyder. Houston: Arte Publico Press, 1992.

Cuentos y relatos indígenas. Mexico City: Universidad Nacional Autónoma de México, 1989.

Cultura y sociedad en América Latina y el Caribe. Paris: UNESCO, 1981.

Cultura popular y técnicas de comunicación en América Latina. Quito, Ecuador: CIESPAL, 1986.

"Cultures of the Americas: Achievements in Education, Science, and the Arts." National Conference on UNESCO. Denver, Sept. 29–Oct. 2, 1959.

Cunningham, Michael. "After AIDS, Gay Art Aims for a New Reality." *The New York Times* 26 Apr. 1992: Sec. 2. 1.

Cypess, Sandra M. "From Colonial Constructs to Feminist Figures: Re/Visions by Mexican Women Dramatists." *Theatre Journal* 41.4 (December 1989): 492–504.

———. *La Malinche in Mexican Literature: From History to Myth.* Austin: U of Texas P, 1991.

Dahl, Victor, ed. *Culture and Nationalism in Latin America.* San Diego: San Diego State UP, 1987.

Davis, Jennie. "Engaged and Enraged: L. A. AIDS Activist Artist Transforms Mourning into Militancy." *New Art Examiner* 20.8 (1993) 14–17.

Davis, Madeline and Elizabeth Laposky Kennedy, "Oral History and the Study of Sexuality in the Lesbian Community: Buffalo, 1940–60." *Feminist Studies* 12.1 (Spring 1986).

De Johgh, Nicholas. *Not in Front of the Audience: Homosexuality On Stage.* London: Routledge, 1992.

de la Cruz Cruz, Petrona. "El teatro Maya de los altos de Chiapas: Su influencia cultural y su futuro." *Revista del Consejo* 8 (March 1993): 14–16.

———. "El teatro y los problemas de las mujeres de los altos de Chiapas." Unpublished manuscript.

———. "Importancia de la educación para la mujer indígena." Unpublished manuscript.

———. *Una mujer desesperada.* Unpublished manuscript, 1991.

de la Torre, Adela and Beatríz M. Pesquera. *Building With Our Hands: New Directions in Chicana Studies.* Berkeley: U of California P, 1993.

de Lauretis, Teresa, ed. *Feminist Studies/Critical Studies.* Bloomington: Indiana UP, 1986.

———. *Alice Doesn't: Feminism, Semiotics, Cinema.* Bloomington: Indiana UP, 1984.

———. *Technologies of Gender: Essays on Theory, Film and Fiction.* Bloomington: Indian UP, 1987.

deLeon, Dennis. "My Hopes, My Fears, My Disease." *The New York Times* 15 May 1993: 19.

De Leon, Eloise. REACHING IN. Video tape available through the Centro Cultural de la Raza. San Diego: 1991.

Deleuze, Gilles and Felix Guattari. *Anti-Oedipus: Capitalism and Schizophrenia.* New York: Viking Press, 1977.

———. *Kafka: Pour une littérature mineure.* Paris: Les edictions de minuit, 1975.

Delgado Jr., Louis A. *A Better Life.* Manuscript.

de Man, Paul. *Allegories of Reading.* New Haven: Yale University Press, 1979.

de Vos, Jan. *La batalla del Sumidero. Antología de documentos relativos a la rebelion de los Chiapanecas 1524–1534.* Mexico City: Editorial Katun, 1985.

———. *No queremos ser cristianos: Historia de la resistencia de los Lacandones, 1530–1695, a través de testimonios españoles e indígenas.* Mexico City: Consejo Nacional para la Cultura las Artes e Instituto Nacional Indigenista, 1990.

Dewey, Janice. "Doña Josefa: Blood-pulse of Transition and Change." *Breaking Boundaries: Latina Writing and Critical Readings*. Eds. Asuncion Horno Delgado, Eliana Ortega, Nina M. Scott, Nancy Saporta Sternbach. Amherst: U of Massachusetts P, 1989.

Diago, Alejandro. *Hebe Bonafini: Memoria y esperanza*. Buenos Aires: Ediciones Dialectica, 1988.

Diamond, Elin. "Refusing the Romanticism of Identity: Narrative Intervention in Churchill, Benmussa, Duras." *Theatre Journal* 37.3 (October 1985): 273–77. (Also reprinted in Case, *Performing Feminisms*.)

Díaz, José M. "Panorama Cultural." Rev. of *Noche de Ronda* by Pedro R. Monge Rafuls. *Impacto* (N.Y.) 22 May 1993: 32.

Díaz Castillo, Roberto. *Cultura popular y lucha de clases*. Ciudad de La Habana: Casa de las Americas, 1987.

Díaz Gómez, David. "Zinacantán, pueblo de la flor." *México Desconocido* 197 (July 1993): 62–68.

Dirlik, Arif. "Culturalism as Hegemonic Ideology." *Cultural Critique* 6 (Spring 1987).

Domínguez, Robert. "Writing a Wrong." Rev. of "A Better Life." *Daily News* 9 Aug. 1993.

Donkin, Ellen, and Susan Clement. *Upstaging Big Daddy: Directing Theatre as if Race and Gender Matter*. Ann Arbor: U of Michigan P, 1993.

Douglas, Mary. *Purity and Danger: An Analysis of the Concepts of Pollution and Taboo*. New York: Routledge, 1984.

Dovring, Karin. *Frontiers of Communication: The Americas in Search of Political Culture*. Boston: Christopher Pub. House, 1975.

Downing, David B. "The Theory and Politics of Cultural Criticism." *Works and Days: Essays on the Socio-Historical Dimensions of Literature and the Arts* 3.1 (Spring 1985): 7–10.

Duberman, Martin, and Martha Vicinus, George Chauncey, eds. *Hidden from History: Reclaiming the Gay and Lesbian Past*. New York: Meridian, 1990.

Echevarría Alvarado, Felix. *La Plena: Orígen, sentido y desarollo en el folklore puertorriqueño*. Santurce: Express, n.d.

Edmonson, Munro S. *Heaven Born Merida and Its Destiny: The Book of Chilam Balam de Chumayel*. Austin: U of Texas P, 1986.

———. "Quiche Literature." *Handbook of Middle Americans Indians Supplement 3: Literatures*. Eds. Victoria R. Bricker and Edmonson. Austin: U of Texas P, 1985.

Eagleton, Terry. *Criticism and Ideology*. London: Verso, 1978.

Elias, Norbert. *The History of Manners*. New York: Pantheon Books, 1978.

Ellis, Sure and Paul Heritage. "AIDS and the Cultural Response: *The Normal Heart* and *We All Fall Down*." *Coming on Strong: Gay Politics and Culture*. Eds. Simon Sheperd and Mick Wallis. London: Unwin Hyman, 1989.

Estage Noel, Cayuqui. "Danza dialogada huave *Olmalndiuk* (y texto en zapoteco)." *Tlalocan* (UNAM) 9 (1982): 229–48.

———. "Teatro indígena viviente de México en 1988: Tiempo en retrospectiva." *Diógenes, Anuario crítico del teatro Latinoamericano* 4. Buenos Aires: Asociación de Trabajadores e Investigadores del Nuevo Teatro (ATINT) and Grupo Editor Latinoamericano, 1990: 151–55.

———. "True Theater in Native Dance." *The Christian Science Monitor* 14 March 1989: 16–17.

Favre, Henri. *Changement et continuité chez les Mayas du Mexique: Contribution à l'etude de la situation coloniale en Amérique latine*. Paris: Editions Anthropos, 1971.

Feingold, Michael. "Introduction." *The Way We Live Now: American Plays and the AIDS Crisis*. New York: Theatre Communications Group, 1990.

Feitlowitz, Marguerite. *Lexicon of Terror.* Unpublished manuscript, n.d.

Fierstein, Harvey. *Safe Sex.* New York: Atheneum, 1988.

Finn, William. *Falsettos.* New York: Plume, 1993.

Fekete, John, ed. *Life after Postmodernism: Essays on Value and Culture.* New York: St. Martin's Press, 1987.

Feliú, Virtudes. "La fiesta Cubana." *Revolución y cultura.* 9 (Sept. 1985).

Felman, Shoshana. *The Literary Speech Act. Don Juan with J. L. Austin, or Seduction in Two Languages.* Trans. Catherine Porter. Ithaca: Cornell UP, 1983.

Fem. 10 años de periodismo feminista. Mexico City: Grupo Editorial Planeta, 1988.

Ferguson, Russel, et al., eds. *Discourses: Conversations in Postmodern Art and Culture.* Cambridge: MIT Press, 1992.

Fernandez de la Uz, Violeta Rosario. *Analisis historico-cultural de paseo La Placita, Como exponente del Carnaval Santiaguero.* Unpublished Trabajo de Diploma. Santiago, Universidad de Oriente, 1987–88.

Ferreira, Graciela B. *La mujer maltrada: Un estudio sobre las mujeres víctimas de la violencia doméstica.* Buenos Aires: Editorial Sudamericana, 1989.

Feyder, Linda, ed. *Shattering the Myth: Plays by Hispanic Women.* Houston: Arte Publico Press, 1992.

Fisher, E. *Art Against Ideology.* New York: Harper, 1969.

Fisher, Jo. *Mothers of the Disappeared.* Boston: South End Press, 1989.

Fitzgibbon, Russel Humke. *1902-Latin America: Political Culture and Development.* N.J.: Prentice-Hall, 1981.

Flores, Juan. *Divided Borders: Essays on Puerto Rican Identity.* Houston: Arte Publico Press, 1993.

Flores, Juan, and George Yúdice. "Living Borders/Buscando América: Languages of Latino Self-Formation." *Social Text* 24 (Fall 1990): 58–84.

Fornes, Maria Irene. *Maria Irene Fornes: Plays.* New York: PAJ Publications, 1986.

——. *Promenade and Other Plays.* New York: PAJ Publications, 1987.

Forte, Jeanie. "Women's Performance Art: Feminism and Postmodernism" *Performing Feminisms: Feminist Critical Theory and Theatre.* Ed. Sue-Ellen Case. Baltimore: Johns Hopkins UP, 1990.

——. "Realism, Narrative, and the Feminist Players—A Problem of Reception." *Modern Drama* 32.1 (March 1989): 115–27.

Foster, David William. *From Mafalda to Los Supermachos: Latin American Graphic Humor as Popular Culture.* Boulder: L. Rienner, 1988, 1989.

Fox, Ofelia, and Rose Sánchez. *Siempre intenté Decirte Algo (S.I.D.A.). I Always Meant to Tell you Something.* Trans. authors. Unpublished manuscript, 1989.

Franco, Jean. "Killing Priests, Nuns, Women, Children." *On Signs.* Ed. Marshall Blonsky. Baltimore: Johns Hopkins UP, 1985. 414–20.

——. *Plotting Women: Gender and Representation in Mexico.* New York: Columbia UP, 1989.

——. "Self-Destructing Heroines." *Minnesota Review* 22 (1984): 105–15.

Frank, Peter. "Ignore the Dents." *L. A. Weekly* 14–20 September 1990: n.p.

Freedman, Carl. "The Transformation Problem and Cultural Theory." *Comparative Literature East and West. Traditions and Trends.* Eds. Cornelia More and Raymond A. Moody. Honolulu: U of Hawaii P, 1989.

Freud, Sigmund. *Three Essays on the Theory of Sexuality. The Standard Edition of the Complete Psychological Works of Sigmund Freud.* Ed. James Strachey. New York: Avon, 1962.

Frischmann, Donald H. "Active Ethnicity: Nativism, Otherness, and Indian Theatre in Mexico." *Gestos* 11 (Apr. 1991): 113–26.

——. "El nuevo teatro Maya de Yucatán y Chiapas: Grupos sac nicté y Sna Jtz'ibajom." *Tramoya* (Universidad Veracruzana/Rutgers University-Camden) 33 (Oct.–Dec. 1992): 53–56.

——. *El nuevo teatro popular en México*. Mexico City: INBA/CITRU, 1990.

——. "Mexico. VII Fiesta Nacional de Teatro Comunidad." *Gestos* 12 (Nov. 1991): 180–82.

——. "Misiones Culturales, Teatro Conasupo, and Teatro Comunidad: The Evolution of State-Sponsored Rural Theatre in 20th-Century Mexico." *Rituals of Rule, Rituals of Resistance: Public Celebrations & Popular Culture in Mexico*, Eds. William H. Beezley, et. al. Wilmington, Del.: Scholarly Resources, Inc., 1993.

Fuss, Diana. *Essentially Speaking. Feminism, Nature and Difference*. New York: Routledge, 1989.

Gambaro, Griselda. *Information for Foreigners: Three Plays by Griselda Gambaro*. Ed. Marguerite Feitlowitz. Evanston: Northwestern UP, 1991.

Ganim, John M. *Chaucerian Theatricality*. Princeton: Princeton UP, 1990.

García Canclini, Néstor. *Las culturas híbridas. Estrategias para entrar y salir de la modernidad*. México: Editorial Grijalbo, 1990.

——. *Arte popular y sociedad en América Latina: Teorías Estéticas y ensayos de transformación*. México: Editorial Grijalbo, 1977.

——. *Las culturas populares en el capitalismo*. México, D.F.: Editorial Nueva Imagen, 1982.

Garza, Roberto J., ed. *Contemporary Chicano Theatre*. Notre Dame: U of Notre Dame P, 1976.

Geertz, Clifford. *The Interpretations of Culture*. New York: Basic Books, 1973.

——. "Art as a Cultural System." *Modern Language Notes* 91 (Dec. 1976).

Giberti, Eva, and Ana María Fernández, eds. *La Mujer y la violencia invisible*. Buenos Aires: Editorial Sudamericana, 1989.

Glasser, Ruth. "The Backstage View: Musicians Piece Together a Living." *Centro Bulletin* (Spring 1991): 25–49.

Glaze, Anita J. *Art and Death in a Senufo Village*. Bloomington: Indiana UP, 1981.

Goldberg, Roselee. *Performance Art: From Futurism to the Present*. New York: Harry N. Abrams, Inc., 1988.

Garzón Céspedes, Francisco, ed. *El teatro colectivo de creación colectiva*. La Habana, Cuba: Casa de las Américas, 1978.

Goldstein, Richard. "The Implicated and the Immune: Responses to AIDS in the Arts and Popular Culture." *A Disease of Society: Cultural & Institutional Responses to AIDS*. New York: Cambridge UP, 1991. 17–42.

Gómez-Peña, Guillermo. "Death on the Border: A Eulogy to Border Art." *High Performance: A Quarterly Magazine for the New Arts* 12 (Spring 1991): 8–9.

——. "A Binational Performance Pilgrimage" and "Border Brujo: A Performance Poem," *TDR* 35.3 (Fall 1991).

——. *Warrior for Gringostroika*. Minnesota: Graywolf Press, 1993.

González, Yolanda Broyles. "Toward a Re-Vision of Chicano Theatre History: The Women of El Teatro Campesino." *Making a Spectacle: Feminist Essays on Contemporary Women's Theatre*. Ed. Lynda Hart. Ann Arbor: U of Michigan P, 1989.

Goodland, J. S. R. *A Sociology of Popular Drama*. London: Heinemann, 1971.

Goodman, Walter. *The Pearl of the Antilles or An Artist in Cuba*. London: Henry S. King & Co., 1873.

Gossen, Gary. "Life, Death, and Apotheosis of a Chamula Protestant Leader: Biography as Social History." *Ethnographic Encounters in Southern Mesoamerica.* Eds. Victoria Bricker and Gary H. Gossen. Albany: State U of New York; Austin: U of Texas P, 1989. 217–29.

Gracia, Jorge, ed. *Latin American Philosophy in the Twentieth Century: Man, Values, and the Search for Philosophical Identity.* New York: Prometheus Books, 1986.

Graña, María Cecilia. "Buenos Aires en la imaginación del 80. El teatro como paradigma." *Letterature D'America* 16 (1983): 89–121.

Graziano, Frank. *Divine Violence: Spectacle, Psychosexuality, and Radical Christianity in the Argentine "Dirty War."* Boulder: Westview Press, 1992.

Grover, Jan Zita. "The Convergence of Art and Crisis." *High Performance* 36 (1986): 28–31.

Gunn, Giles. *The Culture and Criticism and the Criticism of Culture.* New York: Oxford UP, 1987.

——. *The Interpretation of Otherness: Literature, Religion, and the American Imagination.* New York: Oxford UP, 1979.

Gutiérrez, Sonia, ed. *Teatro popular y cambio social en América Latina: Panorama de una experiencia.* Costa Rica: Editorial Universitaria Centor Americana, 1979.

Habermas, Jurgen. *The Structural Transformation of the Public Sphere.* Cambridge: MIT Press, 1989.

Hacket, Regina. "Whose Art is It?" *The Seattle-Post Intelligencer* 20 August 1991: "Living" Section C.

——. *The Seattle-Post Intelligencer* 7 August 1991: A14.

Hall, Stuart. "New Ethnicities: Black Film, British Cinema." *ICA Documents* 7 (1988): 27–31.

Handelman, Don. *Models and Mirrors: Towards an Anthropology of Public Events.* Cambridge: Cambridge UP, 1990.

Harasym, Sarah, ed. *The Post-Colonial Critic: Interviews, Strategies, Dialogues.* New York: Routledge, 1990.

Haraway, Donna. "Manifesto for Cyborgs." *Coming to Terms: Feminism, Theory, Politics.* Ed. Elizabeth Weed. New York: Routledge, 1989.

Hinds, Harold E., Jr. *Handbook of Latin American Popular Culture.* Westport, Conn.: Greenwood Press, 1985.

Harris, Louis K. *The Political Culture and Behavior of Latin America.* Kent, Ohio: Kent State UP, 1974.

Hart, Lynda, ed. *Making a Spectacle: Feminist Essays on Contemporary Women's Theatre.* Ann Arbor: U of Michigan P, 1989.

Hart, Lynda, and Peggy Phelan, eds. *Acting Out: Feminist Performances.* Ann Arbor: U of Michigan P, 1993.

Hartnoll, Phyllis and Peter Found, eds. *The Concise Oxford Companion to the Theatre, Second Edition.* Oxford and New York: Oxford UP, 1993.

Haskell, Barbara. *BLAM! The Explosion of Pop, Minimalism and Performance 1958–1964.* New York: The Whitney Museum of American Art, 1984.

Haviland, John Beard. *Gossip, Reputation, and Knowledge in Zinacantan.* Chicago: U of Chicago P, 1977.

Hays, Michael. "Theatrical Texts and Social Context." *Theatre* (Winter 1983): 5–7.

Herrera-Sobek, María, ed. *Beyond Stereotypes: The Critical Analysis of Chicana Literature.* New York: Bilingual Press, 1985.

——. Unpublished ms. *Chicano Literary Criticism: New Essays in Cultural Studies and Ideology.* Ed. Hector Calderón. Durham: Duke UP, forthcoming.

Hicks, D. Emily. *Border Writing: The Multidimensional Text.* Minneapolis: U of Minnesota P, 1991.

———. "Border Performance Texts: Robo-Raza at the Crossroads." *Romance Languages Annual* (1991): 469–73.

Hodge, Robert. *Literature as Discourse.* Johns Hopkins UP, 1990.

Hoffman, William M. *As Is.* New York: Vintage Books, 1985.

Holden, Stephan. "Laughs That Mask the Fears of Gay Manhattan." Rev. of "Jeffrey." *New York Times* 21 Jan. 1993: The Arts. C15–20.

hooks, bell. "Third World Diva Girls: Politics of Feminist Solidarity." *Yearning: Race, Gender and Cultural Politics.* Boston: South End Press, 1990. 89–102.

———. *Talking Back.* Boston: South End Press, 1989.

Horno-Delgado, Asunción, et al., eds. *Breaking Boundaries: Latina Writing and Critical Readings.* Amherst: U of Massachusetts P, 1989.

Huerta, Jorge. *Chicano Theatre: Themes and Forms.* Tempe: Bilingual Press, 1982.

———. ed. *Six Plays About the Chicano Experience.* Houston: Arte Público Press, 1989.

Ifeka-Moller, Caroline. "Female Militancy and Colonial Revolt: The Women's War of 1929, Eastern Nigeria." *Perceiving Women.* Ed. Shirley Ardener. London: Malaby Press, 1975.

Ingenieros, José. "Psicología de los simuladores." *Archivos de Psiquiatría y Criminología* II (1903): 449–487.

Instituto Nacional de Estadística, Geografía e Información. *La población de México en 1990.* Aguascalientes: INEGI, 1992.

Jaiven, Ana Lau. *La nueva ola del feminismo en México. Conciencia y acción de lucha de las mujeres.* Mexico City: Editorial Planeta, 1987.

Jameson, Fredric. *The Political Unconscious.* Ithaca: Cornell UP, 1981.

———. "La política de la teoría. Posiciones ideológicas en el debate sobre el postmodernismo." *Criterios* 25–28 (Enero 1989–Dic. 1990).

JanMohamed, Abdul R. "The Economy of Manichean Allegory: The Function of Racial Difference in Colonialist Literature." *"Race," Writing and Difference.* Ed. Henry Louis Gates. Chicago: U of Chicago P, 1986.

———, and David Lloyd, eds. *The Nature and Context of Minority Discourse II.* Special Issue *Cultural Critique* 7 Special Issue (Fall 1987).

———. *The Nature and Context of Minority Discourse. Cultural Critique* 6 Special Issue (Spring 1987).

———. "Dominance, Hegemony, and the Modes of Minority Discourse." *Cultural Critique* 7 (Fall 1987).

Jaquette, Jane S., ed. *The Women's Movement in Latin America: Feminism and the Transition to Democracy.* Boston: Unwin Hyman, 1989.

Jelin, Elizabeth, ed. *Women and Social Change in Latin America.* London: Zed Books Ltd., 1990.

Johnson, Barbara. *A World of Difference.* Baltimore: Johns Hopkins UP, 1987.

Jones, James W. "The Sick Homosexual: AIDS and Gays on the American Stage and Screen." *Confronting AIDS Through Literature: The Responsibilities of Representation.* Urbana: U of Illinois P, 1993. 103–23.

Juárez Espinosa, Isabel. "Cuento del gallo y la mujer." Unpublished short story.

———. "El hombre y la serpiente." Unpublished short story.

———. *La familia: Drama en dos actos*. Unpublished manuscript, 1991.

———. "La mujer maya como fuente de cultura." Unpublished manuscript.

———. "Tul antz ch'ay ta uk'um/Una mujer cayó al río." *Ya'yejik te mamaletik/Palabras de los Ancianos*. Tuxtla Gutiérrez, Chiapas: Secretaría de Educación y Cultura 3 (1983): 23–31.

Juárez Espinosa, Isabel, and Petrona de la Cruz Cruz. *La desconfiada (diálogo dramático)*. Unpublished manuscript, 1992.

Kadvany, "Verso and Recto: An Essay on Social Change." *Cultural Critique* 1 (Fall 1985): 183–215.

Kanellos, Nicolás. *The History of Hispanic Theatre in the United States, Origins to 1940*. Austin: U of Texas P, 1990.

Kanellos, Nicolás, and Jorge Huerta, eds. *Nuevos Pasos: Chicano and Puerto Rican Drama*. Houston: Arte Público Press, 1989.

Kara, Vinzula. Interview with María Teresa Marrero. October 1991.

Kellner, Douglas. *Critical Theory, Marxism and Modernity*. Baltimore: Johns Hopkins UP, 1989.

Kirby, Michael. *Happenings*. New York: E. P. Dutton & Company, Inc., 1965.

Koehler, Robert. "Firing New Salvo in Cultural Battle." *Los Angeles Times* 6 Sept. 1990: F4, F8.

Koestenbaum, Wayne. *Double Talk: The Erotics of Male Literary Collaboration*. New York: Routledge, 1989.

Kostelanetz, Richard. *The Theatre of Mixed Means*. New York: The Dial Press, Inc., 1968.

Kramer, Larry. *The Destiny of Me*. New York: Plume, 1993.

———. *The Normal Heart*. New York: Samuel French, Inc., 1985.

———. *Reports from the Holocaust: The Making of an AIDS Activist*. New York: St. Martin's Press, 1989.

Kushner, Tony. *Angels in America. Part One: Millennium Approaches*. New York: Theatre Communications Group, 1993.

LaCapra, Dominick. "History and Psychoanalysis." *Critical Inquiry* 13.2 (1987): 222–46.

Lafaye, Jacques. *Quetzalcoatl et Guadalupe*. Paris: Gallimard, 1974.

Lambert, Bruce. "AIDS Travel New York-Puerto Rico 'AIR Bridge'" *The New York Times* 15 June 1990: B-1.

Landes, Joan B. *Women and the Public Sphere in the Age of the French Revolution*. Ithaca: Cornell UP, 1988.

Lang, Jon. *Creating Architectural Theory: The Role of the Behavioral Sciences in Environmental Design*. New York: Van Nostrand Reinhold Co., 1987.

Laplanche, Jean, and Jean-Bertrand Pontalis. "Fantasy and the Origins of Sexuality." *Formations of Fantasy*. Eds. James Donald, Cora Kaplan, and Victor Burgin. New York: Methuen, 1986.

Lara Figueroa, Celso A. *Cultura popular en Hispanoamérica*. Guatemala: Universidad de San Carlos de Guatemala, 1980.

Larraín, Jorge. *The Concept of Ideology*. Athens: The U of Georgia P, 1979.

Larroyo, Francisco, ed. *Historia de las doctrinas filosóficas en latinoamérica*. México: Porrua, 1968.

Larsen, Neil. *The Discourse of Power: Culture Hegemony and the Authoritarian State in Latin America*. Minneapolis: Institute for the Study of Ideologies and Literature, 1983.

Laughlin, Miriam. "Arts: The Drama of Mayan Women." *Ms.* 2.1 (July–Aug. 1991): 88–89.

———. "Mayan Women Playwrights." *Belles Lettres* Winter 1991/1992: 45 and 47.

Laughlin, Robert M. "As For Me and The Harvard Chiapas Project." *Ethnographic Encounters in Southern Mesoamerica*. Eds. Victoria R. Bricker and Gary H. Gossen. Albany: State University of New York; Austin: U of Texas P, 1989. 51–72.

——. *Of Cabbages and Kings: Tales From Zinacantán*. Washington, D.C.: The Smithsonian Institution Press, 1977.

——. *The Great Tzotzil Dictionary of San Lorenzo Zinacantán*. Washington, D.C.: The Smithsonian Institution Press, 1975.

——. "The Mayan Renaissance: Sna Stz'Ibajom, The House of the Writer." *Native American Cultures: Before and After Columbus*. Hawaii Committee for the Humanities, 1992. 8, 12.

——. "Tzotzil and Tzeltal: Who in the World?" *Gertrude Blom Bearing Witness*. Eds. Alex Harris and Margaret Sartor. Chapel Hill: U of North Carolina P, 1985.

Laughlin, Robert M. and Carol Karasik, eds. *The People of the Bat: Mayan Tales and Dreams from Zinacantan*. Washington, D.C.: Smithsonian Institution Press, 1988.

Laughlin, Robert M. and Grant J. Wenger. "Insuring a Cooperative's Future." *Cultural Survival Quarterly* 15.1 (1991): 61–63.

Lawson, D. S. "Rage and Remembrance: The AIDS Plays." *AIDS: the Literary Response*. New York: Twayne Publishers, 1992. 140–54.

Lechner, Norbert. *Cultura política y democratización*. Buenos Aires: Consejo Latinoamericano de Ciencias Sociales: Facultad Latinoamericana de Ciencias Sociales, 1987.

Lee, Ralph. Personal Interview. 1990.

Lombardo Otero, Rosa María. *La mujer Tzeltal*. Mexico City: n.p., 1944.

López, Josefina. *Real Women Have Curves*. Seattle: Rain City Projects, 1988.

López, Tiffany Ana, ed. *Growing Up Chicana/o*. New York: William Morrow and Co., 1993.

Losada, Alejandro. "Los Sistemas Literarios Como Instituciones Sociales en América Latina." *Revista de crítica literaria Latinoamericana* 1 (1976): 39–60.

——. "Discursos críticos y proyectos sociales en Hispanoamérica." *Ideologies and Literature* 1, 2 (Feb.–April, 1973–75).

Lotman, Jurij M. *Semiótica de la cultura*. Madrid: Ediciones Cátedra, 1979.

Lucas, Craig. *Prelude to a Kiss*. New York: Plume, 1991.

Lukacs, George. *Significación actual del realismo crítico*. Madrid: Ediciones Era, 1963.

Luzuriaga, Gerardo, ed. *Popular Theatre for Social Change in Latin America*. Los Angeles: UCLA Latin American Center Publications, 1978.

Macías, Anna María. *Against All Odds. The Feminist Movement in Mexico to 1940*. Westport, Connecticut: Greenwood Press, 1982.

Mailloux, Steven. *Rhetorical Power*. Ithaca: Cornell UP, 1989.

Mancillas, Aida. "1,000 Points of Fear—The New Berlin Wall: Impressions of a Weekend on the Border San Diego, California/Tijuana, B.C., April 1990." Unpublished manuscript.

Margulis, Merio. "La cultura popular." *La cultura popular*. Adolfo Colombres et. al. México: Premia, 1982.

Márquez, Rosa Luisa. "Modelo para armar: El sí-dá." *Brincos y saltos: El juego como disciplina teatral*. Puerto Rico: Ediciones Cuicaloca, 1992. 80–87.

Marranca, Bonnie, and Guatam Dasgupta, eds. *Interculturalism and Performance*. New York: PAJ Publications, 1991.

Marrero, María Teresa. *Chicano and Latino Self-Representation in Theater and Performance Art*. Diss. U of California, Irvine, 1992.

——. "Chicano-Latino Self-Representation in Theater and Performance Art." *Gestos* 11 April 1991: 147–62.

Martínez, Eliud. "Personal Vision in the Short Stories of Estela Portillo Trambley." *Beyond*

Stereotypes: The Critical Analysis of Chicana Literature. Ed. María Herrera-Sobek. Binghampton, N.Y.: Bilingual Press, 1985.

Masiello, Francine. *Between Civilization and Barbarism: Women, Nation, and Literary Culture in Modern Argentina.* Lincoln: U of Nebraska P, 1992.

Mattelart, Armand. *La ideología de la dominación en una sociedad dependiente: La respuesta ideológica de la clase dominante Chilena al reformismo.* Buenos Aires: Ediciones Signos, 1970.

McPherson, Scott. *Marvin's Room.* New York: Plume, 1992.

Mendoza, Eduardo, and Gustavo Herrera: "Don José Díaz Núñez: Cuarenta años en el Teatro de Muñecos." *Torre de Papel* 1.1–2 (May–Dec. 1985): xlix–liii.

Middleton, Richard. *Pop & the Blues.* London: Victor Gollancz Ltd., 1972. 262–63.

Miller, Francesca. *Latin American Women and the Search for Social Justice.* Hanover: UP of New England, 1991.

Miller, Judith. "Strangers at the Gate." *The New York Times Magazine* 15 Sept. 1991: cover story.

Minc, Rose S. *Literature and Popular Culture in the Hispanic World: A Symposium.* Gaithersburg, Md.: Hispanicamerica; Montclair, N.J.: Montclair State College, 1981.

Minero, Alberto. "El teatro Hispano pone su atención en el SIDA." Rev. of *Noche de ronda* by Pedro R. Monge Rafuls. *El diario la prensa* 17 Feb. 1991: 30.

Minh-Ha, Trinh T. *Framer Framed.* New York: Routledge, 1992.

———. *When the Moon Waxes Red: Representation, Gender and Cultural Politics.* New York: Routledge, 1991.

———. *Woman, Native, Other: Writing Posticoloniality and Feminism.* Bloomington: Indiana UP, 1989.

Mohanty, Chandra Talpade, Ann Russo, and Lourdes Torres, eds. *Third World Women and the Politics of Feminism.* Bloomington: Indiana UP, 1991.

Molinar Castañeda, Israel. *Matanzas en el VII Festival de la Cultura Caribeña.* Santiago de Cuba: Casa del Caribe. May–June 1987.

———. *Las comparsas.* Unpublished manuscript, 1987.

Monge Rafuls, Pedro R. *Noche de ronda.* Unpublished manuscript, 1991.

Monsiváis, Carlos. *Entrada libre: Crónicas de la sociedad que se organiza.* México: Era, 1987.

———. *Amor perdido.* México: Biblioteca Eva, 1988.

———. "Preguntas sobre identidad, religión y derechos humanos." *México Indígena* 21 (Junio 1991): 7–8.

Monteforte Toledo, Mario, ed. *Literatura, ideología y lenguaje.* México: Grijalbo, 1976.

Montemayor, Carlos, ed. *Los escritores indígenas actuales.* 2 vols. México: Fondo Editorial Tierra Adentro and Consejo Nacional para la Cultura y las Artes, 1992.

Moraga, Cherríe. *Giving Up the Ghost, Shadow of a Man and Heroes and Saints.* Albuquerque: West End Press, 1994.

———. *The Last Generation.* Boston: South End Press, 1993.

———. "From a Long Line of Vendidas: Chicanas and Feminism." *Feminist Studies/Critical Studies.* Ed. Teresa de Lauretis. Bloomington: Indiana UP, 1986.

———. *Giving Up the Ghost: Teatro in Two Acts.* Los Angeles: West End Press, 1986.

Morris, Rebecca. "A Better Life." Rev. of *A Better Life* by Louis Delgado, Jr. *Back Stage:* 20 Aug. 1993.

Murphy, Timothy F., and Suzanne Poirier, ed. *Writing AIDS: Gay Literature, Language, and Analysis.* New York: Columbia.

Murray, Gilbert, ed. *Euripides: The Trojan Women*. London: George Allen & Unwin Ltd., 1976.

Najenson, José Luis. *Cultura nacional y cultura subalterna*. México: Universidad Autónoma del Estado de México, 1979.

Nash, June, and Helen Safa, ed. *Women and Change in Latin America*. Boston: Bergin & Garvey Publishers, Inc., 1986.

———. *In the Eyes of the Ancestors: Belief and Behavior in a Mayan Community*. Prospect Heights, Illinois: Waveland Press, 1970/1985.

Navarre, Max. "Art in the AIDies: An Act of Faith." *High Performance* 36 (1986): 32–36.

Navarro-Aranguren, Marysa. "The Construction of Latin American Feminist Identity." *Americas*. New York: Oxford University Press, 1992.

———. "The Personal Is Political: Las Madres de Plaza de Mayo." *Power and Popular Protest — Latin American Social Movements*. Ed. Susan Eckstein. Berkeley: UC Press, 1989.

Navarro, Ray. "Eso, me esta pasando." *Chicano and Film: Representation and Resistance*. Ed. Chon A. Noriega. Minneapolis: U of Minnesota P, 1992. 312–15.

Navarro Sada, Francisco. "La promoción teatral comunitaria en México." *Gestos* 15 (April 1993): 157–59.

Negrón Muntaner, Frances. "Echoing Stonewall and Other Dilemmas: The Organizational Beginnings of a Gay and Lesbian Agenda in Puerto Rico, 1972–1977 (Part 1)" *Centro De Estudios Puertorriqueños Bulletin* 4.1 (1992): 76–95.

———. "Insider/Outsider: Making Films in the Puerto Rican Community." *Centro De Estudios Puertorriqueños Bulletin* 3.1 (1991) 81–85.

Nelkin, Dorothy, et al., eds. *A Disease of Society: Cultural & Institutional Responses to AIDS*. New York: Cambridge UP, 1991.

Nelson, Gary and Lawrence Grossberg, eds. *Marxism and the Interpretation of Culture*. Urbana: U of Illinois P, 1988.

Nelson, Emmanuel S., ed. *AIDS: The Literary Response*. New York: Twayne Publisher, 1992.

Nettleford, Rex. "Implications for Caribbean Development" *Caribbean Festival Arts*. Eds. John W. Nunley and Judith Bettelheim. Seattle: U of Washington P, 1988.

"Nosotras le entramos parejo con las costureras." Seminario Marxista-Leninista Feminista de Lesbianas. *Fem* 10.46 (June–July 1986): 43–45.

Nunley, John W. and Judith Bettelheim. *Caribbean Festival Arts*. Seattle: U of Washington P, 1988.

Ochnesisus, Carlos, y Otros. *Práctica teatral y expresión popular en América Latina: Argentina, Chile, Perú, Uruguay*. Buenos Aires: Ediciones Pualinas, 1988.

O'Connel, Shaun. "The Big One: Literature Discovers AIDS." *New England Journal of Public Policy* Special Issue on AIDS. 4.1 (1988): 485–506.

Offen, Karen. "Defining Feminism. A Comparative Historical Approach." *Signs. Journal of Women in Culture and Society*. 14.1 (Autumn 1988): 119–57.

Oleza Simó, Juan Oleza. "La literatura signo ideológico: La ideologización del texto literario." *La literature como signo*. Madrid: Editorial Playor, 1981.

Ortiz, Fernando. *Nuevo catauro de Cubanismos*. La Habana: Editorial de Ciencias Sociales, 1985 [1923].

———. "Los cabildos Afro-Cubanos." *Revista Bimestre Cubana* 16.1. (Enero 1921).

———. "La fiesta afrocubana del 'Día de Reyes.'" *Archivos del Folklore Cubano* 1 (1925).

Osborn, M. Elizabeth, ed. *On New Ground: Contemporary Hispanic-American Plays*. New York: Theatre Communications Group, 1987.

——. *The Way We Live Now: American Plays & the AIDS Crisis.* New York: Theatre Communications Group, 1990.

Osorio, Nelson. "Las idologías y los esudios de la literatura Hispanoamericana." *Hispánica* (1979): 9–29.

Padial Guerchoux, Anita, and Manuel Vázquez-Bigi. *Quiché Vinak, Tragedia.* Mexico City: Fondo de Cultura Económica, 1991.

Panizza, Oskar. *The Council of Love: A Celestial Tragedy in Five Acts.* Trans. Oreste F. Pucciani. New York: Viking Press, 1977.

Paredes, Raymund A. "Los Angeles from the *Barrio:* Oscar Zeta Acosta's *The Revolt of the Cockroach People.*" *Los Angeles in Fiction.* Ed. David Fine. Albuquerque: U of New Mexico P, 1984.

Parks, Brian. "Theatre Cameos." Rev. of *A Better Life* by Louis Delgado, Jr. *The Village Voice:* Aug. 1993.

Parret, Herman. *Contexts of Understanding: Pragmatic and Beyond.* Amsterdam: John Benjamin, 1980.

Partnoy, Alicia. *The Little School: Tales of Disappearance and Survival in Argentina.* Pittsburg: Cleis Press, 1986.

Pastore, Judith Laurence, ed. *Confronting AIDS Through Literature: The Responsibilities of Representation.* Urbana: U of Illinois P, 1993.

Pavis, Patrice. *Languages of the Stage: Essays in the Semiology of the Theatre.* New York: Performing Arts Journal Publications, 1982.

Paz Gago, José María. "Para acabar con la estilística: Por una pragmática de la literatura." New York: Grove Press, 1961.

Paz Gago, José María. "Para acabar con la estilística: Por una pratmática de la literatura." *Revista de Literatura.* 49.98 (Julio-Diciembre 1987): 531–40.

Peck, Jeffrey M. "Advanced Literary Study of Cultural Study: A Redefinition of Discipline." *Profession* (1985): 49–54.

Pérez, Nancy, et al. *El cabildo carabalí isuama.* Santiago de Cuba: Editorial Oriente, 1982.

Pérez Firmat, Gustavo, ed. *Do the Americas Have a Common Literature?* Durham: Duke UP, 1990.

Pérez Hernández, Manuel. "Como nos identificamos: ¿Por etnia, por región, por cultura?" *Nuestra Sabiduría* 1 (Sept. 1991): 5–7.

——. "Vivencias de nuestra palabra: El resurgimiento de la cultura maya en Chiapas." *Los Escritores indígenas actuales.* Ed. Carlos Montemayor. México: Fondo Editorial Tierra Adentro, 1992. 83–102.

——. "Skuenta jun antz oy ep yosil/Una mujer que tenía mucho terreno." *Literatura indígena, ayer y hoy: Encuentro nacional de escritores de lenguas indígenas.* Tamaulipas: Instituto Tamaulipeco de Cultura, 1990. 217–21.

Perón, Eva. *My Mission in Life.* New York: Vantage Press, 1953.

Philippi, Desa. "The Conjuncture of Race and Gender in Anthropology and Art History, A Critical Study of Nancy Spero's Work." *Third Text* 1 (Autumn 1987).

Pinero, Miguel. *Short Eyes.* New York: Hill and Wang, 1975.

Pintauro, Joe. *Raft of the Medusa.* New York: Dramatists Play Service Inc., 1992.

Players, Loisaida. "Interview: Loisaida Players." *Centro De Estudios Puertorriqueños Bulletin* 5.1 Special Issue: Youth Culture in the 1990s. (1993): 66–79.

Poniatowska, Elena. "La literatura de las mujeres es parte de la literatura de los oprimidos." *Fem* 6.21 (Feb.–March 1982): 23–27.

———. *Nada nadie. Las voces del temblor.* Mexico City: Era, 1988.

Poovey, Mary. "Feminism and Deconstruction." *Feminist Studies* 14.1 (Spring 1988): 51–65.

Portillo, Estela. *The Day of the Swallows. Contemporary Chicano Theatre.* Ed. Roberto J. Garza. Notre Dame: U of Notre Dame P, 1976.

Postiglione, Gerard A. *Ethnicity and American Social Theory: Toward Critical Pluralism.* Lanham: UP of America, 1983.

Pottlitzer, Joanne. *Hispanic Theatre in the United States and Puerto Rico.* New York: The Ford Foundation, 1991.

Pozas, Ricardo. *Juan the Chamula.* Trans. of *Juan Pérez Jolote* by Lysander Kemp. Berkeley and Los Angeles: U of California P, 1962.

Pratt, Mary Louise, and Marta Morello Frosch, eds. *Nuevo texto crítico* 4 (Año II) Segundo Semestre. Stanford: Stanford UP, 1989.

Preston, John. "AIDS Writing: The Imperative to 'Get It All Down,'" *Outweek* 13 Mar. 1991: 60–61.

———. ed. *Personal Dispatches: Writers Confront AIDS.* New York: St. Martin's Press, 1989.

Prida, Dolores. *Beautiful Señoritas and Other Plays.* Houston: Arte Público Press, 1991.

Pye, Christopher. *The Regal Phantasm: Shakespeare and the Politics of Spectacle.* New York: Routledge, 1990.

Rais, Hilda, ed. *Salirse de madre.* Buenos Aires: Croquiñol Ediciones, 1989.

Radical America 20.6 (1987): Special Issue: "Facing AIDS."

Ramirez, Alfonso. *The Watermelon Factory.* Unpublished manuscript, 1991.

Randall, Marilyn. "The Pragmatic of Literariness." *Poetics.* 14 (1985): 415–31.

Reagon, Bernice Johnson. "Coalition Politics: Turning the Century." *Home Girls: A Black Feminist Anthology.* Ed. Barbara Smith. Brooklyn: Kitchen Table: Women of Color Press, 1983.

Reinelt, Janelle G., and Joseph R. Roach, ed. *Critical Theory and Performance.* Ann Arbor: U of Michigan P, 1992.

Rich, Frank. "A Black Family Confronts AIDS." Rev. of *Before It Hits Home,* Cheryl L. West. *New York Times* 11 Mar. 1992: The Arts. C17–22.

———. "Discovering Family Values at 'Falsettos.'" Rev. of *Falsettos,* William Finn. *New York Times* 12 July 1992: 2.1–8.

———. "Laughing at AIDS Is the First Line of Defense." Rev. of *Jeffrey,* Paul Rudnick. *New York Times* 3 Feb. 1993: The Arts. C15–18.

Richards, David. "The Theatre of AIDS: Attention Must Be Paid." *The New York Times* 5 Jan. 1992: 2.1.

Rivera, José. *A Tiger in Central Park.* Unpublished manuscript, 1992.

Roche, Carlos. "El psuedo-hermafrodismo masculino y los androginoides." *Archivos de Psiquiatría y Criminología III* (1904): 421.

Roche-Monteagudo, Rafael. *La policía y sus misterios.* Habana: La Moderna Poesia, 1925.

Rock, David. *Authoritarian Argentina: The Nationalist Movement, Its History and Its Impact.* Berkeley: U of California P, 1993.

Rodríguez, Carlos A. "Actos de amor: Introducción al estudio de la poesía puertorriqueña homosexual y lesbiana." *Desde Este Lado* 1.2 (1990): 21–26.

Rodríguez, Jesusa. "La gira mamal de la coatlicue." *Debate feminista* 1.2 (September 1990): 401–3.

———. Program notes. *Donna Giovanni. Divas.* Pepsico Summerfare. 1987.

Román, David. "Performing All Our Lives: AIDS, Performance, Community." *Critical Theory and Performance.* Ann Harbor: U of Michigan P, 1992.

——. "*Fierce Love* and Fierce Response." *Critical Essays: Gay and Lesbian Writers of Color.* Ed. Emmanuel S. Nelson. New York: Harrington Park Press, 1993.

Rosario Fernández de la Uz, Violeta. *Análisis histórico-cultural de paseo La Placita, como exponente del carnaval santiaguero.* Unpublished Trabajo de Diploma, Santiago, Universidad de Oriente, 1987–88.

Rose, Jacqueline. *Sexuality in the Field of Vision.* London: Verso, 1986.

Rosenbaum, Brenda. *With Our Heads Bowed: The Dynamics of Gender in a Maya Community.* Albany: Institute for Mesoamerican Studies, 1993.

Rossi, Laura. "¿Cómo pensar a las Madres de Plaza de Mayo?" *Nuevo texto crítico* 4 (Año II). Eds. Mary Louise Pratt and Marta Morello Frosch. Stanford: Stanford University Press, 1989. 145–53.

Ruddick, Sara. *Maternal Thinking: Toward a Politics of Peace.* New York: Ballantine Books, 1989.

Rudnick, Paul. "Laughing at AIDS." Editorial. *New York Times* 23 Jan. 1993: 21.

Rus, Diana L. "La crisis económica y la mujer indígena: El caso de Chamula, Chiapas." Documentos de trabajo sobre cambio en el campo chiapaneco. San Cristóbal de las Casas: INAREMAC (Instituto de Asesoría Antropológica para la Región Maya), 1990.

Rus, Jan. "Whose Caste War? Indians, Ladinos, and the Chiapas 'Case War' of 1869." *Spaniards and Indians in Southeastern Mesoamerica. Essays on the History of Ethnic Relations.* Eds. Murdo J. MacLeod and Robert Wasserstrom. Lincoln: U of Nebraska P, 1983. 127–68.

Ryan, Michael. *Politics and Culture.* Baltimore: Johns Hopkins UP, 1989.

Saalfield, Catherine, and Ray Navarro. "Not Just Black and White: AIDS Media and People of Color." *Centro De Estudios Puertorriqueños Bulletin* 2.8 (1990): 70–78.

Sabato, Ernesto. "Estudio preliminar. Tango, canción de Buenos Aires": *El Tango.* Ed. Horacio Salas. Buenos Aires: Planeta, 1986.

Sabato, Ernesto, ed. *Nunca Más: The Report of the Argentine National Commission on the Disappeared.* New York: Farrar Straus Giroux, 1986.

Sahlins, Marshall. *Culture and Practical Reason.* Chicago: U of Chicago P, 1976.

Said, Edward. "Representing the Colonized: Anthropology's Interlocutors." *Critical Inquiry* 15.2 (Winter 1989): 205–25.

——. *The World, the Text, and the Critic.* Cambridge: Harvard UP, 1983.

Saldívar, José David. *The Dialectics of Our America: Geneology, Cultural Critique, and Literary History.* Durham: Duke UP, 1991.

Sambarino, Mario. *La cultura nacional como problema.* Montevideo: Nuestra Tierra, 1970.

Sánchez, Juan Danell. "¿Extinción o exterminio? En peligro de desaparecer 20 etnias." *Etnias* 1.3 (June 1988): 4–5.

Sanchez-Scott, Milcha. "Roosters." *On New Ground.* Ed. Elizabeth Osborn. New York: Theatre Communications Group, 1987.

Sandoval, Alberto. "Dolores Prida's *Coser y Cantar:* Mapping the Dialectics of Ethnic Identity and Assimilation." *Breaking Boundaries: Latina Writing and Critical Readings.* Ed. Asunción Horno-Delgado, et al. Amherst: U of Massachusetts P, 1989.

Santiago, Hector. *Al final del arco iris.* Unpublished manuscript.

——. *Camino de angeles.* Unpublished manuscript, 1992.

——. *El dulce cafecito.* Unpublished manuscript.

Saporta Sternbach, Nancy, et al. "Feminisms in Latin America: From Bogotá to San Bernardo." *Signs: Journal of Women in Culture and Society* 17.2 1992: 393–434.

Sarlo, Beatriz. "Política, ideología y figuración literaria." *Ficción y política* 30–59.

Scarry, Elaine. *The Body in Pain: The Making and Unmaking of the World*. New York: Oxford, 1985.

Schechner, Richard. *Performance Theory*. New York: Routledge, 1988.

———. *Between Theatre and Anthropology*. Philadelphia: U Pennsylvania P, 1985.

Schele, Linda & David Friedel. *A Forest of Kings*. New York: Morrow, 1990.

———. *A Forest of Kings: The Untold Story of the Ancient Maya*. New York: William Morrow and Company, 1990.

Schele, Linda, and Mary Ellen Miller. *The Blood of Kings: Dynasty and Ritual in Maya Art*. New York: George Braziller in association with the Kimbell Art Museum of Fort Worth, 1986.

Schmidhuber, Guillermo. *El teatro mexicano en cierne 1922–1938*. New York: Peter Lang Publishers, Inc., 1992.

Schirmer, Jennifer G. "Those Who Die For Life Cannot Be Called Dead: Women and Human Rights in Protest in Latin America." *Feminist Review* 32 (Summer 1989): 3–29.

Sciorra, Joseph. "We're Not Just Here to Plant. We Have Culture: A Case Study of Rincón Criollo." Unpublished manuscript.

Sedgwick, Eve Kosofsky. *Epistemology of the Closet*. Berkeley: U of California P, 1990.

Segundo censo de la República Argentina. Buenos Aires: Imprenta de la Penitenciaría Nacional, 1895.

Shamsul Alam, Juan. *Zookeeper*. Unpublished manuscript, 1989.

Shatzky, Joel. "AIDS Enters the American Theatre: *As Is* and *The Normal Heart*." *AIDS: The Literary Response*. New York: Twayne Publishers, 1992. 131–39.

Shewey, Don. "AIDS on Stage: Comfort, Sorrow, Anger." *The New York Times* 21 June 1987:H5.

———. ed. *Out Front: Contemporary Gay and Lesbian Plays*. New York: Grove Press, 1988.

Simonson, Rick, and Scott Walker, eds. *The Graywolf Annual Five: Multi-Cultural Literacy*. Saint Paul: Graywolf Press, 1988.

Simpson, John, and Jana Bennett. *The Disappeared: Voices from a Secret War*. London: Robson Books, 1985.

Singer, Merrill, et al. "SIDA: The Economic, Social, and Cultural Contest of AIDS Among Latinos." *Medical Anthropology Quarterly* 4.1 (1990): 72–114.

Smith, Barbara, ed. *Home Girls: A Black Feminist Anthology*. New York: Kitchen Table Press, 1983.

Smith, Barbara Herrnstein. *On the Margins of Discourse*. Chicago: U of Chicago P, 1988.

———. *Contingencies of Value*. Cambridge: Harvard UP, 1988.

Sna Jtz'ibajom. *Dinastía de jaguares*. Unpublished manuscript, 1992.

———. *El burro y la mariposa*. Unpublished manuscript, 1988.

———. *El haragán y el zopilote*. Unpublished manuscript, 1989.

———. *Entre manos burros mas elote. Unpublished manuscript, 1989.*

———. *Herencia fatal*. Unpublished manuscript, 1991.

———. *¿A poco hay cimarrones?* Unpublished manuscript, 1990.

Sna Jtz'ibajom, and Jeffrey Jay Foxx. "The Working Maya." *Icarus* 5 (Winter 1992): 97–116.

Snitow, Ann. "A Gender Diary." *Rocking the Ship of State*. Eds. Adrienne Harris and Ynestra King. Boulder: Westview Press, 1989.

Solberg, Carl. *Immigration and Nationalism*. Austin: U of Texas P, 1970.

Solis, Octavio. *Man of the Flesh*. 3.2 Costa Mesa: South Coast Repertory Hispanic Playwrights Project (1990).

Sollors, Werner. *Beyond Ethnicity: Consent and Descent in American Culture.* New York: Oxford UP, 1986.

Sommer, Doris. *Foundational Fictions: The National Romances of Latin America.* Berkeley: U of California P, 1991.

Sosnowski, Saúl, ed. *Represión y construcción de una cultura: El caso Argentino.* Buenos Aires: Editorial Universitaria de Buenos Aires, 1988.

Spivak, Gayatri Chakrovorty. "Can the Subaltern Speak?" *Marxism and the Interpretation of Culture.* Eds. Gary Nelson and Lawrence Grossberg. Urbana: U of Illinois P, 1988.

———. *In Other Worlds: Essays in Cultural Politics.* New York: Routledge, 1988.

Steele, Cynthia. "Indigenismo y posmodernidad: Narrativa indigenista, testimonio, teatro campesino y video en el Chiapas finisecular." *Revista de Crítica Literaria Latinoamericana* 9.38 (1993): 249–60.

Sten, María. *Vida y muerte del teatro náhuatl.* Xalapa: Universidad Veracruzana, 1982.

Stepan, Nancy Leys. *"The Hour of Eugenics": Race, Gender, and Nation in Latin America.* Ithaca: Cornell UP, 1991.

Stephens, Lynn. *Zapotec Women.* Austin: U of Texas P, 1991.

Stevens, Evelyn P. "Marianismo: The Other Face of Machismo." In *Male and Female in Latin America,* ed. Ann Pescatello. Pittsburgh: U of Pittsburgh P, 1973.

Suárez-Orozco, Marcelo M. "The Hertitage of Enduring a 'Dirty War': Psychosocial Aspects of Terror in Argentina, 1976–1988." *Journal of Psychohistory* 18.4 (1991): 469–505.

Sussman, Elizabeth, ed., *On the Passage of a few people through a rather brief moment in time: the Situationist International 1957–1972.* Cambridge: MIT Press, 1989.

Talens, Jenaro. *La escritura como teatralidad.* Valencia: Universidad de Valencia, 1977.

Taylor, Diana. " 'High Aztec' or Performing Anthro Pop: Jesusa Rodríguez and Liliana Felipe in *Cielo de abajo.*" *The Drama Review* 37.3 (Fall 1993): 142–52.

———. *Theatre of Crisis: Drama and Politics in Latin America.* Lexington: UP of Kentucky, 1991.

———. "Transculturating Transculturation." *Interculturalism and Performance.* Eds. Bonnie Marranca and Guatam Dasgupta. New York: PAJ Publications, 1991.

Takj otskjilal/kja its'bal/kjitskjibil/ja jas waxna'atiki./Jp'ijiltic/kña'tyäbalojoñ/dü musokyuy/nuestra sabiduría. Unidad de Escritores Mayas-Zoques, Instituto Chiapaneco.

Tejera Gaona, Héctor. "¿Y los próximos quinientos años qué?" *Debate Feminista* 3.5 (Marzo 1992): 68–78.

Theweleit, Klaus. *Male Fantasies.* Vols. 1 and 2. Minneapolis: U of Minneapolis P, 1987–1989.

Thompson, Michael, et. al. *Cultural Theory.* Boulder: Westview Press Inc., 1990.

Timerman, Jacobo. *Prisoner Without a Name, Cell Without a Number.* Trans. Toby Talbot. New York: Vintage Books, 1982.

Torres-Rivas, Edelberto. *Interpretación del desarrollo social Centroamericano: Proceso y estructuras de una sociedad dependiente.* Costa Rica: Editorial Universitaria Centroamericana, 1980.

Todorov, Tzvetan. "El cruzamiento de las culturas." *Criterios* 12 (1990): 3–19.

Treichler, Paul A. "AIDS, Homophobia and Biomedical Discourse: An Epidemic of Signification." *Cultural Studies* 1.3 (1987): 263–305.

Thornton, John. "The Coromanatees: An African Cultural Group in Colonial America." National Endowment for the Humanities seminar, Johns Hopkins University, Summer, 1993.

Troncoso, Oscar. *El proceso de reorganización nacional: Cronología y documentación.* Buenos Aires: Centro Editor de America Latina, Vol. 1: 1984.

Turner, Victor. "Social Dramas and Stories about Them." *Critical Inquiry* (Autumn 1980): 141–68.

U.S. Department of Health and Human Sciences. Centers of Disease Control. National Center for Infectious Diseases. *HIV/AIDS Surveillance Report*. Atlanta, 1992.

Usigli, Rodolfo. *Corona de sombra. Teatro completo*. Vol. 2. Mexico City: Fondo de Cultura Económica, 1966.

Valdez, Luis. *Zoot Suit and Other Plays*. Houston: Arte Público Press, 1992.

———. *Luis Valdez-Early Works: Actos, Bernabé and Pensamiento Serpentino*. Houston: Arte Público Press, 1990.

———. *The Shrunken Head of Pancho Villa. Necessary Theatre*. Ed. Jorge Huerta. Houston: Arte Público Press, 1989.

van den Berg, Klaus. "The Geometry of Culture: Space and Theatre Buildings in Twentieth-Century Berlin." *Theatre Research International* 16.1 (Spring, 1991): 1–17.

Van Gelder, Lawrence. "2 Aspects of the H.I.V. Experience." Rev. of *A Better Life* by Louis Delgado, Jr. *The New York Times* 17 Aug. 1993.

Varela, Rafael. "Autoritarismo y dominación de clase en la cultura del Uruguay militarizado." *The Discourse of Power, Culture, Hegemony and the Authoritarian State in Latin America*. Ed. Neil Larsen. Minneapolis: Ideologies and Literature, 1983.

Veyga, Francisco de. "La inversión sexual adquirida." *Archivos de Psiquiatría y Criminología II* (1903).

———. "Invertido sexual imitando la mujer honesta." *Archivos de Psiquiatría y Criminología I* (1902).

———. "La inversión adquirida-Tipo profesional." *Archivos de Psiquiatría y Criminología II*, 1903.

———. "La inversión sexual congénita." *Archivos de Psiquiatría y Criminología I*, 1902.

———. "El amor en los invertidos sexuales." *Archivos de Psiquiatría y Criminología II* (1903).

———. "El sentido moral y la conductas de los invertidos." *Archivos de Psiquiatría y Criminología III* (1904).

Vera, Rodrigo. "Caciques del PRI expulsan a familias chamulas de Chiapas." *Proceso* 807 (20 Abril 1992): 10–14.

———. "Patrocinio propone castigar las expulsiones de chamulas: Un diputado, apoyarlas; otros, rechazan a los dos." *Proceso* 808 (27 Abril 1992): 20–23.

Versényi, Adam. "Getting Under the Aztec Skin: Evangelical Theatre in the New World." *New Theatre Quarterly* 19 (Aug. 1989): 217–26.

———. "Searching for El Dorado: Performance and Ritual in Early Latin America." *New Theatre Quarterly* 16 (1988): 330–34.

———. *Theatre in Latin America: Religion, Politics and Culture from Cortés to the 1980s*. Cambridge: Cambridge UP, 1993.

Vezzeti, Hugo. *La locura en la Argentina*. Buenos Aires: Paidós, 1985.

Vidal, Hernán. *Literatura hispanoamericana e ideología liberal: Surgimiento y crisis*. Buenos Aires: Ediciones Hispamérica, 1976.

———. "Para una redefinición culturalista de la crítica literaria Latinoamericana." *Ideologies and Literature* 4.16 (May–June, 1983): 121–32.

———. "Introduction." *Cultural and Historical Grounding of Hispanic and Luso-Brazilian Feminist Literary Criticism*. Ed. Hernán Vidal. Minneapolis: Institute for the Study of Literature and Ideology, 1989. 1–17.

——. "Political Theatricality and the Dissolution of the Theatre as Institution." *Gestos* 14 (1992): 27–33.

Villareal, Edit. *My Visits With MGM (My Grandmother Marta). Shattering the Myth: Plays by Hispanic Women.* Ed. Linda Feyder. Houston: Arte Público Press, 1992.

Villarreal, Juan Jerez. *Oriente: Biografía de una provincia.* La Habana: Editorial Siglo, 1960.

Villegas, Juan. *Ideología y discurso crítico sobre el teatro de España y América Latina.* Minneapolis: U of Minnesota P, Ediciones Prisma. 1988.

——. "Towards a Model for the History of Theatre." *The States of "Theory."* Ed. David Carrol. New York: Columbia UP, 1990. 255–80.

——. "Historicizing Latin American Theatre." *Theatre Journal.* 41.4 (Dec. 1989) 505–14.

——. "La estrategia llamada transculturación." *Conjunto* (Julio–Septiembre 1991): 3–7.

Villegas, Juan, and Diana Taylor, eds. *Representation of Otherness in Latin American and Chicano Theatre and Film.* Gestos: Teoria y Practica del Teatro Hispano, 1991.

Vogel, Paula. *The Baltimore Waltz.* New York: Dramatists Play Service Inc., 1992.

Vogt, Evon Z. *Bibliography of the Harvard Chiapas Project: The First Twenty Years 1957–1977.* Cambridge: Peabody Museum, Harvard U., 1978.

——. "The Chiapas Writers' Cooperative." *Cultural Survival Quarterly* 9.3 (1985): 46–48.

——. *Tortillas for the Gods: A Symbolic Analysis of Zinacantec Rituals.* Cambridge: Harvard UP, 1976.

Wagley, Charles, and Marvin Harris. "A Typology of Latin American Subcultures." *American Anthropologist* 57 (1955): 428–51.

Walker, Ana Cara. "Cocoliche: The Art of Assimilation and Dissimulation Among Italians and Argentines." *Latin American Research Review* 22 (1987): 37–67.

Waldman, Diane. *Jenny Holzer.* New York: Solomon Guggenheim Museum, 1989.

Wasserstrom, Robert. *Clase y sociedad en el centro de Chiapas.* México: Fondo de Cultura Económica, 1989.

Watkings, Evan. "Cultural Criticism and Literary Intellectuals." *Work and Days: Essays in the Socio-Historical Dimensions of Literature and the Arts.* 46.1 (Spring 1985): 11–31.

Watson-Espener, Maida. "Ethnicity and the Hispanic American State: The Cuban Experience." *Hispanic Theatre in the United States.* Ed. Nicolas Kanellos. Houston: Arte Público Press, 1984.

Weeks, Jeffrey. "Inverts, Perverts, and Mary-Annes: Male Prostitution and the Regulation of Homosexuality in the Nineteenth and Early Twentieth Centuries." *Hidden From History: Reclaiming the Gay and Lesbian Past.* Ed. Marin Duberman, Martha Vicinus, and George Chauncey. New York: Meridian, 1990.

Weiss, Judith A., Leslie Damasceno, Donald Frischmann, Claudia Kaiser-Lenoir, Marina Pianca, and Beatriz J. Rizk. *Latin American Popular Theatre, The First Five Centuries.* Albuquerque: U of New Mexico P, 1993.

West, Cornel. "The New Cultural Politics of Difference." *Out There: Marginalization and Contemporary Cultures.* Eds. Russell Ferguson, et al. New York: The New Museum of Contemporary Art, 1990. 19–36.

Williams, Raymond. *Problems in Materialism and Culture.* London: Verso, 1980.

——. *Culture and Society: 1780–1950.* New York: Columbia UP, 1983.

Wilson, Carter. *Crazy February. Death and Life in the Mayan Highlands of Mexico.* Berkeley: U of California P, 1974.

Winkler, Karen. "A Conservative Plans to Sound the Guns at NEH." *The Chronicle of Higher Education* 16 October 1991: A5.

Wood, Daniel B. "AIDS Now Affecting Lives of Fictional Character." *The Boston Globe* 23 June 1987: 67.

Worth, Dooley, and Ruth Rodríquez. "Latina Women and AIDS." *Radical America* 20.6 (1987): 63–67.

Yarbro-Bejarano, Yvonne. "The Female Subject in Chicano Theatre: Sexuality, 'Race', and Class." *Performing Feminisms: Feminist Critical Theory and Theatre*. Ed. Sue-Ellen Case. Baltimore: Johns Hopkins UP, 1990.

Yudice, George, Jean Franco, and Juan Flores, eds. *On Edge: The Crisis of Contemporary Latin American Culture*. Minneapolis: University of Minnesota Press, 1992.

Zea, Leopoldo. *Dependencia y liberación en la cultura latinoamericana*. México: Editorial Joaquin Mortiz, 1974.

———. *The Latin American Mind*. U of Oklahoma P, 1963.

Zimmerman, Marc. "Latin American Literary Criticism and Immigration." *Ideologies and Literature*. 4.16 (May–June, 1983): 172–96.

———. *Lucien Goldman: El estructuralismo genético y creación cultural*. Minneapolis: Institute for the Study of Ideologies and Literature, 1985.

Contributors

❏

Judith Bettelheim is Professor of Art History at San Francisco State University. She has extensive curatorial experience and in 1988 she cocurated and coauthored *Caribbean Festival Arts* with John Nunley of the Saint Louis Art Museum. Her articles have appeared in the *Jamaica Journal*, *African Arts*, the *Journal of Ethnic Studies* and *Caribbean Quarterly*.

Sue-Ellen Case is Professor of English at the University of California, Riverside. A past editor of Theatre Journal, she has published widely on feminist and German theatre. She is author of *Feminism and Theatre*, and editor of *Performing Feminisms: Feminist Critical Theory and Theatre*, and *The Divided Home/Land: Contemporary German Women's Plays*. She is coeditor with Janelle Reinelt of *The Performance of Power: Theatrical Discourse and Politics*. She is currently completing a book on feminist theory, lesbian theory, and performance.

Juan Flores is Professor of Latin American and Caribbean Studies at the City College of New York and in Sociology and Cultural Studies at CUNY Graduate Center. He is the translator of *Memories of Bernardo Vega: A Contribution to the History of the Puerto Rican Community in New York*. His book *Insularismo e ideología burguesa en Antonio Pedreira* won the Casa de las Américas Prize for best essay. He is also the author of *Divided Borders: Essays on Puerto Rican Identity*, and *On Edge: The Crisis of Contemporary Latin American Culture* (coedited with George Yudice and Jean Franco).

Jean Franco is Professor of English and Comparative Literature at Columbia University. She is the author of several books on Latin America, most recently *Plotting Women: Gender and Representation in Mexico*. She is coeditor with Juan Flores and George Yudiœe of *On Edge: The Crisis of Contemporary Latin American Culture*.

Donald Frischmann is Profesor Titular in the Departamento de Literatura at the Universidad de las Américas in Puebla, Mexico. He is the author of *El Nuevo Teatro Popular en México*. He is also coauthor of *Latin American Popular Theatre, The First Five Centuries*.

Guillermo Gómez-Peña is founder of the Border Arts Workshop/Taller de Arte Fronterizo. He has developed characters such as Border Brujo and the Warrior of Gringostroika to explore issues of cross-cultural identity and U.S./Latin relations. From 1987 to 1990, he was a contributor to the National Public Radio program "Crossroads." He has been published in volumes on multiculturalism and in journals such as *High Performance* and the *Drama Review*, of which he is a contributing editor. Gómez-Peña received the Priz de la Parole at the International Theatre Festival of the Americas (1989) and the New York Bessie Award (1989). In 1991, he won a MacArthur Foundation Fellowship, or "genius" award.

Jorge Huerta is Chancellor's Associate Professor of Theatre at the University of California, San Diego. He is the founder and first artistic director of Teatro de la Esperanza and Teatro Máscara Mágica in California. His books include *Chicano Theatre: Themes and Forms*, and two anthologies of plays: *Necessary Theater: Six Plays About the Chicano Experience* and *Nuevos Pasos: Chicano and Puerto Rican Drama* (coedited with Nicolás Kanellos).

Tiffany Ana López is a doctoral student in English at the University of California, Santa Barbara. She is editor of *Growing Up Chicana/o: An Anthology* and is currently writing a dissertation on Latina theatre in the United States.

Jacqueline Lazú is an Honors student and a Mellon Fellow at Dartmouth College. She is currently finishing a thesis on the connections between Latin American and U.S. Latino theatre.

María Teresa Marrero is Associate Professor in the Departamento de Literatura at the University of the Américas in Puebla, Mexico. She has published articles on Chicano, Cuban, and Puerto Rican theatre and performance art in Los Angeles and New York.

Cherríe Moraga is a Chicana poet, playwright, and essayist. Her critical essays include the ground-breaking anthology *This Bridge Called My Back: Writings by Radical Women of Color* (coedited with Gloria Anzaldúa), *Loving in the War Years*, and *The Last Generation*. Her plays include *Giving Up the Ghost, Shadow of a Man,* and *Heroes and Saints*. She has won numerous awards for her plays and poetry including the Before Columbus American Book Award, the Fund for New American Plays Award, and the National Endowment for the Arts Theatre Playwrights' Fellowship.

Kirsten Nigro is Associate Professor of Spanish at the University of Cincinnati. She is well known for her research on Latin American and feminist theatre. She has published widely in journals such as *Latin American Theatre Review, Gestos, Estreno,* and edited a special issue of *Latin American Theatre Review* dedicated to Mexican theatre.

Jorge Salessi is Assistant Professor of Romance Languages at the University of Pennsylvania. He is currently working on a book on the construction of Argentine homosexual subjectivity at the turn of the century.

Alberto Sandoval is Associate Professor of Spanish at Mount Holyoke College. He has published numerous articles on Spanish baroque theatre, Latin American colonial theatre, and U.S. Latino theatre. He is working on a book on U.S. Latino representations and self-representations on Broadway: *José, Can You See? U.S. Latino Theatrical and Cultural Representations*. He has published a bilingual book of poetry, *Nueva York Tras Bastidoes/New York Backstage,* and he has written a theatrical piece on AIDS, *Side Effects,* produced at Mount Holyoke College in 1993.

Cynthia Steele is Associate Professor of Spanish at the University of Washington in Seattle. She is the author of *Politics, Gender and the Mexican Novel, 1968–1988: Beyond the Pyramid*. She has done extensive research on indigenous theatre in Chiapas.

Diana Taylor is Professor of Spanish and Comparative Literature at Dartmouth. She is the author of *Theatre of Crisis: Drama and Politics in Latin America* and editor of three volumes of critical essays on Latin American, Latino, and Spanish theatre. Since 1982 she has been director of Dartmouth's Latino theatre group, Primer Acto. Currently she is working on a book on theatre and political spectacle during Argentina's recent "Dirty War."

Juan Villegas is Professor of Spanish and Portuguese at the University of California, Irvine. He is author of numerous books and articles, notably *Ideología y discurso crítico sobre el teatro de España y América Latina* and *Interpretación y analisis del texto dramático*. He is editor of the theatre journal *Gestos*.

Marguerite Waller is Professor of English at the University of California, Riverside, where she teaches gender theory, film, and Renaissance literature. She is the author of *Petrarch's Poetics and Literary History,* as well as articles on Dante, Petrarch, Wyatt, Shakespeare, Federico Fellini, Lina Wertmuller, Liliana Cavani, Maurizio Nichetti, George Lucas, and Hillary Clinton.

Index

❏

Library of Congress Cataloging-in-Publication Data
Negotiating performance : gender, sexuality, and theatricality in
Latin/o America / edited by Diana Taylor and Juan Villegas.
Includes bibliographical references and index.
ISBN 0-8223-1504-1 (cl). — ISBN 0-8223-1515-7 (pa)
1. Theater — Latin America — History.   2. Theater and society — Latin
America — History.   3. Hispanic American theater — History.
I. Taylor, Diana.   II. Villegas Morales, Juan, 1934–
PN2309.N45   1994
792'.098 — dc20   94-27647 CIP